D1567892

Historical Dictionaries of Cities of the World

Series Editor: Jon Woronoff

1. *Tokyo,* by Roman Cybriwsky. 1997
2. *Stockholm,* by Dennis E. Gould. 1997
3. *Warsaw,* by Adriana Gozdecka-Sanford. 1997
4. *Paris,* by Alfred Fierro. 1998

Historical Dictionary of Paris

Alfred Fierro

Translated by Jon Woronoff

Historical Dictionaries of Cities, No. 4

The Scarecrow Press, Inc.
Lanham, Md., & London
1998

SCARECROW PRESS, INC.

Published in the United States of America
by Scarecrow Press, Inc.
4720 Boston Way
Lanham, Maryland 20706

British Library Cataloguing in Publication Information Available

Library of Congress Cataloging-in-Publication Data

Fierro, Alfred.
    [Histoire et dictionnaire de Paris. English]
    Historical dictionary of Paris / Alfred Fierro ; translated by Jon Woronoff.
      p.   cm. — (Historical dictionaries of cities ; no. 4)
    Includes bibliographical references.
    ISBN 0-8108-3318-2 (cloth : alk. paper)
    1. Paris (France)—Civilization—Dictionaries. 2. Paris (France)—
History—Chronology. 3. Paris (France)—Maps.   I. Title.
II. Series: Historical dictionaries of cities of the world ; no. 4.
DC704.F5313   1998
944′.36—dc21   97–15669
                                                      CIP

Contents

Editor's Foreword (Jon Woronoff)   v

Maps

1. Paris in France and in Europe   vi
2. Successive Walls of Paris   vii
3. Arrondissements and Quarters (1795–1859)   viii
4. Arrondissements from 1860 to Today   x

Acronyms and Abbreviations   xi

Chronology   xv

Introduction   1

THE DICTIONARY   21

Bibliography   185

Statistical Appendixes   237

About the Author   245

Editor's Foreword

For most people, Paris would rank high on a list of the most beautiful cities in the world, if not at the top, and this would include many people who had never been there and knew it only from paintings and photos. There are numerous reasons for this. The most important is that, unlike many other cities, Paris did not grow haphazardly: it was fashioned. France's leaders, from early kings to recent presidents, have lavished time—and money—on beautifying the cityscape. Talented architects, town planners and engineers have erected palaces and mansions, as well as more ordinary structures; arranged its streets and boulevards; and updated the infrastructure. Paris not only exists, it vibrates and inspires artists, writers, fashion designers and cooks. Even the politicians and bureaucrats have not been untouched. How, then, could this series, *Historical Dictionaries of Cities,* be complete without a volume on Paris?

This book does not contain everything there is to say about Paris, but it has a lot. It covers the city's history in the chronology, introduction and many entries. It describes monuments, palaces and other buildings, parks, squares and various neighborhoods. There are entries on significant figures from political, economic and cultural circles. Some references cover how the city is administered and how it operates, and others reveal what makes it so appealing: the ballrooms and bistros, the cafés and restaurants, the nightclubs and *guinguettes*. This discussion is rounded off with a very substantial bibliography.

It would be hard to find a more suitable author for this volume. Not born in Paris, but having spent most of his adult life there, Alfred Fierro can see the city more perceptively than a native. Too, because of his profession, he has gotten to know it uncommonly well. In 1965, he became a librarian at the National Library and has been, since 1988, chief librarian of the Historical Library of the City of Paris. It is not just for professional reasons, however, that Dr. Fierro has written over 20 books, many of them on Paris, including studies of various arrondissements and the Louvre (most relevant is his comprehensive *Histoire et Dictionnaire de Paris* (1996)). Instead, as this *Historical Dictionary of Paris* shows, Paris is a city that he obviously loves.

Jon Woronoff
Series Editor

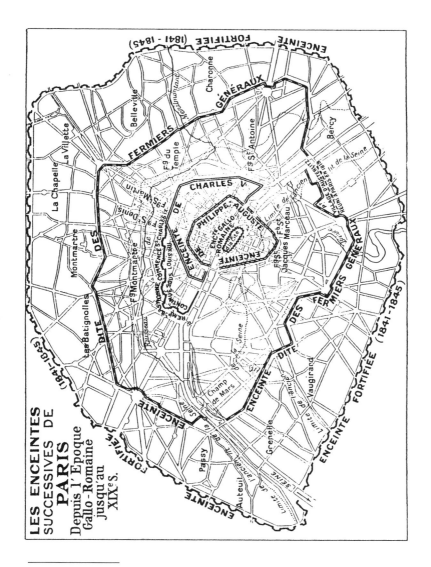

The Successive Walls of Paris from the Gallo-Roman Era until the Nineteenth
Century: Gallo-Roman Wall; Wall of Philippe Auguste; Wall of Charles V;
Rampart Bastion started under Charles IX and continued under Louis XIII; Wall
known as Farmers General; Fortified Wall (1841–1845)

ARRONDISSEMENTS ET QUARTIERS DE PARIS
1795-1859

1er arrondissement:
1. Roule.
2. Champs-Elysées.
3. Place Vendôme.
4. Tuileries.

2e arrondissement:
5. Palais-Royal.
6. Feydeau.
7. Chaussée d'Antin.
8. Faubourg-Montmartre.

3e arrondissement:
9. Mail.
10. Saint-Eustache.
11. Montmartre.
12. Faubourg-Poissonnière.

4e arrondissement:
13. Marchés.
14. Banque.
15. Louvre.
16. Saint-André.

5e arrondissement:
17. Faubourg-Saint-Denis.
18. Bonne-Nouvelle.
19. Montorgueil.
20. Porte-Saint-Martin.

6e arrondissement:
21. Porte-Saint-Denis.
22. Lombards.
23. Saint-Martin-des-Champs.
24. Temple.

7e arrondissement:
25. Mont-de-Piété.
26. Saint-Avoie.
27. Marché Saint-Jean.
28. Arcis.

8e arrondissement:
29. Marais.
30. Popincourt.
31. Faubourg-Saint-Antoine.
32. Quinze-Vingts.

9e arrondissement:
33. Hôtel-de-Ville.
34. Arsenal.
35. Cité.
36. Ile Saint-Louis.

10e arrondissement:
37. Invalides.
38. Faubourg-Saint-Germain.
39. Saint-Thomas-d'Aquin.
40. Monnaie.

11e arrondissement:
41. Luxembourg.
42. Ecole militaire.
43. Sorbonne.
44. Palais.

12e arrondissement:
45. Saint-Jacques.
46. Saint-Marcel.
47. Observatoire.
48. Jardin des Plantes.

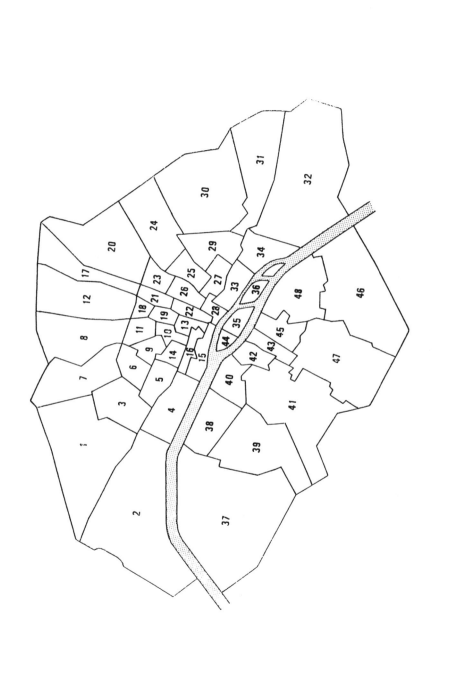

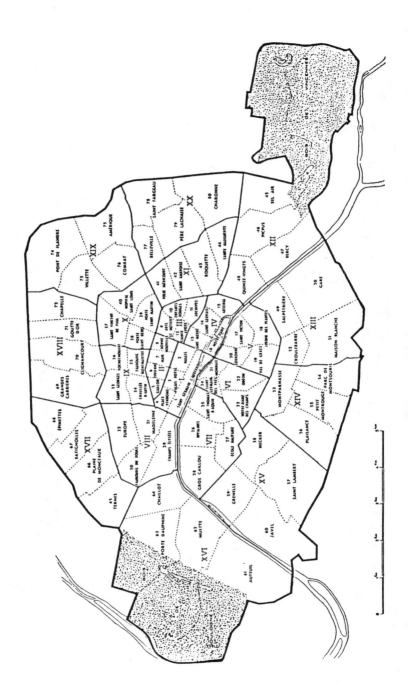

Acronyms and Abbreviations

AP	Assistance Publique (Public Welfare)
APUR	Atelier Parisien d'Urbanisme (Parisian Urbanism Workshop)
BAS	Bureau d'Aide Sociale (Social Aid Bureau)
BNP	Banque Nationale de Paris (bank)
CGO	Compagnie Générale des Omnibus (General Omnibus Company)
CIC	Crédit Industriel et Commercial (bank)
CMP	Compagnie du chemin de fer Métropolitain de Paris (Metropolitan Railway Company of Paris)
CNIT	Centre National des Industries et des Techniques (National Center for Industry and Technology)
CNPF	Conseil National du Patronat Français (National Council of French Employers)
COS	Coefficient d'Occupation du Sol (Ground Occupation Coefficient)
CPAC	Compagnie Parisienne de l'Air Comprimé (Parisian Compressed Air Company)
CPCU	Compagnie Parisienne de Chauffage Urbain (Parisian Urban Heating Company)
CPDE	Compagnie Parisienne de Distribution d'Électricité (Parisian Electricity Distribution Company)
CRECEP	Centre de Recherche, Étude et Contrôle des Eaux de Paris (Center for Research, Study and Control of Water of Paris)
CREPIF	Centre de Recherches et d'Études sur Paris et l'Île-de-France (Center for Research and Studies on Paris and Île-de-France)
CRITER	Centre de Recherche interdépartemental pour le Traitement des Eaux (Interdepartmental Research Center for Water Treatment)
DASCO	Direction des Affaires Scolaires (School Affairs Board)
DASES	Direction de l'Action Sociale, de l'Enfance et de la Santé (Social Action, Childhood and Health Board)

DASS	Direction des Affaires Sanitaires et Sociales (Sanitation and Social Affairs Board)
EDF	Électricité de France (national electricity company)
EPAD	Établissement Public d'Aménagement de la Défense (Public Establishment for Development of La Défense)
FLN	Front de Libération Nationale (National Liberation Front)
GAN	Groupe des Assurances Nationales (insurance company)
GDF	Gaz de France (national gas company)
HBM	Habitation à Bon Marché (low-cost council housing)
HLM	Habitation à Loyer Modéré (moderate-rent council housing)
IAURIF	Institut d'Aménagement et d'Urbanisme de la Région d'Île-de-France (Institute for Development and Urbanism of the Île-de-France Region)
ILM	Immeuble à Loyer Modéré (low-rental building)
INSEE	Institut National de la Statistique et des Études Économiques (National Institute for Statistics and Economic Studies)
MATIF	Marché à Terme International de France (French International Futures Market)
METEOR	Métro Est-Ouest Rapide (Rapid East-West Métro)
MIN	Marché d'Intérêt National de Rungis (Rungis Market of National Interest)
OAS	Organisation de l'Armée Secrète (secret army to keep Algeria French)
PADOG	Plan d'Aménagement et d'Organisation Générale de la Région Parisienne (Plan for Development and General Organization of the Parisian Region)
PCF	Parti Communiste Français (French Communist Party)
PCF	Pouilly-Club de France (?)
POS	Plan d'Occupation des Sols (Ground Use Plan)
PS	Parti Socialiste (Socialist Party)
RATP	Régie Autonome des Transports Parisiens (Autonomous Administration of Parisian Transport)
RER	Réseau Express Régional (Regional Express Network)
RPR	Rassemblement pour la République (Gaullist party)
SAGEP	Société Anonyme de Gestion des Eaux de Paris (Water Management Company of Paris, Ltd.)
SDAU	Schéma Directeur d'Aménagement et d'Urbanisme de la Région Parisienne (Guide Plan for the Development and Urban Planning of the Parisian Region)
SMIC	Salaire Minimum Interprofessional de Croissance (interprofessional minimum wage for growth)

SNCF	Société Nationale des Chemins de fer Français (French National Railway Company)
STCRP	Société des Transports en Commun de surface de la Région Parisienne (Public Surface Transport Company of the Parisian Region)
STIIC	Service Technique d'Inspection des Installations Classées (Technical Service for the Inspection of Scheduled Installations)
SUDAC	Société Urbaine d'Air Comprimé (Urban Compressed Air Company)
TGV	Train à Grande Vitesse (High-Speed Train)
TVA	Taxe sur la Valeur Ajoutée (Value Added Tax)
UAP	Union des Assurances de Paris (insurance company)
UDF	Union pour la Démocratie Française (moderate political party)
ZAC	Zone d'Aménagement Concerté (Concerted Development Zone)
ZAD	Zone d'Aménagement Différé (Deferred Development Zone)
ZUP	Zone d'Urbanisation Prioritaire (Priority Urbanization Zone)

Chronology

circa 4200 B.C.	Excavations on the Bercy site in 1991 reveal evidence of permanent habitation.
circa 100 B.C.	Gold coins minted by the people of Gaul, the Parisii.
52 B.C.	Labienus, Caesar's lieutenant, defeats a Gaulish army before Lutetia, which is burned.
between 14 and 37 A.D.	During the reign of emperor Tiberius, the boatmen raise an altar in honor of Jupiter in Lutetia.
circa 250	The first bishop of Lutetia, Saint Denis, is martyred.
circa 300	A rampart wall is built around the Île de la Cité to protect the inhabitants from Germanic invaders. About then, Lutetia assumes the name of the people whose capital it is and becomes Paris.
508	The Frankish king Clovis makes Paris his capital.
639	King Dagobert I is buried in Saint-Denis Abbey, which becomes the main royal necropolis.
754	Pope Stephen II anoints Pépin the Short and his sons Carloman and Charlemagne in Saint-Denis Abbey.
845	The Norsemen loot the city for the first time.
885–86	The Norsemen besiege Paris.
1021	Education developed at the episcopal school of Notre-Dame, an embryo of the future university.
1112	Louis VI gives preference to Saint-Denis over Saint-Benoît-sur-Loire. Paris becomes the capital, supplanting Orléans.
1121	First evidence of the Paris watermen.
1147	Louis VII leaves on the Crusades and entrusts the regency to Suger, abbot of Saint-Denis.
1163	Reconstruction of Notre-Dame Cathedral begins. It is completed in 1245.
1183	The first Halles are erected.

xv

1190	Before leaving on the Crusades, Philippe II Auguste commands that Paris be surrounded by a fortified wall, which is finished in 1213.
1202	Construction of the Louvre château is completed.
1215	The papal legate grants statutes to the University.
circa 1250	The *Parlement* organizes its first, purely judicial sessions.
1252	Saint Thomas Aquinas begins teaching at the University.
1257	Robert de Sorbon founds a *collège*, the future Sorbonne.
1268	The king's provost Étienne Boileau has the *Livre des métiers de Paris* drawn up, which enumerates 132 professions.
1296	Work is undertaken on the Palais de la Cité in order to accommodate the whole royal administration.
1314	The last grand master of the Knights Templar, whose order was dissolved in 1312, is burned on the Île de la Cité.
1348	The Black Death decimates the population.
1355–58	With King Jean prisoner in England, the provost of merchants, Étienne Marcel, imposes control on Dauphin Charles. The uprising fails and Marcel is killed.
1370	The Bastille, the main fortification on the wall of Charles V, is erected.
1382	The insurrection of the Maillotins against royal taxation results in the discontinuance of the Parisian municipality for 30 years.
1407	The assassination of Louis d'Orléans sets off a 30-year civil war between his supporters, the Armagnacs, and those of the duke of Burgundy, Jean the Fearless, who ordered the assassination.
1420–36	Paris is occuped by an English garrison.
1470	The first book is printed in Paris, at the Sorbonne.
1521	The Sorbonne condemns Luther's theses.
1526	The first martyr of the Reformation, Jean Vallière, is burned.
1530	François I founds the Collège de France to compensate for the fossilization of the Sorbonne.
1533	Dominique de Cortone begins construction of a new Hôtel de Ville.
1546	François I commissions Pierre Lescot to reconstruct the Louvre.

1555	The Calvinists open their first place of worship.
1564	Catherine de Médicis commissions Philibert Delorme to construct the Tuileries.
1572	Saint Bartholomew's Day massacre (August 24–27): members of the Protestant elite, come to attend the wedding of Henri de Bourbon and Marguerite de Valois, are killed at the order of Charles IX.
1578	Henri III lays the cornerstone of the Pont Neuf, which is completed in 1606.
1588	Henri III flees Paris, which is held by the Catholic League.
1589	After the assassination of Henri III, the Protestant Henri IV is rejected by the League.
1594	After abjuring Protestantism, Henri IV makes a triumphal entry into Paris.
1598	The edict of Nantes legalizes Protestant worship.
1610	Henri IV is assassinated by Ravaillac.
1614	Christophe Marie starts building on the Île Saint-Louis.
1615	Marie de Médicis has the Palais du Luxembourg built according to plans by Salomon de Brosse.
1624	Anne of Austria lays the cornerstone of Val-de-Grâce Church.
1629	Richelieu builds the Palais-Cardinal, which later becomes the Palais-Royal.
1634	The Académie Français holds its first meeting.
1648–52	The Fronde, uniting the nobility and the *Parlement* against Mazarin, controls Paris but is ultimately defeated.
1667	The police lieutenancy is established to improve safety in the capital.
1671	Louis XIV leaves Paris permanently for Versailles.
1674	Louis XIV inaugurates the Hôtel des Invalides, built by Libéral Bruant.
1680	The Comédie-Française is formed.
1685	The revocation of the edict of Nantes outlaws the Protestants.
1709	After a particularly harsh winter, widespread misery provokes a popular uprising.
1716–20	John Law sets up a bank for the colonization of Louisiana, but his "system" fails.
1750	The abduction of children by the police to people Louisiana sparks riots.

1753	The king approves Boffrand's design of a new square. Place Louis XV, now called Place de la Concorde, is inaugurated in 1763.
1764	Work begins on the Madeleine and Sainte-Geneviève churches. The former is completed in 1842, the latter, which became the Panthéon, was finished in 1790.
1777	The oldest French daily, the *Journal de Paris,* first appears.
1783	Pilâtre de Rozier and the Marquis d'Arlandes undertake the first human flight on board a hot-air balloon.
1785–88	The Farmers General have a wall built to facilitate the collection of toll duties. Ledoux erects tollgates.
1789	The fall of the Bastille symbolizes the start of the Revolution.
1792	The taking of the Tuileries results in the incarceration and condemnation to death of Louis XVI.
1794	Initiated by Robespierre, the Terror ceases after his execution.
1795–99	The Directory is shaken by a series of coups d'état, during the last of which Napoléon Bonaparte takes power.
1804	Napoléon proclaims himself emperor and is crowned in Notre-Dame.
1806	Construction begins on the Arc de Triomphe de l'Étoile. It is finished in 1836.
1814	Napoléon I abdicates. He is succeeded by Louis XVIII.
1815	After a brief return, the Hundred Days, Napoléon is definitively defeated.
1830	Charles X is overthrown by an insurrection and replaced by Louis-Philippe.
1832	A cholera epidemic and a Republican and Bonapartist insurrection strike the capital.
1834	The Republicans organize a new insurrection but fail again.
1839	The Socialists Barbès and Blanqui initiate an abortive insurrection.
1841	At Thiers's proposal, the parliament votes to build a fortified wall to protect Paris.
1848	A victorious insurrection overthrows Louis-Philippe and proclaims the Second Republic.

1851	The president of the Republic, Louis-Napoléon Bonaparte, carries out a coup d'état and assumes full power.
1852	The Second Empire is proclaimed.
1853–69	Prefect Haussmann directs numerous major projects to modernize the capital.
1855	The first universal exhibition is held, followed by others in 1867, 1889, 1900 and 1937.
1870	France's defeat in the Franco-Prussian War brings about the fall of Napoléon III. The Republic is proclaimed and Paris is beseiged by the German army.
1871	After withdrawing to Versailles, the Thiers government crushes the revolt of the Paris Commune.
1875	After 12 years of work, the Opéra, built by Charles Garnier, is inaugurated.
1889	The Eiffel Tower is inaugurated in connection with the universal exhibition.
1895	Louis Lumière invents the Cinematographe and projects the first films in Paris.
1900	The métro goes into service on the occasion of the universal exhibition.
1910	The capital is afflicted by the worst floods since 1658.
1914–18	Paris is bombed several times during the First World War.
1919	The peace conference meets in Versailles. The Sacred Heart basilica is consecrated after more than 40 years of work.
1925	Modernness is the keynote of the Exhibition of Decorative and Industrial Arts.
1927	Charles Lindbergh achieves the first trans-Atlantic flight between New York and Paris.
1931	An important Colonial Exhibition is organized in the Bois de Vincennes.
1934	A demonstration against parliamentary corruption degenerates into bloody riots.
1936	The leftist parties, united in the Popular Front, win the legislative elections.
1937	The International Exhibition of Art and Technology experiences an ideological confrontation between Hitler's Germany and Stalin's Soviet Union.
1940	Defeated by Germany, France is occupied militarily.

1944   The Allied troops disembark in Normandy. Paris
            is liberated on August 25.
1958   The war in Algeria brings about the fall of the
            Fourth Republic. Charles de Gaulle becomes the
            president of the Fifth Republic.
1964   France is divided into 21 regions. The Parisian re-
            gion is subdivided into eight départements, one of
            which constitutes the city of Paris.
1968   The month of May is marked by riots in the Latin
            Quarter and a general strike that paralyzes the
            country. President de Gaulle steps down in 1969.
1970   The University of Paris is replaced by 13 au-
            tonomous universities.
1973   The peripheral boulevard is completed and the
            Maine-Montparnasse Tower is inaugurated.
1974   Charles-de-Gaulle airport in Roissy is opened.
1977   Jacques Chirac is elected mayor of Paris. The
            métro and the Regional Express Network are con-
            nected at the Châtelet station.
1979   The Forum des Halles is finished.
1984   Nearly two million persons demonstrate in favor
            of freedom of education.
1986   The City of Science and Industry in La Villette and
            the Orsay Museum are inaugurated. Islamic ter-
            rorists carry out a series of bomb attacks.
1989   Several major architectural projects are com-
            pleted: Grand Louvre Museum, Bastille Opéra,
            Grande Arche de la Défense and City of Music in
            La Villette.
1992   Euro Disneyland is opened in Marne-la-Vallée.
1995   Jean Tiberi is elected mayor of Paris to replace
            Jacques Chirac, who became president of France.
1996   The American Center is closed. Former mayor
            Jean Tiberi is accused of malpractices regarding
            low-cost rental apartments of Paris municipality.
            Another Islamic bomb attack. New building of
            French National Library is inaugurated.
1997   The right loses anticipated legislative elections to
            the Socialist Party and its allies.

Introduction

PARIS IN FRANCE AND IN EUROPE

Paris is located at 48° 50′ 11″ north latitude and 2° 20′ 14″ east longitude. It is the capital of France. Although it is a bit to the north of the country's center today, it should be remembered that France did not always have its current borders; Paris was at the geographic center of an earlier entity that did not originally include the Garonne basin (Bordeaux and Toulouse) or the Rhône basin (Lyon and Marseille). Straddling the Seine, in roughly the middle of the sedimentary basin that is known as the Parisian basin at the confluence of the main waterways of that basin—the Seine, Marne and Oise—Paris is the center of a circle with a radius of somewhat less than 500 kilometers that encompasses Belgium and the left bank of the Rhine in Germany: the distance to Brussels is 308 km; to Rotterdam, 457 km; to Cologne, 469 km; to Strasbourg, 462 km; to Lyon, 461 km; to Limoges, 375 km; to Nantes, 374 km; and to Rennes, 348 km. London, too, is less than 400 km away.

Ranking first among the major European metropolises, Paris is the heart of a vast region formed by the river basins of the Loire, the Seine and the pair Meuse/Rhine, which open it to the Atlantic, the English Channel, the other side of the Rhine and the Alps. This location enabled Paris to receive the cultural and economic contributions of England, Germany and Italy and, to a lesser extent, a more distant Spain, and these countries were in turn subject to its influence. It was in the Parisian basin that the Gothic art originated that spread throughout the continent, and it is there that the French language was shaped that reigned over England, Flanders and even Italy during the 13th century; Marco Polo's *Description of the World* was first written in French. Similarly, during the 17th and 18th centuries, monarchical absolutism, classical architecture, and French arts and culture extended from Versailles as far as Stockholm, Saint Petersburg and Lisbon. Yet, as we shall see, Paris was not initially destined to become a great European metropolis, or even the capital of France.

1

FROM THE ORIGINS TO THE END
OF THE MIDDLE AGES (1498)

It has been proven that prehistoric humans lived in the Parisian basin as many as 700,000 years ago. The Gauls settled in the region some 2,500 years ago, and the Parisii people seem to have reached Lutetia around 250–225 B.C. In 52 B.C., the Romans won a decisive victory before Lutetia, which became a Roman possession for five centuries, as did Gaul as a whole. The town was rebuilt with the classical grid layout of the ancient cities. The Right Bank saw the most development; construction was concentrated in the Île de la Cité, site of the governor's palace and Temple of Jupiter, and along the slopes of Mount Sainte-Geneviève, with its baths, theater, amphitheater and, on the summit, the forum: the focus of economic and social life. The core of Roman Gaul, however, consisted of the axis of the Rhône, Saône and Rhine, which linked Italy to the Rhenish boundary, threatened by unruly Germanic tribes. Gaul's capital was established in Lyon, nearly halfway between Cologne and Rome. At that time, Lutetia/Paris was just a small town of some 5,000 to 6,000 souls, a bit off to the side on the secondary route toward England and subordinated to Sens, a town that itself depended on Lyon.

Christianity seems to have made its appearance around A.D. 250, a quarter of a century before the town was looted by Germanic tribes, which event incited the Parisians to fortify the Île de la Cité around A.D. 300 in order to have a place of refuge in moments of danger. With the collapse of the Roman empire, Paris and the fertile Parisian basin fell into the hands of the Franks. This Germanic people crept slowly from the swampy common estuary of the Meuse and the Rhine, presently in the Netherlands, southward to the Somme, the Seine and then the Loire. Clovis, king of the Franks, who had subjected Paris in 486, proclaimed the city his capital in 508. However, at the death of Clovis (511), Paris was fought over by his sons and grandsons, whose other capitals were Soissons, Reims and Orléans. The increasing predominance of the aristocracy of the eastern Franks of Austrasia (a land between the Meuse and Rhine) shifted the axis of the Frankish kingdom eastward. The Merovingians, a dynasty that derived from Mérovée, Clovis's grandfather, was replaced in 751 by the Carolingians, descendants of the mayors of the Austrasian palace. Charlemagne, king of the Franks in 768 and emperor in 800, was their most illustrious representative. His capital was Aix-la-Chapelle, between the Meuse and Rhine; Paris was just one provincial town among others.

Paris's importance was enhanced by the partition of the Carolingian empire in 843, which resulted in the formation of a Western France and an Eastern France. These territories eventually gave rise to the kingdom of France and the Germanic Holy Roman Empire, a precursor of Germany. Western France was limited to the east by four waterways, the Escaut, Meuse, Saône and Rhone, and the Seine and Loire basins formed its center. As of 804, the long ships of the Scandinavian pillagers, the Norsemen, or Vikings, used these two rivers to penetrate and lay waste to the country. The Robertian dynasty developed as a means to combat them. The head of the family bore the title of count of Paris and also the higher and broader title of duke of France. The dynasty was distinguished by Robert the Strong and two of his sons, Eudes (king from 888 to 898) and Robert I (king from 922 to 923), who wrested the crown of Western France from the representatives of the Carolingian dynasty, which was definitively ousted in 987 with the election as king of France of Hugues Capet, the grandson of Robert I.

This third dynasty, named Capetian, played a decisive role in the formation of a France that was dominated by its northern half and in the choice of Paris as the capital. Hugues Capet's possessions were not very extensive. Most of them were located between Laon in the north and Orléans in the south, Dreux in the west and Melun in the east—that is, within a radius of about 100 kilometers around Paris. Hugues Capet and Robert II the Pious preferred residing in Orléans but, under the reign of Henri I (1031–60), Paris won out over its rival. Louis VI the Stout (1108–37) finally opted for Paris and confirmed this choice in 1112 by giving precedence to Saint-Denis (12 kilometers from Notre-Dame) as the principal abbey of his kingdom, to the detriment of Saint-Benoît-sur-Loire (36 kilometers from Orléans). When he left for the Crusades in 1147, Louis VII entrusted the regency to Suger, the abbot of Saint-Denis. The supreme confirmation of Paris's role as capital came in 1190, when Philippe II Auguste left France for the Holy Land. He deposited his treasure in the Temple (the house of the Knights of the Temple), left the key with six bourgeois of the city and commanded that Paris be surrounded with a fortified wall.

During the reign of Philippe II Auguste (1180–1223), Paris really began to look like a major city: a new market with covered halls was built, called Les Halles (1183); its main streets were paved (1186); the king had a new residence constructed, the Louvre (1202); and the pope granted a charter to its university (1215). Paris grew in keeping with the extension and power of the royal domain. In 1328, a census estimated that king Philippe VI had about 16 million subjects, and around 200,000 of them lived in Paris, which was then the most inhabited city in Europe, well ahead of the other metropolises of London, Antwerp, Bruges, Ghent, Florence, Milan, Rome and Venice.

The economic and population growth of France and its political hegemony over Western Europe were being challenged by the 1330s. In addition to the conflict with England, known as the Hundred Years' War, there was the disorganization of the economy, unbearable fiscal pressure and, finally, the plague, the Black Death that killed between a third and a quarter of the population of Europe between 1348 and 1353 and affected France quite severely. This combination of disasters was aggravated by the defeat at Poitiers (1356), which delivered King Jean II the Good into the hands of the victorious English. Charles, the king's elder son and dauphin and future Charles V, was forced to convene the Estates General to ask them to adopt new taxes so the war could be continued and the king's ransom paid. The bourgeoisie, led by Étienne Marcel, the provost of merchants of Paris, agreed, subject to the implementation of extensive reforms that were distasteful to the king's suite. The conflict culminated in 1358 in the assassination by an armed Parisian mob of two of the dauphin's advisors. Already devastated by the war between England and France, the Île-de-France was afflicted in May and June by a terrible uprising of the peasantry, the Jacquerie, against the nobility, which was blamed for not protecting it. Étienne Marcel was killed on July 31, 1358, while trying to open the gates of Paris to the English troops.

The dauphin regained the upper hand while dealing tactfully with the capital's bourgeois. After becoming king in 1364, under the name of Charles V, he took great care of the city and its inhabitants, equipping it with a new wall on the Right Bank that protected those quarters that had developed since 1200. Excessive taxation, however, provoked new disturbances during the minority of Charles VI (born in 1368, king in 1380), namely, the revolt of the Maillotins (March 1, 1382). The uprising was severely repressed, the municipality was abolished and the city came under the administration of the king's provost.

The king's insanity, ascertained in 1392, ushered in a new period of misfortunes. His uncles, the dukes of Berry and Burgundy, and his brother, Louis d'Orléans, fought over power and squandered the kingdom's revenue. Jean the Fearless, duke of Burgundy, had the duke of Orléans killed on November 23, 1407. This act unleashed a civil war between the Burgundians and the victim's supporters, who were known as the Armagnacs because they were commanded by Bernard d'Armagnac, father-in-law of the young Charles d'Orléans, the son of Louis. The Parisians took advantage of the conflict to have their municipality reestablished in January 1412. The butchers' faction, led by Simon Caboche, dominated the city for the Burgundians and installed a reign of terror from April to July 1413. Supported by the moderate bourgeois, the Armagnacs regained control of the city but then alienated the population. On May 29, 1418, the Saint-Germain-des-Prés gate was opened to the Burgundian troops. The heads of the Armagnac party were captured and massacred. Egged on by the executioner Capeluche, uncontrollable elements of the Burgundian party engaged in excesses of brutality until Jean the Fearless restored order by having the ringleaders executed on August 23, 1418.

The assassination of the duke of Burgundy on Montereau bridge, on September 10, 1419—ordered and witnessed by the dauphin, the future Charles VII—stirred up the political situation. The son of Jean the Fearless, Philippe the Good, struck an alliance with Henry V of England to avenge the death of his father and imposed on Charles VI and his suite the treaty of Troyes (May 21, 1420). This finally satisfied the supreme ambition of the English monarchy: the king of England was named regent of the kingdom of France and designated the heir of Charles VI. English garrisons moved into the Louvre, the Bastille and the Vincennes château and, on December 1, 1420, Henry V and Charles VI together made their entrance into a Paris whose citizenry and university had sworn to obey the treaty of Troyes.

Destiny soon thwarted this union of the crowns of England and France when Henry V died on August 31, 1422, at the age of 35, preceeding Charles VI into the tomb by 50 days. In Paris and in France, the power was held by John of Lancaster, the duke of Bedford and brother of Henry V, in the name of his son, Henry VI, an infant born in December 1421. The English garrison was insignificant, a mere 100 to 200 men lost in a city of more than 100,000 souls, and Paris was still administered by French officers and defended by its own bourgeois militia. The war that ensued seriously hurt the city's economic activities and swelled the already hard-pressed population with thousands of refugees from the surrounding countryside who came seeking shelter within its walls.

The city's bourgeoisie tolerated the discreet presence of the English only as long as their military supremacy lasted. Among other things, its militia threw back an attack by Jeanne d'Arc at Saint-Honoré gate on September 8, 1429. But the problems continued multiplying. Henry VI could not get to Reims and had to accept a second-rate crowning in Paris on December 16, 1431. His decision, a month later, to found the University of Caen was a serious political error since it aroused the anger of the University of Paris, which was jealous of its monopoly and a strong force in the capital's life because of its thousands of unruly students. Plots proliferated to open the city gates to the troops of Charles VII, who prowled about outside. The death of Bedford and the reconciliation of the duke of Burgundy and Charles VII in September 1435 put the English in a desperate position. On April 15, 1436, the tiny English garrison surrendered and obtained the authorization to leave Paris for Rouen by boat, taking along its local accomplices among the bourgeois.

Charles VII felt no attraction for a city that had been disloyal for so long and preferred the châteaux in the Loire where he had already been residing most of the time for 20 years. His son, Louis XI (1461–83) did not like the Parisians either and kept the municipal administration under close tutorship, imposing his flunkies as merchant provosts. Paris was subjugated and kept under tight control but was also favored by a king who did not live there but did maintain there his administrative machinery, the *Parlement*. The city got used to having an administrative function where the path to fame and fortune passed through service to the sovereign.

It was during the second half of the 15th century that the city's middle classes turned away from commerce and productive endeavors and fell into the rut of public office, preferring the mediocrity and parasitic security of paperwork and red tape to the risks of business and free enterprise. One particularly striking example of the economic decline of Paris is that, whereas the population increased from 100,000 to 150,000 between 1422 and 1500, cloth manufacturing—which had long been the dominant activity—collapsed: there were 360 master weavers in the city in 1300 and only 42 in 1481. Bankers and money changers abandoned Paris, which ceased even being mentioned in the Italian lists of foreign exchange agencies.

FROM THE REFORMATION
TO THE REVOLUTION (1498–1789)

The 16th century was dominated by religious issues. As of 1484, at the Sorbonne, Jean Lailler set the authority of the Bible against that of ecclesiastical tradition and energetically criticized the pope. In 1491, Jean Langlois denied the real presence of God in the Eucharist and was burned at the stake. The decisive blow, however, came from Germany, where Martin Luther shook the Church of Rome irremediably and brought about the schism. As of 1520, Lutheranism had infiltrated Paris. The Reformation assumed a typically French flavor with Calvin as of 1533. As the new ideas progressed, the tensions grew. Calvinist worship appeared in Paris in 1555 and the first synod was held there in 1559, concluding with the establishment of the French Reformed Church.

The civil war was unleashed by Duke François de Guise and the Catholics in 1562. Until peace was restored in 1598, there were eight religious wars interrupted temporarily by patched-up peaces. Paris, in the hands of the Catholics, was concerned only by the Saint Bartholomew's Day massacre of 1572, which was ordered by Charles IX at the instigation of the queen mother, Catherine de Médicis. It took a toll of between 2,000 and 10,000 victims and almost destroyed the rich Protestant community of the capital, which could no longer play a significant part in the economic and social life of Paris.

The inability of the king's armies to put down the Protestants or Huguenots turned the most warlike Catholics, who had united in the Catholic League, against Henri III, who was supported by the moderate Catholics. To lead the Parisians, an Organization of Sixteen was formed, a sort of League general staff, consisting of representatives of the 16 quarters of the city. On May 9, 1588, although the king had expressly prohibited him from doing so, Henri de Guise, the League's head, entered the city and was acclaimed by an armed mob. On May 12, the Parisians rose, putting up thousands of barricades and massacring the king's Swiss soldiers. Henri III fled and a League-dominated town council was set up that pledged allegiance to the duke of Guise. In an attempt to restore his authority, the king promised reforms and convened the Estates General in Blois. Henri de Guise dominated the debates and tried to subject the king to his power. Henri III resolved to order de Guise's assassination by his guard on December 23, 1588. The League, the Sorbonne and the *Parlement* declared the king dethroned and recognized as sovereign Cardinal Charles de Bourbon, who was being held prisoner by Henri III in Blois. Henri III then formed an alliance with his natural heir, according to the order of succession: the Protestant Henri de Bourbon, king of Navarre. The royal and Huguenot armies were preparing to lay siege to Paris when Henri III was killed in Saint-Cloud on August 1, 1589, by the Dominican monk Jacques Clément.

Now formally king under the name of Henri IV but deserted by part of the Catholics of the royal army, the king of Navarre did not have sufficient resources to take Paris, which he besieged several times between November 1589 and January 1591. Sorely tried by the famine, the Parisians and the moderates sought a compromise solution. The death of Cardinal de Bourbon, the Leaguers' king, sowed confusion in their camp and the candidacy of the infanta, the daughter of King Philip II of Spain, to the French crown, aroused very strong reservations. The Leaguers attacked the moderates, who favored peace, purged the *Parlement* and hanged three of its members. Charles de Mayenne, who had succeeded his brother Henri de Guise as head of the League, was alarmed by the excesses and came closer to the moderates, executing four of the Sixteen. Contact was made with Henri IV, who was asked to convert to Catholicism. "Paris is worth a mass" was supposedly Henri IV's comment, and he solemnly abjured Calvinism on July 25, 1593, in Saint-Denis Abbey. The League then disintegrated rapidly and, on March 22, 1594, Henri IV made a triumphal entry into the city, which had been evacuated by the troops of the king of Spain. Peace with Spain and the edict of Nantes (1598), which recognized the rights of the Protestants, put an end to a third of a century of religious warfare.

The French Renaissance was marked not only by bloodshed and religious fanaticism. Once again the capital of the kingdom in 1528, following a solemn declaration of François I, Paris benefited from the sovereign's generosity and was embellished with several handsome monuments displaying a new taste inspired by Italy: the king's palace, the Louvre, was partially reconstructed by Pierre Lescot, and the municipality received a new town hall (Hôtel de Ville) designed by the Italian Dominique de Cortone, called the Boccador. Catherine de Médicis had the Palais des Tuileries built and the Marais quarter was filled with sumptuous mansions, such as the Hôtel Carnavalet. With peace restored, vast architectural projects were launched and town planning made its appearance. Henri IV created two squares, Place Royale (presently Place des Vosges) and Place Dauphine. He also had the Pont Neuf completed and continued the reconstruction of the Louvre. After his assassination in 1610 by Ravaillac, a student of the Jesuits, his widow, Marie de Médicis, served as regent in the name of Louis XIII. As of 1624, Richelieu held the reality of power on behalf of the king. As long as peace prevailed, the city prospered and splendid buildings were erected: Palais de Luxembourg, Palais-Cardinal (the future Palais-Royal), fine houses on the Île Saint-Louis and private mansions in the Marais.

In 1635, France went to war on the side of the Protestant Germans to break the hegemony of the Habsburgs, who were seated on the thrones of Spain and Austria and who were masters of Italy, the Franche Comté and what was to become Belgium. The military expenditures generated an inordinate growth in taxes and sparked numerous peasant revolts. In Paris, the breaking point was reached in 1648. On May 13, the *Parlement* called on the other sovereign courts to join it to work to "reform the abuses of the state." The very foundation of monarchical power was questioned. Cardinal Mazarin, who governed in the name of boy-king Louis XIV, had the leaders of the parliamentary Fronde arrested on August 26, 1648, but the city was soon covered with barricades and he had to release them.

During the night of January 5–6, 1649, the king, his mother, the regent Anne of Austria, and Mazarin secretly left the capital and took refuge in Saint-Germain-en-Laye. The *Parlement* declared Mazarin a public enemy and received the support of most of the princes and grand lords. A peaceful compromise was signed at Rueil in March 1649, but the tension remained acute. Mazarin bet on the predictable disunity of the Frondeurs, the deep dissensions between the parliamentarians and the princes of the blood, who were united only in their common hatred of him. In February 1651, he went into voluntary exile. The quarrels immediately revived among the Frondeurs, especially between the prince of Condé and Gondi, cardinal of Retz. Condé took up arms. In a hopeless position, driven back to the walls of the capital by Turenne and the royal army, he escaped defeat thanks only to the Grande Mademoiselle, Louis XIV's niece, who had Saint-Antoine gate opened for him on July 2, 1652. No sooner was he in Paris than Condé sought to impose his authority, on July 4, by having his soldiers invade the Hôtel de Ville and kill some of the members of the assembly meeting there. This was done in vain: the

Parisians remained violently hostile to him, and Condé had to flee the city on October 14 and seek refuge with the Spaniards in Namur. On February 3, 1653, Mazarin returned to Paris, acclaimed by the crowds, the ultimate victor of a Fronde destroyed by its own divisions. With Spain's defeat and the Peace of the Pyrenees (1659), peace was finally restored after a quarter century of war. After Mazarin's death (1661), Louis XIV personally exercised power. He preserved particularly unpleasant memories of the disturbing days of 1648 and his shameful nocturnal flight of January 1649 and bore a tenacious grudge against the Parisians. The Sun King commanded the construction of Versailles, a palace in proportion to his unbounded vanity, and abandoned Paris as of 1671. He did not entirely neglect the fallen capital, however. Of the 200 million pounds he lavished on his buildings, about 10 percent were spent on Paris, half of this for the work on the Louvre and the Tuileries, the rest for the Hôtel des Invalides, Place Vendôme and Gobelins factory. Substantial progress was made for public safety with the establishment of the office of lieutenant general of police and the development of public lighting, in particular.

Marked by endless and ruinous wars, the reign of Louis XIV went on and on interminably, creating widespread distress. From 1693 to 1713, life was exceedingly harsh for ordinary people and the middle classes throughout the country. In Paris, that misery assumed the form of more than a thousand people dying of starvation each day during the winters of 1693–94 and 1708–09. The great lord and courtier, the duke of Saint-Simon, acknowledged in his *Mémoires* that on the death of Louis XIV, on September 1, 1715, "the people, ruined, crushed and desperate, thanked God."

After having the *Parlement* annul the hated monarch's will, Philippe d'Orléans assumed the regency in the name of Louis XV, who was only five years old. His first act was to bring the court back to the Tuileries. The economy picked up with the adventuresome speculation of John Law. The king, however, returned to Versailles in 1722, reopening the fateful breach between the court and the city. The public opinion that was solidifying in the scorned capital channeled and guided the popular discontent and exploited the new ideas of the philosophers to challenge the absolute monarchy. The criticism of the parliamentarians, the philosophers and Jansenists converged on Louis XV.

The Jansenists, persecuted throughout the reign of Louis XIV, enjoyed exceptional popularity even among the lower classes. The supposed miracles that occurred as of 1727 at the tomb of Deacon Pâris in Saint-Médard cemetery crystallized a popular fervor that condemned Rome and the scarcely disguised incredulity of the bishops who came from the nobility. The *Parlement,* largely won over by Jansenism, questioned the excessive expenditures of the court and sought to limit the luxurious life of the monarch. The ideology of the Enlightenment exalted the bourgeois values of work, knowledge, merit, tolerance and even religious indifference and expounded on the theme of equality of men, contesting the domination of a parasitic aristocracy based on birth and not on talent. The Parisian masses were led to demonstrate their discontent more and more often: 73 riots were recorded between 1711 and 1766.

On the death of Louis XV in 1774, Louis XVI and his frivolous wife Marie-Antoinette quickly squandered any sympathy they might have earned. The licentiousness and wastefulness of the court and the great lords were the subject of a thousand pamphlets. The queen was compromised in the necklace affair, the king was discredited by his lack of character and his constant indecisiveness, and spending on the American War of Independence increased the state debt catastrophically. One reform after another was proposed, but none was implemented. With his coffers empty and unable to pay his bills, Louis XVI was forced to convene the Estates General to ask them to adopt new taxes.

A CENTURY OF REVOLUTIONS (1789–1871)

The elections of the members of the Estates General were carried out in a feverish atmosphere, and the Estates General met in Versailles on May 5, 1789, although the voting had not yet begun in Paris, where the bloody riot of April 28, 1789, had thoroughly discouraged the police and the army, which were very poorly led, from continuing to maintain order. Very soon, it turned out that Louis XVI had no wish to reform the state and to curb the court's expenses. Urged by the queen and her suite, he decided to call on the troops in the garrisons along the eastern and northern frontiers to forcibly disperse the Estates General, which had proclaimed itself the National Assembly, and restore the absolute monarchy. On July 11, 1789, he showed his true colors and dismissed the reforming minister Necker. On Sunday, July 12, brawling broke out in the Tuileries garden between people out for a walk and horsemen of the Royal German regiment. On July 13, a bourgeois militia was established. Looking for rifles, cannons and powder, on July 14 it attacked the Bastille, an arms depot and prison and the symbol of royal absolutism and despotism.

The weak, indecisive Louis XVI accepted the fait accompli, recalled Necker and went to Paris on July 17. He received the tricolor rosette from Bailly, who had been proclaimed mayor of Paris in the place of the merchants' provost, who was killed on the 14th. The bourgeois militia, named the National Guard, was placed under the command of La Fayette. The revolutionaries completed their undertaking on October

5–6, 1789. A mob of women set out from the Halles, accompanied by National Guards, and walked to Versailles to ask the king for bread. On the 6th, in the morning, the women invaded the royal apartments, which La Fayette had neglected to have guarded, and convinced the vacillating Louis XVI to return to Paris. In the evening of the 6th, the king and his family slept in the Tuileries, henceforth at the mercy of the mob's movements. They were joined there by the National Assembly soon after.

The political life of Paris intensified, and out of nowhere a superabundant press emerged. The municipality assumed real power, in contrast to the merchants' provostship, which, ever since the 15th century, had done nothing more than carry out the decisions of the royal authority. After a year of calm and the great ceremony of national reconciliation, the Festival of the Federation on the Champ-de-Mars on July 14, 1790, the tension resumed because of the king's ill will. Indeed, Louis XVI could not resign himself to becoming a constitutional monarch on the English model. In the night of June 20–21, 1791, he fled with his wife and children but was recognized, arrested in Varennes and brought back to Paris on June 25. The idea of establishing a republic then started gaining ground. A petition hostile to the king was presented to the populace on the Champ-de-Mars on July 17, 1791. Mayor Bailly proclaimed martial law and La Fayette ordered the National Guard to open fire on the assembled crowd. Both had to resign later, having lost their popularity with the masses who were increasingly swayed by revolutionary agitators.

Louis XVI made one last mistake: in declaring war on Austria on April 20, 1792, he hoped that a rapid defeat of France would bring the enemy troops to Paris and that King Francis II of Austria, the brother of his wife Marie-Antoinette, would restore the absolute monarchy and punish the revolutionaries. The first part of this maneuver succeeded: the French armies were defeated. However, on August 10, 1792, the French revolutionaries launched an insurrection that seized the Tuileries. The Republic was proclaimed on September 21. The captive king was judged, condemned to death and then guillotined on January 21, 1793.

Dominated by the Jacobins, the Paris Commune exerted the dominant influence over the nation's elected representatives, the Convention, and over the government. It instigated the massacres of September 1792 in the prisons and allowed permanent political agitation to reign in the 48 sections. The left wing of the Club des Jacobins, the Montagne, rose against the rightist Girondins and organized two insurrections, on May 31 and June 2, 1793. The Commune's cannons were pointed at the Convention, and the terrorized deputies voted to arrest the 29 principal representatives of the Girondist party, who were judged and guillotined.

Paris's representatives to the Convention, Robespierre, Danton and Marat, allied to the Commune's leaders Chaumette, Hébert and Réal, imposed a de facto popular dictatorship that lasted more than a year. The

Revolutionary Tribunal ensured expeditious justice, and the Terror that followed made it possible to control the press and the economy. The *sans-culottes,* most of them artisans or workmen from the Faubourg Saint-Antoine and Faubourg Saint-Marcel, were the armed might of the Revolution: they controlled all the activities and issued passes and certificates of good citizenship. Food was requisitioned, taxed and rationed; paper money was drastically devalued and replaced with *assignats* (promissory notes issued by the government); the churches were closed; and priests and monks were urged to defrock and even marry.

The factions fought bitterly for power. Robespierre managed to eliminate the extreme left of the Enragés by August-September 1793. The Hébertists, who replaced them on the political chessboard, were in turn eliminated in March 1794. Finally, Robespierre turned on the moderate right wing, the Indulgents, associated with Danton and Desmoulins, who were guillotined in April 1794. Robespierre's triumph was short-lived. To impose his absolute authority, he had to do away with most of the leadership of the Parisian Revolution, thus radically narrowing its popular base. On June 8, 1794, to inaugurate the Great Terror (the daily rate of executions leaped from three to 30), the Festival of the Supreme Being consecrated the apotheosis of the Incorruptible, Robespierre's nickname. Since he intended to continue his task of "purification," ceaselessly denouncing the rotten elements within the Convention, a majority of the deputies feared for their lives. A makeshift coalition formed around Billaud-Varenne, Carnot and Collot d'Herbois, deputies and members of the Committee of Public Safety (See Dictionary "Terror"). The Convention brought charges against Robespierre on July 27, 1794. The Paris Commune could bring together only a few hundred men to defend him. Arrested at the Hôtel de Ville, Robespierre and his friends mounted the scaffold on the evening of July 28, 1794.

Paris's role in the Revolution was over. The city was placed under close supervision by the state for nearly two centuries. It lost its right to elect a mayor and representatives. It was divided into 12 arrondissements, whose administrators were appointed by the government. Two riots sparked by destitution and hunger broke out, on April 1 and May 20, 1795, but they were easily put down in the absence of talented political agitators. The majority of the Convention's members, who had won out over Robespierre, had also voted for the king's death. They were regicides, and they feared certain punishment should the monarchy be restored. They therefore established a regime, called the Directoire (Directory), with the aim of maintaining a moderate republic. Their system was quickly destabilized, however, by annual partial elections, and the five directors who governed France had to resort to force after each election. It was no longer the Parisian masses who carried out the coups d'état but the military. The only Parisian insurrection, on October 5, 1795, was undertaken by the royalist sections of the rich quarters, and it was readily crushed by a young general named Napoléon Bonaparte. He put an end to the Directoire and seized power through a last coup d'état on November 9–10, 1799 (Brumaire 18–19, Year VIII, of the Republican calendar). The new master of France preserved the social and economic achievements of the Revolution and confirmed the hegemony of the bourgeoisie. Napoléon I restored the prosperity of the capital and gave it the Vendôme column, the triumphal arches of the Carrousel and Étoile and started construction of the Rue de Rivoli. Then, in 1814, the empire collapsed after 20 years of almost continual warfare against various European coalitions.

Louis XVIII and Charles X did not restore the old order, but they did adopt reactionary policies that worried the bourgeoisie. Liberal ideas made their way through the middle classes, and Paris experienced nearly permanent student unrest. The funerals of Bonapartist or liberal opponents were turned into huge demonstrations by the opposition, such as those of the exchange broker Manuel (1821), General Foy (1825), the actor Talma (1826) and the deputy Manuel (1827). On April 29, 1827, while Charles X was reviewing the National Guard, hostile cries broke out in the ranks: "Long live the Charter! Down with the ministers! Down with the Jesuits! Long live freedom of the press!" The king immediately ordered the corps to be dissolved. Since the bourgeois enrolled in it had paid for their equipment, they kept their uniforms and weapons at home.

In August 1829, the king appointed as head of the government one of his intimate friends, Jules de Polignac, a narrow-minded person generally despised by the French. Without any clearly defined program, he remained inactive for months, doing little more than suing one newspaper after the other in an attempt to muzzle the press. The Chamber of Deputies adopted a no-confidence motion against him on March 16, 1830. The Chamber was then dissolved by the king, but the opposition won the legislative elections. Charles X then decided to resort to force. On July 26, he dissolved the newly elected Chamber even before it could convene, suspended freedom of the press and altered the electoral law in such a way as to reduce the number of property-owner electors who were favorable to the opposition. An insurrection broke out in Paris that lasted three days, the Trois Glorieuses, from July 27 to 29, 1830. The Republican and Bonapartist workers and students were joined by thousands of liberal National Guardsmen bearing arms. Poorly led, the army wore itself out breaking through barricades that were immediately put up again behind it. By July 29, it was obvious that the insurrection was victorious. Charles X fled, and the liberal deputies offered the crown to his cousin Louis-Philippe d'Orléans.

Louis-Philippe I was immediately confronted by the Republicans, who had been cheated of their victory. The first years of his reign were turbulent. A religious service held in memory of the duke of Berry, the son of Charles X, at Saint-Germain-l'Auxerrois church, triggered a riot on February 14, 1831. The church was sacked and the archbishop's palace was burned down. Another uprising occurred during the cholera epidemic of March 1832. In order to limit the risk of contagion, the police commissioner authorized an additional garbage collection at nightfall. This seriously inconvenienced the *chiffonniers,* or ragpickers, who were unable to exercise their trade. They spread the rumor that the government and the bourgeoisie were in favor of the epidemic to "assassinate the people." The funeral of Bonapartist General Lamarque, on June 6, was the signal for the insurrection. The National Guard, however, supported the army, and the 4,000 insurgents were crushed. The social unrest continued with countless strikes, which led the Republicans to believe that their time had come and to organize a new insurrection, from April 12–14, 1834. It quickly failed and ended in a tragedy: soldiers massacred all the innocent inhabitants of a building in the Rue Transnonain.

The July Monarchy then entered a more tranquil phase. New press laws made it possible to penalize the opposition newspapers severely. All the attempts at revolt by the Republicans, Socialists and Bonapartists failed miserably. While the parliamentary opposition gained ground slowly in the provinces, in Paris in 1846 it received 9,000 of the 14,000 property-related votes. The poor harvest of 1845 and 1846, compounded by the credit crunch in 1847, weakened a regime that was founded on economic prosperity. In 1847, the opposition launched a banquet campaign that was to end in February 1848. The last banquet was forbidden. Fearing that this prohibition would spark disturbances, the government called out the National Guard on February 23, 1848, which demonstrated its hostility to Guizot, who headed the cabinet. The king gave in and asked Guizot to resign. The crowds expressed their joy so noisily that the crisis seemed to have been overcome, but later in the evening some scared soldiers opened fire on the rejoicing demonstrators, killing about 100 people. The Republicans immediately issued a call to arms. On February 24, 1848, at dawn, the streets of Paris were bristling with 1,500 barricades. Louis-Philippe I abdicated.

The Republicans and Socialists did not let the bourgeoisie confiscate their victory. They proclaimed the Second Republic and formed a provisional government. Alarmed by the workers' demonstrations, the bourgeois closed their shops and factories while proletarians demanded new rights and the doubling of their wages. The result was a serious economic and social crisis. One hundred thousand unemployed workers received state support within the framework of the "national workshops." At the legislative elections, the moderate Republicans won, even in Paris, where the main Socialist leader, Louis Blanc, came in 27th. The decision of the new government to send some of the workers in the

Parisian national workshops to work in the provinces incited the Socialists to attempt a coup d'état. On June 23, 1848, the eastern half of the capital—everything to the east of the Rues Saint-Denis and Saint-Jacques—was covered with barricades. Some 15,000 armed Socialists faced an army of 30,000 men supported by the National Guard of the bourgeois quarters to the west. The railway quickly brought in more troops from the provinces. By the 26th, the last insurgents were crushed in the Faubourg Saint-Antoine.

In December 1848, a nephew of Napoléon I, Louis-Napoléon Bonaparte, was elected president of France. He had won over the bourgeois by means of the imperial legend forged by the Romantic writers and because of the workers who voted for him out of hatred of the bourgeois right that had massacred them in June 1848. On December 2, 1851, he carried out a coup d'état and, one year later, proclaimed himself emperor under the name of Napoléon III. He undertook a radical modernization of Paris, entrusting this effort to the prefect Haussmann. From 1853 to 1869, the capital was one enormous work site, and a considerable share of the present buildings dates back to that era. So as to better control these projects and the growth of the city, Paris's area was more than doubled on January 1, 1860, through the incorporation of the neighboring communes. The city's administrative limits have hardly changed since, and today's 20 arrondissements were created at that time.

Old and tired, the emperor sought to consolidate his regime by moving it toward liberalism. The plebiscite of May 8, 1870, marked the success of that operation with more than 80 percent voting "yes." Paris, however, was an exception, with 184,000 "no" and 138,000 "yes" votes. The Second Empire seemed to be solidly rooted when Napoléon was lured into declaring war against Prussia on July 19. By September 2, after a disastrous campaign, the emperor and the main French army surrendered at Sedan.

On September 4, 1870, when the surrender was announced, the Republican deputies met at the Hôtel de Ville, proclaimed the Republic and set up a provisional government. On September 19, the Prussians and their allies began the siege of Paris. More than 500,000 men defended the city, 300,000 of them National Guardsmen. Bismarck left a cordon of only 150,000 soldiers around it, because he preferred to starve it out rather than attack. Faced with relatively few but formidable combatants, the Parisian army was little more than a disorderly and undisciplined rabble, whose sorties were driven back time and again. However, the famine was far more deadly than these wretched encounters. During the whole siege, only 3,000 men were killed, while 64,000 civilians died, three times the normal death rate.

The publication of the armistice convention on January 29, 1871, aroused indignation among the Parisians, who felt betrayed. On March 11, their hostility intensified when they learned that the deputies elected in February had decided to meet in Versailles and not in the capital. On March 18, 1871, at dawn, a military operation was launched to disarm Paris and, in particular, to remove 227 cannons located on the mound of Montmartre. The operation dragged on, the city awoke and crowds surrounded the soldiers, who refused to fire on them. The commanding generals, Lecomte and Thomas, were killed by the enraged populace.

The Paris Commune made a clean break with the government. On paper, it was backed by 200,000 National Guardsmen, but their indiscipline and negligence were such that there were never more than 20,000 men under arms. On the other side, Thiers could count on only 22,000 soldiers at first. He got Bismarck to release numerous prisoners of war, which brought his force to 130,000 men by April 16. All of the Communards' attacks ended in disaster. The Commune was undone by its lack of organization, the mediocrity of its political and military leaders and endless personal quarrels. It was dominated by the 42 representatives of the International, who consisted of followers of the Socialist ideas of Blanquists, Proudhonians, "Jacobins" nostalgic of the Revolution of 1789 and unclassifiable romantic hotheads such as Delescluze, Flourens or Pyat. The elections of March 25, 1871, showed that the breach between the bourgeois west and the working-class east persisted. Only four arrondissements, the 10th, 11th, 18th and 20th, all located in the northeast, voted heavily for the proletarian candidates.

It was from the west that the soldiers of the Thiers government, known as the Versaillais, slipped into Paris on Sunday, May 21, 1871, benefiting from the absence of guards near the Saint-Cloud gate. For a week, the "bloody week," Paris was the scene of fighting and fires lit by the Communards, which destroyed dozens of public buildings, among them the Tuileries palace and the Hôtel de Ville. The last Communards perished on May 28, with their backs to the "federalists' wall" of Père-Lachaise cemetery. The number of dead on the Commune side was estimated at 20,000. There were 38,000 arrests, 10,000 condemnations—including 93 with the death penalty—but only 23 executions.

FROM CITY TO MEGALOPOLIS

This bloodshed brought to a close a particularly unsettled period of more than 80 years, during which Parisian insurrections determined the course of France. The capital no longer acts as the driving force of the nation's history, but it remains a sounding board that reverberates and amplifies the country's problems. In practice, Paris often showed extreme reactions. It was passionately Boulangist from 1886 to 1889, triumphantly electing General Boulanger deputy in January 1889, only to forget him a few months later when it became engrossed in the Panama scandal that ruined many people who had bought shares in the Panama Canal Company. The Dreyfus affair then became the prime subject of polemics, although the Republic was never truly threatened. In vain, the ultra-nationalist Déroulède tried to provoke a military coup d'état during the president's funeral in February 1899. His attempt was so ridiculous that the court released him.

The First World War (1914–18) affected Paris only marginally. Bombing by German aviation and artillery caused only 500 deaths and 1,200 wounded in four years, while the Spanish flu killed 300 to 2,000 people a week during the second half of 1918. The interwar period was characterized by social movements that concerned the country as a whole, although there was a specifically Parisian day of rioting on February 6, 1934. On that day, hundreds of thousands of protestors tried unsuccessfully to reach the Palais-Bourbon, where the deputies were meeting, to express their indignation and hostility to the parliamentary corruption that had just been revealed in the Stavisky affair. Reacting with exceptional brutality, the police fired on the crowd and killed 16 demonstrators, wounding hundreds more.

During the Second World War, Paris was occupied by the Germans from June 14, 1940, to August 25, 1944. Its inhabitants were subjected to severe food restrictions, while such items as fuel, heating, clothing, and shoes were rationed or available only at exorbitant prices on a flourishing black market. The Resistance and the attacks it mounted provoked reprisals whose scale has been exaggerated: the French authorities claimed during the Nuremberg Trials that 11,000 persons had been shot at Mont-Valérien alone, whereas it seems that there were not more than 1,400 victims for the whole Parisian region. Similarly, the Liberation of Paris in 1944 caused relatively few casualties: 1,482 Parisians killed, 582 of them civilians, according to official estimates.

Postwar events did not pass Paris by. If anything, the city was in the thick of them, although it never had a decisive role. It also turned against General de Gaulle after the war, electing indecisive and short-lived governments during a painfully long Fourth Republic. It then welcomed de Gaulle back in 1958. The Fifth Republic was still faced with the most wrenching problems of decolonization: whether to keep Algeria French or grant it independence. Part of the struggle between the French settlers (*colons*) and the Algerian Force de Libération Nationale (FLN) was played out in the streets of Paris, which had more than their share of demonstrations, police repression and bomb attacks by the FLN and the Organisation de l'Armée Secrète (OAS), which tried to assassinate de Gaulle.

For a while, there was relative calm. Then, in May 1968, the students took to the streets, complaining about overcrowding of facilities, useless courses and incompetent professors, and harsh living conditions. This was overlaid with anger at the Vietnam War and disenchantment with the de Gaulle regime. Demonstrations and riots broke out and attracted frustrated workers and won the support of many ordinary citizens, although others were sufficiently frightened to back the government. In the end, the students gave up, but de Gaulle stepped down.

The events of May 1968 were the last large-scale demonstrations in Paris. In 1977, the state was so convinced that Paris no longer represented a threat to the government that it restored the capital's right to elect a mayor and have an autonomous political life along the same lines as the other communes of France. This put an end to 182 years of close supervision.

In fact, the foremost issues since 1871 have not been political but rather economic, social and territorial. For a long time, Paris functioned as an administrative capital living off the wages, income and revenue of royal officers and jurists of the *Parlement*. Otherwise, its main activities were commerce and luxury crafts geared to the king and the Versailles court as well as the nobility and upper bourgeoisie. Industry developed only slowly. In 1847, a survey by the Paris Chamber of Commerce recorded nearly 350,000 workers dispersed in 65,000 firms. There were only 7,000 establishments employing more than ten workers. Large-scale manufacturing hardly existed and was limited to the production of railway materials and highly polluting chemical plants located in the periphery, in Javel, Grenelle, Passy, Clichy, Belleville and Pantin.

Napoléon III and Haussmann were opposed to the industrialization of the capital because they perceived in growing masses of workers a threat for the Second Empire. It was partly to avoid the proliferation of factories that, on January 1, 1860, the surrounding suburbs were incorporated into Paris. Even before the end of the Second Empire (1870), the shift of Parisian industries toward the suburbs had begun. Ironworks for the railway, which first appeared in the 1840s, had already disappeared from the capital by 1900.

It was only with the First World War that the Parisian region became a significant industrial pole. It benefited substantially from the transfer of operations from the northern and eastern regions, which were occupied by the Germans between 1914 and 1918, but also from the introduction of new industries such as automaking, aviation and pharmaceuticals.

Between 1920 and 1960, the emergence of a "red" industrial belt in the suburbs, dominated by the Communists, confirmed the fears that had troubled Napoléon III. Paris and its suburbs accounted then for a quarter of the manpower and of the production of French industry. However, in the 1970s there was a brutal deindustrialization of the suburbs, leaving behind thousands of hectares of rusting industrial hulks and hundreds of thousands of unemployed workers. Paris itself, where industry was already less important, has lost more than half its workforce since 1968. At present, it generates less than five percent of the national output.

Nevertheless, Paris is endowed with all the assets needed for a flourishing service sector. With respect to culture and education, the capital behaves like a vampire, sucking up the intellectual life of the rest of the country for its own benefit. Nearly all the publishing houses, major newspapers and important magazines are located in Paris. Its 13 universities host 20 percent of all students, and the bulk of the scientific research organizations are concentrated in the Île-de-France region. The biggest French companies have their headquarters in the capital or the immediate vicinity, especially in the new quarter of skyscraper office buildings, La Défense. However, Paris suffers from a long-term weakness in the areas of banking and finance. As was already noted, this is largely attributable to the attitude of the monied classes under the Ancien Régime, which preferred to invest their money in the offices of the royal state rather than go into business and trade. The turnover of the Paris Bourse is only one-third of the London stock exchange and one-ninth that of the New York and Tokyo stock exchanges. When it comes to international banking transactions, Paris is also greatly overshadowed by London, Tokyo and New York.

Since the incorporation of the peripheral communes in 1860, Paris has partially lost its predominant position in the Île-de-France region. In 1872, the city had 1,851,000 inhabitants, and the suburbs only 325,000. Thereafter, while the capital increased its population by a further million persons to reach its maximum of 2,906,000 inhabitants in 1921, the suburbs added 1.5 million during the same period. They continued growing and expanding, while the number of Parisians decreased. In the 1990 census, the 2,154,000 Parisians represented only a mere 20 percent of a combined population of more than 10,500,000 persons. Paris covered only four percent of the area of a conurbation of more than 2,400 square kilometers. The administration was slow in reacting to this situation. In 1964, it discontinued the Seine département (Paris and 70 peripheral communes, 475 square kilometers) and the Seine-et-Oise département (684 communes, 5,603 square kilometers) and replaced them with seven départements: one for Paris alone, three for the nearby suburbs and the last three for the more distant suburbs.

Henceforth, Paris's progress can be conceived of only within the framework of this vast megalopolis, the largest in Europe. Increasingly, however, it must also be seen within the much broader context of the whole continent and beyond. Paris has not ceased attracting attention and, as the capital of France, it hosts numerous international conferences and meetings. If less so than before, it remains a fertile source of ideas and trends, whether in architecture and the arts or the latest fashions. It is still a magnet for foreigners, some of them students, others intellectuals, and constant flows of immigrants, legal and illegal. More superficially, the millions of tourists and other visitors who come every year leave with something more than just souvenirs.

The Dictionary

-A-

ABÉLARD, PETER (1079–1142). After having studied at Chartres, Abélard arrived in Paris about 1100. There he followed the courses of Guillaume de Champeaux, founder of Saint-Victor (q.v.) abbey. It did not take long before he quarreled with his master and had to leave the city. In 1102, Abélard founded a school at Melun, then another at Corbeil, closer to Paris. In 1113, after Guillaume de Champeaux left for Chalons, where he was appointed bishop, Abélard became the master of the schools at Notre-Dame in Paris. His secret love affair with Héloïse and the birth of a son named Astrolabe aroused the ire of Fulbert, his mistress's uncle, who sought revenge by having him castrated. Abélard then withdrew to the abbey of Saint-Denis while Heloïse took the veil at Argenteuil abbey. Because of his work on the trinity, Abélard was condemned by the council in Soissons in 1121. He sought refuge in Champagne, at Saint-Ayoul, where he wrote his treatise on Christian theology and founded, near Nogent-sur-Seine, the oratory of Paraclet, where in 1129 he brought Héloïse and the cloistered nuns who had been expelled from Argenteuil by the abbot of Saint-Denis. After writing his autobiography *Historia Calamitatum* (*History of My Calamities*) about 1132, Abélard returned to Paris to teach, this time on Mount Sainte-Geneviève (q.v.). He was again condemned for heresy in 1140 by the council in Sens. After he died in 1142, he was interred at Paraclet and Heloïse joined him in the same crypt in 1164. Their common tomb was transferred to Père-Lachaise cemetery (q.v.) in 1817.

ACADÉMIE FRANÇAISE. The French Academy, which was originally founded by Richelieu in 1635 to keep writers under the control of the absolute monarchy, has survived to the present day. It claims to be the guardian of the French language and to this end publishes a dictionary, now in its ninth edition, that no one uses. It also distributes awards to large families, prizes for good conduct and literary prizes

21

that are devoid of any prestige. Its 40 members are co-opted and are sarcastically called "immortals" because most of them will fall into oblivion. Indeed, most of the truly great authors have never been members; they include Descartes, Pascal, Molière, Diderot, Balzac, Stendhal, Flaubert, Baudelaire, Verlaine, Rimbaud, Maupassant, Proust, Gide, Giraudoux, Céline and Sartre, just to mention the most famous. The first woman to be elected was Marguerite Yourcenar in 1980. On the other hand, there have been countless members of the French Academy who never showed the slightest sign of literary talent, as well as many representatives of the aristocracy, church and military. Barbey d'Aurevilly once remarked with wit: "They are forty who think like four."

AIDS (ACQUIRED IMMUNODEFICIENCY SYNDROME). This infectious disease was discovered in the United States in 1981. In that same year, the first cases were detected in Parisian hospitals by Dr. Willy Rozenbaum. In 1983, the virus was identified at the Pasteur Institute by the team of Professor Montagnier. In 1986, Jean Choussat, director general of Parisian Hospitals, submitted a report to the Chirac government on a suitable organization of care for persons suffering from AIDS. In 1988, Minister of Health Michèle Barzach estimated that 200,000 people were HIV positive. Paris and Île-de-France accounted for more than half of the 6,000 deaths registered in 1994, and 6,600 new cases were diagnosed in that same year. This brought the number of AIDS patients (with an average life expectancy of over two years) to 16,000 in France as a whole in 1995.

According to an epidemiological study, some 59 percent of the AIDS patients in Paris were homosexuals. However, statistics based on the records of patients treated in the ten major hospitals of the capital between July 1, 1992, and June 30, 1993, indicated a decrease in the proportion of homosexuals and drug addicts and an increase in the number of persons infected by heterosexual contacts. Thus, the Lariboisière Center, located in a neighborhood with a heavy concentration of drug abusers, recorded a steadily declining percentage when screening for HIV positives: from 7 percent in 1988 to 1.5 percent in 1993. In *Le Sida et les fragilités françaises* (AIDS and French Fragilities) (1995), Jean de Savigny, secretary general for public welfare and former director of the French Agency for AIDS Control, estimated that the peak in the number of persons affected (HIV positives) had been reached in 1990 or 1991, whereas the Ministry of Health had foreseen that it would be reached only around 1993.

AIR POLLUTION. In 1973, the central laboratory of the headquarters of the Paris police (q.v.) introduced air quality control. Airparif, the first network, consisting of 12 monitoring stations, was installed in 1979. Since then, this network has expanded considerably, observing 304 parameters at 173 sites. The reduction in industry has brought about a large decrease in certain substances: pollution caused by sulfur (SO_2 and SO_3) and hydrochloric acids, known as strong acidity, coming from the combustion of fuels and coal, declined from more than 300 micrograms per cubic meter in 1957 to 47 in 1987. Lead, deriving from leaded gasolines, dropped from four micrograms in 1978 to less than two micrograms at the roundabout of the Champs-Elysées (q.v.). At Porte des Lilas, however, 14 micrograms was recorded near the peripheral boulevard (q.v.) during the rush hours. There is a definite increase in the pollution coming from automobiles, such as carbon monoxide, nitrogen monoxides and dioxides. The anticyclones that bring good weather also cause an atmospheric stability that favors photochemical reactions among pollutants. Thus, when the heat and sunshine mount, nitrogen monoxide (NO) joins with other emanations from automobile exhaust to form nitrogen dioxide (NO_2) and ozone (O_3). Thus, Parisians are increasingly worried about the ever larger number of hours when the pollution standards set by the European Community are exceeded and about the spread of respiratory disorders. Thus far, no solution has been found by the city and national authorities.

AIRPLANES. Although a big city is hardly the ideal place for experimenting with aircraft that require considerable room for takeoff, Paris can be regarded as one of the cradles of aviation. It was, in fact, in this city that the first competition of heavier-than-air flying machines took place, at the Galerie des Machines of the Champ-de-Mars (q.v.) on February 11, 1905. About 30 airplanes were launched from the top of a 38-meter pylon and achieved flights of 20 to 40 seconds. On June 8 and July 18, 1905, Gabriel Voisin made his first tests of an airplane with floats on the Seine (q.v.) at the level of Billancourt bridge. Santos-Dumont carried out his first trial in an airplane above the Bagatelle (q.v.) park on July 22, 1906. On May 21, 1911, it was at the airport (*see* Airports) of Issy-les-Moulineaux, presently incorporated in Paris, that the departure took place for the Paris-Madrid airplane race, which was watched by 800,000 spectators. On August 7, 1912, an ordinance of the Parisian police (q.v.) prohibited the landing of airplanes in the capital. Violating this law, Jules Védrines landed on the terrace of the Galeries Lafayette (q.v.) department store on January 19, 1919. On August 7 of the same year, Charles Godefroy flew under the arch of the Arc de Triomphe (*see* Étoile). This exploit was repeated several times, the last time by the "black baron," Albert Maltret, in August 1988. *See also* Balloons.

AIRPORTS. Paris is the site of the oldest airport in the world. Originally located at Issy-les-Moulineaux, it was certificated by a law of July 31, 1890, and its field was purchased by the City of Paris in 1893. That is where the earliest female pilot, baroness de Laroche, was licensed on March 6, 1910. In 1977, this historic place became the Parisian heliport.

The First World War incited the army to install a squadron of seven airplanes at Le Bourget. On August 18, 1918, postal aviation was born there with the first mail services for the American troops who were disembarking at Saint-Nazaire. The first commercial flight also took off from Le Bourget, heading for London, on February 8, 1919. In September 1919, the airport was officially opened for civilian air traffic and military aviation was transferred to Orly. In 1945, Orly also became a civilian airport designated for intercontinental connections, while Le Bourget was used for flights to other parts of Europe and North Africa; private planes landed at Toussus-le-Noble. By 1953, Orly had become more important than Le Bourget and, in May 1969, the latter was closed and reserved for the Paris Air Show.

A new airport was constructed at Roissy-Charles-de-Gaulle between 1966 and 1974. By 1990, it overshadowed Orly. The Aéroport de Paris, which includes both Orly and Roissy, each year handles about 500,000 flights, 50 million passengers and a million tons of freight, which makes it Europe's second busiest airport after London.

ALCHEMY. Alchemy brings together mysticism and chemistry in the quest for the philosopher's stone. Paris has a very rich tradition in this field. Its oldest house (q.v.) (51, Rue de Montmorency) was built in 1407 by Nicholas Flamel, who enjoyed a reputation as a presumed alchemist. At 1, Rue Saint-Claude, the house in which the great magus of the 18th century Cagliostro lived still stands. Saint-Jacques's tower is regarded as one of the pinnacles of alchemy and magic. There are mysterious sculptures with alchemistic figurations at Saint-Gervais and Saint-Merri churches. Saint-Marcel's portal at Notre-Dame Cathedral is also called the "portal of alchemists." There are alchemistic stained-glass windows in the catechistic chapel of Saint-Etienne-du-Mont Church.

ALTITUDE. The height of Paris above sea level varies from 26 meters along the Seine (q.v.) at Grenelle to 129 meters at the location of the Télégraphe métro station. Montmartre (q.v.) lies at 129 meters, Ménilmontant at 118 meters, Belleville (q.v.) at 115 meters, Buttes-Chaumont (q.v.) at 101 meters, Montsouris at 78 meters, Charonne (q.v.) at 65 meters, and Mount Sainte-Geneviève (q.v.) and Butte-aux-Cailles both at 60 meters.

AMERICAN CHURCHES. There are three important places of worship for the American community in Paris. The oldest was built at 48, Rue de Lille, by the American Baptist Church. In 1873, the architect W. Hansen built a temple with metal structures covered by stone in a neo-Gothic style reminiscent of the 15th century. Between 1881 and 1884, the British architect George-Edmund Street constructed the American Trinity Church at 23, Avenue George V. The pro-cathedral of the communion of American Episcopal churches in Europe, it is both a parish church and the seat of the archbishop. This edifice was inspired by the English Gothic of the 13th century. As for the American Church of Paris, it is located at 65, Quai d'Orsay, and replaced a chapel that was constructed in 1858 at 21, Rue de Berri. From 1926 to 1929, it was built of brick in the neo-Gothic style of the 15th century by Carroll Greenough, who surrounded it with schools and sports grounds. There is abundant decoration, most of it provided by American artists such as Charles J. Connick, Ralph Adams Cram, Charles Lorin and Walter G. Reynolds. One of the windows is a memorial to the American soldiers who fell during the First World War.

AMERICAN LIBRARY (10, rue du Général Camou). It was founded in 1920 within the framework of the aid provided by the United States for the reconstruction of France from the devastation of the First World War. At present it contains nearly 100,000 volumes and provides precious services for students who work on the history and literature of the United States.

AMERICANS IN PARIS. Starting with the War of Independence, close ties existed between the emerging United States of America and Paris. Benjamin Franklin (q.v.) and the other members of the American mission to the French court, Arthur Lee, Silas Deane, and later John Adams and John Jay, resided at the Hôtel de Velentinois (62–70, Rue Raynouard) in Passy from 1777 to 1785. Thomas Jefferson was ambassador of the United States from 1785 to 1789. John Paul Jones (q.v.) died in 1792 at 19, Rue de Tournon, where he had been living since 1789. Thomas Paine stayed in Paris several times between 1781 and 1802. In the 19th century, writers such as James Fenimore Cooper, Ralph Waldo Emerson, Washington Irving, Henry Wadsworth Longfellow and Mark Twain lived in Paris. The French capital became a second home for American writers and artists between 1920 and 1939, welcoming Ernest Hemingway (q.v.), Henry James (q.v.), Sinclair Lewis, Henry Miller (q.v.), Ezra Pound, Thornton Wilder and others. It also received a large number of musicians, among them Louis Armstrong, Sidney Bechet, Duke Ellington, George Gershwin and Cole Porter. Many books on the Americans in Paris are included in the Bibliography. *See also* Baker, Josephine; Beach, Sylvia; Black Americans; Franklin, Benjamin; Hemingway, Ernest; James, Henry; Jefferson, Thomas; Jones, John Paul; Miller, Henry Valentine; Monroe, James; Morris, Gouverneur; Paine, Thomas; Wharton, Edith.

AMÉRIQUE. One of the quarters in the 19th arrondissement is called Amérique . . . but not for reasons one might expect. Instead, the cause is almost whimsical. Long ago, under the present square of Rhin-et-Danube, there were immense quarries of gypsum that, according to tradition, produced a plaster of such exceptional quality that it could be exported as far away as America.

APACHES. The name of that American Indian tribe became popular in France toward the middle of the 19th century because of the novels of Gustave Aimard, who stressed just how fierce the Apaches were. Journalists writing for the dailies *Le Matin* and *Le Journal* used the expression "apache" in 1902 to designate gangs of juvenile delinquents in the districts of Belleville (q.v.) and Charonne (q.v.) whose actions were revealed to public opinion by the "golden helmet" affair (a prostitute bearing this nickname for which two gangs engaged in a war). From 1902 to 1907, the *Apaches* were in fashion, and special columns devoted to sordid crimes, entitled "Paris-Apache," proliferated in the newspapers.

ARAGO, ÉTIENNE (1802–92). A Republican politician, Étienne Arago participated in the political struggle against the regimes of Louis-Philippe (1830–48) and Napoléon III (1852–70). When the surrender of the French army at Sedan and the emperor's capture were announced, the Second Empire was overthrown and a provisional government consisting of Republicans was formed on September 4, 1870. This government appointed Arago mayor (q.v.) of Paris. However, since he was unable to overcome the disturbances in the capital, he was replaced by Jules Ferry (q.v.) on November 15.

ARC DE TRIOMPHE. *See* ÉTOILE.

ARCADES. The arcade (usually called *passage,* or passageway, in French) is a typically Parisian phenomenon. It is generally covered with a glass roof, often narrow (4–5 meters wide), reserved for pedestrians and lined with shops. In a city such as Paris used to be, lacking sidewalks and where passersby had to constantly watch out for fiacres (q.v.) and flounder in the mud, these passageways offered welcome comfort because they also sheltered one from rain and cold. The origin of the arcade is traced to the wooden gallery that the duke of Chartres had built in 1786 at the Palais-Royal (q.v.) and to which was added a glass-enclosed gallery in 1792. The exceptional commercial success of the Palais-Royal galleries encouraged the construction of other arcades, such as Passage Feydeau (1790), Passage du Caire (1799), Passage des Panoramas (1800).

The heyday for building such arcades occurred between 1822 and 1848, during which period some 80 percent of the city's passageways were created. Many of them have since disappeared, but new ones are still being opened, only now they are called galleries. Many of them can be found under the large buildings of the Champs-Elysées (q.v.). Walter Benjamin wrote an informative book on Paris's passageways and their economic and social role.

ARCHBISHOP. The bishopric of Paris was raised to the rank of archbishopric only in 1622. Since then there have been 30 archbishops, including the present incumbent, Jean-Marie Lustiger, who was enthroned in 1981. For a long time the seat of the archbishopric was located along the southern side of Notre-Dame Cathedral (q.v.) in a building constructed during the term of Maurice de Sully (1160–96). This building was sacked on July 29, 1830, after the victory of the revolutionaries and the fall of Charles X, to punish the then archbishop Monseigneur de Quélen for having supported the monarch, who was overthrown. On February 14, 1831, the archbishop's palace was again ransacked by a mob and destroyed. The government refused to put up a new building, and Monseigneur de Quélen had no official residence up to his death. In 1840, his successor, Monseigneur Affre, accepted the government's proposal and was installed in the Hôtel de Chenizot (56, Rue Saint-Louis-en-l'Île). From 1849 to 1906, with the law on the separation of church and state, the archbishop resided in a mansion called the Hôtel du duc Du Chatelet (127, Rue de Grenelle, presently the Labor Ministry). After various temporary lodgings, the archbishop moved into the Hôtel de Rambuteau (30, Rue Barbet-de-Jouy) from 1913 to 1972. From 1972 on, he has been living at 8, Rue de la Ville-l'Evêque.

ARGOT. As early as the 15th century, François Villon (q.v.) referred to the "jargon" or "jobelin" that was used by the Parisian underworld to avoid being understood by the rest of the population. The term "argot," or slang, appeared in 1628 in a book by Olivier Chereau, *Le Jargon ou Langage de l'Argot réformé.* However, by the 19th century, this slang was being used by such eminent novelists as Balzac (q.v.), Dumas père and Victor Hugo (q.v.), and by Eugène Sue (q.v.) in *Les Mystères de Paris.* Almost all the novelists who wrote about Paris between 1880 and 1950 used *argot,* and this off-color language or slang really came into its own in detective stories. Alas, with even fewer Parisians by birth in the lower-class neighborhoods and ever more

Portuguese, Africans and Asians, *argot* has tended to disappear and be replaced by the *verlan* of the suburbanites.

ARRONDISSEMENTS. The administrative structure of Paris has evolved over time. Until 1789, it was divided into quarters (q.v.). These 20 quarters were replaced by 60 districts and then by 48 sections by the Revolution. A law of October 11, 1795, reorganized the capital into 12 arrondissements, or municipal districts. On January 1, 1860, by incorporating the nearby communes, Paris expanded from 12 arrondissements to 20, with new boundaries and new numbers, adopting the shape of a snail shell. The size of these arrondissements varies considerably. Those in the center are much smaller than those on the periphery, as can be seen from the following table, which indicates the area in hectares.

1st	182.7	11th	366.5
2nd	99.2	12th	637.7*
3rd	117.1	13th	714.6
4th	160.0	14th	562.0
5th	254.0	15th	850.2
6th	215.4	16th	784.6**
7th	408.8	17th	566.9
8th	388.1	18th	600.5
9th	217.9	19th	678.7
10th	289.2	20th	598.4

*The Bois de Vincennes (994.7 hectares) is not included in the area of the 12th arrondissement.

**The Bois de Boulogne (852.2 hectares) is not included in the area of the 16th arrondissement.

ARTICLES DE PARIS. These fancy goods, which were given the name *articles de Paris,* included a bevy of small objects handcrafted by artisans in the capital and utilized mainly for women's grooming and dressing, for furnishing apartments or as table decorations. There were all sorts of *articles de Paris:* buttons, baubles, little cardboard boxes, fans, implements for sewing or grooming, parasols and umbrellas, combs, feathers and artificial flowers, purses and wallets and other small fancy leather goods, and many more. A survey undertaken by the Chamber of Commerce in 1860, the last on this branch of handicrafts, enumerated 5,142 makers or owners and 25,748 workers. By now the local production of these fancy goods has almost completely disappeared because of competition from low-cost labor in the Far East.

AUBRIOT, HUGUES (c. 1320–c. 1387). Born in Dijon, Hugues Aubriot was appointed bailiff of Dijon in 1359. He was such an energetic administrator that Charles V (q.v.) had him appointed provost of Paris (q.v.) in 1367. He had the new city walls (q.v.) completed and built the Bastille (q.v.), and he regulated the bearing of arms and protected the Jews. As a reward, the king raised him to the nobility in 1374. However, his struggle against the University's (q.v.) privileges and his ruthless repression of disturbances created by the students made him many enemies. In 1380, fighting broke out over the question of precedence during the funeral of Charles V. Aubriot had the troublemakers, essentially students, arrested. The University demanded, and then obtained, the release of the imprisoned students and then instituted proceedings for heresy against the provost. He was condemned to life imprisonment in May 1381, this being seen as the University's revenge against royal authority. Aubriot took advantage of the revolt of the Maillotins against royal taxes in March 1382 to flee and place himself under the protection of the pope in Avignon, where he died.

AUTEUIL. Located in the 16th arrondissement, the quarter of Auteuil was originally a village of winegrowers. Its name was first recorded in 1109. It was raised to a parish in 1190. There were fewer than 500 inhabitants in 1672, at a time when Molière (q.v.) and Racine lived there, later joined by Boileau in 1685. Lying between Paris and Versailles (q.v.), Auteuil was always well frequented, but its greatest hour of glory came in the 18th century. It was then that it housed the literary salons of Mademoiselle Antier, of the Marquise de Boufflers and, above all, of Madame Helvétius, better known as "Notre-Dame d'Auteuil," whose visitors included Voltaire, Diderot, Chamfort, Condorcet and Benjamin Franklin (q.v.). Its population kept growing, from 1,040 inhabitants in 1801 to 6,200 in 1860, when Auteuil was incorporated into Paris. There are still many gardens but they are gradually disappearing because of real estate speculation and the burgeoning of the population, which reached 29,000 inhabitants in 1900 and twice that 30 years later before stabilizing.

-B-

BAGATELLE. This little chateau, which Marshal d'Estrées had built in 1720 in the Bois de Boulogne, was called the Bagatelle or Babiole, which translates into English as "bauble" or "trifle." Nonetheless, this building cost its owner more than 100,000 francs of that time. The Bagatelle pavilion became famous as a place used by Louis XV for lover's trysts until 1760. In 1775, it was bought by the count of Artois, the brother of Louis XVI, who had it razed and rebuilt by the architect Bélanger for the tidy sum of 1,200,000 francs. Renamed the Folie d'Artois, the Bagatelle was surrounded by gardens that spread over 15 hectares and were arranged in a picturesque Anglo-Chinese style by the

English landscape gardener Thomas Blaikie. The marquis of Hertford, its owner from 1832 to 1870, bequeathed it to Sir Richard Wallace (q.v.), who had a Trianon erected. The city of Paris bought the Bagatelle in 1904 and turned it into a place for exhibitions and a garden containing precious collections of trees, bushes and ornamental plants.

BAILLY, JEAN SYLVAIN (1736–93). Bailly, who was a famous astronomer, hoped to become the Benjamin Franklin (q.v.) of France and went into politics as soon as the Revolution began. He was elected chairman first of the Assembly of the Third Estate and then of the Constituent Assembly on June 17, 1789. After the fall of the Bastille (q.v.) on July 14 he was proclaimed mayor (q.v.) of Paris. Bailly, who was hated by the monarchists and criticized for his moderation by the revolutionaries, and who also was not much of a politician, rapidly lost popularity. He was completely discredited after the shooting on the Champ-de-Mars (q.v.) on July 17, 1791, and resigned, although he stayed on until his successor, Pétion (q.v.), was elected in November 1791. Bailly was arrested on November 6, 1793, and guillotined on November 12 on the Champ-de-Mars after a ceremony of atonement for the massacre of July 1791.

BAKER, JOSEPHINE (1906–75). Born in St. Louis, Missouri, Josephine Baker was a chorus girl on Broadway by the age of 15. She became a star in Paris in 1925, when she appeared with the Revue Nègre of the Black Birds. Almost naked, a belt of bananas draped around her waist, she excited and scandalized the public with her expressive dancing to the rhythm of the Charleston, which was then unknown in France. In 1927, she began to sing as well. Her American accent seduced the Parisians and she became the toast of the town with songs such as "La Petite Tonkinoise" and "J'ai deux amours." She participated in the Resistance in France and in Morocco from 1940 to 1942. Returning to Paris just after the city was liberated in August 1945, she sang before the wildly rejoicing crowds: "J'ai deux amours, Mon pays et Paris" (I have two loves, my country and Paris). Josephine Baker was granted the Legion of Honor, and she continued singing successfully until her death while also devoting herself to the struggle against racism and to the orphanage she had founded at Milandes in Périgord.

BALLOONS. Along with Annonay (80 kilometers south of Lyon), Paris can be considered the cradle of lighter-than-air craft. On June 4, 1783, the Montgolfier brothers, papermakers in Annonay, flew a hot-air balloon there. On August 27, 1784, on the Champ-de-Mars (q.v.) in Paris, a Montgolfier rose up into the sky. On September 19, in the courtyard of the palace of Versailles (q.v.), Louis XVI himself witnessed the flight of a balloon made of blue cotton that carried a sheep, a rooster and a duck. On October 15, the first man to achieve Icarus's dream was François Pilâtre de Rozier. Standing in a gondola suspended by ropes from a balloon, he rose to a height of 80 meters above the garden of the wallpaper manufacturer Réveillon, at Rue de Montreuil in Paris. The first free flight in the history of the world took place on November 21, 1783. This time it was Pilâtre de Rozier and François Laurent, the marquis d'Arlandes, who took off in a Montgolfier from the Muette garden, east of the capital, rose as high as 1,000 meters and then set down on Butte-aux-Cailles in the southeast. The first woman to go up alone in a balloon was Jeanne-Geneviève Labrousse, the future wife of Garnerin, the inventor of the parachute (q.v.), on November 10, 1798. The first company of military balloon pilots was formed and posted to Meudon, at the gates of Paris, on April 2, 1794. During the siege of 1870, communications with the rest of France were ensured by postal balloons (q.v.).

BALZAC, HONORÉ DE (1799–1850). Born in Tours, Honoré de Balzac arrived in Paris in 1814 and spent most of his life there. The author of 85 novels, he drew an extraordinary social portrait of that city in the series of novels grouped under the heading of *La Comédie humaine.* These books meticulously described not only aristocratic but also lower middle-class circles, not only the underworld but also the world of high finance. *Le Père Goriot, César Birotteau, Illusions perdues, Splendeurs et Misères des Courtisanes, La Cousine Bette* and *Le Cousin Pons* are the main masterpieces of this prolific and precise novelist who created exceptional characters who were nevertheless inspired by reality, such as the social-climber Rastignac or the criminal Vautrin. The house at 47, Rue Raynouard, where Balzac lived from 1840 to 1847, was turned into a museum (*see* Museums) dedicated to his memory in 1949.

BARRICADES. Popular uprisings in Paris were often marked by the construction of barricades in order to turn the rebelling quarters into fortresses and to slow down the advance of the police (q.v.) force. The first day of barricades in the capital's history took place on May 12, 1588, when the virulent Catholic League stirred up the inhabitants against King Henri III, who was accused of not conducting the war against the Protestants energetically enough. The second day occurred on August 27, 1648, and was the start of the Fronde (q.v.), a revolt of the *Parlement* (q.v.) and the nobility against the power exercised by Mazarin in the name of the child king Louis XIV (q.v.) and the regent, Anne of Austria. During the revolutionary period (1789–96) there were uprisings in which barricades were raised, but their role was minor.

The situation was very different on July 27, 28 and 29, 1830, when the city was covered with thousands of barricades and the insurrection precipitated the fall of Charles X. There were only about 30 barricades erected during the aborted uprising of April 12–14, 1834. At least 1,500 were counted on February 24, 1848, which convinced Louis-Philippe to abdicate. On June 23–26, 1848, although the capital was covered with barricades, the working-class and socialist insurrection was crushed. On December 3–4, 1851, the Faubourg Saint-Antoine (q.v.) revolted feebly against the coup d'état of Louis-Napoléon Bonaparte, the future Napoléon III: just 70 barricades were erected. The bloody week of May 21–28, 1871, witnessed the end of the Commune de Paris (q.v.) in a city in flames in which the paving stones of many streets were torn up to construct thousands of barricades. Not many were built during the liberation of Paris (q.v.), between August 19 and 25, 1944, since they were not of much use against tanks.

BASOCHE. The unmarried clerks of the courts of justice who were not filling the function of attorney were grouped into a fraternity called the *basoche,* which, according to tradition, had been recognized by Philippe IV the Fair in 1303. This association elected its own "king" who collected an entrance fee from new members, or "yellow beaks," and each year organized a "display," or parade, of clerks who marched through the city. The ceremony finished with a satirical show that was staged at the Palais de Justice (q.v.). This show was the origin of French comic theater. The *basoche*'s court held audiences and organized contests of farcical pleadings, or "fat suits," until 1789.

BASTILLE. The main fortification on the walls (q.v.) constructed by Charles V (q.v.), the Bastille was built between 1370 and 1382 near the Saint-Antoine gate. It was shaped like a rectangle, about 66 meters by 30 meters, and flanked by eight towers 24 meters high. These towers served as state prisons during the 17th and 18th centuries and were reserved especially for high-ranking or prestigious political opponents. These included Marshal de Bassompierre, Superintendent of Finance Fouquet, the Man in the Iron Mask, Voltaire, Cardinal Louis de Rohan and Marquis de Sade. There were never many prisoners, 43 at most, and only seven when the Bastille was taken by the people of Paris on July 14, 1789. In September 1789, the fortress—a symbol of absolutism and despotism, not least because of the royal warrants of arrest—was razed.

But what should take its place? Over the years many projects were mooted, but none was accomplished. Napoléon I had decided, back in 1808, to have a monumental fountain built in the shape of an elephant (q.v.), but nothing came of this apart from a scale model. After the victory of the insurrection of July 27, 28 and 29, 1830, it was decided to erect a column in memory of the persons who died during those three days, known as the Trois Glorieuses (q.v.). This "July" column was inaugurated at Place de la Bastille in 1840. With a total height of more than 50 meters, its foundation sinks into the location of the basin for the elephant fountain and the Saint-Martin canal flows under it. A crypt guards the remains of the 504 victims of the insurrection of July 1830 whose names are inscribed on the column. The column has a diameter of nearly four meters and is hollow, leaving room for a stairway that leads to the upper platform. This is graced with a statue of "Liberty," a winged spirit who flies off, holding her broken chains in her left hand and the torch of liberty in her right. To the east of the square, since 1989, is the Bastille Opéra, designed by the architect Carlos Ott.

BATEAU-LAVOIR (13, Place Emile-Goudeau). Built in about 1860 in Montmartre (q.v.) on the side of a collapsed quarry, the Bateau-Lavoir was inhabited as of 1880 by numerous artists who gave it its name, which translates into the "wash-house boat." This may have been because there was only one source of water and because the many doors of its tiny one-room dwellings made one think of the passageway of a steamer. From 1900 to 1914, the Bateau-Lavoir was the cradle of modern painting, with Renoir, Van Dongen, Picasso (q.v.) and others living there. It was there that cubism was born.

BATEAU-MOUCHE. The first of these steamboats designed to transport travelers on the Saône were built in 1864 in the Mouche quarter of Lyon (hence their name). They first took to the Seine (q.v.) during the world exhibition of 1867. They were so successful that they remained in service even after the exhibition closed. In 1886, the various companies running them merged into the General Company of Parisian Boats, which served a network of 39 kilometers with 47 pontoon stations and 107 bateaux-mouches carrying eight million travelers a year at an average speed of 16 kilometers an hour. Over the years, however, water transport lost out to competition from trams (q.v.), buses (q.v.) and the métro (q.v.) so that by 1918 the boats existed only through the custom of tourists.

BAUDELAIRE, CHARLES (1821–67). Baudelaire spent his youth in the Latin Quarter (q.v.); he studied at Collège Louis-le-Grand (q.v.) and went for walks in the Luxembourg gardens. With the exception of a trip to the island of Reunion, which was imposed on him between 1841 and 1842, he spent his whole life in his hometown, where he frequently moved from one place to another and led a Bohemian (q.v.)

existence as an art critic and poet. Everything he created is devoted to this city, *Les Fleurs du Mal* (1857) with their "Parisian pictures," *Les Paradis artificiels* (1860), *Petits Poèmes en prose* and *Le Spleen de Paris* (1869).

BEACH, SYLVIA (1887–1962). Sylvia Beach, who was born in Baltimore, Maryland, opened the first American bookshop and lending library in Paris on November 17, 1919. Her shop, which was called "Shakespeare and Company," played an eminent role in literary history between 1919 and 1939. James Joyce, whose *Ulysses* was published by her in 1922, called it "the great literary workshop." Ernest Hemingway (q.v.), T. S. Eliot, Samuel Beckett, Thornton Wilder and many other writers who are now famous browsed in that magic place, located at 8, Rue Dupuytren, and which moved to 12, Rue de l'Odéon in 1921. Even today, at 37, Rue de la Bûcherie, an American bookshop carries on the name of "Shakespeare and Company."

BEAUBOURG CENTER. *See* POMPIDOU CENTER.

BELLEVILLE. On the highest site in Paris (129 meters), there was originally the Savies farm, first referred to in 862, then the hamlet of Poitronville, which appeared in the 12th century, and finally the village of Belleville, which was first mentioned in 1451. The hamlet of Ménilmontant depended on this village of winegrowers. On these pastoral heights, well-to-do Parisians of the 18th century built country houses, while just across the border with the city taverns and cafés (q.v.) sprang up that sold the "guinguet" wine, the light wine produced by the vineyards on the neighboring slopes, duty free and thus much cheaper than that from within Paris's limits.

Between 1825 and 1860, this still-rural village began turning into a working-class district, while its population rose from 2,876 inhabitants in 1817 to 57,699 in 1859, just before it was incorporated into the capital. At that time, Belleville was the 13th-largest town in France and a hotbed of intense Socialist unrest. In 1871, its inhabitants made up a significant share of the Communards, and it was in Bas Belleville that the last fighting of the civil war took place, on May 28. Since the end of the 19th century, Belleville has become home to large numbers of foreigners. Even today, it is still one of the places with the highest number of leftist Parisian voters. Belleville's territory corresponds to the 20th arrondissement, to which are added adjacent sections of the 19th, 10th and 11th arrondissements.

BERCY. Nowadays Bercy is a quarter in the 12th arrondissement, but it is also the site of the oldest known human settlement in Paris. In September 1991, excavations brought to light tools, pottery and pirogues bearing witness to permanent human occupation going back at least 6,000 years. The name Bercy was first mentioned in a deed of 1134 by which Louis VI confirmed the ownership of this village by the abbey of Montmartre. This area is damp and thinly inhabited. Its market gardens and its lovely dwellings were part of the commune of Charenton and of the Parisian parish of Saint-Paul until Bercy was raised to an independent commune in 1791. At that time, its population was less than 1,400 inhabitants and it had risen only to just over 10,000 by 1860, when it was incorporated into Paris.

The townscape has changed considerably over the past two centuries. The sumptuous country estates, Folie Rambouillet, châteaux of the Paris brothers and Petit-Bercy have all disappeared and been replaced by a port and huge wine warehouses, which were built between 1809 and 1820. These warehouses were recently torn down, and a new quarter is under construction. Its main buildings are the Palais Omnisport de Paris-Bercy, erected in 1984 by Michel Andrault, Aydin Guvan and Jean Prouvé; the Ministry of Finance, completed in 1989 by Paul Chemetov and Borja Huidobro; and the American Center (51, Rue de Bercy), designed by Frank Gehry.

BERNHARDT, SARAH (1844–1923). Born Henriette-Rosine Bernard in Paris, Sarah Bernhardt was the daughter of a milliner from Berlin and a Havre magistrate. After a stint at the Comédie-Française (q.v.) from 1861 to 1863, she was given a series of minor roles until finally she was noticed in *Le Passant,* by François Coppée in 1869. She returned to the Comédie-Française in 1872 after her triumph during the revival of *Ruy Blas,* by Victor Hugo (q.v.). However, her eccentricities were such that she was forced to leave the Comédie-Française again in 1880. She then went on a tour of Europe and the United States and was greeted with wild applause when she played in *La Dame aux Camélias,* by Alexandre Dumas fils, and *Adrienne Lecouvreur,* by Eugène Scribe and Ernest Legouvé. For years she created roles and contributed to the success of plays in Paris, which she then introduced abroad, thereby becoming the ambassador of French theater. Her triumph in *La Tosca,* by Victorien Sardou, in 1887 was unforgettable. In 1899, she founded her own theater at Place du Châtelet, where *Hamlet,* by Marcel Schwob, and *L'Aiglon,* by Edmond Rostand, were staged and applauded. She continued acting there herself until 1914, but made only rare appearances after she had a leg amputated in 1915. She is buried in the Père-Lachaise cemetery (q.v.).

BIBLIOTHÈQUE NATIONALE. *See* NATIONAL LIBRARY.

BIÈVRE, LA. The Bièvre, whose name derives from the Gallic words for "river of beavers," is the only waterway of any size that flows into the Seine (q.v.) in Paris. Its source is near Versailles (q.v.), in the small valley of Bouviers; it then crosses Buc, Jouy, Bièvres, Igny, Verrières, Antony, Fresnes, Bourg-la-Reine, Cachan, Arcueil and Gentilly before entering Paris through the passage at Peupliers. Then it flows along the Rue des Peupliers toward Moulin-des-Prés, winds around the Butte-aux-Cailles from the west, and squeezes Gobelins between its two arms, which meet again at Rue Broca before following the Rue du Fer-à-Moulin and Rue Poliveau (a distortion of Pont-Livault). From that point on, the junction of the Bièvre with the Seine varies. In prehistoric times, it flowed parallel to the Seine, which it joined at the level of the Alma bridge. Later it flowed into the Seine at the location of the Rue de Bièvre. Finally, the monks of Saint-Victor (q.v.) diverted it toward the east so they could use it to water their garden. The result was that it flowed into the Seine initially at the level of Sully bridge and subsequently at the level of Austerlitz bridge. During its whole passage through Paris, the Bièvre is covered by a cement vault and today is not much more than a sewer.

BISTROS. The bistro (*bistrot* in French) is a typically Parisian institution. It can be defined as follows: an apparently modest café (q.v.) or restaurant (q.v.), with reasonable prices, attracting regular customers who contribute to creating a convivial atmosphere. The origin of the word is uncertain. Some believe it appeared in 1814, during the Russian occupation, when the Cossacks asked to be served rapidly (*bistra* means fast in Russian). Others think that it derives from *argot* (q.v.) and comes from *louchebem,* the butchers' language.

Physically, not much distinguishes one bistro from another; the only originality comes from the clientele: idlers, workers, employees, retirees, and, especially, the pillars of the bistro with their "counter calluses," who are present from opening time to closing time and consume alcoholic beverages.

The habitués always drink the same thing: coffee with or without cream for the abstemious, a small "morning" white wine for the fans of alcohol, then a rosé or a big red, and an apéritif for the office employees at noon and on leaving the office. There is often a dart board, with the loser paying for the round. They speak in a code, and the orders are often incomprehensible to outsiders. The "little black" is a coffee, and the "kir," "tomato" and "parrot" designate different colored mixtures. Sometimes the names are affected by politics. About 1955, a glass of red wine was called a "Stalin," a glass of rosé a "Socialist" and milk was known as "Mendès-France." Mineral water, which is not often ordered, was a "jobless."

Nowadays the bistros are in decline. People move about too much and the former habitués tend to disappear. Meanwhile, white- and blue-collar workers have less time for lunch and hurry to catch the packed trains to the suburbs at the end of the day. However, the bistros are doing their best to resist this mad dash and the general worsening of working and living conditions.

BLACK AMERICANS. At the beginning of the 19th century, many Black Americans were fascinated by the image of France, the nation of human rights and the abolition of slavery. The first Black literary club in the United States was founded in New Orleans in the 1840s and its main members, Armand Lanusse and Victor Séjour, studied in Paris. Black artists appeared successfully before Parisian audiences: Louis Gottschalk, Thomas Brown Bethune, Elizabeth Greenfield, James Bland and Ira Aldridge. Other Blacks traveled around France as tourists, such as William Wells Brown and Booker T. Washington.

France became much better known to the Black American population as a whole during the First World War. More than 200,000 Black soldiers told their families in their letters home that they had not been subjected to segregation by the French population. It was in Paris, in 1919, that W. E. B. Du Bois and Joel Spingarn organized the first Pan-African Congress. Between 1918 and 1939, most of the writers from Harlem— Countee Cullen, Jessie Fauset, Langston Hughes, Harold Jackman, Claude McKay, Jean Toomer, Walter White, and others—spent some time in Paris. Large numbers of musicians, singers and dancers also came, with Josephine Baker (q.v.) obtaining the greatest success.

After the Second World War, a new wave of Black writers arrived in Paris, first Richard Wright, followed by James Baldwin, William Gardner Smith and Chester Himes. Alongside them were the designer Ollie Harrington, the painters Walter Coleman, Beauford Delaney, Herb Gentry and Larry Potter, as well as countless musicians. During the 1950s they formed a remarkable Black colony that met in the Latin Quarter, in the Monaco and Tournon cafés (q.v.), and then in the "soul" restaurant of LeRoy Haynes.

Africa's independence and the retreat of racism in the United States during the 1960s weakened the image of France in the Black community, all the more so since France was itself caught up in a colonial war in Algeria. Nevertheless, there are not many Black American writers and artists presently active who have not visited Paris at least once.

BOATING. Boating, which appeared around 1825, was above all an activity for ordinary people and an excuse to have lunch on the grass, take a drink or two and sing songs. It was first practiced by young artists and students and caught on more broadly only toward 1850, when the canalization of the Seine (q.v.) made the pastime much easier. The number of pleasure craft registered with the police (q.v.) climbed from 1,200 in 1850 to 4,000 in 1854. Civil servants, clerks and shopkeepers started to go boating. Between 1860 and 1880, most of the boating parties got back to their home port in the suburbs by train, using the Bastille station for those upstream (Bercy, Charenton, Joinville, Nogent) and Saint-Lazare for those downstream (Neuilly, Asnières, Argenteuil, Chatou, Bougival). After that, boating faded away, a victim of industry and pollution as the banks of the Seine lost their charm and the smiling countryside turned into gloomy suburbs. Boating as a hobby did not survive the First World War.

BOBINO (20, Rue de la Gaîté). The Bobino music hall (q.v.) was inaugurated in 1873 but it was not very successful until it came under the management of Bernard Richain in 1894. He had the auditorium refurbished in 1901 and attracted new talents such as the singer Henri Alibert. The audience continued to dwindle, though, preferring the cinema (q.v.) instead, until the hall was closed in 1926. Bobino was then bought by the Lutétia-Empire company, which renovated the auditorium luxuriously. Fernandel made his Parisian debut there in 1928. Still, despite lavish shows that were changed every week, Bobino continued slipping until Alcide Castille and his son took over the management in 1936. They gave it a new lease on life by staging modern operettas and featuring artists such as André Dassary, George Guétary, Yves Montand, Bourvil, the Compagnons de la Chanson, Line Renaud, Aznavour, Henri Salvador, Robert Lamoureux, the Frères Jacques, Patachou, Juliette Gréco, Raymond Devos, Georges Brassens, Gilbert Bécaud, Jacques Brel, Léo Ferré and others. The company was run by Félix and then Gilles Vitry between 1958 and 1981. The last show was given by Guy Bedos in January 1981. Bobino was torn down in 1984.

BOHEMIANS. The Bohemian was born in Paris about 1840. This was a new social category of students or artists, happy revelers, lazy and noisy, who did not care what tomorrow would bring. This image was modified by Henri Murger's book, *Scènes de la vie de bohème,* which was published in 1847. The Bohemian was now a young man who departed from bourgeois rules of social life to profit from his youth and sow his wild oats before settling down and entering good society. About 1880, a third type of Bohemian was created. This was a *révolté* who refused all compromise with the world of money and the vulgar pleasures of the crowd and denounced the "leveling of pleasures." These new Bohemians refused to live like the others and stuck together in the Latin Quarter (q.v.) or Montmartre (q.v.). The Bohemian almost disappeared after 1914 because of the social upheavals of the First World War.

BOILEU, ÉTIENNE (c. 1200–70). After serving as provost (q.v.) of Orléans until 1260, Étienne Boileau was distinguished by Louis IX (Saint Louis), who put him in charge of Paris. As the first royal provost of the capital whose name is known, he is remembered for having ordered the compilation of all the regulations of guilds in the city, which provided an authentic picture of the Parisian economy and society of about 1268–70.

BONNOT, JULES JOSEPH (1876–1912). On December 21, 1911, at Rue Ordener, an armed holdup was carried out by gangsters in an automobile for the first time in Paris—well before the exploits of Al Capone popularized this sort of crime. The frequency and brutality of this type of holdup, which was always bloody and often fatal, aroused public opinion. The gang's leader was Bonnot, backed up by François Raymond Callemin (born in 1890) alias "Scientific" Raymond, both of whom spouted anarchistic ideas. The police (q.v.) finally arrested Raymond on April 7, 1912. On April 24, Bonnot shot down the deputy head of the detective squad and managed to escape from a group of policemen. On April 28, he was surrounded in a house in the suburbs, at Choisy-le-Roi. There he was besieged, yet he held out against a small army of 500 policemen and gendarmes, directed by Chief Commissioner Louis Lépine (q.v.) in person, until he was killed. At least 20,000 people from the neighborhood and all of Paris witnessed the battle, the dynamiting of the house and the final assault. The following May 4, a special criminal brigade of the police was set up to stamp out the urban gangsterism of which the Bonnot gang was the first example.

BOUCICAUT, ARISTIDE (1810–77). First just a peddler, then an employee in a linen-draper shop, Boucicaut joined with Paul and Justin Videau in 1853 to operate the drapery and fancy goods store "Au Bon Marché" (22–24, Rue de Sèvres). He allowed free admittance, with no obligation to buy, set fixed prices that did away with bargaining, permitted returns and accepted small profits, hoping to compensate for the narrow margin with larger sales. Bon Marché's turnover skyrocketed from 500,000 francs in 1852 to more than 72 million at his death, and the number of employees rose from 12 to 1,788.

BOUFFES-PARISIENS (Theater) (4, Rue Monsigny). In order to have his operettas played, Jacques Offenbach (q.v.) bought a theater made of boards, in a corner of the garden of the Champs-Elysées (q.v.), from the prestidigitator Lacaze. Named Bouffes-Parisiens, it was inaugurated in July 1855 in the midst of the world exhibition. It was a great success, but this rundown theater was unusable in inclement weather.

Thus Offenbach started looking for a more comfortable auditorium. He bought and renovated the Théâtre des Jeunes Acteurs in the Rue Monsigny, which was created in 1826 by Charles Comte, and opened it on December 29, 1855, under the same name of Bouffes-Parisiens. The first important work of the famous composer, *Orpheus in the Underworld*, was staged there in 1858. It was an unheard-of success for the time, with a run of 228 performances.

Offenbach withdrew from the management of the theater in 1861, but it continued to stage operettas until 1913. These included *Les Mousquetaires au couvent* (1880), by Varney, and *Véronique* (1898), by Messager. In 1918, the operetta was again in vogue with the colossal success of *Phi-Phi*. Albert Willemetz took over the management of the theater in 1929 and staged both comedies and operettas. However, the latter were increasingly expensive, and the auditorium could not hold an audience of more than 700. The Bouffes-Parisiens was therefore gradually confined to being a variety theater, at which it still excels today.

BOULEVARDS. The first boulevards in Paris, called the Grands Boulevards, were created by Louis XIV (q.v.) who, in 1670, ordered that the city walls (q.v.) be torn down and replaced by thoroughfares 36 meters wide and lined with trees. The Grands Boulevards start at the Bastille (q.v.) and end at the Madeleine (q.v.). They remained fairly countrified, a place for family promenades bordered by some lovely residences, until the beginning of the 19th century. About that time, theaters (q.v.) were opened and became the heart and soul of Parisian life until about 1900.

There are also two other boulevards that are less well known but that also replaced old walls. The outer boulevards, which surround Paris from Place de la Nation to Place de l'Étoile (q.v.) and passing by Place Clichy and Place Denfert-Rochereau, were traced along the location of the wall built by the Farmers General between 1783 and 1787 (*see* Tollgates). The marshals' boulevards delimit present-day Paris. They correspond to the military road, a rampart walk inside the fortifications that Louis Adolphe Thiers (q.v.) had built between 1841 and 1845 and that were razed as of 1919. They bear the names of marshals of Emperor Napoléon I. The peripheral boulevard is the highway that has circled the capital since 1973 and that runs just a few dozen meters outside the marshals' boulevards.

BOULOGNE (Woods). What remains of the great forest of Rouvray, which stretched to the west of Paris, the woods or Bois de Boulogne received their name about 1308 from a chapel that King Philippe the Fair had built in memory of a pilgrimage to Boulogne-sur-Mer.

François I had a chateau constructed there that was called Madrid, to recall the king's captivity in the Spanish capital. In the 18th century, the châteaux of La Muette and Neuilly, the Saint-James, Bagatelle (q.v.) and Renelagh follies (q.v.) were built there. Napoléon III commissioned the engineeer Alphand, the architect Davioud and the landscape gardener Barillet-Deschamps to turn the woods into an English-style park. From 1852 to 1858, two lakes and three streams were dug and a race course was built at Longchamp. Later additions on its 852 hectares are the Jardin d'Acclimatation (a children's amusement park), the estate of Bagatelle, the Municipal Flower Garden and the Shakespeare Garden, as well as the Museum of Popular Arts and Traditions.

BOUQUINISTES. Paris is the only city in the world to have bookseller's stalls lining the quays. These stalls hold the stock in trade of the *bouquinistes,* small dealers in secondhand books. They first appeared in the 16th century and competed with the booksellers who owned shops. These humble dealers display their books on a trestle table or laid out on a cloth on the pavement. Some of them hawk their books in the streets with a wooden or wicker basket hanging from their necks by a strap. The proprietors of bookshops complained bitterly about the great harm they suffered from the *bouquinistes.* Thus, in 1578, it was decided that only 12 of them should be authorized and that they should sell their goods, two by two, at six locations, all of them along the banks of the Seine (q.v.). No sooner had the Pont Neuf (q.v.) been completed in 1606 than the *bouquinistes* invaded it, although they had been prohibited from doing so. Despite hassling from the police, the *bouquinistes* multiplied. There were estimated to be about 120 of them in 1732 and 300 in 1796. The first official count was made by the police headquarters in 1857, when they numbered only 67, and each one was allocated ten meters of parapet along the quays of the 1st, 4th, 5th and 6th arrondissements. In 1904, they set up a trade association, and today there are about 250 *bouquinistes.*

BOURSE (Place de la Bourse). The first exchange was officially established in 1724 at the Hôtel de Nevers in the Rue Vivienne. It moved several times during the Revolution. From 1818 to 1827, it was housed in the stage settings store of the Opéra (q.v.) in the Rue Feydeau. In 1828, it moved into a palace built by Brongniart at the orders of Napoléon I. Today, in this pastiche of an ancient temple is located the French stock exchange. Women have been admitted since 1967 but access has been strictly supervised ever since the bomb attack of October 20, 1980.

At present the operations are extensively computerized, and the

Paris Stock Exchange ranks fourth in the world after New York, Tokyo and London, although the volume of transactions is a tenth that of New York and a third that of London. The creation of the international futures market, the Marché à terme international de France (MATIF), and the end of exchange control stimulated the expansion of the Paris Bourse. However, the high proportion of investors controlled by the state, nationalized banks and insurance companies greatly limits the market's ability to fluctuate.

BRIDGES. The lay of the land around Paris is influenced by the passage of the Seine (q.v.), which in turn is influenced by the existence of the Île de la Cité (q.v.). The Romans built two stone bridges, the Grand Pont between the island and the right bank and the Petit Pont to the left bank. During the 14th century, two footbridges were erected, the Pont aux Meuniers and Pont de la Planche-Mibray, that were used mainly to access the watermills (q.v.). At the end of the 14th and beginning of the 15th centuries, two new bridges were built, the Pont Notre-Dame and Pont Saint-Michel. As of 1607 these four bridges were joined by the Pont Neuf (q.v.). Five new bridges were constructed under Louis XIII, between 1620 and 1635. The 11th bridge, presently called Pont de la Concorde, was inaugurated in 1791. Napoléon I (1804–14) put up three more. Seven new bridges went into service between 1827 and 1834, four during the Second Empire (1852–70), and the Third Republic offered Paris eight new bridges between 1876 and 1905. Two bridges were built in 1968–69 as part of the peripheral boulevard. Along with the bridges for the métro (q.v.) and for pedestrians, there was a total of 38 bridges on the Seine within the limits of Paris in 1997.

BUSES. One of those forgotten pioneers, Charles Dietz successfully experimented in 1834–35 with an ancestor of the bus on the Paris-Versailles route. This was a steam car pulling a coach. At that time, however, steampower was authorized only on railway tracks, so the trams (q.v.) developed first. It was not until 1906 that the General Omnibus Company put into service the first automobile-drawn omnibuses, which were soon called autobuses, or just buses. They ran on the AM line from Montparnasse (q.v.) to Saint-Germain-des-Prés (q.v.) and carried 30 passengers each. In 1912, there were more than 1,000 of these buses running on 43 lines. From 1921 to 1939, 16 different models were launched, one after the other, with Renault eventually taking over the market. The gradual discontinuance of trams by 1929 encouraged a proliferation of buses, there being 4,000 in 1937. The invasion of public thoroughfares by the private automobile by the 1950s was a serious setback for the buses, which, caught in traffic jams, were forced to move ever more slowly, so that at present they move only at about 10 kilometers an hour on the average. By now they account for only 10 percent of urban travel, and the number of passengers has fallen from 900 million a year in 1948 to a bit more than 300 million people, using the 60 or so lines covering somewhat more than 500 kilometers.

BUTTES-CHAUMONT (Park). Napoléon III wanted to offer the inhabitants of the working-class neighborhoods of the north and east of the capital a place for recreation and relaxation. To that end, he chose the hillock of Chaumont ("bare or bald mound"), a spot not far from which the sinister gallows of Montfaucon had stood for centuries and from which open and underground quarries had since the 18th century mined thousands of tons of gypsum, which was turned into plaster in the nearby furnaces. It was also close to the municipal rubbish dumps and a knacker's yard. Hordes of tramps and vagabonds sought refuge in this lugubrious place. The engineer Alphand and the landscape gardener Barrillet-Deschamps filled in part of the quarries but preserved the wild and picturesque landscape, dug an artificial lake, put up a belvedere and made a grotto of the entrance to the old quarry. Thus, 27 hectares of desolation was transformed into a romantic English-style park, which was inaugurated in 1867 after four years of massive labor. This "invented landscape," as it was described by the poet Louis Aragon, is the most original and pleasing of Paris's green spaces.

-C-

CABARET. The cabaret is the ancestor of the restaurant (q.v.). It differed from the tavern in that the tavern sold "by the jug" whereas the cabaret sold "by the plate," that is, the wine was served on a table, covered with a tablecloth, at which it was possible to eat. During the 15th and 16th centuries, François Villon (q.v.), François Rabelais and Mathurin Régnier celebrated the good food and joyous companionship of the Parisian cabarets. In the 17th century, La Fontaine, Molière (q.v.) and Racine frequented Le Mouton Blanc and La Croix de Lorraine. Marivaux went to L'Epée de Bois, while Rousseau and Diderot dined at Au Panier Fleuri. Excited by the drink, the table mates often finished the meal by breaking into a song.

No mention was made of singers or musicians in the cabarets until 1880. At the end of the 18th century, two prestigious establishments, the Café des Muses and the Café d'Apollon, presented sketches, pantomime and prestidigitation acts, precursors of the café-théâtres. Two associations organized meetings in the cabarets and sang there, both of them named Société du Caveau. The first was founded in 1733 in the Cabaret du Caveau, in the Rue de Buci, by Collé and other writers, poets, painters and musicians to compose and sing poems, but it disappeared in 1742. A second group was formed at the initiative of the writer Crébillon fils and lasted from 1762 to 1792, only to be reconstituted from 1796 to 1802 and from 1806 to 1816 with Goffé, Désaugiers and the chansonnier Béranger. Its meetings were held on the 20th of each month at Au Rocher de Cancale, in the Rue Montorgueil.

The modern cabaret was born on November 18, 1881, with Le Chat Noir (q.v.) of Rodolphe Salis, which was located at the foot of Montmartre at 84, Boulevard de Rochechouart. A multitude of imitators followed: Le Mirliton, L'Ane Rouge, Les Décadents, Les Soirées Parisiennes, Le Chien Noir, Le Lapin Agile, and so on. The cabaret revue, a musical satire of current political events, was invented in 1899 by Henri Dreyfus in La Boîte à Fursy. As of 1914, the cabaret was supplanted by the café-chantant (q.v.) or café-concert.

CABOCHE, SIMON LECOUSTELIER, alias JEAN. A flayer at the slaughterhouse near Châtelet, Jean Caboche was mentioned for the first time in September 1411, when the duke of Burgundy, Jean the Fearless, tried to foist his authority on the mad king Charles VI (q.v.) and win over the Parisians. The powerful butcher's guild rallied to the duke, and Caboche became the spokesman of the Burgundian faction. In 1413, he led an armed mob in an attack on the dauphin's residence. His name remains attached to the Cabochien ordinance of May 25, 1413, which provides for all sorts of reforms that never saw the light of day. In August 1413, Armagnac's party won in Paris, and Caboche had to flee. He returned to the capital in 1418, close behind the Burgundian troops, but he no longer played any political role since the supporters of Jean the Fearless were being taken away by the executioner Capeluche.

CAFÉ. Coffee, which was produced in the Arabian peninsula, entered Europe through Venice and reached Paris in about 1643–44. This beverage became fashionable only in 1669, thanks to the Turkish ambassador. In 1672, an Armenian named Pascal opened the first café, or coffee house, first at the Saint-Germain fair and then on Quay de l'École. Starting off as a waiter in Pascal's service, the Sicilian Procopio dei Coltelli made drinking coffee the "in" thing with the establishment he founded, which still exists today under the name of Procope (q.v.). As a place for meetings and literary, and later political, discussions, the cafés proliferated: there were 380 in 1723, nearly 1,800 in 1789 and more than 4,000 in 1807.

The Palais-Royal (q.v.) and then the Grands Boulevards boasted the most famous cafés in the 19th century, such as Tortoni, Café de Paris, Café Anglais, Café Riche and others. Around 1910, the painters turned Montparnasse (q.v.) into a center of intellectual life and got together at La Coupole (q.v.) and Le Dôme (q.v.). In Saint-Germain-des-Prés (q.v.), the existentialist crowd of the 1945–55 period frequented Café de Flore (q.v.), the Deux Magots (q.v.) and Lipp (q.v.). Nowadays, cafés are dying out as places for socializing and the sole survivor of their age of glory is the Café de la Paix (q.v.), which has become little more than a tourist attraction. *See also* Café-Chantant; Café de la Paix; Coupole, La; Deux Magots, Les; Dôme, Le; Flore, Le; Lipp; Procope; Rotonde, La.

CAFÉ-CHANTANT or CAFÉ-CONCERT. The first café (q.v.) where the public could watch sketches and pantomimes was mentioned about 1740 under the name of Café des Bouts de Chandelle. It did not take long for other cafés to imitate it, in particular the Café des Muses and Café d'Apollon. The real vogue of café-chantants began in 1839–40 on the Champs-Elysées (q.v.), which at that time was little more than a promenade through the countryside where Parisians could quench their thirst in popular cafés. Small bands and singers appeared successfully at the Café du Bosquet, Café du Midi and Café des Ambassadeurs. From there, the fashion spread throughout Paris with Estaminet Lyrique and Café de France on the Grands Boulevards, Casino Français at the Palais-Royal (q.v.) and the pagoda of Ba-Ta-Clan on the Boulevard Voltaire. The biggest and best known of the café-chantants were near the Faubourg Poissonnière, such as the Alcazar d'Hiver and Eldorado (q.v.) on the Boulevard de Strasbourg. The heydey of the café-chantant came between 1880 and 1900, when it was the main entertainment for the lower classes, but it was rapidly supplanted by the cinema (q.v.). The only ones that remained after the First World War were Bobino (q.v.), L'Européen, Pacra, Le Petit Casino and Les Folies Belleville. The café-chantant passed from the scene around 1950.

CAFÉ DE LA PAIX (5, Place de l'Opéra). Inaugurated in 1863, the Café de la Paix, which is located at the corner of Place de l'Opéra and the Boulevard des Capucines, occupies the ground floor of the Grand Hotel. From the day it opened, it has been an extraordinary success. Seated on its terrace, the biggest in Paris at that time, the Parisian bourgeois could hail acquaintances passing by. Since it is next door to the Opéra (q.v.), the Café de la Paix rapidly became the rendezvous of people in artistic, literary and even political circles, with whom mingled the foreign tourists lodged in the Grand Hotel. The original Napoléon III decor, the work of Charles Garnier, who was the architect of the

Opéra, has been preserved, and it still attracts throngs of tourists who crowd its terrace, which was enclosed with glass in 1976.

CANCAN. The rowdy dances popular among the common people of Les Halles (q.v.) quarter at the end of the 18th century seem to be the origin of the cancan. In 1832, it was launched under that name by Alton-Shée and Lord Seymour (called Milord Blackguard) and played at the Bal Musard. The dancers Pomaré and Céleste Mogador raised it almost to an art form in 1844 at the Bal Mabille (q.v.). Offenbach (q.v.) introduced the French cancan in *Orpheus in the Underworld* (1858); but by that time the fashion was already passing. There was a revival at the end of the 19th century at Moulin Rouge (q.v.) with La Goulue, Grille d'Égout, Nini-Patte-en-l'air and Rigolboche, who were immortalized by Toulouse-Lautrec (q.v.).

CARDIN, PIERRE (1922–   ). Cardin started out as a cutter for a men's tailor, then became an assistant of Christian Dior (q.v.), before founding his own fashion house in 1949. He is one of the eminent representatives of Parisian *haute couture*. Among other things, he won the Golden Thimble in 1977, 1979 and 1982 and was granted the Fashion Oscar in 1985. Cardin has been a member of the Academy of Fine Arts in the Institute of France since 1992. His store is located at 82, Rue du Faubourg-Saint-Honoré.

CARNAVALET (Museum) (23–25, Rue de Sévigné). As of 1548, Jacques des Ligneris had built one of the most beautiful mansions (hôtel) of Paris. Pierre Lescot, Jean Bullant and Androuet du Cerceau may have worked on it, and the rich sculpture is attributed to Jean Goujon. In 1578, this mansion was bought by Françoise de la Baume-Montrevel, the widow of a Breton gentleman, François de Kernevenoy, from whose distorted name the present name of Carnavalet originated. As of 1654, François Mansart further embellished this sumptuous residence and added a floor. The Marquise de Sévigné (q.v.) lived there from 1677 until her death in 1696. In 1866, the city of Paris bought the hôtel to house its historical collections.

CARROUSEL (Arch). The triumphal arch of Septimus Severus in Rome served as the model for the architects Percier and Fontaine when they built the Arc de Triomphe du Carrousel between 1806 and 1808. It was dedicated to Napoléon's Grande Armée, but the emperor objected to having his effigy placed at the summit of the arch, installed in a chariot pulled by the famous ancient horses taken from the basilica of San Marco in Venice but returned in 1814. The Arc de Triomphe was used as the entrance to the palace of the Tuileries (q.v.), which was burned by the Commune (q.v.) in 1871. The name Carrousel comes from the great equestrian tournament, or carousel, that Louis XIV (q.v.) held on June 5–6, 1662, to celebrate the birth of the dauphin.

CARTIER. In 1847, Louis-François Cartier set up shop as a jeweler in the Rue Montorgueil. The quality of his jewelry was such that he was an immediate success and, in 1859, he moved to the heart of Paris's commercial and society center at 9, Boulevard des Italiens. Allied with the Worths, the Cartier family represented the elite of the gifted Parisian craftsmen, who were sought after everywhere. In 1899, the Cartier store was transferred to an even more prestigious address, 13, Rue de la Paix. In 1902, a branch was opened in London (4 New Burlington Street) and in 1909 another was established in New York (712 Fifth Avenue). The Cartier company presently embodies the highest quality and the most refined taste in Parisian and worldwide jewelry.

CARTOUCHE, LOUIS DOMINIQUE (1693–1721). Once a schoolmate of Voltaire at Collège Louis-le-Grand (q.v.), Cartouche left school at the age of 12 to follow a troupe of Bohemians (gypsies). Later he served in the army for a while and ended up as the head of a gang of highway robbers who relieved Parisians of their valuables for nearly ten years. He was betrayed by one of his accomplices, arrested and condemned to death by being broken on the wheel at Place de Grève (q.v.). By then his popularity had reached such a peak that even before the execution took place a play was staged at the Comédie-Française (q.v.) that depicted his rakish existence. The first French bandit to enjoy the sympathy of public opinion, Cartouche can be regarded as a French counterpart of Robin Hood.

CASINO DE PARIS (16, Rue de Clichy). The Palace-Théâtre was built in 1880 on the site of an earlier amusement park, the Tivoli, which was turned into a skating rink in 1867. In 1890, it was renamed Casino de Paris. Its shows and revues attracted a huge public. Mistinguett (q.v.) made her debut there in 1893. The Casino's greatest time of glory began in 1917 when it came under the management of Léon Volterra, who organized spectacular revues with, among others, Gaby Deslys and Harry and Murray Pilcer, who brought the Rag Time Band to Paris. In 1920, Mistinguett and Maurice Chevalier (q.v.) triumphed in the revue of "Paris qui Jazz." The Hollywood star Pearl White played there in 1922. From 1929 to 1966, Oscar Dufrenne and Henri Varna ran the music hall. During that time Josephine Baker (q.v.), Cécile Sorel and Tino Rossi were unforgettable hits, and the greatest lead dancers appeared, including Line Renaud, Mick Micheyl, Mary Meade, June Richmond and Zizi Jeanmaire.

CASTEL BÉRANGER (14, Rue La Fontaine). In 1894, Hector Guimard (q.v.) received an order for a block of flats for rental purposes in a neighborhood that was then rather seamy, poorly served by public transport and close to warehouses and gas plants. He was able to take advantage of a narrow plot of land and put up three buildings of five to six stories and decorated them exuberantly in what became known as the *art nouveau* style. When Castel Béranger won the first competition of façades of the city of Paris, in 1898, Guimard became a celebrity.

CATACOMBS (1, Place Denfert-Rochereau). Deep under Paris numerous quarries had been dug ever since Gallo-Roman times to extract limestone for building, clay for pottery and gypsum for plaster. In 1776, it was decided for hygienic reasons to forbid cemeteries (q.v.) within the cities. The old quarries of Tombe-Issoire were then chosen for storing the bones from Parisian cemeteries and especially the largest of them, the Innocents cemetery near the Halles, which contained more than two million corpses. The transfer took place from 1786 to 1788 for Innocents and from 1792 to 1814 for 16 other Parisian cemeteries. To this were later added human remains disinterred during Haussmann's (q.v.) major projects. All in all, the bones of six million persons were carefully piled up over 11,000 square meters some 20 meters underground. In a questionable allusion to the ancient catacombs of Rome, this ossuary received its name.

CATHERINETTES. The custom of celebrating the festival of Saint Catherine of Alexandria as patron saint of the seamstresses and milliners appeared only in the 1850s at about the same time that *haute couture* (q.v.) was developing. The word *catherinette* was used in 1882 to designate the unmarried women who put a cap on the statue of Saint Catherine in the churches on November 25, when they had reached the age of 25. The seamstresses who had reached that age wore on that day a bonnet with green and yellow ribbons, which was gradually replaced by more outlandish headgear. Saint Catherine's festival generated a joyful atmosphere in the fashion district toward Avenue Montaigne and around the Champs-Elysées (q.v.). The Catholic Church, namely, the parish of Notre-Dame-de-Bonne-Nouvelle, participated in this event from 1925 to 1969, when Saint Catherine of Alexandria was dropped from the Roman calendar.

CATHOLIC LEAGUE. *See* LEAGUE.

CEMETERIES. In early Paris there were as many cemeteries as there were places of worship—more than 300. Persons of note were buried inside the church and the rest of the population in the cemetery surrounding the parish sanctuary. These cemeteries were often quite small, less than 100 square meters for those of Saint-Landry or the Sainte-Chapelle. The largest, that of Saints-Innocents, did not exceed 7,000 square meters (compared to Père-Lachaise (q.v.), which covered 440,000). Nonetheless, it contained over two million corpses, which caused the soil to rise more than two meters and gave out a constant stench that plagued the Halles (q.v.) quarter.

In 1776, the king decided to close all the cemeteries located within the cities. The bones extracted from the Parisian burial grounds were transferred to the Catacombs (q.v.). New cemeteries were then established outside of the city at the beginning of the 19th century, those of Père-Lachaise in the east, Montmartre (q.v.) in the north and Montparnasse (q.v.) in the south. The further extension of the city limits brought those three, as well as those of 11 incorporated communes, within the capital. New cemeteries for Parisians were then opened in the suburbs: Saint-Ouen (1872), Ivry (1874), Bagneux and Pantin (1886), Valmy in the Bois de Vincennes (1906) and Thiais (1929). There is also a private necropolis, the Picpus cemetery (35, Rue de Picpus), reserved for the descendants of persons guillotined during the Revolution, where Lafayette, among others, rests.

Excluded from the cemeteries, the Jews and Protestants buried their dead more or less secretly. During the Middle Ages, the Jews had a burial ground on the Left Bank (near Rue Pierre-Sarrazin and Rue Galande) and perhaps another on the Right Bank (Rue de la Verrerie). When their community was reestablished toward the end of the 17th century, they had two small cemeteries at 46 and then 44, Rue de Flandre and at 94–96, Rue Gabriel-Péri in Montrouge.

In 1576, the Protestants were granted the Trinity cemetery (20–22, Rue de Palestro) and another, the so-called Plague-Stricken cemetery (186, Boulevard Saint-Germain), which they had to abandon in 1604 for the Saints-Pères cemetery (30, Rue des Saints-Pères). In 1598, the edict of Nantes gave them a third burial place in the Rue des Poulies (corner of the present Rue Amyot and Rue Laromiguière). When they were outlawed in 1685, the Protestants were forced to bury their dead secretly in fields, gardens and building sites. As of 1725, the police allowed them to inter the dead in the lumberyard at Quay de la Rapée as long as this was done very discreetly. In 1777, Louis XVI authorized the French Protestants to bury their dead in the cemetery for foreign Protestants in the Rue de la Grange-aux-Belles. The Revolution of 1789 put an end to this discrimination and opened the cemeteries to all.

CHAILLOT. On top of Chaillot Hill, made of Lutetian limestone, was a village that was mentioned in a bull of Pope Urban II in 1097 but that had already existed since at least the sixth century. Mining was carried out there, while vines grew above. On the eve of the Revolution, it was the biggest village to the west of Paris, with a population of 2,000 in 1785. Since 1659, Chaillot has had the status of a suburb of Paris. It was incorporated into the capital in 1783. There was enormous rivalry among architects as to what should be placed on top of the hill, and countless projects were drawn up. It was not until 1878, though, on the occasion of the world exhibition (q.v.), that the Trocadero Palace was built. In 1937, within the context of a new world exhibition, the palace was replaced by the present Chaillot Palace. The work of Jacques Carlu, Louis Hippolyte Boileau and Léon Azéma, this huge building houses the Museum of Mankind, the Maritime Museum, the Museum of French Monuments, and the Cinema Museum and Film Library, as well as two theaters, one of which is the People's National Theater, made famous in the early 1950s by Jean Vilar.

CHAMBER OF COMMERCE. In 1602, Barthélemy de Laffemas got Henri IV to create a Commercial Assembly of Paris, which seems to have disappeared at the death of the king in 1610. In 1616, François Du Noyer got Louis XIII to establish the General Chamber of Commerce, which, again, apparently became dormant on the death of the king in 1643. In 1664, Louis XIV (q.v.) set up the Commercial Council, whose scope covered France as a whole. He replaced it in 1700 with a General Council of Commerce, which also covered the whole country. The Chamber of Commerce of Paris was created in 1803. First housed in the Hôtel de Ville (q.v.), it was transferred in 1826 to Place de la Bourse. In 1923, it moved to Hôtel Potocki (27, Avenue de Friedland), where it remains. The Chamber of Commerce took the initiative in establishing the École Supérieure de Commerce (1819), the École des Hautes Études Commerciales (1881) and various other schools. Together with the Municipal Council, it is responsible for running such events as the Paris Fair (q.v.) and the Tourist Board.

CHAMP-DE-MARS. Covering 35 hectares between the Seine (q.v.) and the École Militaire, the Champ-de-Mars (Field of Mars)—as its name indicates—was originally a parade ground for the cadets of the school. It was laid out in 1765 at the same time that the École Militaire was built. This vast open space played a historic role during the Revolution. On July 14, 1790, the Festival of Federation was celebrated there. On July 17, 1791, the signing of a petition demanding the abolition of the monarchy degenerated into a bloody massacre. In 1798, it was there that the earliest French trade fair was held, the Exhibition of Industrial Products. The world exhibitions (q.v.) of 1867, 1878, 1889 and 1900 were also held there, with the Eiffel Tower (q.v.)

being the last souvenir of the 1889 exhibition. The Champ-de-Mars also witnessed the first balloon (q.v.) flights. Horse races were organized there from 1780 until the race track was opened at Longchamp in 1855.

CHAMPS-ELYSÉES. It was not until the 17th century that this area was gradually integrated into Paris. Marie de Médicis had the Cours-la-Reine laid out, a broad path extending from the Tuileries (q.v.) garden and forming an avenue leading to Chaillot (q.v.). The Champs-Elysées (Elysian Fields) became a promenade in 1676 when Le Nôtre widened that avenue and planted trees along it as far as the present Rue Marbeuf. In the 18th century, the present traffic circle of the Champs-Elysées was built. Along it sprang up bowling greens, dairies, restaurants, *guinguettes* (q.v.), a dance hall and the Coliseum, most of them hastily thrown together, which were visited by Parisians on Sundays and holidays when the weather was nice.

On August 15, 1806, when the cornerstone of the Arc de Triomphe at Place de l'Étoile (q.v.) was laid, the avenue began to assume a more grandiose dimension. Yet, at that time, only six houses had been built along the Champs-Elysées. During the Second Empire, the Carré Marigny became one of the main entertainment districts of the capital, with its dance halls, in particular Mabille (q.v.); its cafés (q.v.), such as the Alcazar and Ambassadeurs; and the Impératrice circus. That is also where Offenbach (q.v.) opened the first Bouffes-Parisiens (q.v.). On both sides of the avenue luxurious private mansions were built, the most prestigious being those of the duke of Morny (at number 9), and La Païva (at number 25). The Champs-Elysées gradually replaced the boulevards (q.v.) as the center of social life and it kept that position until just after the Second World War. Even today it is the triumphal way par excellence, closely tied to the most brilliant moments of French history, such as the victory parade in 1919 and the parade celebrating liberation in 1944.

CHANEL, GABRIELLE, known as COCO (1883–1971). The sailor blouse, a short jacket with a sailor collar that she designed in 1913, launched Coco Chanel's career. In 1916, for the first collection of her fashion house, which she had just opened, she presented a knitted sweater and short dress that gave women a more relaxed image in clothing that was both elastic and comfortable and that played down the bust. In 1921, her perfume, Chanel No. 5, was an exceptional hit and is still popular. Her fashion house was closed in 1939 but opened again in 1954, at 31, Rue Cambon. Until she passed away, it continued producing the famous jersey suits to which she held the secret.

CHARLES V THE WISE (1338–80). Charles V was the oldest son of Jean II the Good and the first heir to the throne of France who bore the title of dauphin, in 1349. He had the difficult task of running the kingdom during his father's captivity in England between 1356 and 1360. Among other things, he had to face enormous financial problems, foil the intrigues of Charles the Evil, the king of Navarre, and put down the revolt of the Parisians led by Provost of Merchants Étienne Marcel (q.v.). Living almost entirely in Paris and the immediate vicinity, he had the city surrounded by a new wall crowned with the Bastille (q.v.), founded the royal library at the Louvre (q.v.), and bought the Hôtel Saint-Paul near the Bastille, where he resided, although he also stayed frequently in the châteaux of Vincennes (q.v.) and Beauté.

CHARLES VI THE MAD (1368–1422). Like his father Charles V (q.v.), Charles VI spent most of his life in Paris. His reign began with the revolt of the Maillotins, an uprising of Parisians against the royal taxes in 1382. His insanity, already evident by 1392, subjected the kingdom to the ambitions of his uncles and cousins. Two factions clashed in a civil war that broke out in 1407 with the assassination of Duke Louis d'Orléans and that lasted until 1435: the Burgundians, who were supporters of the duke of Burgundy, Jean the Fearless, confronted the Armagnacs, backers of Duke Charles d'Orléans led by his father-in-law Bernard d'Armagnac. Paris suffered the consequences of this conflict because it joined the Burgundian camp from 1411 to 1413 and again in 1418. The assassination of Jean the Fearless at Montereau in 1419 at the orders of the dauphin, the future Charles VII, resulted in the conclusion of the Treaty of Troyes by which Charles VI made Henry V of England his successor to the throne of France. However, Henry V died several weeks before Charles VI, leaving under the guardianship of his brother, John of Lancaster, the duke of Bedford, his son Henry VI, a baby less than one year old.

CHARONNE. Charonne is first mentioned in 1008 in a deed by which Robert II the Pious granted the rights over this village to the abbey of Saint-Magloire. For a long time it remained a small village of winegrowers. At the time of the Revolution in 1789, it counted only about 600 inhabitants living along four roads. Quite close to Paris, it boasted numerous taverns and *guinguettes* (q.v.), which sold the wines produced on its slopes to the trade tax-free. The village saw a burst of growth in the 19th century, with the population spurting to 6,000 inhabitants in 1850 and then 16,000 in 1860, when the commune was incorporated into Paris and became a quarter in the 20th arrondissement. All that remains of Charonne's rural past is Saint-Germain church, the only one aside from Montmartre church that retained its cemetery (q.v.), and the remains of Bagnolet château, namely, the Ermitage pavilion, which dates from 1734.

CHARTIER (Restaurant) (7, Rue du Faubourg-Montmartre). Founded by Camille Chartier in 1898 or 1899, this *bouillon* (the name for a low-price restaurant) has preserved its original decor to the present day. Located at the end of a courtyard, the Chartier is still a place where ordinary Parisians can have a decent lunch or dinner for a very modest price. They share tables with an ever-increasing number of tourists attracted by the picturesque setting and the accessible prices.

CHAT NOIR, LE (Cabaret). The first cabaret (q.v.) in the modern sense of the word was Le Chat Noir, opened on November 18, 1881, by Rodolphe Salis at 84, Boulevard de Rochechouart. It was decked out with its catchy iron signboard of a black cat with golden eyes perched on a French croissant, which was designed by Willette. This place, into which 40 patrons could barely squeeze, was frequented by the cream of artistic and literary society: Alphonse Allais, Paul Bourget, François Coppée, André Gill, Jean Moréas and others. Poets such as Charles Cros, Maurice Rollinat and Albert Samain read their verses there. In 1885, Le Chat Noir moved into larger premises at 12, Rue de Laval, which also housed a Petit Théâtre, which Jules Claretie described as the "Bayreuth of shadow theaters." There the side-splitting comedies of Caran d'Ache, Maurice Donnay, Henri Rivière and Robida were played. Although Le Chat Noir did not survive the death of its founder in 1897, it was by far the best Parisian cabaret.

CHÂTELET (Square). On the same spot as the present Palace du Châtelet stood until 1802 a gloomy fortress called the Grand Châtelet. Its origin can probably be traced back to a big wooden tower erected in about 870 in front of the Grand Pont (presently Pont au Change) to prevent the Norsemen, or Vikings, from going up the Seine (q.v.). Around 1130, this tower was replaced by a small fortified castle or barbican made of stone, which became the seat of the provost of Paris (q.v.). In this capacity, it served both as a court and a prison for persons awaiting judgment. Among those detained, most of them common criminals, were some celebrities, such as the poet Clément Marot, who composed his *Enfer* around 1526; the count of Rochefort, who was forced to stay there during the Fronde (q.v.); and the famous bandit Cartouche (q.v.), who spent his last days there in 1721. The Grand Châtelet was torn down between 1802 and 1810.

There was also a Petit Châtelet, erected on the left bank in front of the Petit Pont at the location of the present Place du Petit-Pont. It was originally a wooden tower also constructed to keep the Viking ships from going up the Seine. It was rebuilt in stone in 1369 and was used as an annex to the Grand Châtelet's prison. It was demolished in 1782.

CHEVALIER, MAURICE (1888–1972). Born in Ménilmontant in modest circumstances, Maurice Chevalier began singing at the age of 12 in the cafés-chantants (q.v.). He was discovered by Mistinguett (q.v.) in 1904 and went from triumph to triumph, appearing in the finest music halls (q.v.) and leading revues at the Casino de Paris (q.v.). In 1921, he appeared on stage for the first time with the legendary straw hat that became his trademark. In 1929, he acted in the first talkies. In 1936, songs such as *Ma Pomme* and *Y a de la joie* became worldwide hits. With his good-natured banter of the Parisian *titi*, Maurice Chevalier became a symbol of Paris throughout the first half of the 20th century. In 1958 he received a Special Academy Award for his contributions over more than 50 years as an entertainer.

CHIFFONNIERS. Collectors of used materials, old clothing and shoes, broken glass, and scraps of paper and cardboard, the *chiffonniers*, or ragpickers, were one of the poorest groups in society. The police (q.v.) mistrusted them, and an ordinance in 1698 forbade them, in vain, from wandering around the streets and the suburbs before the break of day. An ordinance of 1828 required that they wear badges with their names and descriptions so as "to distinguish them from night prowlers who try to mix with them." With a basket on their backs, a lantern in one hand and a hook in the other, the *chiffonniers* scoured the city by night, rummaging in the piles of garbage. The number of these ragpickers was estimated at 1,800 in 1832 and 15,000 in 1880. When they were forbidden from exercising their activity during the cholera epidemic of 1832, in order to limit the risks of contagion, they unleashed a bloody riot. Since the *chiffonniers* needed room to sort their harvest, they were forced to move to the outskirts of the city, usually staying in wooden shacks at the foot of the fortifications, in what was called the Zone (q.v.). Oddly enough, the *chiffonniers* disappeared during the 1960s at a time when Paris was producing more and more recyclable waste.

CHINATOWN. Since the beginning of the 1980s, the name Chinatown has been given to the quarter of Porte de Choisy where large numbers of "boat people" who fled Vietnam, most of them of Chinese origin, have congregated. There they have recreated the atmosphere of their home country, with stores, exotic products, restaurants, Buddhist temples, newspapers and so on. This quarter is expanding ever further on both sides of the Avenue de Choisy and reaches as far as Place d'Italie.

CHIRAC, JACQUES (1932–   ). Chirac went into politics in 1962, in the wake of Prime Minister Georges Pompidou, and became the Gaullist deputy of Corrèze as of 1967. As secretary of state for employment, he negotiated with the strikers in May 1968. He made a name for himself as minister of agriculture in 1972. In 1974, he distanced himself from the Gaullist candidate Chaban-Delmas and rallied to Giscard d'Estaing. When the latter was elected president, Chirac was rewarded by being appointed prime minister. Ousted in August 1976, Chirac got himself elected mayor (q.v.) of Paris in March 1977. Campaigning in the presidential election of 1981 against Giscard d'Estaing and François Mitterand, he stood down grudgingly in favor of the outgoing president, who was beaten. After defeating the Socialists in the legislative elections of 1986, Chirac became Mitterrand's prime minister in what was called "cohabitation" until 1988. Meanwhile, he won the municipal elections in 1983 and 1989, each time achieving a "grand slam," taking all 20 arrondissements of the capital. On May 7, 1995, Jacques Chirac finally achieved his highest ambition and became president of France, carrying 60 percent of the Parisian vote. He was succeeded as mayor by Jean Tiberi (q.v.), who has had great difficulties since mid-1996 owing to the mismanagement of the low-rental buildings.

CHOLERA. Coming from India, cholera struck for the first time in France in 1832, causing 18,402 deaths in Paris between March and September. It reappeared in March 1849 and killed 16,165 Parisians by the end of the summer. From September to November 1865, it claimed only 4,349 victims because the authorities had learned to control it through improved hygiene and isolating the ill. In 1873, it killed only 869 persons, less than the typhoid that was always rampant because of the poor quality of drinking water. The November 1884 epidemic killed only 980 persons. In July 1892, the beginnings of an epidemic were quickly stemmed. There has been no further major outbreak in Paris.

CHRISTOFLE. Charles Christofle, the jeweler, founded a company in 1830 that had specialized in custom-made silver and gold-plating by 1845. In 1914, it became the foremost goldsmith in France. After the Second World War, Christofle set up shop in Argentina, Brazil, Italy and elsewhere. In 1981, a sales outlet was opened in the United States. Today, Christofle is one of the world leaders in the goldsmith's art and a symbol of quality and taste.

CINEMA (Filmmaking). The production of films began in the Parisian region almost immediately after the famous first public paid showing on December 28, 1895. George Méliès built his studio in Montreuil, where Charles Pathé also settled in 1904 before moving to Vincennes, right next door. Léon Gaumont was located in the 19th arrondissement, near the Buttes-Chaumont (q.v.), in the Rue des Alouettes. The Société Éclair was established in 1907 at Epinay-sur-Seine, and Louis Aubert set up his studios in 1915 at Saint-Maurice. In 1919, Henri Niepce converted his airplane factory into a motion picture studio, where the 1925 film *Napoléon* by Abel Gance was produced. Cinéromans Films de France opened its studios at Joinville in 1922 and later, in 1926, transferred them to Montmartre (6, Rue Francoeur).

The talkies stimulated the construction of new studios in 1930 and 1936 in Neuilly-sur-Seine and Courbevoie. New studios were also built in Boulogne, in the Avenue Jean-Baptiste-Clément in 1941, then in the Rue de Silly in 1946, where they enjoyed an exceptional period of prosperity during the 1960s and until they were closed in 1972. A studio was opened in the Rue du Fief in Billancourt and another in Paris, in the Rue François Ier. The increase in outdoor shooting and a crisis in filmmaking wiped out many of the production studios during the 1980s. Still, there have been some newcomers: the studios of the Société Française de Production in Bry-sur-Marne and Studio 91 in Arpajon.

CINEMA (Theaters). In 1895, the cinema was born in Paris, where it was immediately crowned with success. In 1907, Pathé set up the first commercial circuits and opened the first theaters for this new form of entertainment. In 1913, there were about 180 theaters of various sizes, the Gaumont Palace being able to accommodate 6,000 filmgoers. After that the number of movie theaters stagnated until talkies came on the scene and stimulated a resurgence: 191 theaters in 1930, 336 in 1940 and 354 with room for 240,000 filmgoers at the peak in 1954. The cinema's decline was caused by the triumph of television as of 1960. Since 1980, Paris has lost half of its movie theaters, and there were only about one hundred left in 1996. *See also* Rex.

CITÉ (Island). The Île de la Cité is the historic cradle of Paris. That is where the little Gallic village stood and where the Romans established their administration, the same spot that was successively occupied by the king's palace, the *Parlement* (q.v.) and then the Palais de Justice (q.v.). The religious authorities also resided on the island. Excavations brought to light the pillar dedicated to Jupiter that the boatmen's corporation had erected during the reign of Emperor Tiberius (14–37). It was found under the chancel of Notre-Dame, showing that the Christian religion had literally taken the place of the pagan cult. Built in the shadow of the seventh-century cathedral, the Hôtel-Dieu was for many centuries the only place where the poor and sick could find comfort. The University (q.v.) grew out of the episcopal school located in Notre-Dame cloister. Aside from the cathedral, the Sainte-Chapelle and the Conciergerie, there remains almost no trace of the island's past since Haussmann (q.v.) razed the network of back streets with their squalid and decrepit medieval houses, which Victor Hugo (q.v.) knew and described in his novel *Notre-Dame de Paris (The Hunchback of Notre-Dame)*.

CITÉ INTERNATIONALE UNIVERSITAIRE (Boulevard Jourdan). The law of June 28, 1921, provided for the establishment of a university residential campus on the location of bastions 81, 82 and 83 of Thiers's wall (q.v.), which had been condemned. The oil tycoon Emile Deutsch de la Meurthe financed the construction of the first building, which was inaugurated in 1925 and named after him. Sixteen other foundations followed over the next seven years, and in 1939 there were 19 halls with a total of 2,400 beds. Canada, Belgium, Argentina, Japan, the United States and others had their own houses. They were sometimes the work of famous architects: Le Corbusier designed the Swiss hall, and Willem Marinus Dudok that of the Netherlands. Twelve new foundations were established in the 1950s, and another five in the following decade. There are presently about 5,000 residents in the Cité Internationale Universitaire belonging to 120 different nationalities: 37 percent are French, 22 percent are nationals of other European countries, 22 percent are Africans, 12 percent are Americans and 7 percent are Asians.

CLEMENCEAU, GEORGES (1841–1929). Earlier a doctor in Montmartre (q.v.), Clemenceau was appointed mayor of the 18th arrondissement, on the fall of Napoléon III, in September 1870 and confirmed by an election in November. He was then elected a deputy in February 1871. He tried in vain to block the formation of the Commune (q.v.) and had to flee Paris on March 23, 1871. Although he was reelected a deputy of the Seine département by Montmartre and became one of the leaders of the Radical party, Clemenceau left Paris for the département of Var in 1885 and remained its deputy and then senator until 1920. He served as prime minister and minister of the interior from 1906 to 1909 and later as prime minister and minister of war from 1917 to 1920.

CLOCHARDS. The word *clochard*, or tramp, appeared in 1895. Previously, one had spoken of beggars and vagabonds. The *clochard*, a typically Parisian character, is a person who lives in public places and has no home to call his own. Until the end of the 18th century, indigents and vagrants accounted for about 10 percent of the population and represented a threat to law and order. It was not until the end of the 19th century that full employment was gradually achieved and the living standards of the poorest were improved significantly. By then the *clochard* appeared to be a very marginal being, inoffensive and picturesque, leading a solitary, carefree and unfettered life.

These tramps scrounged food at the Halles (q.v.) and the markets and rolled their own cigarettes, made from butts they picked up off the floor. They had their own favorite cafés (q.v.) and restaurants (q.v.) in the Rue Mouffetard and Rue Lagrange, at the Halles, near the Saint-Ouen, Clignancourt, Pantin and Montreuil gates. On occasion, they also worked as *chiffonniers* (q.v.), or ragpickers. Each commercial district had its own *clochards*, who provided petty services in exchange for something to eat or drink. These *clochards* made up only a tiny share of the population until the beginning of the 1970s, no more than one or two Parisians in a thousand. This happy day is gone, and the recession has multiplied by 10 or 20 the number of persons of no fixed abode who have become tramps whether they like it or not, and the voluntary and satisfied *clochard* is just a memory.

CLOVIS I (c. 466–511). Clovis, king of the Franks in 481, founded the Merovingian dynasty. He negotiated with Saint Geneviève (q.v.) to have Paris submit to his authority. Married to Clotilda, a Catholic Burgundian princess, he was baptized in Reims, probably in 496, and made Paris his capital in 508.

CLUNY (Museum) (6, Place Paul-Painlevé). The Cluny museum, which was opened in 1844, is devoted to the Middle Ages. It is actually located in two very different monuments. One is the ancient Roman baths, one of the most impressive remains of Gallo-Roman Lutetia, whose main room is 14 meters high and still has its vaulting and consoles in the form of ship's prows, which recall the importance of the boatmen or water-going merchants in the life of the Cité (q.v.). The other is the Hôtel Cluny. Next to the ruins of the Roman baths, the abbot of the powerful order of Cluny, in Burgundy, had a mansion built around 1330 where he could reside during his stays in Paris. Jacques d'Amboise, who was abbot of Cluny from 1485 to 1510, replaced it with the present building, which is richly sculpted in the flamboyant Gothic style. Among the many treasures of the museum are medieval tapestries, in particular the enigmatic *Lady and the Unicorn.*

COAT OF ARMS. The growth of cities and the spread of communal liberties is at the origin of the first municipal seals. The boat or ship that appears for the first time in the 13th century on an official document coming from the watermen's community of Paris symbolized the river trade activities of this guild. The coat of arms remained unchanged until the death of Étienne Marcel (q.v.). At the end of 1358, it was embellished by a fleur-de-lis, which symbolized the royal authority that had been restored in the city. In 1415, the fleur-de-lis was turned into a seedling in the chief (upper portion) of the seal. The seal's inscription remained in Latin until it had to be translated into French in the 16th century: "Seal of the provost of merchants of the city of Paris." As for the small boat that had originally appeared, it got bigger and bigger until it became a proud warship. During the Revolution the fleur-de-lis and the ship disappeared. Napoléon I restored the ship and replaced the fleur-de-lis with bees. When the monarchy was reestablished, it brought back the fleur-de-lis in 1817. The present coat of arms of Paris was defined by a prefectural decision of November 24, 1853, which read: "gulls, a ship rigged with silver, floating on waves of the same, with a blue chief sown with fleurs-de-lis of gold; the escutcheon timbred with a mural crown of four golden towers."

COGNACQ, ERNEST (1839–1928). First a clerk and then a salesman in a draper's shop, in 1867 Cognacq opened his first store, Au Petit Bénéfice, in the Rue de Turbigo. He later abandoned this location and set up shop on the Pont Neuf, sitting behind a hawker's tray sheltered by a big red umbrella, which earned him the nickname of the "Napoléon of the clearance sale." On January 1, 1870, he took out a lease on tiny premises near Pont Neuf, which he named À la Samaritaine (q.v.) in memory of the pump of the same name installed on that bridge by Henri IV. In 1872, Cognacq married Louise Jay (1838–1925), a salesgirl at Bon Marché who played a major role in the success of their joint effort. The Samaritaine department store (q.v.) took off like lightning, with four employees in 1870, 25 in 1875 and 3,000 to 5,000 depending on the season in 1925, and a turnover of 840,000 francs in 1874, 2 million in 1877, 40 million in 1895 and more than a billion in 1925. The art collections that the couple left were the basis for the Cognacq-Jay Museum. *See also* Samaritaine.

COLETTE, GABRIELLE SIDONIE (1873–1954). Thanks to her first husband, Willy, Colette discovered Paris and its pleasures and learned the writer's trade. The first four novels of the *Claudine* cycle (1900–04) were an account of that initiation in love and literature in the setting of a city she would never leave. In *La Vagabonde* (1910) and *L'Envers du Music-Hall* (1913), she narrated her career as a mime at Moulin Rouge (q.v.). She died in a suite at the Palais-Royal (q.v.) where she had resided for many years and it is there that the government held her public funeral.

COLLÈGE DE FRANCE (Place Marcelin-Berthelot). In 1530, François I founded the Royal College, or Collège de France, at the suggestion of Guillaume Budé. Unlike the Sorbonne, which stubbornly rejected all innovations, this school was intended to disseminate the knowledge of the Renaissance and to teach in three languages, Latin, Greek and Hebrew. The Collège de France has remained a citadel of French thought. Its roster of professors is impressive, including the philosopher Ramus, who disappeared in 1572 during the Saint-Bartholomew's Day (q.v.) massacre, Gassendi, Roberval, La Hire, Tournefort, Rollin, Daubenton, Champollion, Laënnec, Claude Bernard, Michelet, Edgar Quinet, Ernest Renan, Marcelin Berthelot, Henri Bergson, and Paul Valéry. The present buildings were erected between 1774 and 1780 by Chalgrin and reconstructed and expanded between 1831 and 1842.

COLLÈGES. Originally, the *collèges* were sorts of hostels or family pensions where provincials and foreigners who came to Paris could live. The oldest was the Collège des Dix-Huit, founded in 1711 by a pilgrim who had returned from Jerusalem, Josse de Londres. He had acquired a hall in the Hôtel-Dieu and converted it into a dormitory for 18 "pupils," the word used in the Middle Ages to designate students at the University (q.v.). In 1208, a second *collège* was established, the Collège des Bons-Enfants Saint-Honoré (Rue des Bons-Enfants). All of the subsequent *collèges* were located on the Left Bank, in what would become the University quarter, or the Latin Quarter (q.v.).

There were two categories of *collèges*. The secular *collèges*, about 50 of them, were almost all founded between 1250 and 1350. They did not have many pupils, only 680 of them at the beginning of the 15th century, while the University (q.v.) had 4,000 masters and students. There were not many religious *collèges*, but they had many boarders belonging to the order that financed them: Dominicans, Franciscans, Cistercians or Bernardines, Premonstrants, Carmelites, Cluniacs, Augustinians and so on. Most of these were established between 1218 and 1300. However, by the beginning of the 18th century only 39 *collèges* attached to the University were still in existence, and even they were sinking into decay and did not have many boarders. In 1763, when the scholars of 29 small *collèges* were regrouped in the Collège Louis-le-Grand (q.v.), they added up to only 193 pupils. The Revolution of 1789 put an end to the *collèges* and the University.

COLORS OF PARIS. The history of the colors of the city of Paris is not simple. The provost of merchants (q.v.) and magistrates (q.v.), until the end of the Middle Ages, wore robes that were half red and half white, red on the left and white on the right. Later on, and until 1789, they were red on the left and tan (brownish, almost maroon) on the right. The coat of arms (q.v.) of Paris has a red foundation that corresponds to the color of the banner of the Abbey of Saint-Denis, this being the banner of the patron saint of Paris. The ship is white. At the end of 1358 was added the golden fleurs-de-lis (yellow) on a blue field (foundation). It is therefore incorrect to claim that the old colors of Paris are blue and red, the present official colors of the municipality. In fact, this union of red and blue was the sign that the supporters of Étienne Marcel (q.v.) had been won over from January to July 1358, with the red being worn on the left and the blue on the right.

COMÉDIE-FRANÇAISE. Established on October 21, 1680, at the personal order of Louis XIV (q.v.), the Comédie-Française resulted from a merger of the Illustre Théâtre of Molière (died in 1673) and its rival, the troupe of the Hôtel de Bourgogne. It appeared first at Théâtre Guénégaud (in the present Rue Jacques-Callot), and later, from 1689 to 1770, at 14, Rue de l'Ancienne-Comédie, which explains its name. From 1770 to 1782, the Comédie's actors and actresses played in the palace of the Tuileries (q.v.). They left it for a new theater named the Odéon. In 1794, the troupe moved to the Palais-Royal (q.v.), where the present Théâtre-Français is still located. The Comédie-Française received its present charter from Napoléon I, by the Moscow decree of October 15, 1812. Whereas it initially staged only the classics by Corneille, Racine, Molière (q.v.) and others, more recently it has been presenting plays by modern French and foreign authors.

COMMUNE DE PARIS. There were actually two Communes in Paris. The first was established in the evening of July 14, 1789, and replaced the administration of the Ancien Régime. It was turned into an insurrectional Commune on August 10, 1792, and contributed to the fall of the monarchy. During the Terror (q.v.), it became an instrument of the dictatorship of the *sans-culottes* (q.v.) and was dissolved on August 24, 1794.

The second Commune was a consequence of the Franco-German War and France's defeat. The Central Committee of the National Guard of Paris seized power on March 18, 1871. It then elected a Municipal Council, which proclaimed the Commune on March 27 and refused to obey the Thiers (q.v.) government, which had sought refuge in Versailles. It was crushed militarily during the "bloody week" of May 21–28, 1871.

CONCIERGE. The *concierge* is a typically Parisian character. Originally, there were not many *concierges* and porters, and their job was basically to open and close the entrance gates of large mansions or of noble and royal estates. Their responsibilities also included keeping an eye open within the houses as well to prevent the help from stealing. The tax rolls of the year 1292 counted 24 *concierges*, 13 porters and two "closers." The Louvre (q.v.) had two porters but no *concierge*, whereas the Palais de la Cité had a concierge who was lodged in what is still called the Conciergerie.

At the beginning of the 19th century, use of a *concierge* became common in larger buildings, and he or she acted as the representative of the owner in commercial blocks of flats, collecting the rent on the owner's behalf. The number of *concierges* peaked at 85,000 in 1939 and has been decreasing rapidly since the 1960s. By now the bulk of the *concierges* are women, ever fewer of whom originate from Paris or the provinces and ever more of whom come from Portugal, Spain, Yugoslavia and sometimes even North Africa. The increasingly widespread use of coded locks to get into buildings is one of the causes of the gradual disappearance of the *concierge*.

CONCORDE, PLACE DE LA. In 1748, the city of Paris decided to offer an equestrian statue to Louis XV, and the king provided a site for it on a plot of land located between the Tuileries (q.v.) and the Champs-Elysées (q.v.). Working from a plan by Germain Boffrand, as of 1753 Jacques-Ange Gabriel cleared a vast esplanade that opened to the south on the Seine (q.v.) and to the east and west on the gardens of the Tuileries and the Champs-Elysées and was closed to the north by the two palaces that divide Rue Royale. In 1793, Louis XVI was guillotined in this square, which was called Louis XV Square and was later renamed Square of the Revolution and then Place de la Concorde in 1795. It was in the center of this square that, in 1836, Louis-Philippe had an Egyptian obelisk (q.v.) from Luxor erected and set off by a fountain on each side. This architectural setting was completed by statues of the eight principal cities of France.

CONCOURS GÉNÉRAL. In 1733, Abbot Louis Legendre, canon of Notre-Dame, took out an annuity on his personal fortune to initiate a competition of poetry and music. This was the origin of the Concours général, whose organization was entrusted to the University (q.v.). The first contest was held in 1747, and the prizes were given out at the Sorbonne. Among the winners in the 18th century were the poets Jacques Delille and André-Marie Chénier, the critic Jean-François Laharpe and Maximilien de Robespierre (q.v.). The Concours général, which was discontinued in 1793 and resumed in 1801, was initially reserved for the four *lycées* of the capital, Louis-le-Grand (q.v.), Charlemagne, Condorcet and Henri VI. Prizes were awarded for philosophy as of 1810 and for history as of 1815. Four additional schools were allowed to compete: Saint-Louis, Collège Stanislas, Collège Sainte-Barbe (q.v.), and Lycée de Versailles. In 1863, the Concours général was opened to all the *lycées* in France. It was discontinued again in 1904, was reinstated in 1921, and exists to the present day.

CORDELIERS (Club). The Société des Amis des Droits de l'Homme et du Citoyen was founded on April 27, 1790. Because it met in the former convent of the Franciscan friars, or *cordeliers* (15, Rue de l'École-de-Médecine), it was called simply the Club des Cordeliers. Harassed by the municipal administration led by Bailly (q.v.), the club was forced to leave on May 17, 1791, and moved to the Hôtel de Genlis (18, Rue Dauphine). Its members played an important role in submitting the petition calling for the abolition of the monarchy and in the massacre that followed at the Champ-de-Mars (q.v.) on July 17, 1791. After Bailly's resignation, the club returned to the former convent.

The Cordeliers had a much more democratic structure than the Club des Jacobins (q.v.) and were not dominated by any one leader. Among the main spokesmen were Chaumette, Danton, (q.v.), Hébert, Legendre, Marat (q.v.), Momoro and Vincent. It was not until the fall of the Girondins in June 1793 that the Club des Cordeleirs exerted an influence comparable to that of the Jacobins. Robespierre (q.v.), however, who held the reality of power by working through the Committee of Public Safety, persecuted them, had their provincial committees dissolved and managed to relegate the Cordeliers to the level of a neighborhood club that was influential only in part of the Left Bank. He had the leading members arrested and executed in March 1794, and the Club des Cordeliers ceased meeting regularly before being forced to merge with the Club des Jacobins.

COUNT OF PARIS. Mention is made of a count of Paris under the Merovingian and Carolingian kings. The title belonged to the royal family or the highest Frankish nobility. Charles the Bald granted this title to Eudes, who distinguished himself during the siege of Paris by the Norsemen in 885–86. When he became king of France in 888, Eudes passed the title of count of Paris to his brother Robert. Robert's son, Hugues the Great, gave himself the title of duke of France and left the title of count of Paris to the counts of Vendôme, who bore it from 941 to 1007. This title ceased to exist until King Louis-Philippe reestablished it for his grandson Henri at his birth in 1838. Since that date, the title of count of Paris is borne by the pretenders to the crown of France descended from the Bourbons-Orléans branch.

COUPOLE, LA (Brasserie) (102, Boulevard du Montparnasse). On the evening of December 20, 1927, La Coupole was added to the many meeting places that already existed in Montparnasse (q.v): Le Sélect, La Rotonde (q.v.), Le Dôme (q.v.), La Palette, Le Jockey and La Closerie des Lilas. Among its first customers were Aragon, Blaise Cendrars, Foujita, Kisling, Soutine and Vlaminck. Thirty-two artists were each asked to paint a canvas, all of which were attached to pillars to decorate the establishment. Today, 70 years later, La Coupole remains a cultural institution where the art of conversation, eating and drinking—in short, the art of living in society—is still held in high esteem.

COUR DES MIRACLES. The name "court of miracles" was used ironically in referring to the places inhabited by beggars because they faked various infirmities to beg for alms and then, miraculously, found their eyes, arms and legs well again as soon as they returned to their own quarters. The oldest court of miracles was located in the vicinity of Les Halles, in the Rue de la Truanderie. A second was located around 1350 in the Rue des Francs-Bourgeois. The most recent and the largest was contiguous to the convent of Filles-Dieu (237, Rue Saint-Denis) and opened on a network of back streets near the Rue Montorgueil, Rue Saint-Denis and Rue Neuve-Saint-Sauveur (presently Rue du Nil). In 1668, shortly after he was appointed lieutenant-general of police (q.v.), La Reynie led a small army of policemen and gendarmes who assaulted this last court of miracles, which was immediately razed.

COURRÈGES, ANDRÉ (1923–). After learning his trade with Balenciaga between 1950 and 1960, André Courrèges opened his own haute couture establishment in August 1961 in the Avenue Kléber, with only two seamstresses. In 1965, his collection revolutionized the world of fashion. It was designed for the modern working woman who gets about by car and leads as active a life as any man. His theory was that a woman's clothing should not constrain her and that she wants to express through the way she dresses her will to be the equal of any man. Since then, Courrèges has remained as successful as ever and even more modern than before. His showroom is presently located at 40, Rue François Ier.

COUTURIÈRES. For centuries, tailors were the only people authorized to clothe men and women. The term *couturière* at that time applied to the humble activities of sewers and seamstresses, who were limited to altering or repairing garments. However, in 1675 the *couturières* finally obtained recognition of their profession. However, their trade was still limited to undergarments, such as camisoles, slips and petticoats, while the tailors maintained a monopoly for dresses and everything else that went over them. The tailor's monopoly was abolished by the Revolution of 1789. The 19th century was a golden age for the *couturières*, whether they ran a small business of their own, took orders to clothe women in the neighborhood, worked as assistants in fashion houses or toiled away as workers in the garment factories.

Ready-to-wear clothing has almost completely done away with both tailors and *couturières*. Even in today's garment industry, the *couturière* is more likely to be a man than a woman and more likely to be Turkish, Kurdish or Chinese than French. Most of them are hidden away in lofts of the Sentier quarter or in the suburbs.

CRÉDIT MUNICIPAL. The first pawnshop was opened in Perugia (Italy) in 1462 by the monk Bernabo de Terni to lend money at low interest rates to poor people who until then had had to resort to usurers. In Paris in 1637 Théophraste Renaudot founded the first pawnshop, which lasted until 1644. There were no other pawnshops until 1777, when Louis XVI created one. In 1804, Napoléon Bonaparte confirmed its monopoly of lending money in return for pledged goods in the capital. This pawnshop, which has been located at 55, Rue des Francs-Bourgeois ever since it was founded, reached its peak in 1890 with 26 branches in Paris and the suburbs.

In 1918, it was turned into the Crédit Municipal de Paris. It went through a long period of decline until, under the banking law of January 24, 1984, it was put in the same category as other credit institutions. This change allowed it to adopt more dynamic policies. Since 1987, the Crédit Municipal has opened a series of eight branches in the suburbs and as far away as Melun and Chartres. It has also introduced new services, including the organization of one hundred public auctions a year. These innovations have increased its turnover tenfold between 1983 and 1989 so that it now exceeds a billion francs.

CRIES OF PARIS. The cries of Paris go back as far as the city itself. Doubtlessly from ancient times, the streets teemed with itinerant dealers whose distinctive cries reverberated as they tried to attract the attention of potential customers. A book of trades compiled in 1268 or 1270 laid down rules of proper conduct so that the itinerant dealers would not harm the trade of merchants who ran shops. Around 1300, Guillaume de Villeneuve listed the street cries of Paris in *Les Crieries de Paris*. There were also public criers who proclaimed the decisions of the royal or municipal administrations on the streets and at crossings. At the beginning of the 19th century, there were still about one hundred itinerant trades whose cries could be heard. In 1904, only about 20 remained. Automobile traffic has killed off the last of the itinerant trades, and it was an exception in 1997 to hear the calls of the rare knife grinders and glass sellers who still roam the streets.

CRILLON (Hotel) (10, Place de la Concorde). Two impressive buildings dominate the northern side of Place de la Concorde (q.v.) on either side of the Rue Royale. The one on the right, originally the royal storehouse, is presently occupied by the Ministry of the Navy. The one on the left took its place in history on February 6, 1778, when the first Franco-American treaty of alliance was signed by Benjamin Franklin (q.v.) and Arthur Lee on behalf of the 13 American states. In 1788, it was acquired by the Count de Crillon, whose name it still bears. On March 11, 1909, it was inaugurated as a luxury hotel and a competitor of the Grand Hotel, the Ritz (q.v.) and the Meurice (q.v.). From 1914 to 1918, the Crillon was requisitioned and served first as the headquarters of the British chief of staff and then the American chief of staff. In 1919, it was used for meetings of the committee appointed by the Preliminary Peace Conference to establish the League of Nations, the predecessor of the United Nations. Its most ostentatious period came between the two world wars when its bar was patronized by the greatest names of American literature, such as William Faulkner, Scott Fitzgerald and Ernest Hemingway (q.v.). During the Second World War, it was again the headquarters of the Allied chiefs of staff in 1939, only to be replaced by the German chief of staff from 1940 to 1944. Next, it became the residence of the head of the expeditionary corps of the Allied forces in Europe before returning to its function as a hotel for a well-heeled international clientele.

The Crillon Hotel has three suites, known as the "grands appartements," which have housed the likes of Elizabeth Taylor, Michael Jackson and Julia Migenes, as well as 160 rooms. Three huge halls, named The Eagles, The Battles and Marie-Antoinette, frequently house international conferences. Still a refuge for millionaires, the Crillon no longer has any year-round paying guests. The last long-term resident was the granddaughter of Alexander Fleming, the discoverer of penicillin, who lived there for 30 years.

CRIME (Boulevard). The Boulevard du Temple was nicknamed the "boulevard of crime" between 1825 and 1860 because of the bloody melodramas that were played in its many theaters (q.v.) that catered to popular tastes. Among these theaters were the Variétés Amusantes, Délassements Comiques, Funambules, La Gaîté, L'Ambigu-Comique and then the Folies-Dramatiques, Cirque Olympique and Théâtre Historique, the last of which was founded in 1846 by Alexandre Dumas père and became the Théâtre-Lyrique in 1848. Among the most successful plays were *L'Auberge des Adrets* and *Robert Macaire,* both great triumphs for Frédérick Lemaître, and *Trente Ans de la Vie d'un Joueur, Fualdès, Paillasse, Le Courrier de Lyon* and *La Reine Margot* by Dumas. The boulevard of crime was done in by Haussmann's (q.v.) construction projects, which destroyed its theaters in 1862.

-D-

DAGUERRE, LOUIS JACQUES MANDÉ (1787–1851). Initially a painter and maker of panoramas, dioramas and scenery for the Opéra (q.v.), Daguerre also carried out research on photography as of 1824. In 1829, he joined the Nicéphore Niepce to develop a process that was named "daguerreotype" and was purchased by the French government in 1839, which offered the whole world the first process of photographic reproduction. Provided by the state with a lifetime pension, in 1840 Daguerre retired to Bry-sur-Marne.

DANTON, GEORGES JACQUES (1759–94). Danton was a lawyer who practiced at the Cour du Commerce. During the Revolution, he joined the nearby Club des Cordeliers (q.v.) and became one of the ringleaders while also playing an important role in the Club des Jacobins (q.v.). An eloquent speaker who had the common touch, he fought the monarch and urged the deposition of the king. He is thought to have been the author of the petition that resulted in the shooting at the Champ-de-Mars (q.v.) on July 17, 1791. Danton was one of the main instigators of the insurrection of August 10, 1792. Appointed minister of justice, he allowed the massacres of September 1792 to take place. He was elected to the Convention, where he was allied with Robespierre (q.v.) and Marat (q.v.) to combat the government and the Girondin deputies, who were eventually arrested on June 2, 1793. From April to July 1793, he was a member of the Committee of Public Safety and an advocate of all-out war against the foreign monarchies but of relative clemency in domestic repression. For this, Danton was accused of "moderatism" by Robespierre, summarily judged by the Revolutionary Tribunal (q.v.) and guillotined on April 16, 1794. To those who had advised him to flee in order to escape death, he had replied: "Can one carry the motherland under the soles of one's shoes?"

DAUPHINE (Square). In 1601, Henri IV commissioned the head of the *Parlement* (q.v.), Achille de Harlay, with constructing a triangular square contiguous on the west with the Palais de Justice (q.v.). The work was undertaken from 1607 to 1619 and Place Dauphine was subject to strict rules in its design. The ground floor had to have arcades surmounted by two stories and an attic, all of this constructed in three colors: red bricks with clamps of dressed white stones and a slate roof. To avoid the agitation that prevailed on the Pont Neuf (q.v.), only two openings were provided, one at the western tip connecting with the bridge, the other at the opposite end opening onto the Rue de Harlay. Unfortunately, Place Dauphine has been disfigured by elevations and reconstructions of its façades, and the third side, facing the Rue de Harley, was demolished in 1874 to build the monumental but cold western façade of the Palais de Justice.

DÉFENSE, LA. In 1931, a competition was held for an extension to the west of the architectural axis running from the Louvre (q.v.), to the obelisk and Place de la Concorde (q.v.), the Champs-Elysées (q.v.) and the Arc de Triomphe de l'Étoile (q.v.). This project of a triumphal way was taken up again as of 1950. The first phase was finished with the opening in 1958 of the National Center for Industry and Technology. Then began an immense enterprise covering 760 hectares of the communes of Puteaux, Courbevoie and Nanterre intended to equip the capital with a huge center of office buildings and tertiary activities. Three generations of towers were built. The first did not exceed 100 meters. The second, beginning after 1970, created skyscrapers with the Gan (182 m), Fiat (230 m) and Assur (152 m) towers. During the 1980s, the last generation of towers appeared, more economical and with more windows to take advantage of the natural light, such as the Elf (180 m) and Descartes (130 m) towers. A shopping center, Les Quatre Temps, was opened in 1981. Métro line no. 1 was extended to La Défense in 1992, where it connected with the Regional Express Network (RER). Since 1989, La Défense has been crowned by the Great Arch by the Danish architect Johan Otto von Spreckelsen, an open cube with sides of 110 meters. The name La Défense derives from a statue that was erected there in 1883 to commemorate the defense of Paris in 1870–71, during the siege of the capital by the Germans.

DEGAS, EDGAR DE GAS, called (1834–1917). Son of a banker, Degas had enough money to devote his life to his passion for painting, engraving and sculpture. A pupil of Ingres, he participated in the exhibitions of the impressionists between 1877 and 1886 but refused to be categorized in any specific school. A misanthropist, although he liked crowds and people, Degas was a purely urbanite and Parisian genius. Nature appears in his works only in the form of some presentations of horse racing fields. As an artist, he preferred painting such things as the inside of bistros (q.v.), cafés-chantants (q.v.), theaters (q.v.), and the shops of laundresses. He engaged in a pitiless portrayal of reality, of effort and work, but also of the drunkard's decay. He was particularly inspired by the tutus of the Opéra dancers and the vulgar coquetry of ordinary women. A painter of gestures, brilliantly capturing the attitude of a fleeting moment, Degas was not only a very great painter and engraver but also an admirable sculptor.

DENIS (Saint). According to Grégoire de Tours, an author of the end of the sixth century, Saint Denis was one of the seven bishops sent by the Church of Rome around 250 to evangelize Gaul. Denis's companions were the priest Eleutherius and the deacon Rusticus who suffered martyrdom with him. Saint Denis is regarded as the first bishop of Paris. The Basilica of Saint-Denis was erected on the site of his tomb.

DEPARTMENT STORES. The forerunners of the department store were the fancy goods shops that went in for "novelties," that is, articles that had recently appeared on the market and appealed to a female clientele. They consisted largely of clothing and accessories such as fabrics, lingerie and jewelry. The first of these novelty shops was Au Tapis Rouge, thought to have been founded in 1784. This type of store really took off as of 1820 with La Belle Jardinière (1824), Aux Trois Quartiers (1829) and Le Petit Saint Thomas (1830). Department stores as such developed during the Second Empire with Au Bon Marché (1852) (q.v.), Au Louvre (1855), the Bazar de l'Hôtel de Ville (1857), Au Printemps (1865) (q.v.), La Samaritaine (1870) (q.v.) and others. Meanwhile, the pioneer, Au Tapis Rouge, was entirely refurbished at 65–67, Rue du Faubourg-Saint-Denis. In 1869, La Paix opened a completely renovated store at the corner of Rue Neuve-Saint-Augustin and Rue de la Michodière. This is the store that Zola took as a model for his novel *Au Bonheur des Dames (The Ladies' Paradise)*.

The golden age of the department stores lasted from 1880 to 1914. As the suburbs expanded and large stores were opened there, the situation became critical. By 1996, the only department stores that remained were Au Bon Marché on the Left Bank, at Rue de Sèvres; the Bazar de l'Hôtel de Ville and La Samaritaine on Rue de Rivoli; and Au Printemps and its neighbor, Galeries Lafayette (q.v.), on Boulevard Haussmann. *See also* Boucicaut, Aristide; Cognacq, Ernest; Galeries Lafayette; Samaritaine, La.

DEUX MAGOTS, LES (Café) (6, Place Saint-Germain-des-Prés). Established in 1873 in the place of a textile store that was decorated with two *magots* (grotesque porcelain figures from China), the café (q.v.) Les Deux Magots became the rendezvous of the intellectual elite of the Latin Quarter (q.v.) in 1885. Verlaine, Rimbaud and Mallarmé were regular customers and then, at the beginning of the 20th century, patrons included Guillaume Apollinaire, Léon Daudet, Alfred Jarry and Oscar Wilde. After the First World War it was frequented by

André Breton and the surrealists Gide, Garaudoux, Mac Orlan, and Saint-Exupéry; foreign writers such as Ernest Hemingway and James Joyce; and the painters Derain, Dunoyer de Segonzac, Fernand Léger, Miro and Picasso (q.v.).

Well before the Second World War, along with Le Flore (q.v.) and Lipp (q.v.), Les Deux Magots was one of the great cultural centers that created the myth of Saint-Germain-des-Prés (q.v.). In 1933, a Deux Magots literary prize was instituted and the first winner was Raymond Queneau for *Le Chiendent*. From 1945 to 1955, the café was the rendezvous of the existentialists. Albert Camus, Jean-Paul Sartre and Simone de Beauvoir fled Le Flore, where they were besieged by curiosity seekers, and sought refuge at Les Deux Magots, where they joined Juliette Greco, Mouloudji, Roger Vadim and Boris Vian. Nowadays, the terrace is crowded mainly with tourists.

DEVICE OF PARIS. Originally, Paris had no symbol other than the boat or ship of the watermen's community, an image that spoke for itself. The trade tokens issued by the merchants' provost (q.v.) as of the end of the 15th century bore devices that changed almost every year. In 1581, the Latin device *Fluctuat at nunquam mergitur* (it floats and never sinks) was used for the first time. It was modified to *Fluctuat nec mergitur* (it floats and does not sink) on the tokens issued in 1582, 1584, 1585 and 1586. This device disappeared later, but it was mentioned by Pierre Palliot in 1660 and Durey de Noinville in 1757 as being the motto of Paris. However, the patent registering the coat of arms of Paris in 1697 and the Armorial General of France of 1696 make no mention of any motto of the city. Legally, the adoption of the device *Fluctuat nec mergitur* dates only from Haussmann's (q.v.) prefectural decision of November 24, 1853.

DIOR, CHRISTIAN (1905–57). Originally a picture dealer who was ruined by the depression in 1930, Christian Dior managed to survive by selling fashion sketches to Schiaparelli and working as a stylist with Robert Piguet until he was recruited by Lucien Lelong. In 1947, thanks to financial backing from Marcel Boussac, he opened his own fashion house at 30, Avenue Montaigne, and his "new look" collection was a big hit. Dior created a new profile for women, with a lengthened and flared skirt, the shoulders set back and the waist pinched. In 1954, he launched the H-line and then, in 1955, the Y-line, which concealed the bust. After his death, his pupil Yves Saint-Laurent (q.v.) carried on his work.

DISNEYLAND PARIS. Inaugurated on April 12, 1992, with the name of Euro Disneyland, this amusement park was designed along the same lines as those that already existed in California and Florida. Although built in a rural area, some 32 kilometers to the east of Paris, it is linked to the capital by the Regional Express Network (RER) and to the Roissy-Charles-de-Gaulle international airport by shuttle buses and lies just off the A4 highway. Disneyland Paris is thus ideally located to welcome the millions of visitors who come from all over Europe. Nonetheless, during its first years the park attracted fewer visitors than anticipated and ran up serious losses. Recent adjustments may have improved the situation.

DOISNEAU, ROBERT (1912–95). Born in the nearby suburb of Gentilly, Robert Doisneau devoted his life to photographing the ordinary, often working-class people of Paris and its surroundings. His first photo essay, in 1932, focused on the Marché aux Puces (flea market). Winner of the Kodak prize (1947) and the Niepce prize (1956), he left the Parisians and suburbanites images that they will cherish.

DÔME, LE (Café) (108, Boulevard du Montparnasse). Founded in October 1897, the Café Le Dôme is located in the heart of Montparnasse (q.v.). It quickly became the favorite spot of American students and artists who played poker and billiards in the back room while Germans, Austrians, Swedes and German-speaking Swiss were taking up the front room by 1903. The painter Jules Pascin, a Bulgarian Jew who joined this German colony, estimated that 500 artists and writers of all nationalities had frequented Le Dôme between 1908 and 1914. Along with Matisse and Picasso (q.v.), other famous "Dômiers" included Adolf Basler, Walter Bondy, Alfred Flechtheim, Otto Freundlich, Richard Goetz, Rudolf Grossmann, Hermann Haller, Hans Hoffman, Moïse Kisling, Erich Klossowski, Rudolf Levy, Eugen Spiro and Hugo Troendle. Since the First World War, Le Dôme is just one café (q.v.) among others, still visited by a crowd of cosmopolitan artists, but it is now La Coupole (q.v.) that draws the greater talents.

DOUCET, JACQUES (1853–1929). An outstanding representative of haute couture (q.v.), Jacques Doucet discovered many talented people, including the dress designers Paul Poiret (q.v.) and Madeleine Vionnet, who presented their first collections in his fashion house. The Doucet style was based on the suppleness and transparence of the material chosen, usually chiffon, tulle or satin in pastel shades. Doucet was also a patron and collector of art, paintings and books, which could be admired in his mansion in the Rue Spontini, then Avenue du Bois-de-Boulogne. His fashion house was located at 21, Rue de la Paix.

-E-

EIFFEL TOWER. When preparing for the world exhibition that would also celebrate the centenary of the Revolution of 1789, the government wanted something that would strike the public's imagination and consolidate the Republican regime. It could best be marked by an exceptional monument and the government adopted the project of the engineer Gustave Eiffel of a tower 300 meters high. It was erected between January 28, 1887, and March 30, 1889. On April 2, the guests invited to the inauguration had to walk up the 1,710 steps—the elevator was put into service only on May 19. Despite the unanimous criticism of writers and artists, the Eiffel Tower appealed to the people and received nearly 12,000 visitors a day during the exhibition. By the end of the first year, the entrance fees had amounted to 6 million francs, compared to the cost of construction, which was only 7 million francs. The tower weighs 7,000 tons and consists of 15,000 metal pieces assembled with 2.5 million rivets. The Eiffel Tower has three platforms at heights of 57, 115 and 274 meters. In 1957, its total height was increased by 20 meters with the addition of a television relay.

ELDORADO (4, Boulevard de Strasbourg). This, the oldest French music hall (q.v.), was built in 1858. Businessman and manager of actors André Lorge gave its huge hall the first place among the Parisian cafés-chantants (q.v.) and introduced music-hall shows there in 1867. Paulus made his debut there in 1868, Yvette Guilbert in 1889, Polaire in 1891 and Mistinguett (q.v.) in 1897, while Dranem achieved his greatest successes there. Alas, this temple of French songs was eclipsed by the cinema (q.v.) and the Eldorado was closed in 1932 and turned into a mere movie theater.

ELECTRICITY. *See* PUBLIC LIGHTING.

ELEPHANT. For the Parisians, the almost mythical king of the beasts is the elephant. Admittedly, they did not see the prehistoric *Elephas primigenus* whose tooth was discovered on the slopes of Belleville (q.v.) when the métro (q.v.) was being built, nor Hannibal's elephants, which crossed Languedoc, Provence and the Alps to fight with Roman legions, nor the one that the caliph of Bagdad, Harun al Rashid, sent to Emperor Charlemagne at Aix-la-Chapelle between 801 and 803. However, the chroniclers do note the extraordinary enthusiasm of the Parisians when, in 1254, on Saint Louis's return from the crusades, they saw the elephant that Henry III of England had offered the king of France. It was not until 1626 that they saw a second elephant, this one presented to Louis XIII by the Dutchman Sevender. The animal had captured the public imagination to such an extent that it was the object of several architectural plans. In 1758, a plan was devised to construct a stone elephant on the hill that later became Place de l'Étoile (q.v.) and where the Arc de Triomphe now stands. In 1808, Napoléon I took up that project for Place de la Bastille. A plaster model was cast and was not demolished until 1847. In his novel *Les Misérables*, Victor Hugo (q.v.) made this Gavroche's (q.v.) hiding place. An enormous hollow elephant graced the garden of the Moulin Rouge (q.v.) music hall in 1889.

ELYSÉE (Palace) (55, Rue du Faubourg-Saint-Honoré). This palace, which was built between 1718 and 1720, initially bore the name of its first owner, the count of Evreux. The Marquise de Pompadour, the mistress of Louis XV, acquired it in 1753. On her death in 1764, the mansion reverted to the king, who used it to lodge ambassadors during their stay in Paris. The financier Beaujon bought it in 1773 and had it renovated by Boullée. The duchess of Bourbon, who became the owner in 1787, had the garden—which reached as far as the Champs-Elysées (q.v.)—redesigned, which led to the palace being called Elysée-Bourbon. From 1805 to 1808, Joachim Murat, the marshal of Napoléon I who later became the king of Naples, had the inside redecorated again. The emperor himself resided there several times and signed his abdication there on June 22, 1815. After becoming state property and being inhabited periodically, Louis-Napoléon Bonaparte chose the Elysée palace as his residence when he was elected president at the end of 1848. He left it for the Tuileries (q.v.) when he was proclaimed emperor in 1852 but had major work undertaken that gave the palace its present appearance. Since 1873, the Palais de l'Elysée has been the official residence of the French president.

ENVIRONMENTAL PROTECTION Concern about protecting the environment emerged with the industrial society. The decree of October 15, 1810, laid down the first rules for supervising dangerous, noxious or unsanitary establishments. A technical body of inspectors of scheduled installations was formed in 1863. The regulatory framework was completed by the laws of December 19, 1917, and July 19, 1976. By virtue of the decree of September 21, 1977, the chief commissioner of police was entrusted with supervising the environmental protection of Paris. Some 12,000 installations are monitored by the Service Technique d'Inspection des Installations classées (STIIC) (Technical Service for the Inspection of Scheduled Installations). The Agence de Bassin Seine Normandie (Agency for the Seine Normandy Basin), the Direction départementale de l'Equipment and the Centre de Recherche interdépartemental pour le Traitement des Eaux (CRITER) (Interdepartmental Research Center for Water Treatment) carry out closer supervision of the surface treatment companies, which have the principal responsibility for water pollution. *See also* Air Pollution.

ÉTOILE (Arch and Square). In 1806, Napoléon I decided to erect, on the site of the Étoile tollgate (q.v.), a triumphal arch to the glory of the Grande Armée. The monument, which was designed by Chalgrin (died in 1811) rose only slowly and was not completed until 1836. This enormous and imposing structure is nearly 50 meters high and 45 meters wide, with more than 29 meters for the vault of the great arch. Since 1919, the Arc de Triomphe has become the apex of French patriotism, as the delegations of the victorious armies marched under its arch on July 14. On January 28, 1921, the Unknown Soldier was buried and the flame of remembrance has never ceased burning over his tomb since then. The square, now officially called Place Charles-de-Gaulle but still commonly known as Place de l'Étoile, assumed its present appearance during the Second Empire. By a decree of August 13, 1854, Baron Haussmann (q.v.) added five avenues to the seven that already existed, thereby forming a star (*étoile*) with 12 points. These are bordered by a dozen mansions, the so-called Marshals' hôtels, built by Hittorff and Rohault de Fleury between 1860 and 1868.

ETYMOLOGY OF PARIS. The name Paris appeared around A.D. 300 to replace the earlier name of Lutetia. The capital's name was derived from that of the Gallic tribe of the Parisii. The original name of Lutetia probably comes from the Celtic word *lut*, which means swamp.

-F-

FAIRS. The fairs are major markets that are held on specific dates. They played a very important role in the Middle Ages. The principal fair, the Lendit Fair, was held not in Paris, but in Saint-Denis. In Paris, the oldest fair is doubtlessly the Saint-Ladre Fair, also known as the Saint-Lazare Fair, which was granted in 1110 by King Louis VI the Stout to the monks of the leprosarium of Saint-Lazare. Philippe II Auguste bought the rights to it in 1181 and transferred it to the Halles des Champeaux, which he was having built. It was then held at the tip of Saint-Eustache Church until it ceased to be held at the beginning of the 17th century. Meanwhile, in 1183, the monks of Saint-Lazare initiated a new fair to finance the leprosarium. Called the Saint-Laurent Fair, it was held in the vicinity of Saint-Laurent Church but faded away in the 18th century.

The year in which the Saint-Germain Fair was begun is not known; but the event was referred to in 1176 and was held not far from Saint-

Germain-des-Prés abbey. It lasted until 1789. In 1222, Philippe II Auguste granted the bishop a fair on the parvis of Notre-Dame. This pork, fat and lard fair was limited to one day, Holy Thursday at first, and then Holy or Shrove Tuesday as of 1664. Abolished by the Revolution, it resumed in 1840 on Boulevard Bourdon as a fair for ham and for scrap iron. In 1869, it was transferred to the Boulevard Richard-Lenoir. The Saint-Ovide Fair was born in 1665 with the gift of the relics of Saint Ovide that the pope made to the duke of Créqui. The crowds of pilgrims on Saint-Ovide's Day (August 31) who gathered at the Capucine monastery, located near the present Place Vendôme, where the relics were stored, spontaneously generated a fair. The disruption that it caused led it to be transferred in 1770 to Louis XV Square (now Place de la Concorde). A fire destroyed the huts and stalls in 1777 and the fair did not survive.

The Temple Fair also dates back to the 17th century. It was held in the Temple (q.v.) courtyard on October 28, and was the origin of the secondhand goods market at the Temple. The only fair to survive to the present takes the form of the so-called Throne Fair (q.v.), which is held on the Reuilly Lawn of the Bois de Vincennes (q.v.). It is a nondescript food fair that seems to have been held since the 13th century in the enclosure of the abbey of Saint-Antoine. Gingerbread was sold there, which is why it is also called the Gingerbread Fair. *See also* Paris Fair.

FATTED OX FESTIVAL. The procession of the fatted ox (*boeuf gras*) dates back to the Middle Ages and seems to have been introduced by the butchers' guild. Rabelais refers to it in *Gargantua*. This procession started from the Apport-Paris, near the central slaughterhouse opposite the Châtelet (q.v.), crossed the Seine (q.v.) and went to greet the *Parlement* at the Palais de Justice (q.v.) before retracing its steps and ending with the killing of a fatted ox. A young boy, the king of the festival, was perched on the ox, which was escorted by butcher's boys in disguise who played music. Once the abattoirs were opened at La Villette (q.v.) in 1867, the festival was transferred there. It gradually lost its prestige until in 1952 it was prohibited on the pretext that it disturbed automobile traffic.

FAUCHON (Grocer-Caterer) (26, Place de la Madeleine). Auguste Fauchon opened this store in 1886, and it has been an incredible success ever since. It grew until it occupied the whole northeastern corner of Place de la Madeleine, adding to the high-class grocery a pastry shop and catering operations. It is possible to buy more than 2,000 products there, including the most rare and exotic, among them a very special honey that is not well known but that is in heavy demand: it is collected from beehives hanging from the Opéra's (q.v.) roof. Fauchon also has an exceptional wine cellar whose oldest bottle is a cognac from 1840.

FAVART, SIMON (1710–92). Initially an author of vaudevilles, Simon Favart began writing for the comic opera in 1760. His plays were a big hit at the Opéra-Comique (q.v.), whose director he became, and at the Théâtre-Italien. His work was plentiful, about 60 plays in all, but fairly mediocre. Still, mention must be made of *La Chercheuse d'esprit* (1741) and *Bastien et Bastienne*, which Mozart set to music. With the composers Grétry and Philidor, the librettist and songwriter Favart can be regarded as the father of French musical comedy.

FERRY, JULES (1832–93). A deputy of Paris and Republican opponent of the Second Empire, Jules Ferry was appointed prefect of the Seine (q.v.) by the government that was formed on September 4, 1870, on the announcement of the capture of Napoléon III by the Prussians. On November 15, 1870, he replaced Étienne Arago (q.v.) at the town hall. He put down attempted coups d'état by the extreme left and organized rationing in the besieged capital. For this he won his nickname of "Famine Ferry." After the Commune (q.v.) was formed on March 18, 1871, he fled the city, but he remained mayor (q.v.) at least in name until June 5, 1871. Elected deputy by his native Vosges, he became prime minister in 1881–82 and at the same time minister of public education, in which capacity he carried out basic reforms. Prime minister again from 1883 to 1885, he had to resign following the failure of his policy of colonial conquest in Tonkin (North Vietnam).

FIACRES. Nicolas Sauvage is presumed to have invented the fiacre in 1612. This small horse-drawn carriage, known as a four-wheeler, hackney or cab in English, was the oldest form of public transport in Paris. However, carriages for hire were first mentioned only in 1623, in an order of the *Parlement* (q.v.). The word "fiacre" apparently came from Brother Fiacre, a discalced Carmelite of the Petits Frères monastery, who had such an impressive reputation for saintliness that his picture was pasted on the carriages by the cabmen as protection against accidents. A regulation of 1669 required that the carriages be identified with yellow numbers painted on the back and the sides. In 1789 there were 800 fiacres, and in 1853, 2,600.

In 1855, Napoléon III granted the monopoly for fiacres to the Compagnie impériale des Voitures de Paris (Imperial Carriage Company of Paris). This monopoly was abolished in 1866, but the company maintained its dominant position. In 1896, it owned more than 5,000 of the 10,000 fiacres in the city. By 1900, however, the horse-drawn cab ran into competition from the motorized cab: in that year, there were 10,863 fiacres and 115 taxis and in 1907, 9,409 fiacres and 2,359 taxis. The last horse-drawn fiacre for hire disappeared in 1922. Until the 1950s, there was still a handful of fiacres for rich foreign tourists who wanted a ride around the Champs-Elysées (q.v.) neighborhood.

FIREMEN. Fire prevention and control were very poorly organized in the Middle Ages. The Parisians always had buckets of water at the disposal of the watchmen (q.v.). Those who really distinguished themselves in putting out fires were the monks of the mendicant orders (Franciscans, Dominicans, Augustinians and Carmelites). The fire pump had already been invented by the beginning of the 16th century, but it did not appear in Paris until 1699, when the king purchased a dozen of these pumps and offered them to the city. A company of pump guards was formed in 1722, a forerunner of the present-day fire brigades. From 60, the number of men rose to 108 in 1767. In view of the deficient organization of the rescue work during the fire at the Austrian embassy in 1810, Napoléon I decided to issue the decree of September 18, 1811, that reorganized and militarized the corps of firemen. This structure has remained almost intact to the present day: the firemen are quartered in barracks and wear a uniform. Their numbers have not ceased growing. The initial battalion became a regiment of more than 1,500 men in 1867. A century later, on February 28, 1967, the firemen's brigade of Paris was established with responsibility for an area including the capital and the three neighboring départements that make up the nearby suburbs. While there were 5,000 firemen in 1967, there are now about 7,000, with impressive equipment and nearly 300 mechanical pumps.

FIRES. The city's history is marked by fires, some of which were particularly noteworthy. The oldest recorded fire in Paris occurred in 52 B.C. The inhabitants of Lutetia set fire to everything that would burn on the Île de la Cité (q.v.) to prevent Labienus, Caesar's lieutenant, from taking over the place. Another fire completely destroyed the Cité again in 585. Although no other calamity took place that affected the whole city, as happened in London in 1666, some fires were disastrous and have lived on in people's memories.

In 1618, the main hall of the Palais de Justice (q.v.), where the *Parlement* (q.v.) met, was consumed by flames. In 1621, the Marchands (merchants') and Changeurs (money-changers') bridges, built of wood, were destroyed and 14 monks of the mendicant orders perished while fighting the fire. In 1631, the Sainte-Chapelle (q.v.) was saved from destruction only by the courage of these monks, forerunners of today's firemen (q.v.). In 1661, the small gallery of the Louvre (q.v.) caught fire and then, in 1671, the tower of the Sorbonne (q.v.) was damaged. In 1718, the Hôtel-Dieu (q.v.) and the Petit Pont burned. The year 1737 was marked by two catastrophes: the Hôtel-Dieu burned again and the Auditor General's Office, located in the Palais de Justice, went up in smoke with all its archives. The Hôtel-Dieu burned again in 1772 and the Palais de Justice in 1776. The Opéra (q.v.) was destroyed by fire in 1763, then again in 1781.

Theaters (q.v.), illuminated by candlelight, were a particular hazard: the Théâtre-Français was destroyed in 1799, the Odéon in 1818, and the Théâtre-Italien in 1838. In 1860, the explosion of a ton of alcohol caused an immense conflagration in the Bercy (q.v.) warehouses. That, however, was nothing compared to the fires set by the defeated Communards (*see* Commune) at the end of May 1871, which destroyed the Ministry of Finance, the palace of the Legion of Honor, the Tuileries (q.v.), the Hôtel de Ville (q.v.), and the warehouses at La Villette (q.v.)—more than 200 buildings in all. The last major disaster caused by fire was the blaze at the Charity Bazaar on May 4, 1897, the day after it opened, which left 135 casualties.

FLEA MARKETS. The flea markets emerged around 1860 on the periphery of Paris in places where the *chiffonniers* (q.v.), or ragpickers, lived. At the various gates, they sold items they had recovered from the capital's garbage. Such markets were particularly numerous in the town of Saint-Ouen in the immediate vicinity of Paris. That is where the main flea market is located today, a vast maze subdivided into smaller, specialized markets: Jules Vallès, Paul Bert, Serpette, des Rosiers, Cambo, Biron, Venaison, des Malassis and Malik. There are nearly 1,500 stalls, which are open Saturdays, Sundays and Mondays and where one can buy everything from antiques and furniture to army surplus clothing. There are two other fair-sized flea markets, at the Montreuil and Vanves gates. In Paris, at the Aligre market (Place d'Aligre), there is still a small market for secondhand goods and frippery held every day next to a larger market for fruits and vegetables.

FLEURIOT-LESCOT, JEAN-BAPTISTE ÉDOUARD (1761–94). Born in Brussels, Fleuriot-Lescot participated in the Belgian revolt against Austrian domination (1789) and sought refuge in Paris after the uprising collapsed. Sort of a student of architecture and sculpture, and a shady participant in the activities of the revolutionary clubs, he began to play a significant role only when he was elected substitute for Public Prosecutor Fouquier-Tinville of the Revolutionary Tribunal (q.v.) (March 13, 1793) with the support of Robespierre (q.v.). The latter had him chosen on May 10, 1794, to replace Mayor Pache (q.v.), who was forced to resign. Fleuriot-Lescot tried in vain to stir up the Parisian people in favor of his protector when he was ordered to stand trial by the Convention. Fleuriot-Lescot was guillotined along with Robespierre shortly after his defeat on July 28, 1794.

FLOODS. The location of Paris is prone to floods. The oldest recorded one occurred in 583 and stretched as far as Saint-Laurent Church, with the rising Seine (q.v.) overflowing into its former bed at the foot of the hills of Belleville (q.v.) and Montmartre (q.v.). Chroniclers mentioned 10 years of high waters in the 13th century, six in the 14th, 15 in the 15th and 19 in the 16th. The maximum high-water mark occurred in 1658, when the river reached nine meters on the scale of the Tournelle bridge, exceeding by 30 centimeters the flood of 1910, which was immortalized by untold thousands of photographs and picture postcards. The construction of a series of dams upstream on the Seine has made it possible to control the floods effectively.

FLORE LE (Café) (172, Boulevard Saint-Germain). Probably founded in 1865, Le Flore was just an ordinary café (q.v.) until the end of the 19th century. Then it began to be frequented by Remy de Gourmont and Huysmans and, somewhat later, by the opponents of Dreyfus, who grouped around Charles Maurras. In 1912, Guillaume Apollinaire founded the poetic movement Soirées de Paris there. The surrealists were in evidence there during the interwar period. It was there that Lawrence Durrell and Truman Capote founded the P.C.F. (Pouilly-Club de France). As of 1939, Le Flore became the cradle of existentialism with Jean-Paul Sartre and Simone de Beauvoir. Nowadays, more than anything, it is a place of pilgrimage for tourists.

FOLIES-BERGÈRE (32, Rue Richer). On May 2, 1869, the first Parisian theater specifically designed to serve as a music hall (q.v.) was inaugurated. For an entrance fee of one franc, customers could attend a stage performance while being able to come and go, drink and smoke as in a café (q.v.). The shows included operettas, ballets, pantomimes and acrobatic feats. Among the most popular international acts were the American acrobat Leona Dare, famous for her "iron jaw"; the marksman Ira Paine; and Hanlon-Lee, a combination of clowns, mimes, gymnasts and musicians. Edouard Marchand, the director, invited the first troupe of "girls," the Barrison Sisters, to visit France in 1890. The stage of the Folies-Bergère revealed the talents of Caroline Otéro, Liane de Pougy, Emilienne d'Alencon and Loïe Fuller (q.v.), whose dances were a tremendous success. The last star recruited by Marchand, in 1901, was the opera dancer Cléo de Mérode. The first variety show was given in the Folies-Bergère in

1886. Maurice Chevalier (q.v.) made his debut in 1909, and Mistinguett (q.v.) made hers in 1911. As of 1919 Paul Derval gave his reviews an exceptional glamor and, in 1926, revealed the "black pearl" Josephine Baker (q.v.). Since the Second World War the Folies-Bergère has lost some of its prestige, Still, after Derval's death in 1966, his widow and then Hélène Martini have kept up the music hall tradition as best they could.

FOLLIES. The word *folie* in French (folly in English) derives from the Latin word *folia*, which means "leaf" and was used to designate a country pleasure home surrounded by greenery. These follies existed in the Middle Ages, and the street names Rue de la Folie-Méricourt and Rue de la Folie-Regnault recall follies of the 14th and 15th centuries. The Folie-Rambouillet of Bercy, which was famous for its size and wealth, was built by the financier Nicolas de Rambouillet between 1633 and 1635.

However, it was especially with the passing of Louis XIV (1715), that the follies, or "little houses," began to proliferate. After an interminable end of a reign marked by bigotry and prudishness, the nobility felt an intense need to break loose socially and sexually. In these smiling and discreet places the great lords caroused in the company of their mistresses. Most of the follies were located on the Right Bank, in particular in the eastern faubourgs, in Bercy (q.v.), Picpus and Saint-Antoine (q.v.), where the lavish Titon Folly (Rue Titon) could be found. The Montmartre (q.v.) faubourg also had a large number of follies reaching as far as Chaussée d'Antin. Faubourg Saint-Honoré (q.v.) could boast the richest of all, that of the financier Beaujon.

FORAIN, JEAN-LOUIS (1852–1931). Painter, designer and caricaturist, Forain was related to the impressionists. A friend of Verlaine, Rimbaud and Huysmans, for the latter he illustrated the *Croquis parisiens* (Parisian Sketches) (1880). While working for the *Journal*, *Figaro* and *L'Assiette au Beurre*, he was one of the best caricaturists of the Belle Epoque. With his cynical humor he caustically portrayed scenes of Parisian life, which were the object of several of his collections such as *La Comédie parisienne* (The Parisian Comedy) (1892), *Temps difficiles* (Hard Times) (1893) and *Nous, vous, eux* (Us, You, Them) (1894). Along with Daumier and Toulouse-Lautrec, Forain was one of the keenest observers of the Parisians.

FORTS DES HALLES. Tradition has it that the *forts des Halles* or market porters were introduced by Louis IX, doubtlessly after 1250. An ordinance of 1415 mentioned them under the name of "sworn porters" and gave them the title of town officers, appointed by the merchants' provost (q.v.). Discontinued during the Revolution but restored at the beginning of the 19th century, their appointments were henceforth granted and revoked by the police commissioner. Numbering 700 and called the "700 muscular ones," they were assigned to five companies for the wholesale pavilions of fruit and vegetables, meat, butter and eggs, poultry and fresh fish. The *forts* not only transported the goods, they were responsible for them and patrolled the area in order to prevent theft.

As the operations were mechanized and forklifts appeared, this sort of manual labor, with porters carrying loads on their backs, was doomed. As of 1952, there was no more recruitment and the porters gradually dispersed as they left the trade or went into retirement. In 1969, when the Rungis market was opened, there were only 269 remaining *forts des Halles*. Not a single one was still active by 1996.

FRANKLIN, BENJAMIN (1706–90). Both a scientist and a statesman, Benjamin Franklin was sent to London in 1757 to defend the interests of the American colonists. Ceasing to believe in the possibility of his country developing under British domination, he rallied to the revolution of the 13 colonies. He was elected as the representative of Pennsylvania to the first Continental Congress in 1774 and participated in drafting the Declaration of Independence. Benjamin Franklin then went to Paris to negotiate an alliance against England and remained there until 1785. In Paris, he gained the sympathy of public opinion, the salons and even the court through his good-natured simplicity. He obtained France's commitment to aid the United States during the War of Independence (1778–83).

FRONDE. Fronde is the name given to the civil unrest that troubled France from 1648 to 1653. This period began in Paris in May 1648 when the *Parlement* (q.v.) joined with the Grand Council, the Audit Office and the Court of Aids to form a political body that interfered in the affairs of state. Cardinal Mazarin, who governed in the name of the young Louis XIV (q.v.), had the ringleaders arrested, which provoked an uprising of the Parisians and the Day of Barricades (August 26, 1648). The cardinal gave in, had Louis XIV and Anne of Austria leave the city (January 5, 1649), and besieged Paris until the compromise peace of Rueil (April 1, 1649).

However, the parliamentary Fronde was then followed by a Fronde of princes, led by Condé, Conti, Retz and Turenne and encouraged by Gaston d'Orléans, the king's uncle. Mazarin relinquished office and went into exile (February 1651), betting that the princes would fall out with one another, which soon happened. Rallying to the royal cause, Turenne beat Condé at Faubourg Saint-Antoine (July 2, 1652).

However, Condé was able to take refuge in the capital when the Grande Mademoiselle, the daughter of Gaston d'Orléans, had the city gates opened for him. Finally, the citizens of Paris could no longer take Condé's arrogance and he had to seek refuge with the Spaniards. Louis XIV and Anne of Austria returned triumphantly to Paris (October 21, 1652) and Mazarin came back as well (February 3, 1653). Meanwhile, the Fronde disintegrated.

FRONT DE SEINE. In 1967, the City of Paris initiated a major urban renewal program for the old industrial district bordering the Seine (q.v.) in the 15th arrondissement, along the Quay de Grenelle and Quay André-Citroën. The architects Raymond Lopez, Henri Pottier and Michel Proux were entrusted with supervising a project that was inspired by the American model. Dozens of high-rise apartment blocks and office buildings were projected. The first two were the Evasion Tower and the Seine Tower; the latter, which was built in 1990, was also known as the Crystal Tower because it was covered with mirrors. This program is not yet completed and is continuing along the Quay André-Citroën. However, much more space is being reserved now for greenery.

FULLER, LOÏE (1862–1928). Loïe Fuller was a child prodigy who first appeared on stage in Chicago at the age of four. In 1889, she left the theater to devote herself to dancing. She was a hit when she performed the Fire Dance at the Folies-Bergère (q.v.) in 1892. Edison made a film of that performance: *Annabelle the Dancer, or Loïe Fuller's Serpentine Dance*. Between tours in Europe and the United States, Loïe Fuller spent most of her time in Paris. Among other things, she danced at the 1900 world exhibition, at which she revealed two new talents, Isadora Duncan and Maud Allen. In 1923, although in her sixties, she played in Gounod's *Damnation of Faust* at the Paris Opéra. Loïe Fuller was drawn by Toulouse-Lautrec (q.v.) and Jules Chéret and also posed for the sculptor Auguste Rodin (q.v.). Her memoirs, *Quinze ans de ma vie* (Fifteen Years of My Life) (1908), deal at length with her stays in Paris. Loïe Fuller invented a new way of dancing, with an accent on suppleness.

FULTON, ROBERT (1765–1815). Fulton, a mechanic born in Pennsylvania, was at the origin of the modern navy. Living in England, and then France as of 1797, he designed the *Nautulus*, which was later called the *Nautilus*, a propeller-driven submarine that navigated with sails on the surface. Napoléon Bonaparte, however, having no understanding of maritime matters, dismissed his invention. On August 9, 1803, Fulton made the first demonstration of a steamboat on the Seine (q.v.). After returning to the United States in 1806, he built the *Clermont*, which was the first steamship to make a regular commercial run between New York and Albany, as of 1808.

FUNICULARS. Although Paris is relatively flat, two funiculars were built to climb the hills of Belleville (q.v.) and Montmartre (q.v.). The Belleville funicular was designed using the technique of a continuously running endless cable like the one used since 1873 in San Francisco. It was put into service on August 25, 1891. About two kilometers long, it ran from Place de la République to Belleville Church along the Rue du Faubourg-du-Temple and Rue de Belleville. It carried five million passengers a year at a speed of 12 kilometers per hour. In 1924, it was replaced by a bus (q.v.) service.

The Montmartre funicular was built in 1900 to serve the Sacré-Coeur Basilica (q.v.). It worked with a system of water counterweights and was modernized in 1991. It is operated by the Régie Autonome des Transports Parisiens (RATP).

-G-

GALERIES LAFAYETTE (40, Boulevard Haussmann). The last of the major department stores (q.v.), the Galeries Lafayette were founded in 1894 by Théophile Bader and Alphonse Kahn. The store gradually expanded around two vast halls. In 1926, the architect Pierre Patout increased the intimacy of the buildings and their decoration by playing down the appearance of an Oriental bazaar, which had been the original intention of Bader. Unfortunately, when the buildings were modernized and the ceilings raised in 1958, much of the old decoration disappeared, and only traces can be found now in the grand hall. The Galeries Lafayette were enlarged to the east and the west with two other stores.

GAMIN. Parisian kids were not very different from other children before the beginning of the 19th century, and the *gamin des rues*, or "street urchin," is mentioned for the first time in 1802. The Parisian *gamin* type was shaped after the Revolution of July 1830. In 1836, the Théâtre du Gymnase staged a play called *Le Gamin de Paris*. The *gamin* became a special category: with a lower-class background, he is the opposite of the bourgeois child because he grows up in the streets and becomes streetwise, away from family control rather than being hemmed in by countless prohibitions. He rejects all forms of authority and order and participates in all forms of revolt. The painter Charlet portrayed this sort of *gamin*, followed by Daumier, Gavarni and many other artists. In literature, it was Eugène Sue (q.v.) who provided the best description in the character of Tortillard in *Les Mystères de Paris,* "sceptical and cheeky like a child of Paris, corrupted as it were with his mother's milk," doomed to crime and the scaffold. *See also* Gavroche.

GARDENS. Paris does not have anywhere near as many green spaces as London or New York. In theory, 20 percent of the capital is covered with greenery, but the Bois de Boulogne (q.v.) and Bois de Vincennes (q.v.), which are located on the periphery and not within the city, are included in this estimate. In reality, if these woods are not counted, the two million Parisians can enjoy only about 500 hectares situated within the built-up areas. This is less than six percent of the total space. Some arrondissements, such as the 2nd, 9th and 10th, do not have even one percent of green space and six others have between two and three percent. Nearly all of the 400 green and wooded spaces recorded by the municipality are smaller than one hectare. Since 1977, the town hall has taken some account of the demands of the citizens and ecologists and created 103 more hectares of squares and gardens dispersed among 126 sites.

GARNIER-PAGÈS, LOUIS ANTOINE (1803–78). Louis Antoine Garnier-Pagès was a Republican who fought on the barricades (q.v.) in July 1830. He was elected deputy of Eure in 1841. When the Republic was proclaimed on February 24, 1848, he became the minister of finance in the provisional government and was also appointed mayor (q.v.) of Paris. He held the post only until March 5, when he was replaced by Armand Marrast (q.v.). Elected a deputy in 1864, Garnier-Pagès was one of the leaders of the Republican opposition and became a minister in the Government of National Defense that was formed on September 4, 1870, after the fall of Napoléon III.

GAS. The first patents relating to gas were taken out between 1796 and 1801. Philippe Lebon in particular invented a process generating both light and heat. But gas lighting was not available until 1816 in a café (q.v.) at Passage des Panoramas. Public lighting (q.v.) with gas began in 1829 in the Rue de la Paix and at Place Vendôme. In 1855, all the private companies merged into the Compagnie parisienne d'éclairage au gaz (Parisian Gas Lighting Company), which was replaced by the Société du Gaz de Paris.

Gas was nationalized at the same time as electricity to create Electricité de France-Gaz de France (EDF-GDF). The gas stove was introduced in 1840. The network grew from less than 500 kilometers in about 1850 to 1,700 kilometers in 1905. At the end of 1899, 30 percent of the dwelling places were equipped with gas and at least half of the population was using gas. By now the gas network has reached 2,300 kilometers serving more than 800,000 consumers.

GASTRONOMY. By the end of the Middle Ages Paris was already known as a temple of good eating. In the 16th century, the Venetian ambassador was amazed by the quantity and quality of the food that could be found in the capital and noted that it was possible to taste the rarest and most refined dishes. Gastronomy became an art early in the 19th century with Brillat-Savarin, Grimod de La Reynière and Carême. The Palais-Royal (q.v.) was then at the pinnacle of French cooking. Around 1845, the Grands Boulevards (q.v.) pulled ahead with the Café Anglais, Café Riche, Maison Dorée and Café de Paris, all of them located on the Boulevard des Italiens. During the 1860s, the heart of Parisian haute cuisine shifted to the west: Café de la Paix (q.v.) at Place de l'Opéra, Durand on the Boulevard de la Madeleine, but also to the Champs-Elyseés (q.v.) and the Bois de Boulogne (q.v.), with the Armenonville pavilion. The most famous dishes of "international cuisine" were fashioned in Paris during the 19th century: Béarnaise sauce, bouchée à la reine, vol-au-vent, lobster Thermidor, veal Marengo and Orloff, sauté potatoes, crêpes Suzette, and many more. Parisian cuisine still maintains its prestige today.

GAULTIER, JEAN-PAUL (1952–). After getting started in 1970 with Pierre Cardin (q.v.), Jean-Paul Gaultier worked for Jacques Esterel from 1971 to 1973. He presented his first collection in 1976 and quickly rose to the top with a strikingly modern and often provocative style. In 1988, he received the Oscar for the best ready-to-wear collection.

GAVROCHE. Gavroche was a character created by Victor Hugo (q.v.) in *Les Misérables*, a novel that was published in 1862 but depicted events in the 1830s. He gave a new image to the *gamin* (q.v.), a more positive one of a generous and sensitive child with a social conscience. In 1872, in his *Grand Dictionnaire*, Pierre Larousse noted the disappearance of this Parisian type.

GENEVIÈVE (Saint) (c. 420–c. 502). Born in Nanterre, Geneviève is said to have taken the veil at the age of seven and received the blessing of Saint-Germain d'Auxerre. In 451, according to legend, with her prayers she turned back the Huns who wanted to attack Paris. Very popular with the people, she apparently negotiated Paris's rallying to the side of Clovis (q.v.) in 486. After she died, she was buried at the summit of the mountain that bears her name, and Clovis had a basilica built, later called Sainte-Geneviève, at the place of her tomb. Saint

Geneviève became the patron saint of Paris and she was invoked in times of calamity, when the shrine containing her relics was carried in a procession through the city.

GEORGE V (Hotel) (31, Avenue George V). Inaugurated in 1928, the George V Hotel was the work of the architects Lefranc and Wybo, who designed a neoclassical façade for its nine floors. Attracted by its technical advances, the hotel was quickly adopted by a well-heeled American clientele, and Greta Garbo, Terence Young, Gene Kelly, Buster Keaton and Cecil B. DeMille, among others, stayed there. After the liberation of Paris in August 1944, General Eisenhower installed his headquarters there for a while. From 1989 to 1992, its 310 rooms and suites were completely renovated. The halls were decorated with luxurious Flemish, Beauvais and Aubusson tapestries. A gastronomical restaurant, "Les Princes," was opened by André Sonier. The Parisian poet Léon-Paul Fargue described the George V as a polished and powdered transatlantic liner that reigned over the most aristocratic avenue in Paris.

GOBELINS (Factory) (42, Avenue des Gobelins). Jean Gobelin, a dyer, set up shop in the 15th century on the banks of the Bièvre (q.v.). The reputation of his factory soon overshadowed that of the other firms that had already opened factories along that river, and his name eventually designated the whole quarter. In 1667, Colbert established the Manufacture royale des Meubles et Tapisseries de la Couronne (Royal Factory of Furniture and Tapestries of the Crown) specifically to produce goods to decorate the palaces of Louis XIV (q.v.). It still exists in an assortment of buildings from various periods, and the name of Gobelins has been given to the 13th arrondissement.

GOUTTE D'OR (Quarter). For the longest time the Goutte d'Or was an uninhabited place covered with vineyards (q.v.). During the 18th century, the vines were replaced by gypsum quarries and plaster furnaces. The hamlet of Goutte d'Or was established around 1814 within the commune of La Chapelle. It was incorporated into the capital in 1860 and formed one of the quarters of the 18th arrondissement. That is where Zola situated *L'Assommoir (The Dram Shop)*, his novel about alcoholism.

Ever since 1945, the Goutte d'Or quarter has been gradually transformed into a medina, a North African town inhabited mainly by people coming from Algeria, Morocco and Tunisia. It has its own cafés (q.v.) and its own restaurants (q.v.) where you can eat excellent couscous and *tadjines*. Its various shops, most of them run by North

Africans, sell everything from groceries to jewelry, to say nothing of textiles and tapes of Arab music.

GOVERNOR OF PARIS. As the king's representative, the governor played an important role until 1660. Fearing the ambition of the great lords to whom this office was entrusted, Louis XIV (q.v.) limited the term of his governors to three years and forbade them from residing in their government without his authorization. Henceforth, they played a purely honorary rule until the office was done away with during the Revolution of 1789.

GRAND VÉFOUR, LE. *See* VÉFOUR, LE GRAND.

GRAND-GUIGNOL (Theater) (Impasse Chaptal). In 1897, Oscar Métenier founded a theater at the foot of Montmartre (q.v.). The Grand-Guignol was to stage the naturalistic dramas that were rejected elsewhere and send a cold shiver down the backs of the spectators. Until it was closed in 1962, the Grand-Guignol was the theater of horror, the macabre and blood and gore. Among the many authors who wrote for it, the most memorable were André-Paul Antoine, Alfred Binet, Charles Foley, Gaston Leroux, Maurice Level, André de Lorde, Max Maurey, André Moüezy-Eon and Maurice Renard.

GRANGE-BATELIÈRE. *See* SEINE, LA.

GRÈVE (Square). Presently called Place de l'Hôtel de Ville, the earlier Place de Grève was initially just that, a *grève*, or bank of the river sloping gently toward the Seine (q.v.). It was there that at the beginning of the 12th century the Grève port (q.v.), one of the main ports of Paris, developed. In 1357, Étienne Marcel (q.v.) established the headquarters of the municipality there, in the Maison aux Piliers (Pillared House), the forerunner of the Hôtel de Ville (q.v.). This square, which was then about a quarter of the size of the present one, was the center of city life. It is where the official festivities, the annual Saint-Jean fire, but also the executions, took place. It is also where the guillotine (q.v.) was inaugurated. In 1853, Haussmann (q.v.) had all the tiny streets around the Hôtel de Ville razed to create the present square. Two barracks, erected behind the Hôtel de Ville, were linked to it by an underground passage. The purpose was to prevent the building from being taken by rioters, as had occurred several times during the Revolution, in 1830 and 1848, and as would happen again in 1870–71. *See also* Strikes.

GRÉVIN (Museum) (10, Boulevard Montmartre). Initiated in 1882 by the caricaturist Alfred Grévin, the Musée Grévin is a waxworks museum. At a time when there was no cinema, this reconstruction of the bloody deeds that were reported in the newspapers was a great success. There were lifesize likenesses of the celebrities of the period: Victor Hugo (q.v.), Sarah Bernhardt (q.v.) and many others. Later on, historical scenes were added: Marat (q.v.) stabbed in his bathtub, Louis XVII at the Temple prison, Napoléon and Joséphine at Malmaison, and so on. In 1900, a playhouse was opened, the Théâtre Joli, with sculptures by Bourdelle and a stage curtain by Jules Chéret. The Musée Grévin still receives many visitors who admire the faithful reproductions of important policymakers of the present day, such as Edouard Balladur, Jacques Chirac (q.v.), Bill Clinton, and others. Indeed, it was so popular that it opened an annex at the Forum des Halles (q.v.). This branch consists of 22 realistic scenes out of Paris's past, such as a performance at the Opéra, the Café Napolitain at the time of the Belle Epoque (1885–1900), the universal exhibition (q.v.) of 1900 and the world imagined by Jules Verne.

GUILLOTINE. In the name of equality and progress, Dr. Joseph Ignace Guillotin had the various instruments of torture used by the Ancien Régime abolished and replaced them with one sole method of execution, the guillotine. Initially called Louison, the guillotine was developed by a piano maker, Tobias Schmidt or Schmitt, and a surgeon, Antoine Louis, although it was promoted by Dr. Guillotin, whose name it borrowed.

The guillotine was inaugurated at Place de Grève (q.v.) on April 25, 1792, and its first victim was the thief Nicolas Jacques Pelletier. After the insurrection of August 10, 1792, and the fall of the monarchy, the guillotine was set up at Place du Carrousel. An exception at that time, Louis XVI was beheaded at Place de la Concorde, on January 21, 1793. From May 17, 1793, until June 7, 1794, however, the guillotine was transferred to the Place de la Concorde, which was then called Place de la Révolution. From June 9 to 12, it was located at Place de la Bastille. On June 13, it was relegated to the eastern outskirts of Paris, to Place du Trône-Renversé (presently Place de la Nation). After the execution of Robespierre (q.v.) (July 28, 1794), the Terror (q.v.) came to an end and the guillotine returned to its original location at Place de Grève (presently Place de l'Hôtel de Ville) in 1795.

Now used on common criminals rather than royalty or revolutionaries, the guillotine continued moving. It remained at Place de Grève until 1830. In 1832, it was transferred to the tollgate (q.v.) of Saint-Jacques or d'Arcueil (corner of Boulevard Saint-Jacques and Rue du Faubourg-Saint-Jacques). In 1851, it was installed at the Roquette prison (Rue de la Roquette), where it stayed until 1899. When the prison was demolished, it was set up near the Santé (q.v.) prison in the

Boulevard Arago. In 1939, the executions ceased being public and the machine operated within the courtyard of the Santé prison. The last execution took place on November 28, 1972. The death penalty was abolished in 1981.

GUIMARD, HECTOR (1867–1942). After designing the Electricity Pavilion for the 1889 world exhibition (q.v.), the architect Hector Guimard became a professor at the École des Arts Décoratifs. Between 1893 and 1903, he constructed a dozen buildings, including Castel Béranger (q.v.). Their hallmark was a particularly polished style of decoration. He also launched Art Nouveau. As of 1899, Guimard made the entrances for the métro stations out of iron and cast iron with a luxuriant and pliant floral and vegetable decor that its detractors put down with the name of "noodle style." Almost all of these entrances were destroyed until they were listed in the inventory of historic monuments in 1978. The Museum of Modern Art in New York bought one for its collections. In March 1923, Guimard founded the Groupe des Architectes Modernes with Frantz Jourdain and Henri Sauvage, but his ideas were regarded as too daring and he received no more orders. He left France for the United States in 1938 and died in New York.

GUINGUETTES. There have always been bars and taverns located right next to Paris but outside the limits of the city toll (*see* Tollgates) to avoid paying the heavy taxes levied on wines and spirits. The name *guinguette* appeared during the Régence (1715–23) and seems to come from *guinguet*, a rather mediocre but also rather cheap beverage wine that was sold there. To entertain their customers, *guinguette* owners would hire two or three performers to play music to which one could dance. When the surrounding communes were incorporated into Paris in 1860, the *guinguettes* moved further out into the suburbs. Henceforth it was along the Seine (q.v.) and the Marne, to Nogent, Joinville, Suresnes, and so on, that the Parisians went by train for eating, drinking and entertainment.

-H-

HALLES, LES (Market). In 1137, King Louis VI bought some land at Champeaux and set up a market selling corn from Beauce. In 1141, it was joined by merchants who had left the Place de Grève (q.v.), which had become too small for the business that was conducted there. Between 1181 and 1183, Philippe Auguste had the market surrounded by walls against which the shops and stalls leaned. He also had two halls built to protect the goods from bad weather and theft.

Les Halles, the central market of Paris, was born. Saint Louis added three new halls and Philippe III, another two in 1278. Around 1320, the whole market was completed with many small halls, each one bearing the name of the town from which the merchants came: the halls of Saint-Denis, Gonesse, Pontoise, Beauvais, Douai, Amiens, Brussels, etc. By then foodstuffs took up less room than other products, such as hides, cloth and textiles.

The Halles were reorganized between 1543 and 1572, with seven covered halls and uncovered halls divided into five groups. Since it had become much too small for a city of more than a million inhabitants, these Halles were torn down in 1847 and replaced by 10 iron girder and glass pavilions designed by Baltard. In 1963, these Halles were also condemned and they were all destroyed except for one, which was moved to Nogent-sur-Marne. They were replaced by the Marché d'Intérêt National (MIN) (Market of National Interest) in Rungis, which is the biggest wholesale food market in the world and was inaugurated in 1969.

HAUSSMANN, GEORGES EUGÈNE (1809–92). Haussmann, who had been the prefect of the départements of Var, Yonne and then Gironde, was noticed by Napoléon III, who appointed him prefect of the Seine département on June 22, 1853. He was assigned the task of modernizing a Paris that was still partly medieval. He launched numerous projects that largely reshaped the city. Among other things, he recreated the axes of Paris: the east-west one by finishing the Rue de Rivoli and building the Champs-Elysées (q.v.) and the north-south one by laying out the Boulevards de Strasbourg, de Sébastopol and Saint-Michel. He was particularly proud of the numerous gardens (q.v.) he made, the biggest of which are the parks of Montsouris and Buttes-Chaumont (q.v.). He also refashioned the Bois de Boulogne (q.v.) and Bois de Vincennes (q.v.).

Haussmann's work was enormous but also greatly criticized, mainly because it caused the destruction of many old buildings. The financial aspects of the policy of renovation and real estate speculation were also questioned. After he was dismissed on January 5, 1870, by Napoléon III, who wanted to give his regime a more liberal appearance, Baron Haussmann wrote his *Mémoires* to justify his actions.

HAUTE COUTURE. The origin of haute couture is sometimes traced back to the end of the 18th century, to Rose Bertin, who provided clothing for Marie-Antoinette, and to Hippolyte Leroy, who clothed Empress Joséphine. It is more generally accepted, however, that it was Charles Frederick Worth (q.v.) who was the first, back in 1857, to give his clothing and store a luxury image while organizing the production side of the operation like an industry. Thanks to Napoléon III and his wife, Empress Eugénie, Worth's showrooms and workshops ended up occupying the whole building at 7, Rue de la Paix, thereby endowing that avenue, which until then was not particularly commercial, with an exceptional prestige.

The trade did so well that, at the 1900 world exhibition, a special pavilion was devoted to haute couture, and 20 Parisian houses displayed their models. Most of these firms were located at Place Vendôme (q.v.) and Rue de la Paix. During the 1920s, haute couture assumed a new dimension. There were no fewer than 72 couturiers at the International Exhibition of Decorative Arts in 1925, but they were decimated by the depression and there were only 29 houses at the 1937 world exhibition. The Second World War hastened the decline: by then, fewer than 2,000 women were still clothed by a famous couturier. Thus, haute couture had to find expedients and cooperated with the ready-to-wear industry.

Since the 1930s, the fashion district's center of gravity shifted toward the west to get closer to its well-to-do customers. The showrooms are now clustered around the Champs-Elysées (q.v.), Avenue Montaigne, Rue François Ier, Rue Marbeuf and Rue du Faubourg-Saint-Honoré. By 1996, only 18 fashion houses were able to cover the costs of showing two collections a year: Pierre Balmain, Pierre Cardin (q.v.), Carven, Chanel (q.v.), Dior (q.v.), Louis Féraud, Givenchy, Christian Lacroix, Ted Lapidus, Guy Laroche, Lecoanet Hemant, Hanae Mori, Paco Rabanne, Nina Ricci, Yves Saint-Laurent (q.v.), Jean-Louis Scherrer, Torrente and Ungaro. Six other houses present their collections from time to time or have recently given up the fashion parade and devoted themselves to luxury ready-to-wear: Courrèges, Jacques Faith, Grès, Lanvin, Jean Patou and Per Spook. *See also* Chanel, Gabrielle; Courrèges, André; Dior, Christian; Doucet, Jacques; Gaultier, Jean Paul; Lagerfeld, Karl; Lanvin, Jeanne; Poiret, Paul; Rabanne, Francisco Rabaneda-Cuervo; Ricci, Maria Nielli; Saint-Laurent, Yves; Worth, Charles Frederick.

HÉDIARD (Grocery-Caterer) (21, Place de la Madeleine). Tradition has it that the young Ferdinand Hédiard was undertaking his tour of France as a journeyman when he discovered his vocation on seeing tropical fruits unloaded in the port of Toulon. In 1854, he set up shop at 21, Place de la Madeleine, where he introduced rich and refined Parisians to the consumption of these fruits. Among other things, he initiated Alexandre Dumas père in the delights of eating pineapples. The present establishment carries on the tradition of purveying high-quality products from around the world and has added a catering operation.

HEIGHT OF MONUMENTS. Several monuments stand out in the Parisian skyline because of their height. The tallest are the Eiffel Tower (320.75 meters) (q.v.), the Main-Montparnasse Tower (210 m), the dome of the Invalides (105 m) (q.v.), the dome of the Panthéon (83 m) (q.v.), the Sacré-Coeur Basilica (80 m) (q.v.), Notre-Dame Cathedral (69 m) (q.v.), the Opéra Garnier (54 m) (*see* Opéra), the Arc de Triomphe at the Étoile (49.54 m) (q.v.), the July Column at Place de la Bastille (47 m), the column at Place Vendôme (45 m) (q.v.) and the Georges-Pompidou Center (42 m) (q.v.).

HEMINGWAY, ERNEST (1899–1961). Ernest Hemingway was the most illustrious representative of the "lost generation," the young Americans who participated in the First World War and stayed on as expatriates in France and Europe during the interwar period. The novel *The Sun Also Rises* (1926) tells of that voluntary exile. Hemingway also devoted a whole book to his Parisian experience, *A Moveable Feast*, which was published posthumously in 1964.

HERMÈS. In 1837, Thierry Hermès founded a company that specialized in making quality harnesses for the carriage horses of high society. The first saddles were made in 1900. After the First World War, with the passing of horse-drawn carriages, the Hermès company had to seek new products. It began producing ladies' handbags and opened a clothing department that was an immediate hit. In 1937, the silk scarf appeared that made Hermès famous around the world. Marlene Dietrich, Ingrid Bergman and Grace Kelly were among its best-known and most faithful customers. Located at 24, Rue du Faubourg-Saint-Honoré, the Hermès firm still symbolizes Parisian and French luxury and elegance.

HISTORICAL LIBRARY OF THE CITY OF PARIS (24, rue Pavée). On his death in 1759, the procurator of the king and the city of Paris, Antoine Moriau, bequeathed his library in the hôtel de Lamoignon (24, rue Pavée) to the city of Paris on the condition that the municipality turn it into a public library. This library was closed in 1795 and transferred to the library of the Institut de France (q.v.). In 1804, the city reestablished a municipal library several times at different locations before installing it in the Hôtel de Ville (Town Hall) (q.v.) in 1847. On May 24, 1871, it perished when the building was burned down (see Fires) by the Communards (see Commune). A new library was established in the Hôtel Carnavalet (23, rue de Sévigné) but was moved to 29, rue de Sévigné in 1898 to make room for the Carnavalet museum (q.v.).

In 1969, the Bibliothèque de la Ville de Paris was established at its present location, the same place where it had been created two centuries before. (An administrative library separate from the historical library had been organized at the Town Hall after it was rebuilt during the years 1870–1880.) The present library is devoted to the history of Paris and contains more than 600,000 volumes as well as 20,000 maps, 20,000 manuscripts, and 30,000 old photographs of the capital.

HORSE RACING. The first horse race in Paris took place in 1651 in the Boulogne woods. The first permanent racetrack was opened in 1776 in Neuilly, on the Sablons plain. Races were also held now and then in the Vincennes woods, on the Champ-de-Mars (q.v.), and at Chantilly on the racetrack laid out by Lord Seymour, where in 1835 the first horse racing prize was contested, that of the Jockey-Club (q.v.). Napoléon III endowed Paris with a racecourse (hippodrome) located in the Bois de Boulogne (q.v.) on the Longchamp plain, where the first Grand Prix de Paris was run in 1863. The steeplechase built its own racecourse in Auteuil, in 1873. The first trotting races were organized in 1880 on the racetrack of the Bois de Vincennes (q.v.). There are also several other racecourses in the suburbs, such as those at Saint-Cloud, Maisons-Laffitte and Enghien.

HORSES. The horse played a constantly growing role in Paris until, suddenly, it disappeared. The horse market was held in the Middle Ages near the Porte Saint-Honoré. From 1565 to 1605, it was held at the Hôtel des Tournelles (presently Place des Vosges). From 1605 to 1633, the location was the Butte Saint-Roch (at the crossing of Rue Molière and Rue de l'Échelle), then from 1633 to 1687 it took place in the bastion of Louis XIII's wall (between Boulevard des Capucines and Rue Louis-le-Grand). Later on, between 1687 and 1857, it occurred on the city's outskirts, at Faubourg Saint-Victor (between Boulevard de l'Hôpital and Rue Duméril). The next site, between 1857 and 1907, was on the Boulevard de l'Hôpital between the Rue Jeanne-d'Arc and Boulevard Saint-Marcel. Finally, it ended up at the abattoir of the Rue Brancion.

The number of horses continued increasing until 1900. Official statistics were kept as of 1880, when there were 78,908 horses, while in 1912 there were only 55,418. The horse-drawn coaches were being quickly displaced by motor vehicles as of 1906: they used 15,000 to 17,000 horses between 1892 and 1900, but fewer than 10,000 in 1912. The First World War put an end to the use of horses: the last fiacre (q.v.) disappeared in 1928. Today there are only about one thousand horses in the capital, half of them in about a dozen riding clubs and the rest in the Célestins barracks of the Republican Guard.

HOSPITALS. According to tradition, the oldest hospital, the Hôtel-Dieu (q.v.), was founded in 651. The second Parisian hospital, established in 1171, was called Saint-Anastase or Saint-Gervais, because it was just an ordinary house opposite St. Gervais church. Two hospices were opened shortly after to lodge travelers and pilgrims, the Trinité and Sainte-Catherine hospitals. During the 13th and 14th centuries quantities of other "hospitals" sprang up but the Hôtel-Dieu was the only hospital in the modern sense of the word. The other establishments only sheltered the transient poor or the city's own needy but did not provide any medical treatment as such.

In order to look after the plague-stricken, in 1606 the Sanitat Saint-Marcel, or Santé, was created. Henri IV ordered the construction of a large hospital to isolate persons with infectious diseases: Saint-Louis Hospital, which was opened in 1616. The Hôpital Général, set up in 1656 by Louis XIV (q.v.), only served the purpose of locking up vagrants, beggars and the destitute and subjecting them to forced labor. It was a prison and not a place for medical care. It was not until the 19th century that genuine hospitals developed in Paris. Much of this occurred within the framework of public welfare (q.v.). In 1996, there were about 40 major hospitals in the capital. The evolution of Parisian hospitals can be followed at the Musée des Hôpitaux de Paris at the Quai de la Tournelle.

HÔTEL DE VILLE (Town Hall). The first location of the municipal administration was at Place de Grève (q.v.), which was later called Place de l'Hôtel-de-Ville, in the Maison aux Piliers (Pillared House). As of 1533, François I had a new town hall built. Intended to reflect the prestige of the capital, it was constructed according to plans by the Italian Dominique de Cortone, known as Il Boccadoro. Interrupted by the wars of religion, the work dragged on until 1628. The Hôtel de Ville was enlarged in 1837 and then disappeared in May 1871 in a fire (q.v.) set by the Communards. The architects Ballu and Deperthes reconstructed it between 1871 and 1882, maintaining the style of the Boccadoro façade but lengthening and heightening the building, which gave it its present appearance. The mayor (q.v.) resides in the Hôtel de Ville, and the majority of the head offices of the city administration are housed in this huge building, which also has many reception halls for various ceremonies.

HÔTEL-DIEU (Place du Parvis-Notre-Dame). Possibly founded in 651 by Saint Landry, bishop of Paris, until the end of the 12th century the Hôtel-Dieu was the only center for medical care in Paris. It was located on the southern bank of the Île de la Cité (q.v.), on the same spot as the present Square Charlemagne. Its buildings from the 12th and 13th centuries, contemporary with Notre-Dame Cathedral (q.v.), were devastated by two fires (q.v.), in 1718 and 1737. It was reconstructed by Germain Boffrand in 1749. The Hôtel-Dieu was razed to make way for the projects of Haussmann (q.v.) and reconstructed between 1864 and 1877 on the northern side of the Notre-Dame parvis, where it still stands.

HOTELS. There were already innkeepers and hotel keepers, the two words signifying much the same thing, in Gallo-Roman Gaul, and there has never been a time when Paris had no "hotels." In fact, the tax rolls of 1292 listed 24 hotel keepers. In 1788, the city counted 439 hotels, most of them poorly kept. They were so bad that visitors from the provinces and abroad preferred lodging with the citizens of the capital. With the exception of Hotel Meurice (q.v.), there was not a single hotel that was capable of meeting the sanitary requirements of British tourists until the major projects of Haussmann (q.v.) in the 1850s and 1860s. At present, there are about 2,000 hotels with 100,000 rooms in Île-de-France, three-quarters of them located in Paris. Along with Hotel Meurice, there are a number of prestigious hotels for the well-to-do and many more reasonable hotels for those of modest means. The bulk are fairly old, although sometimes charming or cozy, with relatively few new hotels. *See also* Crillon; George V; Inter-Continental; Lutétia; Meurice; Plaza-Athénée; Ritz.

HOUSE (OLDEST). The oldest house in Paris is located at 51, Rue de Montmorency. It was built by Nicolas Flamel, who designed it as a hospice for the poor. This information has been certified by the deed of foundation of November 17, 1406, as well as the inscription of 1407 that can be found on the façade between the ground floor and the first floor. *See also* Alchemy.

HUGO, VICTOR MARIE (1802–85). Victor Hugo, one of the originators of the French Romantic movement, was among the most highly admired writers during his lifetime. He showed remarkable independence by refusing to support the Second Empire and living in voluntary exile in Jersey and Guernsey from 1852 to 1870. After his death, the government held national funerals but respected his last wishes, namely, that his body should be carried in a pauper's hearse and there should be no religious ceremony. Hugo was buried in the Panthéon (q.v.). There is an interesting museum in the Victor Hugo House at Place des Vosges.

Victor Hugo was a poet of Paris of an exceptional lyricism,

whether he wrote in prose or verse. He drew powerful pictures of medieval Paris in *Notre-Dame de Paris* (1831) (*The Hunchback of Notre Dame*) before it disappeared under the projects of Baron Haussmann (q.v.). He was especially famous for his descriptions of revolutionary Paris of the 1830s in the Romanesque epic *Les Misérables*, which he began writing in 1845 and which appeared in 1862, and which contains such extraordinary characters as Jean Valjean and Gavroche (q.v.).

-I-

INSTITUT DE FRANCE (Palace) (23, Quai de Conti). At his death in 1661, Cardinal Mazarin bequeathed two million francs to found a college to educate 60 young persons drawn from the nobility and bourgeoisie of the four provinces annexed by France as a result of the Treaties of Westphalia (1648) and the Peace of the Pyrenees (1659): Alsace, Artois, Piedmont and Roussillon–hence the name of College of Four Nations borne by the college of Mazarin. Le Vau, who designed the building, created a harmonious semicircular composition modeled on Saint-Agnes church in Rome. Ever since 1805 the French Institute has been located there. It consists of the Académie Française (q.v.) and the Academics of Inscriptions and Belles Lettres, Science, Fine Arts and Moral and Political Sciences.

INTER-CONTINENTAL (Hotel) (3, Rue de Castiglione). Built on the site of the former Ministry of Finance, which was burned down by the Communards in May 1871, the Continental Hotel (its first name) was inaugurated in June 1878 on the occasion of the world exhibition (q.v.). The architect, Henri Blondel, had to obey the strict town-planning rules that applied to the Rue de Rivoli and Rue de Castiglione. Its 500 rooms were arranged around a huge courtyard, which has now been turned into a summer restaurant and garden. The hotel's very meticulous decoration was inspired by the Louis XIV and Louis XV styles. The suites are particularly grand and imposing: Napoléon suite (220 square meters), Imperial suite (380 sq m) and Aiglon suite (165 sq m).

It was at the Inter-Continental Hotel in July 1880 that the meeting was held of the members of the Franco-American Union for the Statue of Liberty, with the participation of the sculptor Frédéric Auguste Bartholdi, who was entrusted with casting the statue. Eugénie de Montijo, the widow of Napoléon III, was a regular guest of the hotel for 20 years from May to July; her last stay was in 1919, less than a year before her death.

INVALIDES (Hôtel and Church). In 1670, Louis XIV (q.v.) decided to build a hospice to shelter poor, old or invalid soldiers and officers who had shed their blood for his glory. Libéral Bruant constructed the initial building between 1671 and 1676. The present hotel can accommodate 7,000 veterans. The Dome Church, designed by Hardouin-Mansart, was finished and inaugurated only in 1706. Its crypt holds the tomb of the Emperor Napoléon I as well as those of several other eminent French soldiers and statesmen (Joseph Bonaparte, Marshal Turenne and Marshal Foch).

At present, the military governor of Paris resides at the Invalides. It also contains a large and impressive Army and Artillery Museum, with a gallery of models, the museum of the Order of Liberation and a military hospital.

ISLANDS. Nowadays there are only three islands on the Seine (q.v.) in Paris. The largest, the Île de la Cité (q.v.), birthplace of the capital, measured only eight hectares at the time of Gallo-Roman Lutetia. Now there are 17 hectares because of encroachments on the river, embankments built on the eastern end and the incorporation of three small islands at its western tip. The island of Saint-Louis (which originally consisted of two tiny islands, Île aux Vaches and Île Nôtre-Dame) remained uninhabited until it was subdivided into lots, and construction began in 1614. The third existing island, the Île des Cygnes (Island of Swans), is an artificial dike that was built in 1825. It should not be confused with the true Île des Cygnes, which was attached to the Left Bank at the beginning of the 19th century and corresponds to a narrow sliver of land running between the Rue de l'-Université and the Seine, starting on the east at the Rue Jean-Nicot and ending on the west at Champ-de-Mars (q.v.). The Île Louviers was attached to the Right Bank in 1841. It was located between the Boulevard Morland and the Quai Henri IV. There was a small island, called Merdeuse, just opposite the National Assembly, which has been incorporated in the Quai d'Orsay.

-J-

JACOBINS (Club). The Breton Club, founded in May 1789 at Versailles (q.v.) by the delegates from Brittany to the Estates General, became the Club des Jacobins when the Constituent Assembly moved to Paris in October 1789. Although its real name was the Society of Friends of the Constitution, its more popular name is attributed to the fact that it was located in the convent of the Jacobins, or Dominican friars, at the Rue Saint-Honoré. Originally the club was in favor of a constitutional monarchy along the British model, but it split after the attempted flight of Louis XVI in June 1791, and its more moderate members, such as Barnave, La Fayette (q.v.) and Lameth, left it to found the Club des Feuillants. Dominated by Pétion (q.v.) and Robespierre (q.v.), the group remaining with the Club des Jacobins gradually adopted democratic principles and, soon after, the Republican idea.

The Club des Jacobins spread into the provinces and created more than 1,200 clubs, which formed the spearhead of the Revolution. In Paris, the club organized the fall of the monarchy (August 10, 1792) and the elimination of the Girondins (May 31 and June 2, 1793). The Jacobins exerted constant popular pressure on the delegates to the Convention and imposed a disguised dictatorship, that of Robespierre. When he fell, on July 28, 1794, the Club des Jacobins was held responsible for the excesses of the Terror (q.v.). It was closed on November 12, 1794. There was an attempt at reconstituting the club in July–August 1799 with the Néo-Jacobins.

JAMES, HENRY (1843–1916). Born in New York, Henry James became a famous novelist in the United States as of 1871. Shortly thereafter he left his country for Europe and preferred living in Paris, where he mixed with Flaubert and Zola (q.v.). He described his fellow expatriates in *The American* (1874), the aristocracy of the Faubourg-Saint-Germain in *Madame de Mauves* (1878) and the life of Bohemians (q.v.) in *The Ambassadors* (1903). His novels provide some of the best descriptions of Paris during the Belle Epoque.

JANSENISM. Cornelis Jansen (1585–1638), the bishop of Ypres, gave his name to Jansenism, although he played only a minor role. This religious movement was essentially French and largely Parisian, deriving its inspiration from Saint Augustine. It tried to introduce into Catholic thought some of the themes coming from the Protestant Reformation. The Jansenists countered the optimism, opportunism and spiritual flexibility of the Jesuits with austerity, moral rigor and a refusal to compromise. The authorities were soon annoyed by the uncompromising nature of the doctrine. In 1638, Richelieu had Saint-Cyran imprisoned at Vincennes. After his death in 1643, Antoine Arnauld became the new spiritual leader of Jansenism. Blaise Pascal supported the Jansenists in the *Lettres provinciales* (1656). Quesnel took over from Arnauld when he died in 1694.

Louis XIV (q.v.), a friend of the Jesuits, persecuted the Jansenists, expelled the nuns from Port-Royal (q.v.) de Paris in 1664 and packed them off to Port-Royal-des-Champs, which he had razed in 1709. This persecution only gave Jansenism more popular appeal, since it became a form of opposition to a corrupt monarchy that indulged in debauchery. Jansenism and Gallicanism merged in their refusal of Roman Ultramontanism and their assertion of the right to a specifically French Catholicism. Both collapsed at the beginning of the 19th century when Napoléon Bonaparte imposed his control on the papacy.

JARDIN DES PLANTES. The Jardin des Plantes, or Botanical Garden, originated in 1626 at the initiative of two physicians to Louis XIII, Jean Héroard and Guy de La Brosse. Its first buildings were put up in 1635. Later called the Jardin du Roi (King's Garden), it developed impressively under Buffon, who was appointed curator in 1739 and who turned it into a center for scientific study and expanded it from seven to 17 hectares. In 1793, the Jardin des Plantes became the National Natural History Museum, a scientific institute endowed with 12 chairs of learning. Later on a menagerie was opened and greenhouses were built. Nowadays the museum occupies 24 hectares and employs 1,500 persons while dispensing education through its 25 chairs.

JEFFERSON, THOMAS (1743–1826). Thomas Jefferson was one of the main architects of the independence of the United States and served as governor of the state of Virginia from 1779 to 1781. In 1785, he replaced Benjamin Franklin (q.v.) as ambassador and remained in Paris until 1789. His contacts with philosophers and his visits to the court of Versailles only strengthened his hostility to monarchical despotism and inequality. After serving as American secretary of state from 1790 to 1793, he served as the third president of the United States from 1801 to 1809. In 1803, he bought Louisiana from Napoléon Bonaparte. Jefferson refused to stand for a third term.

JOCKEY-CLUB (2, Rue Rabelais). Modeled after its British counterpart, the French Jockey-Club was founded on November 11, 1833, with the elaborate name of the Society for the Encouragement and Improvement of the Equine Races of France. Its founders were 15 members of the nobility, and they elected Lord Henry Seymour as their first president. Initially, the Jockey-Club was housed at 2, Rue de Helder, on the corner of the Boulevard des Italiens, at the heart of high society of the time. It subsequently moved about, next locating at the Rue de la Grange-Batelière, then the Rue de Gramont, and later the Rue Scribe, before ending up in 1924 at its present location near the Champs-Elysées (q.v.). Its rosters include about one thousand members.

JONES, JOHN PAUL (1747–92). A Scotsman who joined the American side when the War of Independence broke out, John Paul Jones was one of the most formidable adversaries of the British navy, carrying his raids as far as the British coast. In 1789, he settled in Paris, where he died on July 18, 1792, at his home at 19, Rue de Tournon. He was buried in the cemetery reserved for foreign Protestants at 41–47, Rue de la Grange-aux-Belles. After extended research undertaken at the request of the American government, on April 14, 1905, the lead coffin in which he was buried was found with his body perfectly preserved. He was brought back to the United States and interred in the chapel of the Naval Academy at Annapolis, Maryland.

JULY FOURTEENTH. At present, July 14 is celebrated as France's National Day in memory of the taking of the Bastille (q.v.) on July 14, 1789, which traditionally marks the beginning of the French Revolution. On July 14, 1790, the reconciliation and unity of all the French within one nation was celebrated on the Champ-de-Mars (q.v.) on the occasion of the Festival of the Federation. July 14 was celebrated annually until 1802. It was then discreetly forgotten by Napoléon Bonaparte. After he was proclaimed emperor in 1804, he consecrated Saint Napoléon's day, August 15th, as the national festival. The Third Republic restored July 14 as the National Day in 1880.

-L-

LA FAYETTE, GILBERT MOTIER DE (1757–1834). By fighting in the American War of Independence in 1777, La Fayette became a celebrity at the age of 20. He soon became the spokesmen of the aristocrats who adopted the ideas of the philosophers. Chosen as a delegate for the nobility to the Estates General in May 1789, he was appointed commander of the National Guard (q.v.) when it was created on July 15, 1789. On October 5–6, 1789, his inaction and negligence—which some considered deliberate—allowed a mob from Paris to invade the château of Versailles (q.v.) and bring the royal family back to the capital almost as captives. It was his negligence again that allowed Louis XVI to escape from the Tuileries (q.v.) with his family on June 20,1791.The last straw for the Parisians, who already distrusted La Fayette, was that he had troops fire into the crowd at the Champ-de-Mars (q.v.) on July 17, 1791.

He made an additional mistake by giving up the command of the National Guard to run for mayor (q.v.) of Paris, only to be beaten by the revolutionary Pétion (q.v.), for whom Queen Marie-Antoinette preferred to vote. Placed in charge of the armies, he was defeated by the Austrians in the north and vainly attempted to have his troops march on Paris, where Louis XVI had just been overthrown on August 10, 1792. La Fayette surrendered to the Austrians on August 20 and disappeared from the political scene.

He reappeared a quarter of a century later. As a representative of the liberal opposition in the Chamber of Deputies from 1818 to 1830, he helped put Louis-Philippe on the throne in July 1830. For several months he was again the commander of the National Guard before being cast into the opposition. Simple-minded and credulous, foolish and politically inept, La Fayette was a plaything of history rather than a principal actor.

LAGERFELD, KARL (1938–). In 1954, at the age of 16, Karl Lagerfeld won the fashion competition organized by the International Wool Secretariat, tying with Yves Saint-Laurent (q.v.). He worked with Pierre Balmain and then with Jean Patou as a dress designer until 1963. He became one of the trendsetters of ready-to-wear through the Cloé company and had his own brand name by 1984. Since 1983, he has been directing the Chanel (q.v.) house. In 1992, he received the Golden Thimble, the highest award for haute couture (q.v.) in France.

LANDRU, HENRI DÉSIRÉ (1869–1922). In April 1919, Henri Landru, an elegant man in his fifties, bald and bearded, was arrested in Montmartre (q.v.), suspected of swindling and fraudulent misuse of funds. The police (q.v.) looked for the women whose savings he had stolen but could not find them. They soon became convinced that Landru had lured at least a dozen women to his country home in Gambais, killed them and then burned their corpses in his stove. Despite the absence of material evidence of these murders, Landru was condemned to death and guillotined. Charles Chaplin brought this story to the screen in the movie *Monsieur Verdoux* (1947).

LANVIN, JEANNE (1867–1946). In 1889, Jeanne Lanvin opened her first shop, where she sold hats she had made. Her success was such that she expanded her activities to dressmaking and even added a children's department. In 1926, she created the first haute couture (q.v.) house for men. The Lanvin style was characterized by taste and moderation. The Lanvin house, located at 15, Rue du Faubourg-Saint-Honoré, kept up with fashion trends by launching a labeled line of ready-to-wear in 1967.

LATIN QUARTER. Initially called the University Quarter, the Latin Quarter is rather imprecisely defined. It developed with the University (q.v.) in the second half of the 12th century. In order to escape the tutorship of the bishop of Paris, the students of the École Notre-Dame of that time left the Île de la Cité and settled on Mount Sainte-Geneviève (q.v.). This was a large, turbulent community with its own practices that spoke a dog Latin that was the official language of the medieval University; this is what gave the name "Latin" to the area these students frequented. This area stretched to the present-day Odéon intersection—where the quarter of Saint-Germain-des-Prés (q.v.) begins—to the west and to the east, as far as the Faculty of Science of Jussieu and the Censier university center, roughly to the limits of the present 5th and 13th arrondissements.

Until 1968, this area remained the heart of University life, a boisterous Latin Quarter as ready to revolt then as in the Middle Ages. The division of the Sorbonne (q.v.) into 13 autonomous universities in 1970 marked the decline of the Latin Quarter, which became home only to several thousand students. Most of the bookshops have disappeared and been replaced by clothing and shoe stores as well as fast food joints. Even the publishers, including the largest, Hachette, have been moving out recently. Yet, thousands of tourists still flock to the area in a vain search for the atmosphere of the riots of May 1968.

LEAGUE. The Catholic League was founded in June 1576 at the initiative of the Guise family, which reproached King Henri III with not pressing the struggle against the Protestants energetically enough. The king took charge of the League in an attempt to neutralize Henri, the duke of Guise, and his younger brother Louis, cardinal of Lorraine. The death of the duke of Anjou, the younger brother of Henri III, in June 1584, only made the situation worse because Henri III was a homosexual who had no children, his heir, according to the order of succession, was Henri of Bourbon, the king of Navarre and the head of the Protestant party. On December 31, 1584, the Guises signed the treaty of Joinville with King Philip II of Spain and had it approved by Pope Gregory XIII. This treaty excluded from the French crown any non-Catholic prince and designated as heir Charles, cardinal of Bourbon. With the financial aid of Spain, the League raised troops all around France. In Paris, it enjoyed the support of numerous priests and monks who taught at the University (q.v.) and preached in the churches.

Despite his concessions, Henri III still aroused considerable distrust among the League members. The defeat of the royal troops by the Protestants at Coutras, on October 20, 1587, further weakened his position. In Paris, the Sixteen, the representatives of the 16 quarters of the capital, openly prepared the struggle against the king. On May 9, 1588, although Henri III had forbidden him from visiting the capital, Henri de Guise made a triumphal entry into Paris. The king accused him of treason and brought 4,000 Swiss mercenaries into the city on May 12, which set off a popular insurrection. Paris was covered with barricades (q.v.) and the Swiss were massacred. The king took flight. The League supporters elected new municipal authorities who swore allegiance under the control of Henri de Guise. Henri III made a last attempt to save his throne and convened the Estates General in Blois. Henri de Guise dominated the debates and tried to impose his will on the king, who resolved on December 23, 1588, to have him and Cardinal de Guise killed.

In Paris, Charles d'Aumale, a cousin of the victims, was appointed governor of the city by the League. The Sorbonne (q.v.) and the *Parlement* (q.v.) declared Henri III dethroned and recognized Cardinal de Bourbon as king of France. The younger brother of Henri de Guise, Charles de Mayenne, arrived in Paris on February 12, 1589, and had himself proclaimed lieutenant general of the kingdom. Allied to his heir, Henri of Navarre, Henri III prepared to lay siege to Paris, but he was assassinated in Saint-Cloud on August 1, 1589. Now titled Henri IV, the king of Navarre besieged Paris in vain several times between November 1589 and January 1591. In the starving city, the advocates of peace gathered a majority, but the League followers remained in power through fear. Among other things, they had three eminent members of the *Parlement* executed on November 16, 1591. With the death of Cardinal de Bourbon in 1590, the League was divided. Mayenne and the aristocracy were opposed by the Parisian people and the Sixteen, who held that the choice of king depended on the people's will.

The Estates General met in Paris on January 1593, and King Philip II of Spain tried to have his daughter Isabelle elected queen of France. With Henri IV's renunciation of Protestantism on July 25, 1593, at Saint-Denis Abbey, the League disintegrated. Its moderate members went over to the side of the king who had become Catholic again. On March 22, 1594, Henri IV entered Paris without a fight and the troops of the king of Spain withdrew. In January 1596, Mayenne and the last of the League holdouts submitted. This put an end to a civil and religious war that had begun in 1562.

LÉPINE, LOUIS (1846–1933). Chief commissioner of police (q.v.) from 1893 to 1897 and 1899 to 1913, Louis Lépine occupied that post longer than any of the 78 commissioners since 1800. He was in office during a particularly difficult period in the history of the Third Republic. He had to stifle the agitation arising out of the Dreyfus affair, overcome the intrigues of the nationalist leagues, and impose the inventory of property after the separation of church and state in 1905. He also had to react to the first occurrences of modern gangsterism with the Bonnot (q.v.) gang. Lépine endeavored to modernize the Parisian police by forming bicycle brigades and the river brigade (q.v.) and developing scientific policing techniques. He also tried—without much success—to make the Parisians love their police force. In November 1901, he established the Lépine Competition, initially an exhibition of toys and then an annual exhibition of inventions, which still exists today.

LIBERATION OF PARIS. After the landing in Normandy on June 6, 1944, the Allied forces advanced toward the east. The German authorities evacuated Paris on August 17, 1944, and the military governor General von Choltitz received the order to mine the city and blow it up. Although this was a personal order from Hitler, he refused to carry it out. The Parisians rose up on August 19 and seized the police headquarters as well as the main administrative buildings. On August 24, the first troops of the French second armored division of General Leclerc arrived at the Hôtel de Ville (q.v.). The German garrison surrendered on the 25th. The fighting that broke out in various parts of the capital resulted in a few more than one thousand casualties. On the 26th, General de Gaulle, the head of the Free French, walked down the Champs-Elysées (q.v.) to the applause of a million Parisians.

LIBERTY (Statue) (Allée des Cygnes). The sculptor Frédéric Auguste Bartholdi (1834–1904) designed the statue of "liberty lighting the world," which France offered to the city of New York for the centenary of the American declaration of independence. A bronze replica of that statue, nine meters tall and mounted on a pedestal seven meters in height, was offered to the city of Paris by the American Parisian community. Since 1889, it has been located on the Île des Cygnes, an artificial island created in 1825.

LIDO DE PARIS (116 bis, Avenue des Champs-Elysées). In 1929, Edouard Chaux opened, under the gallery of the arcades (q.v.) of the Champs-Elysées (q.v.), at no. 76, a sort of casino that also served as a thermal bath, where Parisians would come to bathe or to have tea or an apéritif, watch fashion parades or listen to jazz bands. The name Lido referred to the famous beach in Venice. In 1948, the Clerico brothers converted the Lido into a huge theater. While dining, the public could enjoy revues with songs and dances, the most famous of which were staged by the Bluebell Girls. Nowadays the Lido is located a bit further up the Champs-Elysées. The revue is presented to an international audience in a space of 6,000 square meters surrounded by a panoramic hall with 1,200 seats. The Lido is the largest private theatrical enterprise in France and employs 450 persons.

LIEUTENANT GÉNÉRAL DE POLICE. The office of lieutenant general of police was created on March 15, 1667, by Louis XIV (q.v.) to combat the civic problems in Paris. The functions of the office were very broad and were not limited to maintaining law and order. The lieutenant general of police was also responsible for the maintenance, cleanliness and lighting of public thoroughfares, traffic, water supply, and so on. His power corresponded to those of both the police commissioner (q.v.) and the prefect (q.v.) of Paris combined. There were 16 lieutenants general of police until that office was discontinued on July 16, 1789. Some held the job for an extended period and played an important role, such as the first, Gabriel Nicolas de La Reynie (1667–97), the second, Marc René de Voyer d'Argenson (1697–1718), the eighth, René Hérault de Fontaine

(1725–39) and the 12th, Jean Gualbert de Sartine (1759–74). *See also* Police; Police, Chief Commissioner of.

LIPP (Brasserie) (151, Boulevard Saint-Germain). About 1880, the Alsacian Léonard Lipp founded a brasserie that was soon known simply by the name of its proprietor. The present decor dates back to the 1900s. It is the work of the ceramist Léon Fargue and his brother, who were the father and uncle respectively of the Parisian writer Léon-Paul Fargue, who wrote: "Paris, two million inhabitants, one single bistro, Lipp." Marcellin Cazes bought the brasserie in 1920 and had it expanded by the architect Léon Madeline, which increased the number of tables from ten to 100. The second floor was turned into a restaurant and the ceilings of the two halls on the ground floor were decorated with African scenes by Charley Garry. The terrace dates from 1947.

This decor made the brasserie a big success. From the early 1920s, it received countless deputies and senators as well as men of letters and of theater, the likes of Gallimard, Gide, Giraudoux, Max Jacob and Saint-Exupéry, but also Copeau and Jouvet. Lipp was consecrated as a political café (q.v.) with the introduction on Fridays of the Molé-Tocqueville lectures, and its role as a literary café was confirmed with the creation of the Cazes prize in 1934, awarded at Lipp by its owner Marcellin Cazes.

LOUIS XIV (1638–1715). Louis XIV, who succeeded his father, Louis XIII, in 1643 at the age of five, began to exercise his personal rule only with the death of Mazarin in 1661. As a child he was deeply disturbed by the disorders of the Fronde (q.v.) and he bore an abiding grudge against Paris. He abandoned the city in 1671, preferring the palace of Versailles (q.v.), which he had built. He was interested in Paris only as it affected his glory. He had the Victoires and Vendôme squares built, opened up the boulevards (q.v.) by tearing down the city walls (q.v.) and appointed a lieutenant general of police (q.v.) to look after law and order. The breach between Paris and its remote king absorbed in the futile pleasures of the court of Versailles played a fundamental role in the emergence of an intellectual and political opposition that culminated in the Revolution of 1789 and the fall of the monarchy.

LOUIS-LE-GRAND (Lycée) (123, rue Saint-Jacques). Along with Sainte-Barbe (q.v.), Louis-le-Grand is the oldest secondary school in Paris. It was founded by the Jesuits in 1564 under the name of Collège de Clermont, where they introduced their new teaching called *modus Parisiensis* (Parisian method). The *collège* (q.v.) was renamed Louis-le-Grand in 1674 in tribute to Louix XIV (q.v.). It was the only *collège* in Paris to remain open during the Revolution, under the name of "equality *collège*," and became the first lycée in 1803 under the name of Lycée de Paris. It had many illustrious pupils: Molière (q.v.), Voltaire, Diderot, Desmoulins, Robespierre (q.v.), Saint-Just, Delacroix, Hugo (q.v.), Baudelaire (q.v.), Littré and others. Even today it is one of the best lycées in Paris, if not the best.

LOUVRE (Palace and Museum). The first Louvre was built between 1190 and 1202 at the orders of Philippe II Auguste (q.v.). When he left for the crusades, the king sought to protect his capital with a fortified wall (q.v.) that was reinforced on the west with a castle. The Louvre was almost square (72 meters by 78 meters) and on the inside was erected a donjon with a diameter of 15 meters and a height of 30 meters. It is possible to see remains of this castle in the archeological crypt under the Cour Carrée (square courtyard). Charles V had the Louvre renovated during the 1360s. Mullion windows were opened in the walls to allow some light into this austere fortress.

When François I decided to make Paris the capital of the kingdom again in 1528, he ordered vast projects. The medieval Louvre was gradually torn down to make way for a Renaissance palace that was constructed by Pierre Lescot in 1546. Henri IV had the south wing of the Cour Carrée completed, the Petite Galerie raised and the Grande Galerie along the Seine (q.v.) erected. Later, the work continued at a slower pace. Under Louis XIV (q.v.), Le Vau redecorated the inside and doubled the size of the Petite Galerie. He also put up three of the four wings of the Cour Carrée, but they were not roofed until the beginning of the 19th century. Claude Perrault succeeded him and built the colonnade that closed the Louvre on the east. Louis XIV left Paris for Versailles in 1671, and the Louvre was abandoned from 1678 to 1793.

Napoléon I resumed the work on the Louvre, which had been turned into a museum in 1793. He had the Arc de Triomphe du Carrousel (q.v.) built, as well as the northwest wing on the Rue de Rivoli. Napoléon III completed the "grand design" by linking the Louvre to the Tuileries (q.v.). The Cour Napoléon was finished in 1857 by Lefuel according to the plans of Visconti. The fire (q.v.) in the Tuileries in May 1871 opened the Louvre to the west on the Tuileries garden and created the magnificent perspective toward Place de la Concorde (q.v.), the Champs-Elysées (q.v.) and the Arc de Triomphe de l'Étoile (q.v.).

President François Mitterrand gave a new impulse to the Louvre by having the Ministry of Finance vacate the east wing on the Rue de Rivoli. He had the museum refurbished and the entrance was henceforth located under the glass pyramid by Ieoh Ming Pei. The "Grand Louvre" museum was inaugurated on March 29, 1989. The opening of the Richelieu wing on November 20, 1993, made it the biggest museum in the world. The museum's vast collections cover all periods and concern the major parts of the world, with the exception of prehistoric times and of primitive arts. The ancient period is particularly well represented with the Victory of Samothrace. From the Italian Renaissance, there are many paintings by Michelangelo and Raffaello including the *Gioconda* (*Mona Lisa*) by Leonardo da Vinci.

LUTÉTIA (Hotel) (45, Boulevard Raspail). The only deluxe hotel on the Left Bank, the Lutétia was built between 1907 and 1910 based on the plans of Louis Boileau and Henri Tauzin. Its façade was richly decorated and sculpted by Léon Binet and Paul Belmondo. Art déco prevailed in the interior decoration. Between 1919 and 1939, the American bar at the hotel received everybody who was anybody in Parisian literary circles. After 1945, the Lutétia was a neutral meeting point between the rival existentialist crowds of Montparnasse (q.v.) and Saint-Germain-des-Prés (q.v.). During the 1980s, its 12 halls and 300 rooms were redecorated by Sonia Rykiel and Sybille de Margerie.

LUXEMBOURG (Palace) (15, Rue de Vaugirard). Marie de Médicis, the widow of Henri IV, had the Luxembourg Palace built between 1615 and 1630 by Métezeau, who was sent to Florence to be inspired by the Pitti Palace. It was constructed on the location of the mansion of François de Luxembourg, whose name was borrowed. Part of the lavish interior decoration was painted by Rubens. In 1799, the palace was assigned to the Senate, which still occupies it. The inside was refurbished as of 1835 by Alphonse de Gisors, and the library was decorated by Eugéne Delacroix.

-M-

MABILLE (Ballroom). In 1840, Mabille bought a small ballroom at the Champs-Elysées (q.v.), in the Allée des Veuves (at 51–53 of the present Avenue Montaigne). This ballroom had been frequented by servants from the neighborhood; but he transformed and upgraded it for a high-class clientele. The gardens graced with zinc palm trees were lighted with gas, and a Chinese-style kiosk was erected to hold a big dance band of 30 musicians. Under the shrubbery, tables awaited the diners, and a huge open shelter kept the dancers dry on rainy days. This ballroom is where a new dance, the polka, triumphed and where the famous dancers of the time, described by Baudelaire (q.v.), were introduced: Queen Pomaré, Céleste Mogador, Rosalba, Finette, Alice-la-Provençale and others. The war of 1870 and real estate speculation in the Champs-Elysées area were fatal for the Bal Mabille, which was closed in 1875 and then demolished.

MADELEINE (Church) (Place de la Madeleine). In 1757, Pierre Contant d'Ivry was entrusted with building a new church, Sainte-Marie-Madeleine. The plans were altered several times, and by 1789 the foundation work had just been completed. Napoléon I decided in 1807 to make this church a temple to glory—naturally, his own military glory. He commissioned Pierre Vignon, who gave it the form of an ancient Greek temple, 108 meters long, 43 meters wide and 30 meters high. The Restoration maintained this plan, but the building was converted for Catholic worship. Jean-Jacques Huvé replaced Vignon (who died in 1828) and finished the church in 1842. The decoration and the sculptures of the church are typical of the art of the 1820s and 1830s.

MAGISTRATES. Up until 1789, the Parisian municipality consisted of the provost of merchants (q.v.) and four magistrates, who were also called "jurors of merchandise" or "jurors of the fraternity of merchants." The magistrates (called *échevins*) were elected for two years and half were renewed, starting in 1450, on August 16 of each year. In the 15th century, this election was purely a formality since the king imposed his candidates, choosing officers in his service, members of the *Parlement* (q.v.), the Court of Aids and the Audit Office, while the commercial upper middle class was gradually supplanted. From the beginning of the 17th century, some specialization became necessary. The first magistrate dealt with the budget, the second with working sites and ports, the third with boulevards and squares and the fourth with fountains and sewers. The king's procurator was responsible for having the city supplied with wood and coal.

MAIGRET, JULES. The most famous of all Parisian policemen, Jules Maigret, never existed. He was born in the fertile imagination of a Belgian writer, Georges Simenon (1903–89). The first Maigret book was *Pietr le Letton* (1930) but the series really started in 1931 when the publisher, Editions Fayard, celebrated the event of an "anthropometric ball" at the Boule Blanche in Montparnasse (q.v.). The pipe-smoking commissioner of the judicial police and his office on Quai des Orfèvres (q.v.) achieved worldwide celebrity thanks to a hundred novels and short stories of which they were the heroes and locus. Simenon, who knew that most Parisians come from the provinces or abroad, had Maigret born in the center of France, in Bourbonnais, near Moulins.

MARAIS, LE (Quarter). The marshy region on the Right Bank of the Seine (q.v.) to the east of the Rue Saint-Martin was known as the Temple Marsh until the beginning of the 17th century. Eventually, the name was shortened to marsh, or *marais*. This area was drained and improved as of the 13th century, and the heyday of the Marais quarter came in the 17th century. Henri IV gave the signal for real estate speculation by ordering the construction of Place Royale (q.v.) (presently Place des Vosges). Dozens of mansions were built throughout that century for nobles and clergymen, financiers and rich bourgeois. The greatest architects designed them, including Androuet Du Cerceau, Le Muet, Le Vau, Mansart and Bruant. Literary salons were held by Scarron and his wife, Françoise d'Aubigné, later the mistress of the aging Louis XIV (q.v.), when she bore the titles of Marquise de Maintenon, Mademoiselle de Scudéry, Madame de Sévigné (q.v.). Nowadays, the name of Marais covers the whole part of Paris that is bordered on the north by the Rue de Turbigo and Rue du Temple, on the east by the Boulevard Beaumarchais and Boulevard du Temple, on the south by the Seine and on the west by the Rue du Renard and Rue Beaubourg.

MARAT, JEAN-PAUL (1743–93). Born in Neuchâtel (now in Switzerland), Marat moved to Paris in 1776 when he was appointed doctor for the guards of the count of Artois, the future Charles X. In September 1789, he founded the newspaper *L'Ami du Peuple* (The People's Friend) and adopted intransigent positions that resulted in lawsuits and forced him to flee to London twice to avoid being put in prison. He was one of the first to question the monarchy and demand the establishment of the Republic. Marat participated in the preparations for the uprising of August 10, 1792, which overthrew Louis XVI. His calls for expeditious justice were at the origin of the massacres of September 1792. In that same month, he was elected as a delegate for Paris to the Convention, where he was among those who voted for the creation of the Revolutionary Tribunal (q.v.) and the Committee of Public Safety. He contributed to the fall of the Girondins on June 2, 1793. On July 13, 1793, Marat was killed in his bathtub by Charlotte Corday. His disappearance rid Robespierre (q.v.) of a dangerous rival.

MARCEL, ÉTIENNE (c. 1315–58). Étienne Marcel, a merchant draper, was elected provost of merchants (q.v.) in 1354. He dominated the Estates General, which was held in Paris as of 1356, and committed the representatives of the urban bourgeoisie to refusing any financial aid to Dauphin Charles as long as far-reaching reforms were not undertaken. Charles, the future Charles V (q.v.), grudgingly issued a grand enactment of reforms in March 1357. Étienne Marcel then joined the royal council where he noticed the ill will of the dauphin's noble counsellors, who were hostile to any reform of the state. He therefore decided to impose his reforms with the support of the cities and to carry out an urban revolution inspired by the movements then taking place in Flanders and Italy. Marcel organized huge demonstrations of armed Parisians who raised red and blue hats, which were their emblem. On February 22, 1358, during one of these demonstrations, the marshals of Champagne and Normandy, two of the dauphin's principal noble counsellors, were killed by the crowd before the dauphin's eyes.

The dauphin thereupon convened the Estates General in Senlis, out of reach of the Parisians, on March 25 and subjected Paris to a blockade. At this point, Étienne Marcel became the ally of Charles the Bad, king of Navarre, whom he allowed to enter Paris on May 4. He also supported the Jacquerie, a peasant uprising against the nobles, which broke out on May 28 but was crushed by June 9. The majority of the bourgeoisie, worried about the blockade and the extreme positions of the provost of merchants, went over to the dauphin's side. Hard pressed and abandoned by all, Étienne Marcel was killed on July 31, 1358, while attempting to open the Saint-Antoine gate to the English mercenaries of the king of Navarre. This event signaled the end of the revolution of the people of Paris.

MARKETS. From the very beginning, there were doubtlessly food markets in Lutetia. In the Middle Ages, in the eighth and ninth centuries, there were four markets on the Île de la Cité: the markets of the large and small bridges, the market on the parvis of Notre-Dame and the Palud market. The city's expansion on the Right Bank generated a market on Place de Grève (q.v.) (presently Place de l'Hôtel-de-Ville), another at the Baudoyer gate (Place Baudoyer) and a third in front of the Châtelet (q.v.), whose main element was the slaughterhouse. The principal Parisian market was opened in 1137 at Champeaux and adopted the name of the Halles (q.v.). There were special markets for oxen, cows and calves, sheep, pigs and horses.

With urban growth, numerous food markets sprang up during the 17th and 18th centuries. Napoléon I introduced the first covered markets. In 1860, there were 51 markets (21 of them covered), and 13 new covered markets were built between 1860 and 1970. These covered markets fell victim to real estate speculation, and the uncovered markets were later threatened because they blocked automobile traffic. At present, there are 82 markets (14 of them covered), of which 13 are for food and the 14th, the Temple square, is reserved for secondhand goods. There are 57 uncovered food markets offering more than 5,000 places, three flower markets, one bird market, a stamp market and several flea markets (q.v.).

MARRAST, ARMAND (1801–52). A journalist with *La Tribune* and then the *National*, Armand Marrast was one of the organizers of the banquet campaign of 1847–48, which ended on February 24, 1848, with the fall of Louis-Philippe and the proclamation of the Second Republic. A member of the provisional government, he was appointed mayor (q.v.) of Paris on March 9, 1848. A moderate Republican deputy in the Constituent Assembly beginning in April 1848, he became president of that assembly when the mayorality was discontinued on July 19, 1848.

MARVILLE, CHARLES (1816–79). A designer and lithographer, Marville was one of the first photographers of Paris, along with Daguerre (q.v.). He walked around with his camera and photographed the buildings that Haussmann's (q.v.) projects had slated for demolition. In 1862, he was rewarded by being named photographer of the city of Paris and of the Imperial Museum of the Louvre (q.v.). In May 1871, he photographed the still-smoking ruins of the buildings burned by the Communards. Thanks to him we can catch a glimpse of the Paris that used to be.

MATIGNON (Hôtel) (57, Rue de Varenne). In 1719, Christian Louis de Montmorency, duke of Luxembourg and then prince of Tingry, bought a plot of land on which he commissioned Jean Courtonne to construct a luxurious *hôtel* (mansion). Unable to meet the enormous expenses, in 1723 he assigned the almost completed edifice to Jacques de Matignon, count of Thorigny, from whom the hôtel derived its name. The mansion's splendor was already celebrated in its time, in particular the façades, which were sculpted with the exuberance characteristic of the Regency style. The hôtel later became the property of the princes of Monaco. From 1801 to 1811, it was the residence of Talleyrand, minister of foreign affairs, who held lavish receptions there. Subsequently passing into the ownership of the Orléans family, the mansion was bought in 1852 by the Genoese banker Raphäel de Ferrari, duke of Galliera, who had the interior redecorated. Hôtel Matignon was the Austro-Hungarian Embassy from 1888 to 1914, when it was sequestered by the French state when war was declared. Since 1935, it has been the residence of the president of the Council of Ministers and, since 1958, that of the prime minister.

MAXIM'S (Restaurant) (3, Rue Royale). Maxime Gaillard, a barman, joined with the head waiter Eugéne Cornuché, to open an establishment in the Rue Royale. It was named Maxim's, using the Anglicized form of Gaillard's first name. Its three salons were decorated by Louis Marnez and a glass roof illuminated the restaurant's (q.v.) main dining room. Initially just a store to sell ice cream and sherbet, Maxim's became a restaurant in 1893. For more than a century it enjoyed an incredible success. It was the meeting place for the beautiful people, and many movie scenes were filmed there. Maxim's was even the theme of various plays such as *La Dame de chez Maxim's* and *Le Chasseur de chez Maxim's*.

MAYOL (10, Rue de l'Échiquier). In 1867, a café-chantant (q.v.) was opened under the name of Grand Concert Parisien. It was quite a success from 1882 to 1885, thanks to Paulus, but then faded away. Yvette Guilbert brought back the public in 1891–92. As of 1895, the singer Félix Mayol created a loyal clientele, then directed the establishment, by then known as "Le Parisien" from 1910 to 1914. He was replaced by Oscar Dufrenne and Henri Varna, who ran it until 1932. They gave the hall its most lasting phase of prosperity by recruiting the best artists known for their songs, launching lavish stage productions and reserving an exceptional place for nudity for that period. Fernandel directed the revues of 1930 and 1931. After Varna left, the Mayol went bankrupt in 1932. Denis, Paul and then René Lefebvre gave it a new lease on life by making it the only nude show in the capital. However, after the death of René Lefebvre in 1975, the Mayol seemed very old-fashioned with its tasteful nudity, which was overwhelmed by a pro-liferation of porno shops. It barely got by until it was closed in 1979.

MAYORS. Until 1789, the municipality was run by a provost of mer-chants (q.v.). The Revolution introduced elected mayors for all the communes in France; but Paris was almost always subject to an ex-ceptional status. After five years of instability, the city was deprived of a mayor in 1794. Only twice, and then just temporarily during sev-eral hectic months in 1848 and in 1870–71, it came under short-lived municipal magistrates appointed by the government. Not until 1977 was Paris aligned on the same common law as the other communes, at which time it also was allowed a mayor. This mayor was able to use his position at the head of the first city of France to be elected presi-dent of the Republic in 1995. The following is a list of mayors of Paris:

- Jean Sylvain Bailly (July 15, 1789 to Nov. 18, 1791)*
- Jérôme Pétion (Nov. 18, 1791 to Oct. 15, 1792, suspended 6–13 July 1792) *
- Philibert Borie (provisional July 6–13, 1792)
- René Boucher (provisional Oct. 15, 1792 to Dec. 2, 1792)
- Henri Lefèvre d'Ormesson (elected Nov. 21, 1792, refused to take office)
- Nicolas Chambon (Dec. 2, 1792 to Feb. 2, 1793)
- Jean Nicolas Pache (Feb. 14, 1793 to May 10, 1794) *
- Jean-Baptiste Fleuriot-Lescot (May 10, 1794 to July 27, 1794) *
- Louis Antoine Garnier-Pagès (Feb. 24, 1848 to Mar. 5, 1848) *
- Armand Marrast (Mar. 9, 1848 to July 19, 1848) *
- Etienne Arago (Sept. 4, 1870 to Nov. 15, 1870) *
- Jules Ferry (Nov. 15, 1870 to June 5, 1871) *
- Jacques Chirac (Mar. 25, 1977 to May 22, 1995) *
- Jean Tiberi (May 22, 1995 to   ) *

* There is an entry on this mayor in the Dictionary.

MÉNILMONTANT. *See* BELLEVILLE.

MERCIER, LOUIS-SÉBASTIEN (1740–1814). Mercier was the au-thor of poems and plays that have since been forgotten. During the Revolution, he espoused Republican views and became a delegate to the Convention and the Council of Five Hundred, but his main claim to fame is that he provided a detailed description of Parisian life on the eve of the Revolution. This was contained in the 12 volumes of the *Tableau de Paris*, which appeared from 1783 to 1789. This work was supplemented by a new description of the city from 1796 to 1797, *Le Nouveau Paris*, which appeared in six volumes in 1798.

MERIDIAN. Because of the great maritime journeys of the 16th century, it became indispensable to create a prime meridian to enable navigators to calculate the longitudes. Each maritime and colonial power had its own. In 1667, when the Paris Observatory was being built, it was decided to make that the zero point (q.v.) of the Paris meridian. Everything located to the west of that observatory was in the western hemisphere and everything located to the east was in the eastern hemisphere. A marker was placed in Montmartre (q.v.) in the axis of that meridian in 1675 and another to the south of the observatory was erected in the park of Montsouris in 1806.

On January 1, 1914, the Paris meridian was done away with and France accepted the English meridian of Greenwich as the prime meridian. Since that date, Paris has been plotted on maps at a longitude of 2 degrees, 20 minutes and 14 seconds east. In November 1994, the Dutch artist Jan Dibbets began to mark out on the ground the location of the Paris meridian with 135 bronze medallions 12 centimeters in diameter and bearing the name of the astronomer Arago, who was the director of the observatory. These medallions stretch from the Cité Internationale Universitaire (q.v.) to the gate of Montmartre.

MÉTRO. It seems that the oldest project for an urban railway was the *métropolitain*, better known as the *métro*. It was conceived for Paris in 1845 by F. de Kerizouet, but the underground in London (1863) and the subways in New York (1868), Berlin (1878), Chicago (1892), Budapest (1896) and Vienna (1898) were actually built earlier. The trouble was that the city and the state presented contradictory plans and the result was a deadlock. The government backed the railway companies, which wanted to limit the metropolitan network to links between the six train stations of the capital. The municipal council wanted a dense urban network but limited to the 20 arrondissements and rejected any extension to the suburbs because that would encourage people to move out. It would also facilitate evasion of the toll (q.v.) fees, which were the main source of income for the communes.

As the world exhibition (q.v.) of 1900 approached, with tens of millions of visitors expected who could not be carried satisfactorily by the existing public transport world (*see* Transport, Public), the state finally gave in and accepted the plans of the municipal council. On March 30, 1898, a law was adopted that declared that the construction of the *métropolitain* was in the public interest. This was an electric train line dug close to the surface. The construction was undertaken by the Belgian group of Edouard Empain under the direction of the engineer Fulgence Bienvenüe. The work was rapid and not very expensive. It consisted simply of ripping up the streets and avenues where the tracks had to pass, building the métro vault and then redoing the pavement.

The first line, from Porte de Vincennes to Porte Maillot, went into service on July 19, 1900. It was an immediate success and it was used by 16 million passengers by the end of 1900. Line 2, from Porte Dauphine to Nation, was opened in 1903. In 1914, lines 1 through 6 and 12 were completed, as were portions of lines 7, 8, 10 and 13. Some half a billion passengers took the métro each year. The network was expanded further during and after the war. In 1939, the network had grown almost to its present configuration, with 159 kilometers of track and 332 stations. After 20 years of stagnation, the Régie autonome des transports parisiens (RATP), the public company that ran the overall urban transit system, launched an ambitious program in 1961. This project linked the capital with the suburbs thanks to the Réseau express régional (RER) (Regional Express Network), which connected Paris to the other départements of Île-de-France. The métro, the RER and the national railway corporation (SNCF) were linked. This gave the overall public transport system an exceptional scope and efficiency.

In 1996, the métro carried more than 1,200 billion passengers, more than 1,500 billion if the RER is included. This amounts to about half of all the motorized travel in the capital. Within the city, the network consists of 158 kilometers of track for the métro and 20 for the RER, served by 317 stations.

MEURICE (Hotel) (228, Rue de Rivoli). After the fall of Napoléon I, Augustin Meurice, an innkeeper in Calais, decided to open a quality hotel in Paris to accommodate the British tourists who flocked to Paris with the restoration of peace between France and Great Britain. In 1817, he established it in a new building in the Rue de Rivoli, which was then being formed. This deluxe establishment, strategically located just opposite the Tuileries (q.v.), the king's residence, gradually spread over ten arcades of that street and attracted a well-to-do clientele. In 1907, Frédéric Schwenter entrusted the architect Henri Nénot with rebuilding part of the hotel, which was expanded with the acquisition of the adjoining Hotel Métropole. The Meurice was then decorated in the Louis XVI style, which was largely inspired by Versailles (q.v.) and equipped with an ultramodern elevator that was a reproduction of Marie-Antoinette's sedan chair. On the roof an open-air restaurant, the Roof Garden, offered an exceptional view along the Seine (q.v.) as far as Saint-Germain-en-Laye.

The hotel's clientele included crowned heads, such as Alfonso XIII, the king of Spain; the Prince of Wales and his brother, the future

George VI; and fashionable writers such as Edmond Rostand. It was there that Coco Chanel (q.v.) held her receptions and Picasso gave his wedding banquet in 1935. From 1940 to 1945, the Meurice was the headquarters of the German military staff of Gross Paris. For 30 years, Salvador Dali spent a month each year in the Royal Suite. Florence Gould held a literary salon there every Thursday from 1946 to 1976. The Meurice has 146 rooms, 41 suites and six salons.

MILLER, HENRY VALENTINE (1891–1980). Henry Miller's writing is haunted by two cities: New York, where he was born, and Paris, where he lived in 1928 and from 1930 to 1940. The apostle of sexual freedom and libertarian and peaceful anarchism, his masterworks were published in Paris: *Tropic of Cancer* (1934), *Black Spring* (1936), *Max and the White Phagocytes* (1938), *Tropic of Capricorn* (1939) and *The Cosmological Eye* (1939). Since it was forbidden to publish his books in the United States until 1960 because they were supposedly pornographic, he also had *Sexus* (1949), *Plexus* (1953) and *Nexus* (1960) published in Paris. His recollections of his stay in the capital appeared in Paris in 1956 with the title of *Quiet Days in Clichy*. Many other aspects of his stay in France can be found in *Letters to Anäis Nin* (1965). *See* Nin, Anaïs.

MINERAL WATER. It is known by relatively few people that Paris actually had spas until the beginning of the 20th century. In fact, around 1650, mineral waters with laxative and antianemic properties were discovered at Passy (q.v.), at the location of the present Rue des Eaux. Other springs were discovered nearby in 1719 on the Quay de Passy (presently Avenue du Président-Kennedy). Boileau, Molière, Condorcet, Benjamin Franklin and Helvétius went to Passy to take the waters. The banker Benjamin Delessert acquired the land in 1800 and had a thermal park built, complete with a Swiss chalet, that existed until 1913. However, excessive building unsettled the ground and the springs dried up.

Auteuil (q.v.) also had springs that were rich in mineral salts, calcium sulfate and iron that were discovered as of the 16th century. In 1842, the Quicherat spring, at 6, Rue de la Cure, was discovered and worked. Some 140,000 bottles a year of its water were sold at the end of the 19th century, but work on the métro (q.v.) put an end to the spring. There were also sources of mineral water in the 17th arrondissement, in the Ternes (21, Rue Pierre-Demours) and Batignolles (11, Rue Sauffroy) quarters. In Belleville (Rue de l'Atlas), a spring provided 350,000 bottles a year from 1853 to 1880 and gave rise to a small spa with a casino.

MISTINGUETT, JEANNE BOURGEOIS, known as (1875–1956). It was with the sketch of the "swaying waltz," which she interpreted with Max Dearly at Moulin Rouge (q.v.) in 1909, that Mistinguett became famous. She appeared regularly in the revues of the Casino de Paris (q.v.), *Paris qui danse*, *Paris qui jazz*, and others. Her biggest hit songs were *Mon homme* (1920), *En douce* (1922), *Ça c'est Paris* (1926), and *C'est vrai* (1935). The quintessential Parisian woman, Mistinguett dominated the music hall (q.v.) between 1914 and 1939, along with Maurice Chevalier (q.v.) and Josephine Baker (q.v.).

MOLIÈRE, JEAN-BAPTISTE POQUELIN, known as (1622–73). The son of a rich tapestry maker from the Halles (q.v.) quarter, Molière studied at the Collège Louis-le-Grand (q.v.) but preferred the theater to his father's trade. After 15 years traveling around France with a wandering group of players, in 1658 he settled in Paris where Louis XIV (q.v.) allowed him to use one of the outbuildings of the Louvre (q.v.), the Petit-Bourbon. Although his plays were not situated in any particular place and although his characters strive for universality, much of his theater can be regarded as typically Parisian. Unquestionably, *Les Précieuses Ridicules* (1659) (*The Affected Young Ladies*), *Le Misanthrope* (1666), *Le Bourgeois Gentilhomme* (1670) (*The World-Be Gentleman*) and *Les Femmes Savantes* (1672) (*The School for Wives*) portray the personae, the social circles and the outlook of the capital.

MONROE, JAMES (1758–1831). After having participated in the American War of Independence, Monroe was elected a representative of Virginia in 1782 and then a senator in 1790. In August 1794, he succeeded Gouverneur Morris (q.v.) as the United States ambassador to France. He moved into 95, Rue de Richelieu, and one of his first acts was to obtain the release of Thomas Paine (q.v.). After he returned to the United States, he served as governor of Virginia from 1799 to 1802, and he negotiated the purchase of Louisiana from France in 1803. He then served as secretary of state in 1811 and was elected president in 1816, and then reelected in 1820. His principles of foreign policy became known as the Monroe Doctrine.

MONT-DE-PIÉTÉ. *See* CRÉDIT MUNICIPAL.

MONTFAUCON (Gallows). Near 53, Rue de la Grange-aux-Belles there was a mound that was flattened in 1782. It was on this site, which remained uninhabited until the beginning of the 17th century, that the king had a gallows erected to hang those condemned to death. Initially of wood, the gallows was reconstructed of stone in about 1325. Those who were hanged were left until they rotted and their remains were thrown into an ossuary that was located in the hollowed-out center of the gallows. Women were not hung but buried alive nearby.

François Villon (q.v.) described the Montfaucon gallows around 1460 in his *Grand Testament*. Many important figures ended their existence there, in particular finance ministers. The Montfaucon gallows stopped being used in 1627 because the foul odors of the rotting corpses detracted from the cleanliness of Saint-Louis hospital, which had been built in the vicinity. A second gallows was put up a bit further north, at 46, Rue de Meaux. It operated until 1790.

MONTMARTRE (Quarter). About halfway between the Île de la Cité (q.v.) and Saint-Denis (q.v.), Montmartre has existed since Gallo-Roman times. On the mound were built a temple dedicated to Mercury and another dedicated to Mars. Christianity carried on the religious tradition of the site, which was the place of martyrdom of Saint Denis and where a church was built. In 1133, Louis VI founded a Benedictine abbey for nuns there, and it owned the whole mound. However, when the abbey fell on hard times during the 14th and 15th centuries, it had to sell some of the land, which encouraged the populating of Montmartre. The vineyards (q.v.) that covered the mound resulted in flourishing sales of wine to the Parisians. In 1729, of the 165 commercial establishments on Montmartre, 134 were *guinguettes* (q.v.), which sold tax-free wine.

In 1790, Montmartre became a commune, but it had only 638 inhabitants by 1806. Then its population began growing rapidly, with 7,802 inhabitants in 1844 and 36,450 in 1857. Around then the Parisians got into the habit of going there to have fun and relax: there were already 16 ballrooms in Montmartre in 1810. Two of them became famous, the Elysée Montmartre and the Bal du Château-Rouge. In 1860, Montmartre was incorporated into Paris and, with the commune of La Chapelle, formed the 18th arrondissement. At the end of the 19th century, Montmartre was one of the main centers of entertainment and the arts, a "New Babylon" decried by the right-thinking.

Toulouse-Lautrec (q.v.) immortalized the dancers of the Moulin Rouge (q.v.). Many painters either lived on the mound or visited it frequently. During the 1820s, Horace Vernet and Géricault took up residence there. Corot moved in around 1830. As of 1850, independent artists would meet at the café (q.v.) under the wing of Manet. It was possible there to encounter Cézanne, Degas (q.v.), Monet, Pissarro, Renoir and Van Gogh. At the beginning of the 20th century, the Bateau-Lavoir (q.v.) became the cradle of cubism. It was there that Apollinaire, Max Jacob, Marie Laurencin, Picasso (q.v.) and Gertrude Stein could be found. But the artist who devoted his career to painting Montmartre was Utrillo (q.v.). In 1997, Montmartre still maintained a reputation as a place for pleasure and wild living and attracted tens of thousands of tourists drawn by the nightclubs and the painters at Place du Tertre.

MONTPARNASSE (Quarter). Presently a quarter (q.v.) in the 14th arrondissement, Montparnasse was for a long time a quarry for the stones needed to construct Paris's buildings. Otherwise, the landscape consisted of windmills (q.v.), pastures and gardens. It was not until the beginning of the 17th century that more people moved into Montparnasse, which became a real suburb of the city. Religious institutions proliferated: Port-Royal (q.v.); the oratory founded by Bérulle; the children's home, Enfants Trouvés of Saint Vincent de Paul; and the Capuchin convent. During the 18th century, lovely country houses, or "follies" (q.v.), were built along the future Boulevard du Montparnasse.

Montparnasse was also a center of entertainment and dining out. At the beginning of the 19th century, numerous *guinguettes* (q.v.) were opened, among the most famous being the Grande Chaumière and the Closerie des Lilas, which later became the Bal Bullier. The Rue de la Gaîté was known for its ballrooms, its cabarets and its infamous brothels. By the end of the 19th century, artists and writers met in the cafés (q.v.) of the Boulevard du Montparnasse such as Le Dôme (q.v.) and La Rotonde (q.v.) and, later, also La Coupole (q.v.) and Le Sélect. They included the likes of Apollinaire, Derain, Max Jacob, Modigliani, Picasso (q.v.), Soutine and Vlaminck. Although Montparnasse has lost its cultural prestige, its nightlife is still popular.

MORRIS, GOUVERNEUR (1752–1816). A businessman from New York, of French Protestant stock on his mother's side, Gouverneur Morris arrived in Paris in February 1789 to represent the commercial interests of the United States. He lived at 63, Rue de Richelieu. In February 1792, he was appointed American ambassador. As such, he turned out to be strongly in favor of Louis XVI and hostile to the Revolution. It was this hostility to the Revolution that led him to have John Paul Jones (q.v.) buried as cheaply as possible, much to the disgust of the Convention, which gave the American hero a national funeral. Similarly, he took no action to have Thomas Paine (q.v.) released from prison. In August 1794, Gouverneur Morris was replaced and returned to the United States in 1798, after traveling around Western Europe.

MOSQUE (1, Place du Puits-de-l'Ermite). On August 19, 1920, the National Assembly allocated funds to build a mosque to honor the memory of the 100,000 Muslims from the Maghreb and Black Africa who died for France during the First World War. A mosque in the Hispano-Moorish style was constructed by the architects Charles Heubès,

Robert Fournez and Maurice Mantout, based on the plans of Maurice Tranchant de Lunel. In was consecrated on July 15, 1926, in the presence of the president of France, the sultan of Morocco and the bey of Tunis. The mosque also houses a Muslim Institute, where the Koran is studied. For a long time it was the only Islamic place of worship in the capital. Although there are now hundreds of others, the Paris Mosque remains the symbol of Islam, which is presently the second largest religion in France—ahead of Protestantism—with about three million followers, 90 percent of them from North Africa.

MOUFFETARD (Street). The Rue Mouffetard is the last village street to survive in the heart of Paris. Originally, it was the starting point of the Roman road running from Lutetia to Rome. It later became the main street of Bourg Saint-Médard, a small district about 700 meters from Paris, surrounded by fields and vineyards (q.v.). The Bièvre (q.v.) marked the southern border and Place de la Contrescarpe was the northern boundary. For a long time the Mouffetard quarter was a poor neighborhood until the real estate speculation of the 1960s and 1970s drove out most of the tenants. They were replaced by young people from well-to-do families who set them up for the duration of their studies in renovated apartments. However, since the market and many shops still exist, this street has maintained its original working-class flavor.

MOULIN ROUGE (82, Boulevard de Clichy). In 1889, two clever businessmen, Charles Zidler and Joseph Oller, built the Moulin Rouge on the ruins of a once-famous dance hall, the Reine Blanche. It was sumptuously decorated by Willette and became the favorite haunt of the rich bourgeois who wanted to let their hair down in Montmartre (q.v.). The huge dance hall was complemented by a garden dominated by an enormous hollow elephant (q.v.). The most spectacular number was the "naturalist quadrille," whose dancers were immortalized by Toulouse-Lautrec (q.v.), namely, La Goulue and Grille d'Égout, accompanied by the contortionist, Valentin le Désossé ("boneless Valentin"). After 1900, the vogue of Moulin Rouge faded and spectacular revues replaced the French cancan (q.v.) dancers. In 1907, Max Dearly and Mistinguett (q.v.) invented the famous "swaying waltz." Unfortunately, manager followed manager, and the financial difficulties continued to mount despite the opening in 1910 of a second hall, the Bal du Moulin Rouge. In 1922, the Moulin Rouge was rebuilt, and Jacques Charles took charge of the shows, introducing Gertrude Hoffmann's American girls, who were a big hit in the revue New York-Montmartre. In 1925, Mistinguett led the revue in which Jean Gabin made his debut. The biggest success was the 1926 revue,

"Ça c'est Paris." The departure of Jacques Charles in 1929 doomed the Moulin Rouge, which was converted to a cinema (q.v.). The Bal du Moulin Rouge, however, has kept going to the present day, with its dinner-dance and its revue.

MUSEUM OF NATURAL HISTORY. *See* JARDIN DES PLANTES.

MUSEUMS. The oldest Parisian museum is the Louvre (q.v.), created on May 26, 1791. The revolutionaries also set up the Museum of Natural History, the Museum of Arts and Crafts and the Museum of French Monuments. Napoléon Bonaparte, in a historical irony, founded the Museum of the Navy in 1801. Between 1815 and 1848, four more museums were established, including the Cluny (q.v.) museum. Napoléon III opened two more. By 1871, more and more were being set up, the city of Paris alone founding five, one of them being the Carnavalet Museum (q.v.). The state instituted the Museum of the Army at the Invalides (q.v.). Three other major museums go back to before 1914: the Museum of Decorative Arts, the Jacquemart-André Museum and the Guimet Museum, which is dedicated to the Far East.

Between 1918 and 1939, the principal new museums to be established were the Museum of Overseas France (presently African and Oceanian Arts), the Museum of Mankind (Musée de l'Homme) and the Palace of Discovery (Palais de la Découverte). After 1945, large numbers of museums were opened, among them the Museum of Modern Art, the Museum of Popular Arts and Traditions, the Museum of Modern Art of the Pompidou Center (q.v.), the Picasso (q.v.) Museum, the Scientific Museum of the City of Science and Industry in La Villette (q.v.) and the Orsay (q.v.) Museum. The extension of the Louvre made it the biggest museum in the world. In 1996, there were more than one hundred museums. *See also* Carnavalet; Cluny; Grévin; Louvre; Orsay; Picasso.

MUSIC HALLS. The birth of the music hall in France can be traced back to February 1, 1867, and it took place on the stage of the Eldorado (q.v.). The first theater purposely built to be run as a music hall was the Folies-Bergère (q.v.), which was opened in 1869. The first establishment to call itself a music hall was the Olympia (q.v.), which was inaugurated in 1893. Other noteworthy examples include the Alhambra, Bobino (q.v.), Casino de Paris (q.v.) and Empire. Competition from the cinema (q.v.) and then television hurt the music hall severely, and only a few still remain, such as the Alcazar, Crazy Horse Saloon, Folies-Bergère, Lido (q.v.), Michou, Moulin Rouge (q.v.) and Paradis Latin. *See also* Bobino; Casino de Paris; Eldorado; Folies-Bergère; Lido de Paris; Moulin Rouge; Olympia.

-N-

NADAR, FÉLIX TOURNACHON, pseudonym (1820–1910). After having led a Bohemian (q.v.) life and published theatrical reviews, short stories and caricatures, Nadar turned to photography. He began to publish the *Panthéon Nadar* in 1854, an album of famous contemporary figures whose portraits were of an exceptional quality and expression. He was also excited by balloon (q.v.) flight and took the first aerial photos of Paris in 1860. In 1870, he organized a balloon corps during the siege of Paris. Strongly attached to artistic and theatrical circles, in 1874 and 1877 Nadar loaned his studio for the first two exhibitions of the impressionists. It is largely thanks to Nadar's talent that photography had been recognized as an art by the end of the 19th century.

NATIONAL ASSEMBLY. *See* PALAIS BOURBON.

NATIONAL GUARD. Established on July 13, 1789, the National Guard was a body of armed citizens along the lines of the bourgeois Parisian militia of the Ancien Régime. Initially under the command of La Fayette (q.v.), it was the spearhead of the Revolution from 1789 to 1794. Napoléon I left it dormant, but it became a bastion of the lower and middle bourgeoisie from 1815 to 1848. The ideas of the liberal opposition gradually spread through its ranks, and the National Guard played a prominent role in the revolution of July 1830, which overthrew Charles X. Its defection in February 1848 precipitated the fall of Louis-Philippe. However, its bourgeois battalions successfully put down the working-class socialist insurrection of June 1848, which was led by worker National Guards of the eastern faubourgs of Paris.

Napoléon III distrusted the National Guard and gave it only insignificant chores. Reorganized on August 12, 1870, at a time when the Franco-Prussian War was turning against France, the National Guard defended the besieged capital. France's defeat propelled many of its members toward an extremist ideology linking nationalism and socialism, and the National Guard played the last act of its existence during the Commune (q.v.), whose army it was. After being crushed during the "bloody week" of May 1871, the National Guard was officially dissolved by Thiers (q.v.), ending the role of armed civilians, whether bourgeois or working-class militia, in French history.

NATIONAL LIBRARY. Originally this was the king's library. It was first created by Charles V, a great fancier of books, but was taken away and dispersed during the English occupation of Paris in 1422–1435. Louis XI reestablished a library which François I installed in the

Fontainebleau château in 1544. It grew rapidly from 1537 thanks to the institution of legal deposit and was gradually transferred to Paris at the end of the 16th century. It was moved to its present location (58, rue de Richelieu) under Louis XIV and catalogued beginning in 1684 using a system that is still in use.

The library was partially opened to the public in 1692, only to become a national library during the Revolution, then an imperial library, then again a royal library, and so on until it was turned into a national library for good in 1870. Constantly remodeled, the buildings were provided with a reading room of 360 places by Labrouste during the reign of Napoléon III. There is no agreement on the estimate of the number of books in the Bibliothèque Nationale, although it is doubtless more than 12 million, not counting the manuscripts and periodicals.

On July 14, 1988, President François Mitterand decided to have a new library constructed. The controversial new building, commissioned from the architect Dominique Perrault, consists of four glass towers in the form of the letter L (the first letter in "livre" or book in French) or the shape of an open book. Inaugurated in 1996, and located at quai François Mauriac, the National Library is gradually developing while awaiting the transfer in 1998–1999 of the printed books and periodicals which are still kept in the old premises at rue de Richelieu.

NIN, ANAÏS (1903–77). Born at the gates of Paris in Neuilly-sur-Seine, Anäis Nin was the daughter of the famous pianist and composer Joaquin Nin. She followed her father on his tours around the world and knew all the famous writers and artists of the time. She was particularly close to Henry Miller (q.v.), for whom she was "half muse, half mother hen." Her romanesque works, many of them autobiographical, and especially her *Diary*, are a first-rate source on the history of the American community in Paris during the interwar period.

NOTRE-DAME (Cathedral). The origins of the cathedral go back to the fourth century. There was a group of buildings existing on the site, including one or two basilicas, the Saint-Jean-le-Rond baptistry, which existed until the 18th century, and an episcopal palace. Bishop Maurice de Sully, who was elected in 1160, decide to have a new building constructed. This work lasted a century. Notre-Dame is one of the monuments of early Gothic architecture, and trial and error by the various successive master builders explains the semiobscurity that envelopes the church. The sculpture on the façade and the gates was destroyed in 1793 by the revolutionaries. During the 19th century, it was restored under the direction of Jean-Baptiste Lassus and Eugène Viollet-Le-Duc, who saved the building, which had almost fallen into ruin, at the cost of very considerable restorations that lasted almost 20 years.

NUMBERING OF HOUSES. After several more or less successful attempts during the 18th century, the numbering of houses according to the system presently in use was defined by the decree of February 4, 1805. Article 4 provides that "the series of numbers shall be formed of even numbers on the right side of the street and of odd numbers on the left side." Article 5 specifies that "the right side shall be determined, in streets perpendicular or oblique to the course of the Seine (q.v.), by the right of a passerby moving away from the river and, in those parallel, by the right of a passerby walking in the direction of the course of the river." To this article 7 adds: "the first number of the series, whether even or odd, shall begin, in streets perpendicular or oblique to the course of the Seine, at the entrance of the street taken at the closest point to the river and, in parallel streets, to the entrance taken going up the river's course, in such a way that, in the former, the numbers increase while moving away from the river and, in the latter, going down it." This means that, to know where the numbering of a street begins, it is necessary to know its location in relation to the Seine, which is not always easy, even for old Parisians.

-O-

OBELISK OF LUXOR (Place de la Concorde). Ever since the Revolution and the destruction of the equestrian statue of Louis XV, the center of Place de la Concorde (q.v.) had remained empty. Under attack from the left and the right by the Republicans, Bonapartists and Legitimate Monarchists, Louis-Philippe wanted to erect a monument whose "neutrality would not arouse any passions." He thus chose the obelisk of Luxor, which the Egyptian pasha, Mohammed Ali, had offered him in 1831. This obelisk dates back to the reign of Ramses in the 13th century B.C. and is a monolith of pink granite, 23 meters high and weighing 230 tons. It was erected on October 25, 1836, before thousands of Parisians, under the direction of the engineer Jean-Baptiste Lebas, who had already had the delicate task of bringing it from Egypt.

OFFENBACH, JACQUES (1819–80). Appointed director of the orchestra of the Comédie-Française (q.v.) in 1849, Offenbach began a remarkable career in 1853 as a composer of operettas with the success of *Pépito*. In 1855, he opened his own theater, the Bouffes-Parisiens (q.v.). His works were only moderately successful until *Orphée aux Enfers (Orpheus in the Underworld)*, which was a tremendous hit in October 1858. His masterpiece, *La Belle Hélène*, was played in 1864. He then produced *La Vie parisienne* (1866), *La Grande-duchesse de Gerolstein* (1867) and *La Périchole* (1868), composing a total of 87 operettas. After 1870, he was less successful, although he did write several popular works such as *Madame Favart* (1878) and *La Fille du tambour-major*

(The Drum-Major's Daughter) (1879). His last composition, *Les Contes d'Hoffmann (Tales of Hoffmann)*, the first to be presented at the Opéra-Comique (q.v.), was staged in February 1881, shortly after his death. Offenbach's light and witty music was admirably suited to the atmosphere of pleasure that prevailed during the Second Empire.

OLYMPIA (28, Boulevard des Capucines). So as to prevent fires, the businessman Joseph Oller had the architect Léon Carle build a music hall (q.v.) entirely of iron in 1887. It was a marvel of comfort and elegance for that day and age, with 2,000 seats and a restaurant (q.v.). Just like the English music halls, it presented a wide variety of acts: acrobats, jugglers, mimes, clowns, animal tamers, dancers, small groups of singers and so on. The public came to see Diavolo on his motorcycle "looping the loop," the transformist dwarf Little Tich, Houdini, Loïe Fuller (q.v.), Fregoli and others. Jacques Charles took charge of the Olympia in 1911, had the hall renovated and produced the best shows of his time. The hall was turned into a cinema (q.v.) in 1929. Then, in 1953, Bruno Coquatrix brought it back to life as a music hall, and until his death in 1979, the best in show business appeared; including Georges Brassens, Léo Ferré, Jacques Brel, Aznavour, Marcel Amont, Juliette Greco, Patachou, Colette Renard, Edith Piaf (q.v.), Gilbert Bécaud, Dalida, Johnny Halliday, Enrico Macias and the Beatles. A bit rundown at present, the hall narrowly escaped destruction and has just been listed as a historic monument.

OLYMPIC GAMES. The Christian emperor of Rome Theodosius I prohibited the Olympic Games in 393 because they were deemed impious. They were eventually restored thanks to the Parisian Pierre de Coubertin. The first were held symbolically in their country of origin, in Athens, in 1896. The second were held in the country of their renovator, in Paris, from May 20 to October 28, 1900. They aroused virtually no interest since all the attention was focused on the world exhibition (q.v.). Very few newspapers even mentioned the events that were held here and there in the city, and then only rarely and briefly. The eighth Olympic Games were also held in Paris from May 4 to July 27, 1924. For this purpose, the Colombes stadium and the Tourelles swimming pool were built. President François Mitterrand wanted Paris to be the site of the 1992 Olympic Games, but his wish was refused by the municipality because of the costs involved.

OPÉRA. French opera resulted from a union of the court ballet danced at the court of the French kings in the 16th century and the Italian opera, which was born in Florence at the same time. The first presentation of an opera took place at the Palais-Royal (q.v.) on February 28, 1645. It was *La Finta Pazza*, a comedy attributed to Marco Marazzoli.

In 1647, Luigi Rossi's *Orfeo* was a great success. The first operas composed by the French were *Le Triomphe de l'Amour* by Beys and Laguerre, and the *Pastorale d'Issy*, by Perrin and Cambert, which were played in 1655 and 1659.

In 1671, Pierre Perrin had the first opera hall built on the site of the present Rue Jacques-Callot. Lully opened his in 1672 on the location of the Rue de Médicis. In 1673, he managed to expel the troupe of the Comédie-Française from the hall in the Palais-Royal, which he took over. The opera remained there until it burned in 1763. Rebuilt, and again destroyed by a fire (q.v.) in 1781, the opera moved to a new theater located at Porte Saint-Martin. In 1794, a new building was dedicated to it, the Montansier hall in the Rue de Richelieu (on the location of Square Louvois). Unfortunately, the duke of Berry was assassinated at the door of that opera house in 1820 and, as a sign of mourning, Louis XVIII had the building torn down. A new opera house was constructed with the material of the old one in the Rue Le Peletier, but it also burned down, in 1873.

At the time, the Opéra of Charles Garnier, which had been commissioned in 1860, was not yet completed. On January 5, 1875, the present hall at Place de l'Opéra was inaugurated. Nowadays only ballets are presented there. At present, operas are staged at the Opéra-Bastille (Place de la Bastille), the work of the architect Carlos Ott, which was inaugurated on July 14, 1989.

OPÉRA-COMIQUE. The Opéra-Comique was born on the boards of the Saint-Germain and Saint-Laurent fairs (q.v.) in the form of popular parodies of the solemn and tedious operas of Lully and Quinault. Despite the efforts of the Opéra (q.v.) and the Comédie-Française (q.v.) to have these presentations prohibited, the king ultimately gave them a legal existence in 1714. This genre eventually triumphed thanks to the genius of Favart (q.v.) and finally, in 1762, the Opéra-Comique obtained a hall that it shared with the Comédie-Italienne, located in the theater of the Hôtel de Bourgogne. Because of the success of Grétry's works, the artists were able to have a hall, called the Salle Favart, built in 1783. In 1838, it was destroyed by a fire (q.v.) and then rebuilt on the same spot. In 1887, it was burned down again. A third Salle Favart was inaugurated in 1898, still at the same place. This is the one that can be seen today at Place Boieldieu.

ORFÈVRES (Quay). The Quai des Orfèvres is a symbol of exceptional continuity. It seems that the goldsmith's trade has been established on the Île de la Cité (q.v.) ever since its Gallo-Roman origins. The name of Quai des Orfèvres (Goldsmith's Quay) recalls this ancient presence.

This name is famous nowadays for another reason. In 1792, the municipality set up its administrative police commission there. In 1800, this site became the headquarters of the Paris police (q.v.), and the chief commissioner of police (q.v.) resided there. In 1871, the Communards set these buildings on fire, and they were rebuilt in the immediate vicinity, at the Boulevard du Palais. Nevertheless, the buildings that were rebuilt on the Quai des Orfèvres still housed part of that administration, namely, the offices of the criminal investigation department. These offices were immortalized by Simenon and his Inspector Maigret (q.v.).

ORSAY (Museum) (9, Quai Anatole-France). This was initially the site of the Orsay palace, the headquarters of the Audit Office and the Council of State, which was burned down in 1871 by the Communards. In 1898, the Compagnie des chemins de fer d'Orléans et du Sud-Ouest acquired the ruins to build a magnificent train station that covered the southwest and replaced the Austerlitz station as the terminal. Constructed by Victor Laloux, it was inaugurated for the 1900 world exhibition (q.v.). In 1939, the traffic on these lines was moved to the Austerlitz station, and the Orsay station became little more than a suburban stop. It served little purpose and was actually slated for demolition when President Giscard d'Estaing decided in 1977 to use it as a museum for art of the second half of the 19th century. The conversion took place between 1980 and 1986 under the direction of the architects Renaud Bardon, Pierre Colboc and Jean-Paul Philippon for the exterior and Gae Aulenti for the interior. One of Paris's most popular museums, it displays works of various schools and periods, classicism, romanticism and symbolism, the Barbizon school, and especially impressionism.

-P-

PACHE, JEAN NICOLAS (1746–1823). The son of the concierge (q.v.) of the de Castries mansion, Pache became the tutor of the children of Marshal de Castries, who got him a job at the Ministry of the Navy. He eventually rose to first secretary. Necker appointed him controller of the royal household. Roland, the minister of the interior, brought him into the ministry, then had him appointed minister of war in October 1792. Pache, however, abandoned the party of the Girondins for that of the Montagnards, which caused him to lose his post as minister in February 1793. His friends in the Mountain then had him elected mayor (q.v.) of Paris on February 14, 1793. He remained in office until May 19, 1794. It was he who had the motto "liberty, equality, fraternity," devised by Momoro, inscribed on public monuments.

Pache played an outstanding role during the insurrectional days of May 31 and June 2, 1793, which culminated in the arrest of the Girondins. Suspected by Robespierre (q.v.) because of his ties with the Hébertists, Pache managed to escape the guillotine (q.v.) but had to resign to make way for Fleuriot-Lescot (q.v.). Pache was imprisoned for a few days after the failure of the insurrection of May 20, 1795. In 1796, after being implicated in the communist conspiracy of Gracchus Babeuf, he withdrew from public life.

PAINE, THOMAS (1737–1809). An Englishman who emigrated to Philadelphia in 1774, Thomas Paine quickly became one of the intellectual leaders of the American Revolution through his pamphlet *Common Sense*. He stayed briefly in Paris in 1781 to obtain financial and military aid from Louis XVI. He returned in 1787 to present a project, a metal bridge, to the Academy of Sciences. A staunch supporter of the Revolution, Paine was granted French nationality by the National Assembly on August 26, 1792. The voters of four départements chose him as their representative to the Convention and he opted for Pas-de-Calais, which was near his native country. Close to the Girondin moderates, he was arrested on December 28, 1793, and thrown into Luxembourg prison from which he was released on November 4, 1794, thanks to the intervention of James Monroe (q.v.).

It was during his imprisonment that he wrote his masterpiece, *The Age of Reason*, a repudiation of religion. He also attacked George Washington, whose cold character he denounced. In 1802, sensing the coming of Bonaparte's dictatorship, he returned to the United States, where Thomas Jefferson (q.v.) had just been elected president. Actually, Napoléon Bonaparte felt a genuine admiration for Paine, saying that he was "the spirit to which a golden statue would be raised in every city in the world."

PALAIS BOURBON (128, Rue de l'Université and 29–35, Quai d'Orsay). It was for the Duchess of Bourbon, the daughter of Louis XIV (q.v.) and Madame de Montespan, and wife of Louis III of Bourbon, that the Palais Bourbon was built. Several architects tried their hand at the task between 1722 and 1728, but the palace is basically the work of Jean Aubert and Jacques V. Gabriel. Originally, it was an Italian-style building consisting of a ground floor covered with a flat roof and surrounded by a vast garden reaching down to the Seine (q.v.). Bought in 1764 by the Prince of Condé, the Palais Bourbon was extended with two wings and a portico on the street.

In 1795, it became the seat of the nation's representatives, the Council of Five Hundred, the Legislative Assembly, the Chamber of Deputies and then the National Assembly. This brought about very considerable alterations, including the installation of a semicircular hall for the people's representatives, the construction of a new façade with a triangular pediment decorated with allegorical sculptures, erection of numerous statues, and painting of frescos by Delacroix in the library. The Palais Bourbon is the counterpart of the Madeleine Church (q.v.) in the axis of the Rue Royale and within the framework of Place de la Concorde (q.v.).

PALAIS DE JUSTICE (Law Courts) (4, Boulevard du Palais). It seems that the location of the present Palais de Justice was, during the Gallo-Roman era, the headquarters of the central authorities. In fact, it is almost certain that the seat of the Roman governor of Lutetia was located at the western tip of the Île de la Cité (q.v.). This governor's palace (Palais de la Cité) remained the residence of the counts of Paris (q.v.) for centuries, and the first Capetian kings lived there until the Louvre (q.v.) was built. The buildings were repeatedly renovated and rebuilt over the centuries.

The Sainte-Chapelle (q.v.) remains from the reign of Saint Louis. The towers on the Seine (q.v.) and the clock date from the 14th century. Most of the buildings disappeared in the fires (q.v.) of the 18th century, and almost all of those we see today date from the 19th century. When the kings left the Palais de la Cité for the Louvre, the central administration, the *Parlement* (q.v.) and the Auditor's Chamber remained there until the Revolution. In 1793, the revolutionary tribunal operated there. Since 1800, it has been the site of the civil tribunal, the court of appeal and the supreme court of appeal, which explains the name Palais de Justice.

PALAIS-ROYAL. In 1629, Cardinal Richelieu, the prime minister of Louis XIII, commissioned the architect Jacques Le Mercier to construct a palace. On his death, in 1642, Richelieu bequeathed his palace to the king, and the Cardinal's Palace became the Royal Palace. Anne of Austria moved there from the Tuileries (q.v.), and it was there that the young Louis XIV (q.v.) witnessed the events of the Fronde (q.v.) in 1648–49. It was doubtlessly because of his unpleasant memories that the king gave the Palais-Royal to his brother, Gaston d'Orléans. The Orléans family kept the Palais-Royal until the Revolution of 1848. During this time, they carried out a number of alterations, among other things changing the southern and northern façades and opening the ground floor with broad doors and arcades.

In 1784, Philippe d'Orléans, the duke of Chartres, needing money, divided the garden into lots and on three sides surrounding the palace built 60 pavilions with three arcades, each of which was rented to cafés (q.v.), restaurants (q.v.), gaming houses and bordellos. Until the prohibition of gaming houses at the end of 1836, the Palais-Royal was the heart of Parisian nightlife. It was later supplanted by the grands boulevards (q.v.) and has been a backwater ever since, housing only stores that sell decorations, stamps, books or antiques. It also contains the Council of State, the Ministry of Culture, the Constitutional Council and the Comédie-Française (q.v.).

PANTHÉON (Place du Panthéon). In 1744, Louis XV promised the canons of Sainte-Geneviève (q.v.) abbey that he would build them a new church. The work began much later, with Jacques Germain Soufflot presenting the first plan in 1757. In 1780, when he passed away, the fabric of the church was well advanced, and it was completed in 1790. Hardly had it been finished than Sainte-Geneviève Church was converted by the National Assembly into a "temple of great men," or pantheon. It received the remains of Mirabeau and Voltaire as of 1791, as well as those of many other illustrious figures of their time. Again used for Catholic worship as of 1806, the monument definitively became a pantheon in 1885. At present, the Panthéon contains the tombs of about 60 of the nation's greats. The most recent, Condorcet, Grégoire and Monge, prominent figures during the revolutionary period, were buried there in 1989 on the occasion of the bicentenary of the French Revolution.

PARACHUTE. Paris can take pride in being the birthplace of the parachute. In 1790, Jacques Garnerin had begun undertaking flights in hot-air balloons (q.v.), and he did his utmost to develop a device that would make it possible to leave the balloon in case of an accident and land safely on the ground without being killed by the fall. On October 22, 1797, he took off from Monceau park in a balloon and plunged into nothingness from a height of 700 meters. His parachute opened and he reached the ground without injury. Garnerin repeated his experience frequently, appearing during official and private festivities. His wife, whose maiden name was Jeanne-Geneviève Labrousse, was the first woman to fly in a hot-air balloon and to parachute on November 10, 1798.

PARC DES PRINCES (Stadium) (24, Rue du Commandant-Guilbaud). The Parc des Princes stadium was built on the site of a cycle-racing track that had been torn down in 1959. Its concrete ellipse takes the form of "a melon with its slices spread apart," as expressed by Michel Dansel. Built by Roger Taillibert and inaugurated on June 4, 1972, it can hold 50,000 spectators. It is where the big soccer and rugby matches are played.

PARIS FAIR. The first Paris Fair was inaugurated on March 17, 1904. Situated at the old market at the Carreau du Temple and covering 10,000 square meters of space, it brought together 495 exhibitors who displayed products manufactured in the capital. This modest commercial event quickly got bigger and bigger. In 1917, it left the Carreau du Temple, which had become too small, and moved to the esplanade of the Invalides (q.v.), where it occupied 70,000 square meters. In 1921, it was transferred to the Champ-de-Mars (q.v.), where it took up 100,000 square meters. Since 1962, it has been held at the exhibition park at the Porte de Versailles, where the space occupied by the Paris Fair has gradually doubled. Its stands now take up nearly 500,000 square meters and are run by almost 13,000 exhibitors, of which 3,000 are foreign. *See also* Fairs.

PARLEMENT, LE. The *Parlement* of Paris was the oldest sovereign court of the kingdom of France. Organized about 1250, it was entrusted with administering justice. It was installed in the king's old palace, which he had left for the Louvre (q.v.) and which is now called the Palais de Justice (q.v.). The *Parlement*'s jurisdiction was vast and covered almost half of the territory of present-day France: Île-de-France, Picardy, Champagne, Centre, Pays-de-Loire, Poitou-Charentes, Auvergne, the northern half of Limousin and Nivernais in Burgundy—about 40 départements in all.

On several occasions, and particularly during the Fronde (q.v.), the *Parlement* tried to mix in the king's politics and play a role comparable to that of the British parliament in London, but the absolute monarchy successfully fended off these attempts to establish a parliamentary regime. Nonetheless, the *Parlement* did play a significant role in the unrest that eventually led to the Revolution and the fall of the monarchy. The *Parlement*'s members formed a well-to-do nobility based on their administrative and judicial posts, which had real importance in the life of Paris.

PASSY. Mentioned for the first time in a document from 1250, Passy was a village of winegrowers. Its population amounted to about 600 inhabitants in 1720. Mineral waters were discovered in about 1650, and the spas were visited until 1868. Jean-Jacques Rousseau and Benjamin Franklin (q.v.) went there to take the waters. For a long time it was a pleasant, rustic place frequented by Parisians tired of the hustle and bustle of the big city. It is still possible to visit Balzac's (q.v.) house. The lord of Passy, Marquis de Boulainvilliers, had a château there, which was converted into a nursing home in the 19th century by Dr. Blanche and where Gérard de Nerval and Guy de Maupassant were treated. Passy was incorporated into Paris in 1860, becoming the Muette quarter of the 16th arrondissement; the name came from a château that had belonged to the kings from 1615 to 1792. Slowly but surely the private parks and gardens have been giving way to blocks of luxury flats for Paris's upper crust.

PAWN SHOPS. *See* CRÉDIT MUNICIPAL.

PÈRE-LACHAISE (Cemetery) (Boulevard de Ménilmontant). In 1776, burials in the cemeteries (q.v.) located inside the cities was forbidden. On March 12, 1801, it was decided to create three cemeteries located outside the city limits for Parisians. The east cemetery, or Père-Lachaise cemetery, was opened on May 21, 1804, on the site of the Montlouis estate, which had belonged to the Jesuits and where Father La Chaise, the confessor of Louis XIV (q.v.), had lived. The cemetery was gradually enlarged from 17 to 44 hectares in 1860, at which time

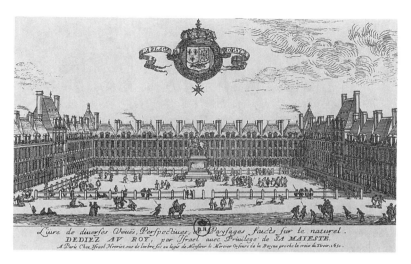

Place Royale (Place des Vosges) in 1651

Palais des Tuileries ca. 1650

The Bastille (July 14, 1789)

The Louvre's New Buildings ca. 1870

Notre-Dame Cathedral at the beginning of the eighteenth century

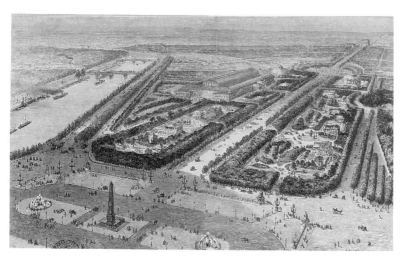

The Champs-Elysées and the Universal Exhibition in 1855

Galeries Lafayette in 1908

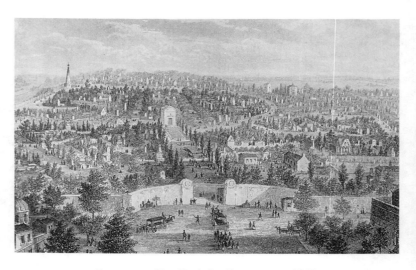

Entrance to Père-Lachaise Cemetery ca. 1850

The Châtêlet in 1780

rtuil et Eglise de SORBONNE, Colege en lVniuersité de Paris fondé l'an 1245 par Robert Sorbon homme fort sçauant; enrichy par St Louis,
basti par le Cardinal Duc de Richelieu l'an 1642. ou ses os reposent sous le grand Autel. Ce bastiment a esté conduit par M. Mercier Architect.

Church of the Sorbonne in 1649

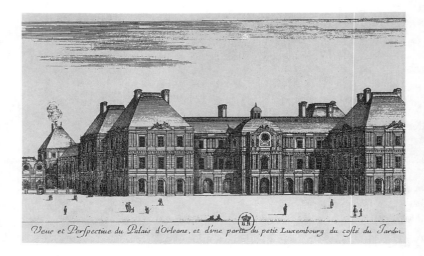

Palais de Luxembourg in 1649

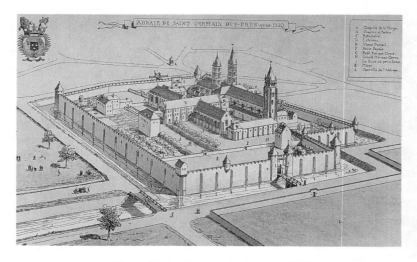

Abbey of Saint-Germain des Prés ca. 1520

Hôtel des Invalides in 1810

Moulin de la Galette ca. 1860

Palais du Trocadéro and Universal Exhibition in 1878

Abbey of Montmartre in 1625

the capital's limits were extended and Père-Lachaise was incorporated into the 20th arrondissement. It was at Père-Lachaise cemetery that the last fighters for the Commune (q.v.) were shot down on May 28, 1871. The cemetery is a remarkable museum of funerary sculpture and holds the remains of numerous French and foreign celebrities, such as Frédéric Chopin, Oscar Wilde, Gertrude Stein and Jim Morrison.

PÉTION, JÉROME (1756–94). A lawyer who was elected to the Estates General in May 1789 by the bailiwick of Chartres, Pétion joined the far left and become a friend of Robespierre (q.v.). He was president of the criminal court of Paris and then elected mayor (q.v.) of the city on November 14, 1791. On June 20, 1792, Pétion allowed the rioters to invade the Tuileries (q.v.) and threaten the king. He was sanctioned and suspended from office from July 6 to 13. On July 14, during the festival on the Champ-de-Mars (q.v.), he was acclaimed by the crowd. He encouraged the victorious insurrection of August 10, 1792, which overthrew the monarchy, and allowed the September massacres to be perpetrated in the prisons. After being elected a delegate to the Convention and subsequently becoming its first president, he resigned as mayor on October 15, 1792, since it was forbidden to hold both posts. By now Pétion had fallen out with Robespierre and become an influential member of the Girondins, and he was proscribed along with them on June 2, 1793. Hunted down by the police, he hid near Bordeaux and eventually committed suicide.

PHILIPPE II AUGUSTE (1165–1223). The son and successor of Louis VII in 1180, Philippe II "Augustus" cleverly took advantage of the rivalry between the king of England, Henry II, and his son, Richard the Lion-Hearted, to weaken the Plantagenets. He participated in the third crusade (1189–91) in the company of Henry II and, before leaving France, ordered that Paris be surrounded by a fortified wall (q.v.). This was constructed on the right bank between 1190 and 1208 and on the left bank between 1209 and 1213. He also had the castle of the Louvre (q.v.) built, between 1190 and 1202. In 1204, Philippe Auguste confiscated the possessions—Maine, Normandy and Touraine—of the brother and successor of Richard the Lion-Hearted, John Lackland. He then routed the coalition formed by England with the Holy Roman Empire and Flanders after his victories at Roche-aux-Moines and Bouvines (1214). On his death he left royal lands that were tenfold larger than when he took the crown, as well as a solidly fortified capital.

PIAF, ÉDITH GASSION, known as (1915–63). Born in the Rue de Belleville to a family of circus performers, Edith Piaf was by far the most popular French songstress of the 20th century. As a child, she wandered from city to city, from neighborhood to neighborhood, with her father, singing in the courtyards and streets to earn a few coins. A real-life Gavroche (q.v.), she often slept out of doors and roamed from Clichy to Pigalle (q.v.), Barbès and Porte des Lilas. Discovered by Louis Leplée, she initiated a brilliant career in 1936, singing on the radio, going on stage, appearing in films and recording one record after another. With Maurice Chevalier (q.v.) and Mistinguett (q.v.), she represented French music and an indomitable Parisian spirit. When she visited the United States in 1945, the students of Columbia University asked her to sing *L'Accordéoniste* in front of the Statue of Liberty.

PICASSO (Museum) (5, Rue de Thorigny). The Picasso Museum was opened in 1985 in one of the largest and most beautiful mansions of the Marais (q.v.). It was built between 1656 and 1659 by Jean Boullier de Bourges for Pierre Aubert de Fontenoy, a tax collector for the salt tax, for which reason the Parisians nicknamed it Hôtel Salé (salted mansion). The noticeable restraint of the façades, without columns and pilasters, is more than compensated for by the rich sculpted ornamentation. Inside the building is one of the finest stairways in Paris, although most of the original decoration has disappeared. The better part of the works left by Picasso in his studio when he died were given by his heirs to the French state to pay the inheritance fees. Paintings, engravings, sculptures, pottery and other objects created by the artist are judiciously displayed within the imposing frame of this mansion.

PIGALLE (Square). The name of the sculptor Jean-Baptiste Pigalle (1714–85) is known around the world thanks to Place Pigalle, the pinnacle of pleasure in Paris. The quarter, which lies astride the 9th and 18th arrondissements, has been an entertainment center since the 18th century. Rue des Martyrs, which at that time had only 58 buildings, boasted no fewer than 25 cabarets. During the Second Empire (1852–70), this calling was further enhanced with the opening of ballrooms such as the Boule Noire, Elysée-Montmartre and Reine Blanche, which later became the Moulin Rouge (q.v.). "Midnight at Place Pigalle" was the rallying call of revelers for a century. Others, however, came to have an apéritif at Place Pigalle. The impressionist painters met at Café Guerbois, and the artists from the nearby Bateau-Lavoir (q.v.) also patronized it. Today, the quarter is a bit run-down, invaded by sex shops and striptease joints, but Pigalle remains extremely popular, and the enduring fame of the place attracts flocks of tourists.

PLAZA-ATHÉNÉE (Hotel) (25, Avenue Montaigne). Built in 1911 by the architect Jules Lefebvre, the Plaza-Athénée was ranked sixth among the best hotels in the world by the American magazine *Institu-*

tional Investor. Its 200 rooms and suites have accommodated many illustrious figures: Charles Lindbergh, Mrs. Joseph Pulitzer, John D. Rockefeller II and Rudolf Valentino, just to mention the Americans between 1919 and 1939. Since 1945, it has been patronized by King Hussein of Jordan, the Kennedy family, Stavros Niarchos, Peter Ustinov, Darryl F. Zanuck and others. The famous spy Mata Hari occupied room 200, but she was in another hotel, the Elysée Palace, when she was arrested in 1917.

POIRET, PAUL (1879–1944). From 1900 to 1924, the couturier Paul Poiret dominated the fashion scene. After having worked for Jacques Doucet (q.v.), he opened his own fashion house, first in the Rue Auber and then in a private mansion in the Rue Pasquier. He launched a revolution in styles, ridding women of the corset and girdle and giving them a straight line that freed and emphasized the bust and the arms. A man of lavish tastes, he held sophisticated parties, surrounded himself with a bevy of artistes and designed numerous costumes. His extravagance ruined him and, hounded by his creditors, he had to give up all his activities in 1924; he died in poverty.

POISSARDES. The women who exercised a trade at the Halles (q.v.) were called "ladies of the Halle" or, more frequently, *poissardes*, an expression that designated the fishmongers, although most of them actually sold vegetables, fruit, flowers, cheese and other foodstuffs. In the official festivities to which the ordinary people were invited, the place of honor was traditionally reserved for the *poissardes* and the charcoal burners, who were regarded as the generally acknowledged representatives of the lower classes. When the queen gave birth to a male child, the *poissardes* went in procession to her bedside to congratulate her. The image of the *poissarde*, or lady of the Halle, was often used in the literature of the 18th and 19th centuries, and she appeared on stage in the character of Madame Angot.

POLICE. The responsibility for policing the city was vested in the king's provost (q.v.) as of the 11th century. Stationed at the Châtelet (q.v.), the provost was a judge, military commander and chief of police all in one. He was aided by the watchmen (q.v.) and, since 1306, by commissioner-examiners (two per quarter), who later became commissioner-investigators and were the ancestors of the present-day police commissioners. The purchase of office generated abuses, disorders and negligence, which made the police force ever less effective. Insecurity in the streets after nightfall was such that Louis XIV (q.v.) decided in March 1667 to establish a lieutenant general of police (*see* Lieutenant Général de Police) endowed with very broad powers. Like the provost, his headquarters were in the Châtelet. His multiple re-sponsibilities of police, administration of public thoroughfares and ur-banism were for the most part carried over when Napoléon Bonaparte set up the police headquarters under the chief commissioner of police (*see* Police, Chief Commissioner of).

It was not until 1829 that the policemen, known as *sergents de ville*, were given uniforms. Hated by the Parisians, the corps of *sergents de ville* was dissolved in 1879 and replaced by a corps of policemen called *gardiens de la paix*, which still exists. Chief Commissioner of Police Lépine (q.v.) modernized the police force at the beginning of the 20th century, setting up bicycle and motorcycle units, companies assigned to traffic duties and the river brigade (q.v.). A high quality scientific police force was formed during the 1880s by Alphonse Bertillon, head of the Criminal Records Office. The first women were recruited in 1935, but they were integrated in the active services only in 1972. The uniform kept changing: the white truncheon of the traf-fic police was introduced in 1896 and the *képi* (peaked cap) was re-placed by the *casquette* (cap) in 1985. At present, the headquarters of the Paris police has about 15,000 *gardiens de la paix* under its orders.

POLICE, CHIEF COMMISSIONER OF. The law of February 17, 1800 (Pluviôse 28, Year VIII), provided for having a prefect at the head of each département. An exception was made for Paris, which, in addition to the prefect of the Seine, had a prefect, or chief commis-sioner, of police with very broad powers that went beyond just the po-lice (q.v.) to include procurement of supplies and traffic in the city. The chief commissioner of police was such an important person that he could present a danger for the political authorities, which is why he was replaced more frequently than the prefect of Paris (q.v.) or prefect of the Seine. Over a period of 197 years, this post was held by 78 per-sons, working out to an average stay of two-and-a-half years. Only three chief commissioners enjoyed a longer stay, exceeding ten years: the first, Louis Joseph Dubois (1800–10); the 20th, Gabriel Delessert (1836–48); and the 46th and 48th, Louis Lépine (q.v.) (1893–97 and 1899–1913).

POLITICAL VIOLENCE. Acts of political violence almost always occur during periods of deep-seated unrest in society. The Black Death of 1348 and the disasters of the Hundred Years War destabi-lized France. After King John II was captured by the English, his son, Dauphin Charles, became the regent. However, the bourgeoisie, led by Étienne Marcel (q.v.), the merchants' provost (q.v.), demanded far-reaching reforms. When the dauphin refused, a mob killed two of his advisors at the Cité palace on February 22, 1358. Étienne Marcel was in his turn killed at the Saint-Antoine gate while trying to let the English enter Paris on July 31, 1358. On leaving the royal mansion of Hôtel Saint-Paul on June 13, 1392, High Constable Clisson was left for dead by hired assassins in the pay of Pierre de Craon, who contested the succession to Brittany. Duke Louis d'Orléans, the brother of Charles VI (q.v.), was assassinated as he left the Hôtel Barbette on November 23, 1407, at the orders of his nephew, Jean the Fearless, duke of Burgundy, who perished in the same way in 1419 on Montereau bridge. Calm was restored with the end of the Hundred Years War and the return of prosperity.

However, the cycle of violence resumed with the outbreak of religious conflicts. The Saint-Bartholomew's Day (q.v.) massacre on August 24, 1572, when thousands of Protestants were killed at dawn at the orders of Charles IX, was the worst bloodshed ordered by the royal power in Paris. Henri III was stabbed at Saint-Cloud on August 1, 1589, by the monk Jacques Clément, and his successor, Henri IV, suffered the same fate at the hands of the Jesuit pupil Ravaillac while his carriage was stuck in traffic at the Rue de la Ferronerie on May 14, 1610. The iron order imposed by the absolute monarchy put an end to such political violence until 1789.

During the Revolution, such acts of violence proliferated, including the assassination of Merchants Provost Jacques de Flesselles on July 14, 1789 and Quartermaster General Bertier de Sauvigny on July 22, 1789; the murder of Deputy Le Peletier de Saint-Fargeau on January 20, 1793; and that of Marat in his bathtub by Charlotte Corday on July 13, 1793. No sooner had he come to power than Bonaparte was the target of royalist attacks: a bomb exploded in his path in the Rue Saint-Nicaise on December 24, 1800. Several periods of assassinations and attempts thereat occurred during the 19th century. The sole heir to the throne of an age to procreate, the duke of Berry, was killed by Louvel on leaving the Opéra (q.v.) on February 13, 1820. Louis-Philippe (1830–48) was the French head of state who faced, without ever being harmed, the largest number of attempts on his life: about ten. The bloodiest one was that of Fieschi on July 28, 1835, which killed 18 people on the Boulevard du Temple. Napoléon III was the victim of four attempts; Orsini's in front of the Opéra on January 14, 1858 left 156 dead and injured. The anarchists unleashed a wave of assassination attempts from 1892 to 1894. Their heros were Ravachol and Auguste Vaillant, whose bomb caused about 60 casualties in the Chamber of Deputies on December 9, 1893.

It is impossible to list all the political crimes committed during the 20th century. Among the most significant were the assassination of Jean Jaurès at Café du Croissant on July 31, 1914, and the murder of French President Paul Doumer at 11, Rue Berryer on May 6, 1932.

The attacks and outrages during the German occupation (1940–44) were particularly numerous, and another major wave of violence occurred during the Algerian war (1954–62), with many bombs set off by the Organisation de l'Ármée Secrète (OAS). The most recent and the bloodiest outrages that took place in 1986 and 1995 and were the work of Islamicists.

POMPIDOU CENTER (19, Rue Beaubourg). In December 1969, President Georges Pompidou launched the project of building a cultural center that would be open to all and that was ultimately called the Georges Pompidou National Center of Art and Culture. The site chosen was on the Beaubourg plateau, a central location that was then empty and that measured a huge 1,850 square meters. Following an international competition, the design of Renzo Piano (Italian) and Richard Rogers (British) was selected. This decision sparked a lively controversy because the center would be ultramodern and thus out of tune with this historic quarter and also because it was so big (a glass and metal quadrilateral 166 meters long, 60 meters wide and 42 meters high) that it would overwhelm the surrounding buildings. Although it was sometimes written off as a refinery or a cultural supermarket, the Pompidou Center has attracted huge crowds, more than eight million visitors a year, or an average of 25,000 a day. It houses the Public Information Library, the Industrial Design Center, the Institute for Acoustic and Musical Research and, especially, the National Museum of Modern Art.

PONT NEUF (Bridge). The Pont Neuf (new bridge) is today the oldest bridge (q.v.) in Paris. Henri III laid the cornerstone for it in 1578. The work was interrupted from 1588 to 1599 by the wars of religion, political turbulence and the financial difficulties they caused. Henri IV inaugurated it in 1607.

Some 233 meters long, the Pont Neuf consists of two separate bridges that meet at a central earthen platform on the western tip of the Île de la Cité (q.v.), which has been graced since 1634 with an equestrian statue of Henri IV. For a long time this bridge was a center of attraction for the whole city. Its breadth, which was exceptional for the period, and the equally exceptional absence of houses on its parapets, immediately made it a very convenient passageway that was frequented by countless itinerant merchants. A hydraulic pump, called La Samaritaine (q.v.), occupied the second arch from the Right Bank from 1608 to 1813.

POOR RELIEF. Four types of assistance had developed up until the Revolution of 1789. The oldest, which may have emerged as early as

651, took the form of the Hôtel-Dieu, which received all the needy without distinction, fed and cared for them. At the end of the 12th century there sprang up charitable foundations established by the kings and queens, the great lords, the church and rich bourgeois. These foundations were usually specialized: the Quinze-Vingts were dedicated to the blind, the Saint-Esprit hospice received the orphans and Saint-Louis Hospital was reserved for infectious diseases and especially those stricken by plague. By 1789, there were already about 50 institutions of this sort, a dozen of them looking after abandoned children, the poor or orphans and about 20 asylums for elderly indigents.

In 1656, under Louis XIV (q.v.), a new type of relief for the poor was introduced, this time of an essentially repressive nature: the Hôpital-Général. This was basically a prison in which were locked up and forced to work the beggars and vagrants, who were accused of creating insecurity in the streets, as well as the prostitutes, the sight of whom offended the prudes. In 1789, some 12,000 indigents were imprisoned there, 1,200 children were in La Pitié, about 6,000 women were incarcerated in La Salpêtrière, and at Bicêtre 4,000 persons were packed in under horrible conditions.

There was a further form of assistance, this one taking various forms and hard to define, but consisting largely of relief distributed directly to the needy by charitable institutions, parishes, religious orders and pious and endowed secular associations. This complex structure was destroyed by the Revolution in 1789 and replaced by a single organization. *See also* Public Welfare.

PORCELAIN. Porcelain production developed in Paris with the discovery in 1769 of a deposit of kaolin in Limousin. Prior to that, there were some small works that made soft-paste porcelain, as well as the royal factory of Vincennes, which was subsequently transferred to Sèvres (q.v.). Between 1768 and 1781, 18 factories were established, 13 of them in Paris and five in the outskirts. Most of these enterprises were located in the Faubourg Saint-Antoine (q.v.). The Revolution of 1789 and the emigration of the well-to-do clientele ruined that luxury industry.

The return of peace in 1815 was not really favorable for any resurgence, since the French market was flooded with English porcelain. Of the 17 manufacturers in Paris in 1850, only four employed more than ten workers, and eight worked alone or with a single worker. However, there were 158 porcelain decorators, who could be found for the most part in the Boulevard Saint-Martin and Boulevard Saint-Denis, in the vicinity of the porcelain shops located in the Boulevard des Italiens, Boulevard de Bonne-Nouvelle, Rue Bleue and Rue de Paradis. Nowadays Paris does not manufacture porcelain, but rather specializes in decoration and marketing. The porcelain trade is concentrated in the Rue de Paradis.

PORT-ROYAL (Abbey, then Hospital) (123–125, Boulevard de Port-Royal). Presently included in the vast complex of Cochin Hospital, the buildings of the former abbey of Port-Royal were at the heart of the spiritual adventure of Jansenism (q.v.). In 1625, the Cistercian nuns of Port-Royal-des Champs (in the Chevreuse valley, several kilometers to the south of Paris) obtained authorization to relocate to the capital. Mother Angélique Arnauld, the convent's superior, had buildings constructed of an exceptional rigor and austerity. As she said, "I love through the spirit of Jesus Christ what is ugly."

On August 26, 1664, Mother Angélique and 75 nuns refused to sign the form recanting Jansenism that was presented to them by the archbishop. Jean Racine witnessed this scene and related it. Henri de Montherlant turned it into the plot of one of his plays. The nuns were then expelled and replaced by sisters of the Visitation, who were dedicated to the education of girls until 1790. The convent was secularized at that time. It was converted into a prison in 1793 with the unintentionally ironic name of Port-Libre (free port). Later on it became and remained a maternity center. In 1802, Chaptal founded a school for midwives there.

PORTS. The Right Bank of the Seine (q.v.), which is low and borders the wider and more rapid arm of the river, is in better condition to establish ports than the Left Bank, which is handicapped by the steep slope of Mount Saint-Geneviève (q.v.) and the narrowness of the smaller arm. Nonetheless, it was on the southern shore of the Île de la Cité (q.v.), to the south of the parvis of Notre-Dame (q.v.), that the Gallo-Roman port was located. This was doubtlessly because the ancient city developed very little on the Right Bank. However, as of the High Middle Ages, this port was transferred to the northern bank of the island, at the location of the Quai aux Fleurs, where the ports of Notre-Dame and Saint-Landry were to be found. Opposite, the port near Place de la Grève (q.v.) (presently Place de l'Hôtel-de-Ville) was developed during the 11th century.

At the height of the traditional river traffic during the 18th century, on the eve of the Industrial Revolution, there were about 20 ports in Paris. By 1840, with the regulation of the course of the Seine, even boats carrying heavy loads could navigate the river. Nowadays, the Autonomous Port of Paris is the leading river port of France. It accounts for half of the country's river traffic, with more than 22 million tons. The port facilities cover 800 hectares and extend along more than 70 kilometers of quays and wharfs. Almost all of the port of Paris, however, is located in the suburbs upstream and downstream from the capital.

PORTZAMPARC, CHRISTIAN DE (1944–   ). There has been a revival of French architecture after 40 years of hideous standardized construction that has generated endless and sinister suburbs. Christian de Portzamparc is the most remarkable example of this new generation of architects. He has worked mainly in Paris and the vicinity, designing among other things the housing complex of the Rue des Hautes-Formes (1975–79), which launched his career; old age homes; the Opéra's dance school, which won him the Silver T-Square of the periodical *Le Moniteur des Travaux publics et du Bâtiment*; and the Cité de la Musique at La Villette (q.v.). The originality and the quality of his work were rewarded in 1993 with the National Grand Prize of Architecture and in 1994 the Pritzker Prize, which is awarded by the Hyatt Foundation and is regarded as the equivalent of a Nobel Prize for architecture.

POSTAL BALLOONS. The postal balloons played a prominent role during the German siege of Paris. The photographer Nadar took the initiative of setting up a balloon company at Place Saint-Pierre in Montmartre (q.v.). The first balloon took off on September 23, 1870. On September 27, the Government of National Defense decreed the formation of the oldest airmail service in the world. Until January 28, 1871, 66 balloons (54 of them carrying 2.5 million letters) left Paris. The balloon *La Ville d'Orléans* went astray and traveled more than 1,300 kilometers to land in Norway, near Lifjeld, thereby establishing the world long-distance record of that time.

POUBELLE, EUGÈNE René (1831–1907). First the prefect of Charente in 1871 and then of Isère, Corsica, Doubs and Bouches-du-Rhône, Poubelle was appointed to head the Seine prefecture in 1883. He was entrusted with foiling the attempts of the municipal council to escape the tight control of the state and then asked to implement measures for the secularization of education and expulsion of the Jesuits. He left the Seine prefecture in 1896. Meanwhile, he had enriched the French language by lending his name to the special boxes that the Parisians were obliged to have to collect their garbage.

POULBOT, FRANCISQUE (1879–1946). A very productive artist, painter, illustrator and designer of posters, Poulbot created a type of *gamin* (q.v.) characteristic of Montmartre (q.v.): facetious, critical and sensitive, living in misery. This street urchin (called *poulbot*) symbolized the deprived, yet mocking and kindly, youth during the whole first half of the 20th century.

PRÉCIEUSES. Preciosity triumphed in Paris around 1650 thanks to the salons of the Marquise de Rambouillet, Madame de Montpensier, Madame de Sablé, Madame Scarron, Madame de Scudéry, Madame de Ventadour and the like. These ladies were the *précieuses* whose main concern was the quest for a refined language and a noble and purified style. Their efforts at purification of manners and language quickly degenerated, however, into worldliness, affectation, sentimentality and gibberish, and incited bitter satires, the best known of which is Molière's (q.v.) play *Les Précieuses Ridicules* (*The Affected Young Ladies*), staged in 1659.

PREFECT OF PARIS. The law of February 17, 1800 (Pluviôse 28, Year VIII), put at the head of each département a prefect who was "alone in charge of the administration." He concentrated in his hands the whole state machinery and possessed extremely broad powers. The prefect depended solely on the minister of the interior. In addition, the prefect of the département of the Seine exercised the functions of mayor (q.v.) of Paris until 1977. After the département of the Seine was abolished in 1964, the prefect assumed the title of prefect of Paris on January 1, 1968.

There have been 37 prefects of the Seine and nine prefects of Paris in 197 years, spending a bit more than four years in office on the average. Some of these prefects were particularly important and remained in office for extended periods: the first, Thérèse Benöit Nicolas Frochot (1800–12); the second and fourth, Gilbert Joseph Gaspard Chabrol de Volvic (1812 to March 1815 and July 1815–30); the eighth, Claude Philibert Barthelot de Rambuteau (q.v.) (1833–48); the 12th, Georges Eugène Haussmann (q.v.) (1853–70); the 20th, Eugène René Poubelle (q.v.) (1883–96); and the 21st, Justin Germain Casimir de Selves (1896–1911). At present, the prefects of Paris rarely stay for longer than five years.

PREFECT OF THE SEINE. *See* PREFECT OF PARIS.

PRÉVERT, JACQUES (1900–77). Closely acquainted with Marcel Duhamel, Raymond Queneau and Georges Sadoul, Jacques Prévert mixed with the surrealists; tried his hand at photography and cinema; got a bit part in *L'Age d'Or*, the first Surrealist film, by Luis Buñuel and Dali; and wrote scenarios for films, chansons and sketches for cabarets, and plays and playlets for the theater. More of an anarchist than a communist, he collaborated with the October theatrical team and went to Moscow with it, but he had the courage to refuse to sign a text in praise of Stalin. Prévert hated all religions, from Catholicism to Communism, and he had the greatest contempt for intellectualism.

A brilliant jack-of-all-trades, he made no particular effort to become known and achieved some success only as late as 1945. His collection of poetry, *Paroles*, published in 1946, sold more than a million copies. After spending almost his whole life treading the streets of Paris, he left the city in 1971 to end his days in the countryside, in Normandy.

PRINTING. Not long after Gutenberg set up his printing press on the banks of the Rhine, printing was born in Paris, in 1470, thanks to three printers from Basel: Martin Crantz, Michel Friburger and Ulrich Gering. The *Lettres* of Gasparino Barzizio, known as Gasparino of Bergamo, was the first book printed on the premises of the Sorbonne. The printers left that location very quickly, though, after being subjected to the persecution of the University (q.v.), which did not cease harassing the Parisian printers until the Revolution. Since most of the printers had converted to Calvinism, they fled Paris after the Saint-Bartholomew's Day (q.v.) massacre in 1572. In Holland, they founded a very powerful and flourishing printing and publishing trade in the French language that flooded France with forbidden books.

Meanwhile, in France, Louis XIV (q.v.) and his successors exercised very strict supervision over the Parisian printers, limiting their number to a maximum of 36 and tolerating only those works that were favorable to the absolute monarchy. It was not until the 19th century that Paris became one of the great capitals of printing. Now, at the close of the 20th century, the lack of space and endless conflicts with the strong leftist book workers' union have forced nearly all of the printers to leave Paris for the provinces, where manpower is cheaper and less affected by political and social agitation.

PROCOPE (Café) (13, Rue de l'Ancienne-Comédie). After he arrived in Paris in 1670, the Sicilian Francesco Procopio dei Coltelli first worked as a waiter for the Armenians Pascal and Maliban, who sold coffee, the then-fashionable "new aroma." In 1684, he set up his own café (q.v.) in the Rue des Fossés-Saint-Germain and was lucky that the Comédie-Française (q.v.) opened soon after just opposite in 1689. The Café Procope then became a meeting place for rich lords and financiers who patronized actresses, actors and writers. During the 18th century, the encyclopedists met there. Voltaire, d'Alembert, Diderot, Rousseau, Beaumarchais and others frequented it. During the Revolution, its clients included Danton (q.v.), Desmoulins, Fabre d'Eglantine and Marat (q.v.). During the Romantic era, Honoré de Balzac (q.v.), Théophile Gautier, George Sand and Alfred de Musset were regular guests. Turned into a restaurant, the Procope still exists, and it is possible to see the table where Voltaire sat.

PROUST, MARCEL (1871–1922). The life and work of Marcel Proust were devoted essentially to Paris. The seven novels making up *A la recherche du temps perdu* (*Remembrance of Things Past*) contain countless descriptions of the atmosphere of the Champs-Elysées (q.v.), the quarter in which he liked to reside; of the Bois de Boulogne (q.v.), where he went on walks; and of the aristocratic circles of the Faubourg Saint-Germain (q.v.), where he placed the Guermantes family. In his books it is possible to rediscover the mood of the city during the Belle Epoque, between 1900 and 1914, and especially to view a meticulous portrait of the life and manners of the aristocracy and the rich upper bourgeoisie.

PROVOST OF MERCHANTS. After Louis IX returned from the crusades in 1255, the Parisian municipality assumed the form it was to maintain until 1789. The head of the watermen's corporation took the title of provost of merchants and directed the municipality's affairs with the help of four magistrates (q.v.). In administering the city, he cooperated with the provost of Paris (q.v.), or royal provost. Some provosts of merchants played an important role and Étienne Marcel (q.v.) even revolted against the royal authority. Some 140 provosts of merchants are recorded, from the first one to be known, Evroïn de Valenciennes (1263), to the last, Jacques de Flesselles, who was killed by the mob on July 14, 1789.

PROVOST OF PARIS. The provost of Paris was an officer designated and removed by the king. He was entrusted with representing the sovereign in the provostry or viscounty of Paris and had both judicial and fiscal powers. His headquarters were at the Châtelet (q.v.). Initially, the provostship was let out for tender, but Louis IX reformed the office and gave it to a royal official paid by the state. The first of these officials seems to have been Étienne Boileau (q.v.) in 1261. By the 16th century the *lieutenant criminel* and *lieutenant civil* shared the bulk of the responsibilities of the royal provost, which were further restricted in 1667 with the introduction of the *lieutenant général de police* (q.v.). There were 84 royal provosts until the office was abolished in 1789.

PUBLIC LIGHTING. The distant origins of public lighting reach all the way back to an ordinance of 1318 that required the maintenance of three public lanterns in a town of 200,000 souls. Several attempts at public lighting were made during the 15th and 16th centuries, especially during times of unrest, so as to improve safety at night, but they never got anywhere because of the cost. The actual birth of public lighting dates back to the ordinance of September 2, 1667, by Louis

XIV, which ordered the permanent installation of lanterns. There were 3,000 of these lanterns by 1669 and 6,000 in 1729. This lighting was improved with the introduction of street lamps between 1745 and 1769, as they provided a much stronger light. There were 5,694 street lamps in 1789. In 1829, the municipality installed the first gas lamps, which became widespread by 1857 and reached their peak in 1890.

These lamps were soon replaced by electricity, which got off to a slow start. The first tests with electric lighting took place in 1843 at Place de la Concorde, but it was not until 1889 that the Municipal Council decided to electrify the capital. This was done progressively, with 130 million kilowatt-hours in 1913, 250 million in 1920 and more than 500 million in 1925. The process was completed in 1938, with consumption reaching a billion kilowatt-hours.

PUBLIC WELFARE. The Ancien Régime's system of poor relief (q.v.) was abolished by the Revolution but, because of a lack of resources, nothing replaced it until Napoléon Bonaparte took power. The consular decree of January 17, 1801, established a general council for the administration of Parisian hospices under the control of the prefect of the Seine (q.v.). A ministerial decree dated April 12, 1813, put under its guidance a relief board for each arrondissement. The law of January 10, 1849, established a General Administration of Public Welfare. Its director, appointed by the minister of the interior at the proposal of the prefect of the Seine, enjoys very broad powers. Since 1855, this administration has occupied its present premises at Victoria Avenue, just opposite the Hôtel de Ville. Public welfare underwent rapid expansion until 1914, with existing hospitals being reconstructed and many new establishments opening. Major work resumed in 1949.

As of 1961, several reforms were adopted to reduce the operating costs and improve the efficiency of an administration that had grown huge. The welfare component per se was withdrawn and was transferred to the public welfare boards of the municipalities of the arrondissements. In return, all the public hospitals in Paris and Île-de-France were attached to the Administration of Public Welfare, which now counts 49 establishments with more than 40,000 beds. *See also* Poor Relief.

-Q-

QUARTERS. Paris seems to have been divided into quarters between the late Roman period and the early Middle Ages. Three of them formed natural units: Île de la Cité (q.v.), Left Bank and Right Bank. In 1190, the construction of Philippe Auguste's wall (q.v.) increased the number to eight: the Cité, the two quarters of Maubert and Saint-André-des-Arts on the Left Bank, and five quarters on the Right Bank: Grève (q.v.), Verrerie, Saint-Jacques-de-la-Boucherie, Sainte-Opportune and Saint-German-l'Auxerrois. In 1380, the new wall built under Charles V (q.v.) brought the number of quarters to 16 with the creation of eight new quarters on the Right Bank: Saint-Antoine (q.v.), Saint-Gervais, Sainte-Avoye, Saint-Martin, Saint-Denis, the Halles (q.v.), Saint-Eustache and Saint-Honoré (q.v.).

The internal subdivision of these quarters was very complicated. To simplify the city's administration, in 1702 the king set up 20 police precincts. In 1789, for the elections to the Estates General, the city was divided into 60 districts. In May 1790, this division was replaced by 48 sections. Finally, in 1795, Paris was divided into 12 arrondissements (q.v.), each with four quarters. On January 1, 1860, with the incorporation of the neighboring communes, Paris went from 12 to 20 arrondissements and 48 to 80 quarters. These quarters are administrative creations and rarely correspond to historical or social entities.

-R-

RABANNE, FRANCISCO RABANEDA-CUERVO, known as PACO (1934–). From his mother, first assistant with Balenciaga, Paco Rabanne inherited his passion for fashion. He designed accessories, shoes and handbags for Balenciaga, Dior (q.v.) and Givenchy. Then, in 1965, he branched out into ready-to-wear accessories, plastic jewelry and glasses. In 1967, he opened his own haute couture (q.v.) house at 23, Rue du Cherche-Midi where he worked with new materials, dresses of plastic, paper, leather and aluminum. He made futuristic costumes for more than 35 films, including *Barbarella* and *Casino Royal*. He won countless awards for his revolutionary creations such as the Golden Tiberius for avant-garde fashion at Capri in 1967, the World Oscar for perfumery in the United States in 1975, the Golden Needle in 1977, and the Golden Thimble in 1990.

RAILWAY LINE AROUND PARIS. This circular railway line was built between 1851 and 1869 in order to connect Paris's six train stations with one another and to carry goods and passengers from one to another. Laid out within the confines of the city, it formed a belt of 34 kilometers in 1875, with 25 stations that were accessible to passengers in the capital. Even in its most prosperous phase, between 1890 and 1900, it never carried more than 10 percent of all public urban traffic. At its peak, in 1900, the year of the world exhibition, it was used by 32 million persons, but its traffic declined rapidly to 24 million in 1910 and 12 million in 1920. In 1934, it was closed to passengers and replaced by a bus line along the same belt route. This railway along the inner or small belt should not be confused with the railway along the outer or large belt, which is 91.5 kilometers long and circles the capital at a considerable distance, serving 33 suburban stations.

RAMBUTEAU, CLAUDE PHILIBERT BARTHELOT DE (1781– 1869). Thanks to his marriage to the daughter of Count Louis de Narbonne, a close associate of Emperor Napoléon I, Rambuteau began a brilliant career as prefect in 1811 in the départements of Simplon (presently Valais in Switzerland) and then Loire. Dismissed in 1815 by Louis XVIII for having rallied to Napoléon during the Hundred Days, he was elected deputy of Mâcon in 1827 and joined the liberal opposition.

On June 22, 1833, Rambuteau was appointed prefect of the Seine (q.v.) and he remained in that office until the Revolution of February 24, 1848, which overthrew Louis-Philippe. He did his best to modernize Paris by expanding the sewer system, building sidewalks along all the streets, installing public lighting (q.v.) with gas, planting trees, creating the first squares and, above all, considerably improving the water supply (q.v.). His work was limited by a lack of financial resources and the half-hearted policy of the government. It was left to Haussmann (q.v.) to carry out the projects that Rambuteau had dreamed of undertaking.

REGISTRY OFFICE. The registers of baptisms, marriages and deaths were kept by the Catholic clergy until the Revolution of 1789 and then by the municipal administration. The oldest of these registers dates back to 1515. The obligation of keeping registers was introduced for the parish priests by the ordinance of 1539. When the Communards set fire (q.v.) to the Hôtel de Ville (q.v.) and then the Palais de Justice (q.v.) in 1871, the originals and copies of about 5,000 registers prior to 1792 and 7,500 others kept by the town halls between 1792 and 1859 were destroyed. The law of February 12, 1872, ordered the reconstitution of the registers that were destroyed but that has been possible for only about a third of the eight million documents that disappeared. Today, each arrondissement keeps its own registers. Registration at churches does not exist legally. Civil registration is compulsory and civil marriage must occur before any religious ceremony.

RENAUDOT, THÉOPHRASTE (1586–1653). The Protestant doctor Théophraste Renaudot was a multifaceted genius. After settling down in Paris, he enjoyed the protection of Richelieu, who appointed him commissioner general of the poor of the kingdom. In 1630, he opened an address bureau that served various purposes: as an information office, a placement agency for servants and workers and a mont-de-piété, or pawnshop (*see* Crédit Municipal). The notices that were printed by the bureau gave him the idea of founding, on May 30, 1631, the first French newspaper, *La Gazette,* the future *Gazette de France.* In 1635, he opened a dispensary from which he provided care free of charge for the poor. After Richelieu's death in 1642, his enemies among the Catholics and doctors saw to it that he was not allowed to practice medicine.

RESTAURANTS. The restaurant, a Parisian invention that grew out of the medieval tavern, can be distinguished by two essential features: the client is served at an individual table and he chooses his dishes from a menu that lists them. The oldest restaurant seems to have been created by a certain Boulanger, in the Rue des Poulies, near the Louvre (q.v.). The first restaurant to become a success because of its refined atmosphere was the Taverne Anglaise of the Palais-Royal (q.v.) run by Antoine Beauvilliers in 1786. The rise of the restaurants during the last years of the 18th century took place at the same time as the emergence of gastronomy (q.v.). The most renowned restaurants could be found at the Palais-Royal. One of them, Le Grand Véfour (q.v.), still exists.

After 1835, the Palais-Royal was supplanted by the grand boulevards (q.v.), with Tortoni, Café de Paris, Café Riche, Café Anglais and Maison Dorée. By 1900 there was an impressive number of restaurants of exceptional quality, such as Laurent and Fouquet's at the Champs-Elysées (q.v.), the Pavillon d'Armenonville and Pavillon de la Cascade in the Bois de Boulogne (q.v.), Weber in the Rue Royale, Prunier in the Rue Duphot, Drouant at Place Gaillon, Tour d'Argent (q.v.) at the Quai de la Tournelle, Lucas and then Carton at the Madeleine and Maxim's (q.v.) in the Rue Royale. The gastronomic tradition continues to this day with the Michelin and the Gault and Millau guides, which distinguish the best tables by granting them four chef's caps. *See also* Bistros; Café; Gastronomy; Lipp; Maxim's; Robuchon; Tour d'Argent, La; Train Bleu, Le; Véfour, Le Grand.

RESTIF DE LA BRETONNE, NICOLAS ANNE EDME RÉTIF, or (1734–1806). Restif de La Bretonne, from Burgundy, arrived in Paris in 1755 where he worked as a printer while writing licentious books. He had some success with *Le Paysan perverti* (1776), *La Vie de mon père* (1779), *Les Contemporaines* (1780), *La Paysanne pervertie* (1784), *Les Parisiennes* (1787) and *Ingénue Saxancourt* (1789). His principal works on Paris are *Le Palais-Royal* (1790, 3 volumes) and *Les Nuits de Paris* (1788–93, 8 volumes), in which he told about his nighttime experiences. A rather dubious character who served as a police informer, Restif was an important witness of Parisian life during the second half of the 18th century, but his writing can be trusted only so far, because he manifests a definite tendency toward exaggeration.

REVOLUTIONARY TRIBUNAL. The uprising in the Vendée and the threat of foreign armies at France's borders put the supporters of the Revolution in a dangerous situation in early March 1793. To face the threat, the Convention voted on March 10, 1793, to establish a Revolutionary Tribunal, whose seat would be in Paris. Its judgments were final and had to be carried out within 24 hours. The Revolutionary Tribunal was presided over by Montané, who, accused of being too moderate, was replaced by tools of Robespierre (q.v.), Herman and then Dumas. Its linchpin was the public prosecutor Fouquier-Tinville.

Some 5,343 persons were prosecuted. Of them, 2,747 were condemned to death and guillotined. Among the victims 20 percent were nobles, nine percent clerics and 71 percent members of the Third Estate, of which 41 percent were artisans and 28 percent farmers. The Revolutionary Tribunal's activities accelerated after the proclamation of the Terror (q.v.) on September 5, 1793, and reached a fever pitch during the Great Terror, from June 11 to July 27, 1794. After Robespierre's execution on July 28, the Revolutionary Tribunal slowed down. It condemned its presidents Dumas and Herman as well as Fouquier-Tinville to death before being disbanded on May 31, 1795.

REX (Cinema) (1, Boulevard Poissonière). Cinema Rex, which was built in 1932 by Auguste Bluysen and John Eberson, was modeled after the fancier American movie theaters. The decoration, the work of Maurice Dufrène, was a decor of an ancient Greco-Roman city enlivened by the lighting. The ceiling represented a starlit sky with passing clouds. Originally, the Rex had 3,300 seats and two balconies. Since 1981, Cinema Rex is listed in the supplementary inventory of historic monuments, which protects it from real estate speculation and debasement.

RICCI, MARIA NIELLI, called NINA (1883–1970). Of Italian origin, Nina Ricci arrived in Paris at the age of 14 and later married Luigi Ricci. Starting as a junior assistant in several haute couture (q.v.) houses, she worked her way up the hierarchy and ended up as the associate of the couturier Raffin, who died in 1929. In 1932, with her son Robert, she founded an haute couture house at 20, Rue des Capucines. Her reputation was guaranteed in 1946 by the success of her perfume "Coeur-Joie," followed in 1948 by another famous perfume, "Air du Temps."

RITZ (Hotel) (15, Place Vendôme). In 1896, the Swiss César Ritz bought the Lauzun Hotel, which had been built in 1705. Behind the classical façade of Mansart on Place Vendôme, the building was refitted by Charles Mewès, who personally designed and chose the decoration and furniture. Inaugurated on June 1, 1898, the hotel (q.v.) immediately received the international high society. One of its first and most faithful clients was Marcel Proust (q.v.), who described in his novels the head waiter Olivier Dabescat, who Edouard Bourdet put on the stage in his play *Le Sexe Faible*. The quality of the cooking was exceptional, thanks to the talent of Auguste Escoffier.

The Cambon bar, which was opened in 1921, was frequented solely by British and Americans, Fitzgerald and Hemingway (q.v.) among others. Coco Chanel (q.v.) made the hotel her permanent residence as of 1934 and stayed there until she passed away in 1971. Louis Bromfield described the hotel's atmosphere during the 1940s in *What Became of Anna Bolton?* The hotel was acquired by Mohamed El-Fayed in 1979 and entirely renovated. The basement was fitted with swimming pool and gym. Nowadays the Ritz has 152 rooms and 35 apartments, 10 of them prestigious suites, and employs 500 persons.

RIVER BRIGADE. Until the Revolution the Seine (q.v.) was policed by the watermen, who were at the origin of the Parisian municipality. In 1800, the policing of navigation in the Seine département was entrusted to the chief commissioner of police. Until 1845, the force had only a rowboat. In 1855, the first pump boat was put into service. On June 30, 1900, on the occasion of the world exhibition, Chief Commissioner Lépine (q.v.) set up the river brigade. It consisted of a punt with oars, diving suits and about 20 divers. As of 1904, it had two motor launches, *La Vigie* and *La Mouette*. Today, the river brigade handles the supervision of the Seine from Ablon to Bougival and is staffed by 64 policemen (47 of them divers) under the orders of the chief commissioner. Its equipment consists, in part, of six motor boats, three rubber dinghies, and a tow-push boat. It carries out nearly 2,000 operations a year. Its headquarters have been located on the Quay Saint-Bernard since 1991.

ROBESPIERRE, MAXIMILIEN MARIE ISIDORE DE (1758–94). After brilliant studies at Collège Louis-le-Grand (q.v.), Robespierre returned to his hometown of Arras to practice as a lawyer. In 1789, he was elected by Artois to the Estates General, where he became one of the principal orators of the Revolution. He exerted great influence on the Club des Jacobins (q.v.) and backed the insurrection of August 10, 1792, which overthrew the monarchy. In September 1792, he was elected as a deputy from Paris to the Convention, where he allied with

Danton (q.v.) and Marat (q.v.) to lead the Montagnards and oppose the moderate Girondins. After they were eliminated on June 2, 1793, Robespierre turned against his allies, eliminating the Hébertists in March and then the Dantonists in April 1794.

By now virtually a dictator and imbued with the ideas of Jean-Jacques Rousseau, he celebrated the Festival of the Supreme Being on June 8, 1794, which marked his apotheosis, and launched the Terror (q.v.) on June 11. Sated with mass executions and fearing for their own existence, the deputies to the Convention finally united against him and had him arrested. Deserted by the Parisian crowds, which were sickened by the executions of Hébert and Danton, he was tried on July 28, 1794, and guillotined the same day, along with 21 of his supporters. Robespierre's disappearance brought to an end the bloodiest period of the Revolution.

ROBUCHON, JOËL (1945–). Often regarded as the best cook in France, and even in the world, Joël Robuchon refined his talents in several restaurants (q.v.) and hotels (q.v.) before setting up on his own with the Jamin restaurant from 1981 to 1994. He then took charge of the Joël Robuchon restaurant at 59, Avenue Raymond-Poincaré. He is the author of several cookbooks, including *Simply French* (1991).

RODIN, AUGUSTE (1840–1917). Fortunately for his genius, Auguste Rodin failed the competition to attend the École des Beaux-Arts three times. He therefore escaped the sterile teaching that was dispensed there and forged his talent in the atelier of the sculptor Carrier-Belleuse, where bronze works of art were cast. His refusal to mix in the political quarrels of the time kept Rodin from receiving official orders, and his works were often turned down by the salons. His bust of Balzac (q.v.) created a scandal and was rejected by the Société des Gens de Lettres. In 1900, he exhibited his own sculptures in a house he had rented at Place de l'Alma. This show was a tremendous success. Rodin left his works to the state, and his atelier at 77, Rue de Varenne, was turned into the Rodin Museum.

ROLAND-GARROS (Stadium) (2, Avenue Gordon-Bennett). The architects Roussel and Faure-Dujarric built the initial Roland-Garros stadium in 1928 to receive the Challenge Round of the Davis Cup. The success of the French Open tennis championships in 1970 brought new installations and considerable expansion. To the central court, which can hold 16,500 spectators, has been added Court No. 1 for 4,500 persons. The complex, located in the Bois de Boulogne (q.v.), covers 5.7 hectares and includes 32 tennis courts: 19 outdoor clay courts, eight covered courts and five indoor courts. The encounter at

Roland-Garros has become a must for tennis players around the world and for Parisian snobs during the French Open, which is held in late May or early June.

ROTONDE, LA (Café). Opened in 1911, the Café de la Rotonde, along with the Dôme (q.v.) and the Coupole (q.v.), was one of the in places for the artistic and literary crowd of Montparnasse (q.v.) during the first 40 years of the 20th century. Among the Rotonde's regular clients were Apollinaire, Derain, Max Jacob, Modigliani, Picasso (q.v.), Salmon, Vlaminck and others. In 1923, it was expanded and the café (q.v.) was joined by a nightclub, dance hall and art gallery. In 1958, it was replaced by a cinema (q.v.), later becoming a restaurant (q.v.) with the name of La Rotonde en Montparnasse. The Rotonde was located at 105, Boulevard du Montparnasse.

ROULE (Faubourg). *See* SAINT-HONORÉ (Faubourg).

ROYAL RESIDENCES. Until the beginning of the 13th century, the only residence the kings had in Paris was the one that had already been occupied by the Roman governors, the Palais de la Cité, presently called Palais de Justice (q.v.). When the Louvre (q.v.) was completed in 1202, Philippe II Auguste (q.v.) moved in. Charles V (q.v.), who was king from 1364 to 1380, resided in the Palais, the Louvre, the château of Vincennes (q.v.) and the Hôtel Saint-Paul, or Saint-Pol, near the Bastille (q.v.). The Hôtel des Tournelles, which belonged to the dukes of Orléans, became the royal residence in 1498, when Louis d'Orléans became King Louis XII. It was demolished after Henri II died there in 1559, and Place des Vosges (q.v.) now occupies that location.

When he died in 1642, Richelieu bequeathed his Palais-Cardinal to the king, and the young Louis XIV (q.v.) lived there. It was in that building, renamed Palais-Royal (q.v.), that he experienced the painful events of the Fronde (q.v.). The Tuileries (q.v.), built as of 1564 for the queen mother Catherine de Medicis, housed Louis XVI and his family from October 1789 to August 1792, then Napoléon I, Louis XVIII, Charles X, Louis-Philippe and Napoléon III. In May 1871, it was burned down in a fire (q.v.) set by the Communards. Three of the six Parisian residences of the kings of France still exist: the first, the Palais de Justice; the second, the Louvre; the fifth, the Palais-Royal.

-S-

SACRÉ-COEUR (Basilica) (Place du Parvis-du-Sacré-Coeur). When Rome was annexed to the Kingdom of Italy in September 1870,

Pope Pius IX locked himself in the Vatican and claimed to be a prisoner. In December 1870, a group of Catholics decided to raise up a sanctuary dedicated to the Sacred Heart and consecrated to the salvation of France as well as to the deliverance of the pope. In December 1873, the National Assembly declared that it was in the public interest to construct this basilica and authorized the purchase of the necessary land on the hill of Montmartre (q.v.). The construction of the Sacré-Coeur aroused a controversy that still exists, with leftist and secular politicians regarding the Sacré-Coeur as a religious provocation and an act of atonement for the Commune (q.v.) of 1871.

In 1875, the cornerstone was laid, but it was not until 1919 that the basilica was consecrated. The architect, Paul Abadie, had to bore 83 holes 33 meters deep, fill them with concrete, and connect them with archs, in order to have sufficiently solid foundations, since the hill was riddled with quarries. As the plot of land was rather narrow (85 meters long and 35 meters wide), he was also forced to design a building organized around a large rotunda but with very short arms. An architectural hodgepodge, the Sacré-Coeur was patterned after the Romanesque churches of Charente for its façade, Saint-Front in Périgueux for its porch and Byzantine churches for its general arrangement and domes. Although this incongruous monument is unquestionably ugly, seen from a distance it does possess a certain majesty because of the exceptional site and the whiteness of its stones. Along with the Cathedral of Notre-Dame (q.v.), the Arc de Triomphe at the Étoile (q.v.) and the Eiffel Tower (q.v.), it is a building known worldwide that symbolizes Paris.

SAINT-ANTOINE (Faubourg). Straddling the Rue du Faubourg-Saint-Antoine, its main artery, the Faubourg Saint-Antoine is presently divided between the 11th and 12th arrondissements. Born with the Royal Abbey of Saint-Antoine, founded in 1198, this eastern faubourg of Paris underwent an exceptional development thanks to the ordinance of 1471, which freed its craftsmen from the constraining regulations of the guilds. Woodworking then assumed particular importance and, at the end of the 15th century, the Faubourg Saint-Antoine became a melting pot that fused the tastes and techniques coming from Burgundy, Flanders, Germany and Italy. Here it was that Renaissance art was applied to furniture making, giving rise to the Henri II style. During the 17th century, a mirror factory was established at 20, Rue de Reuilly. Porcelain (q.v.) and china works prospered in the Rue de Charonne, Rue de la Roquette, Rue Amelot and the intersection of Rue de Reuilly and Rue de Montreuil. Réveillon, the manufacturer of printed wallpaper, opened a factory in the Rue de Montreuil, and coppersmiths and tinsmiths from Auvergne set up shop in Saint-Louis Court and the Rue de Lappe.

On the eve of the Revolution of 1789, the Faubourg Saint-Antoine accounted for about one-tenth of the area of Paris. Its workers and craftsmen formed the vanguard of the Revolution and provided the broad masses of *sans-culottes* (q.v.). A majority of those who took the Bastille (q.v.) on July 14, 1789, came from this faubourg, which laid claim to the title of "Faubourg of Glory" for its feats. The Faubourg Saint-Antoine was in the forefront of all the mass movements of the 19th century, notably during the revolutions of 1830 and 1848 and the Commune (q.v.) of 1871. Today, industry has left the faubourg, but woodworking has been preserved with the famous Boulle School and prestigious firms.

SAINT BARTHOLOMEW'S DAY MASSACRE. This is the name given to the worst bloodshed in the history of Paris. It arose out of a reversal in royal policy with regard to the Protestants. Catherine de Médicis had given up trying to break their resistance and wanted closer relations with their leader, Henri de Bourbon, king of Navarre. Since her children were degenerate and incapable of procreating, she suggested to her son, Charles IX, that he reconcile himself with the heretics. However, the feeble-minded king soon fell under the influence of Admiral Coligny, one of the heads of the Protestant party, who urged him to support the Protestants in the Netherlands who had revolted against the king of Spain. The marriage of the king's sister, Marguerite de Valois, to Henri de Bourbon was to seal the alliance between the monarchy and the Calvinists.

Catherine de Médicis could not tolerate being supplanted by Coligny as the advisor to the king, her son, and feared a war with Spain. She therefore sought to have Admiral Coligny killed, this in cooperation with the ultra-Catholics of the Guise family, but on August 22, 1572, Coligny was only wounded. Rushing to his bedside, Charles IX swore to punish the authors of this attempted assassination. Catherine then admitted to her son that she had participated in the plot and managed to convince this inconsistent being to order the massacre of the Protestants who had flocked to Paris to attend the wedding of their leader.

The signal for the carnage was given on August 24, 1572, shortly before dawn, around 4:00 A.M., by the bells of Saint-Germain-l'Auxerrois sounding the matins for the feast of Saint Bartholomew. Within the walls of the Louvre (q.v.), the flower of the Protestant nobility was cut down, including the Caumonts, La Rochefoucaulds, Pardaillans and Soubises. Many members of the *Parlement,* professors, doctors, printers and booksellers had their throats slit while they slept. The bloodbath continued until August 27 and, according to eyewitnesses, cost the lives of at least three thousand people; some even estimate the number of victims at ten thousand. The looting of their houses, according to the Venetian ambassador, brought the killers at least two million golden crowns.

SAINT-DENIS (Basilica). Some 12 kilometers to the north of the Cathedral of Notre-Dame (q.v.) is the town of Saint-Denis. It is there that according to legend the tomb of Saint Denis was located. The Parisians went there on pilgrimages, and Saint Geneviève (q.v.) had a church built on that spot in about 475. King Dagobert had an abbey constructed there around 625. It became the main burial place of the kings of the Merovingian and Capetian dynasties. Charlemagne had it rebuilt in 775. Suger, the principal advisor to Louis VI, had the church rebuilt again, and it was one of the first monuments of Gothic art. Only part of that edifice, dating from 1137 to 1144, remains because Pierre and Eudes de Montreuil redid the nave, center of the choir and transept between 1231 and 1265.

Until the Revolution, the basilica of Saint-Denis was intimately connected with the history of the monarchy. That is where the queens of France were crowned, the kings being crowned in Reims, and it is where Henri IV abjured Protestantism. The chronicle written by the monks of Saint-Denis served as the official history of the kingdom during the Middle Ages. The abbey's buildings were reconstructed during the 18th century and, as of 1809, used as the educational house of the Légion d'Honneur. During the Revolution, the basilica barely escaped being torn down, but the royal tombs were profaned and the sculptures damaged. It was restored by Viollet Le Duc between 1848 and 1870. Saint-Denis was also an important economic center during the early Middle Ages thanks to the annual Lendit Fair.

SAINT-EUSTACHE (Church) (2, Rue du Jour). It was on the site of a small church dating back to 1210 that the cornerstone was laid in 1532 for a new edifice that François I wanted to serve as an example of the new Renaissance style. However, the king preferred spending his own money on the châteaux of the Loire so the bourgeois of the Halles (q.v.) had to foot the bill. The church rose slowly and was finished only in 1640. Its architecture was inspired much more by the late Gothic than the spirit of the Renaissance, which appears only in the interior decoration. Saint-Eustache is nearly as large as the Cathedral of Notre-Dame (q.v.), on which it was modeled. The church lost its spire, and the main façade, of mixed style and incomplete, was redone in the 18th century.

SAINT-GERMAIN (Faubourg). The construction of the abbey of Saint-Germain-des-Prés (q.v.) in 558 or 559 gave rise to the development of a small market town within the orbit of the monastery. It was not absorbed within the wall (q.v.) of Philippe Auguste in 1209 and remained outside the limits of the expanding city. Until the end of the Middle Ages the town of Saint-Germain remained a fairly rural place where the students from Mount Sainte-Geneviève (q.v.) went to enjoy themselves at the Pré-aux-Clercs. However, their turbulence and acts of violence, sometimes actually criminal, generated countless conflicts between the University (q.v.), which protected them, and the abbott of Saint-Germain-des-Prés, the local lord who protected the inhabitants.

Under Henri IV, the Faubourg Saint-Germain was integrated into the city with the construction of the Pont Neuf (q.v.) and the opening of the Rue Dauphine. At this time, magnificent residences surrounded by gardens sprang up, and it became the favorite place for the nobility, which settled between the Seine (q.v.) and Palais du Luxembourg (q.v.), which was built for Marie de Médicis. As of 1625, the Faubourg Saint-Germain expanded westward, beyond the Rue du Bac and as far as the Quai d'Orsay, which was still called the Grenouillère at that time. As of 1671, Louis XIV (q.v.) had the Invalides (q.v.) erected at the western limit of the Faubourg Saint-Germain.

During the 18th century, new mansions were built, many of which still exist, in particular the Hôtel Matignon (q.v.), the Palais Bourbon (q.v.) and the present Rodin Museum (*see* Rodin, Auguste). The arrogance of that well-to-do aristocracy, which kept to its own sort, was admirably described by Honoré de Balzac (q.v.) and Marcel Proust (q.v.). By 1919, the wealthy had become more discreet and gradually moved away from "the Faubourg," selling the magnificent private mansions, which were turned into embassies and administrative offices.

SAINT-GERMAIN-DES-PRÉS (Church) (Place Saint-Germain-des-Prés). Consecrated in 558 or 559, the church of Saint-Germain-des-Prés was part of an abbey that was first named Saint-Vincent. It assumed the name of the bishop Saint Germain, who was buried there in 576, after that saint was canonized. Several Frankish kings were also interred there during the sixth and seventh centuries. The abbey was sacked by the Norsemen during the ninth century. The church was reconstructed: between 990 and 1014 for the belfry porch, and between 1025 and 1030 for the nave. The choir was repaired during the second half of the 12th century and the monastic buildings were reconstructed during the 13th century.

As the mother house of the Benedictine Congregation of Saint-Maur as of 1631, the abbey of Saint-Germain-des-Prés was at the forefront of historic research during the 17th and 18th centuries, with such erudite scholars as Mabillon. During the Revolution, the monastic buildings were sold and destroyed, aside from the abbatial palace, which was partially saved. Although now just a parish church, it has survived and remains one of the oldest monuments of religious architecture in Paris.

SAINT-GERMAIN-DES-PRÉS (Quarter). A quarter in the 6th arrondissement located near the church of the same name, Saint-Germain-des-Prés took on its own identity only at the end of the 19th century. The presence of numerous publishing houses in that neighborhood near the Latin Quarter (q.v.) attracted writers such as Alphonse Daudet, Edmond de Goncourt, Remy de Gourmont, Joris Karl Huysmans and Emile Zola (q.v.), then the group from the *Nouvelle Revue Française* consisting of Gallimard, Jacques Copeau, André Gide and Jean Schlumberger. Ever since the beginning of the 20th century, 200 snobs of Saint-Germain-des-Prés have been manufacturing famous authors of a French literature that is increasingly inward-looking and decreasingly read. This writer factory operates discreetly, and only insiders and upstarts frequent its literary cafés (q.v.).

It was not until 1945, when two inhabitants of the quarter, Jean-Paul Sartre and Simone de Beauvoir, launched the fashion of existentialism that Saint-German-des-Prés became an international beacon. Then the Café de Flore (q.v.), Brasserie Lipp (q.v.) and Les Deux Magots (q.v.) achieved a boisterous celebrity while local wine cellars were turned into nightclubs animated by emulators of Boris Vian and Juliette Greco. This artificial and adulterated world has had its day.

SAINT-GERMAIN-EN-LAYE (Château). In 1126, King Louis VI had a castle built alongside the forest of Saint-Germain-en-Laye, about 20 kilometers to the west of his palace on the Île de la Cité (q.v.). Burned down by the English in 1346 but restored in 1367, the castle was razed under François I, and the architect Pierre de Chambiges constructed a Renaissance palace in its place as of 1539. In this château Henri II and his son Charles IX were born. King James II of England lived there after being overthrown in 1688. Louis XIV (q.v.) and his court stayed at Saint-Germain-en-Laye frequently while waiting for Versailles (q.v.) to be ready to receive them in 1682. Le Nôtre built a magnificent terrace with an exceptional view in 1672. The château was restored in 1862 and converted into a museum of Gallo-Roman antiquities.

SAINT-HONORÉ (Faubourg). When Louis XIV (q.v.) died in 1715, the limit of Paris was to the west of Porte Saint-Honoré (Rue Royale). Beyond that, there were only vegetable gardens until the little village of Roule. Gradually the restrictions on building were relaxed and, by

1765, houses stretched all the way to the faubourg of Roule, whose name was given to a quarter of the 8th arrondissement. In 1847, the roadway, or faubourg, of Roule was renamed Rue du Faubourg-Saint-Honoré. Wealthy aristocrats, bankers and financiers had lovely country houses, or follies (q.v.), built there during the 18th century. During the following centuries, while the proud porches of the private mansions remained, what truly distinguished the Faubourg Saint-Honoré were the luxury shops. Dressmakers, men's shirtmakers, and perfumers occupied premises right next to antique shops, book stores and galleries of contemporary art. The presidential Palais de l'Elysée (q.v.) and the British and American embassies are among the most prestigious buildings in the quarter.

SAINT-JACQUES (Tower) (Square de la Tour-Saint-Jacques). The parish church of Saint-Jacques-de-la-Boucherie was built between 1508 and 1522. During the Revolution, it became national property and was torn down in 1797. However, one of the towers remained. It was consolidated and restored in 1853 by Théodore Ballu. It has three stories and ends with a terrace on which Blaise Pascal carried out his experiments on the weight of air in 1648 and that presently serves as a meteorological station. The many allegorical sculptures of the tower have aroused curiosity and contributed to the spread of an esoteric legend about this edifice. *See* Alchemy.

SAINT-LAURENT, YVES (1936–). The associate of couturier Christian Dior (q.v.) in 1954, Yves Saint-Laurent succeeded him as the director of the haute couture (q.v.) house. For nearly 40 years, he has symbolized French and Parisian fashion and taste. He has won many awards. In 1958, he received the Neiman-Marcus Oscar for Couture in Dallas. In 1966, he obtained the Harper's Bazaar Oscar. In 1985, his life's work was crowned with the Fashion Oscar. His establishment is located at 5, Avenue Marceau.

SAINT-LOUIS (Island). First called Notre-Dame island, the Île Saint-Louis remained uninhabited until the beginning of the 17th century. Cows grazed peacefully in the pastures, lumber merchants stored their planks and beams, and washerwomen spread out their sheets on the fields to let the sun bleach them whiter. In 1614, Christophe Marie obtained authorization to divide the island into lots and to put up houses on the sole condition that he build bridges (q.v.) to link the two banks. These became the Marie and Tournelle bridges. In association with two financiers, Lugles Poulletier and François Le Regrattier, Marie went to work. Within 30 years, in the heart of Paris, there emerged a modern city designed with taste and symmetry and endowed with

straight and regular streets. In fact, admiring Parisians of that time often called it the "enchanted island."

Magnificent mansions, many of them built by Le Vau, made this
one of the favorite places of residence for the well-to-do aristocracy
of the 17th century. Renamed Saint-Louis in 1726, the island had
ceased being fashionable by the 18th century and was inhabited only
by less well-off businessmen. In 1783, Mercier (q.v.) described the Île
Saint-Louis as a "third-rate provincial town." Looking a bit cold and
constrained, the island is at present a village of 6,000 inhabitants in
the middle of the capital, away from the hustle and bustle, without a
métro (q.v.) or much automobile traffic and served by only one bus
(q.v.) line. It is almost a museum of 17th-century architecture.

SAINT-SULPICE (Church) (Place Saint-Sulpice). The first church of
Saint-Sulpice, which had been built around 1211, had become too
small by the beginning of the 17th century, so it was decided to rebuild
it. The queen mother Anne of Austria laid the cornerstone of the new
edifice on February 20, 1646. However, since money ran short, the
construction work was frequently interrupted and one architect was
replaced by another: Gamard, Le Vau, Gittard, Oppenord, Servan-
doni, Patte, Oudot de Maclaurin and Chalgrin. Each of them altered
his predecessor's designs and the building, which was completed only
in 1780, is marked by heterogeneity and mediocrity: an austere and
massive façade with dissimilar towers and a nave cluttered with heavy
pillars that obstruct the view and get in the way.

SAINT-VICTOR (Abbey). Once a prestigious rival of the abbeys of
Saint-Germain-des-Prés (q.v.) and Sainte-Geneviève (q.v.), nowadays
Saint-Victor is largely forgotten and remembered only because of the
Rue Saint-Victor. In 1108, Guillaume de Champeaux, the famous professor of theology at the school of Notre-Dame Cathedral (q.v.),
founded a hermitage that was turned into an abbey for regular canons in
1113. Under his direction, Saint-Victor abbey became one of the leading centers of Gregorian reform and the teaching of theology. Its professors came from everywhere: Hugues de Saint-Victor was Flemish;
Archard de Saint-Victor, Norman; André de Saint-Victor, English; and
Richard de Saint-Victor, Scottish or Irish. Saint-Victor's prestige was
so great that in 1148 Pope Eugene III entrusted it with the reform of the
neighboring abbey of Sainte-Geneviève. This reform was carried out so
successfully that by 1176 the convent on the mount had eclipsed Saint-
Victor, particularly because of the dynamism of Sainte-Geneviève's abbot, Étienne de Tournai. While closely connected with the life of the
University (q.v.), Saint-Victor's existence ended in 1790. In that year,
it became national property, only to be sold off and destroyed in 1811.

SAINTE-BARBE (Collège) (4, Rue Valette). Founded in 1460, the Collège Sainte-Barbe is the last survivor of about 50 medieval *collèges* (q.v.) that were scattered over the Mount Sainte-Geneviève (q.v.). Among its pupils were John Calvin and Ignatius of Loyola, and it was involved in all the religious controversies that stirred up the University (q.v.). It was closed in 1789 but its buildings were brought back and teaching resumed in 1798. In 1802, it reverted to its name of Sainte-Barbe. Its buildings were reconstructed in 1841 by Théodore and Henri Labrouste. Despite several periods of financial difficulty, Sainte-Barbe has never ceased functioning, thanks to the generosity of its former pupils, who include Paul Bourget, Gustave Eiffel, Léon Gaumont, Jean Jaurès and Charles Péguy.

SAINTE-CHAPELLE (Chapel) (4, Boulevard du Palais). Pious King Louis IX, better known as Saint Louis, paid substantial amounts of gold to Baudouin II, the emperor of Constantinople and king of Jerusalem, to acquire some dubious fragments of the cross and of Christ's crown of thorns. To house these relics, he had the Sainte-Chapelle built between 1241 and 1248. Pierre de Montreuil is often regarded as the architect. The building is 36 meters long, 17 meters wide and 42.5 meters high, which gave it an exceptional upward thrust and the appearance of the jewel-encrusted reliquaries of that time.

The edifice consists of two superimposed chapels. The one on the ground floor was for parish worship of the inhabitants of the Palais de la Cité or Palais de Justice (q.v.). The upper chapel was reserved for the king and his retinue and housed the precious relics. The immense windows of the upper chapel have preserved their admirable stained glass, but the statues suffered considerably from vandalism during the Revolution and had to be restored between 1837 and 1857. At the same time, there was a clumsy restoration of the painted decorations.

SAINTE-GENEVIÈVE (Abbey and Mount). On the heights dominating the Seine (q.v.) to the south of the Île de la Cité (q.v.), the Gallo-Romans built the most important part of Lutetia. There could be found the baths, arenas, theater and forum on top of a "mountain" that hardly deserved the name, since it was not even 60 meters high. It was named Mount Sainte-Geneviève after Saint Geneviève was buried on the top of that supposed mountain in about 502. An abbey was constructed above her tomb, first named after the holy apostles and then Saint Geneviève herself. It was consecrated in 520.

To get away from the burdensome tutorship of the bishop and his chapter of canons, the students deserted the Île de la Cité as of the second half of the 12th century and sought refuge at the foot of the mount, under the easy-going authority of Sainte-Geneviève, which allowed scholarly establishments to proliferate and even became a prestigious center of theological studies after being reformed by Saint-Victor (q.v.) in 1148. Until 1789, the same topographical reality was referred to indifferently by the three terms of University (q.v.), Latin Quarter (q.v.) and Mount Sainte-Geneviève. Louis XV decided to have a new church built for Saint Geneviève, which became the Panthéon (q.v.). After becoming national property in 1790, the abbey was torn down and all that remains is the Clovis tower, which is incorporated in the Lycée Henri IV, which was built on the same spot and still preserves the main reading room of the convent library.

SAMARITAINE, LA (Department Store) (19, Rue de la Monnaie). A pump installed on the second arch of the Pont Neuf (q.v.), on the downstream side, supplied water from the Seine (q.v.) for Parisians from 1608 to 1813. It was named the Samaritaine because the bas-relief that decorated it portrayed the woman of Samaria giving Jesus water from Jacob's well. This name of Samaritaine was adopted by Ernest Cognacq (q.v.) when he set up his novelty shop on the corner of the Rue de la Monnaie and Rue du Pont-Neuf. With his wife, Louise Jay, he turned it into the biggest of the department stores (q.v.) in Paris. Its sales figures, which had already reached 840,000 francs in 1874, exceeded 100 million francs in 1914.

As of 1883, the Samaritaine's architect was Frantz Jourdain, one of the best and most original of that time. In 1904, he began reconstructing the buildings and made them a manifesto of Art Nouveau with the consent of Cognacq, who wanted something eye-catching. The Samaritaine was built around an unconcealed metal frame that opened outward with huge windows, while inside it was bathed in light from the glass roof overhead. In 1925, then associated with Henri Sauvage, Frantz Jourdain was forced by the Seine prefecture to conceal the metal frame of the new store with a stone covering. A third store was inaugurated in 1930. Today the Samaritaine is one of the leading department stores of Paris, and its architecture remains a model of modernity.

SANS-CULOTTES. In 1789, townsmen were usually dressed in knee-breeches. Only the poor wore pants. To mock them, the aristocrats referred to the partisans of the Revolution as *sans-culottes*. They proudly adopted this name, and long striped pants and the Phrygian, or "liberty," cap became the standard dress of the revolutionaries. The five additional days that ended the Republican year of 12 months of 30 days each were named the *sans-culottides*. As the spearhead of the Revolution, the sans-culottes played a fundamental role from 1789 to 1794, participating in all the riots and bringing down first the monarchy and then the Girondins. These *sans-culottes,* who were especially numerous in the Faubourg Saint-Antoine (q.v.), were for the most part artisans and workers, many of them out of work and often illiterate—but they were led by educated men: architects, teachers, lawyers and doctors. This gave that mass an exceptional organization and effectiveness.

SANTÉ (Prison) (42, Rue de la Santé). Marguerite de Provence, the widow of Saint Louis, had a hospital called Maison de Santé built at the end of the 13th century. Anne of Austria had it moved a bit further south in 1652, when it was renamed Sainte-Anne's hospital. On the location of that Maison de Santé, from 1861 to 1867, the architect Emile Vaudremer built the Santé prison, the only penitentiary that still remains in Paris. Technically very advanced for that day and age, it is now somewhat obsolete. It houses between 1,500 and 2,000 prisoners who have reached the end of their sentence or been given light penalties. Near this prison, on the sidewalk and under the fifth tree of the Rue de la Santé, the guillotine (q.v.) did its ghastly work from 1909 to 1939. From 1939 to 1972, the executions were held within the prison walls. The prison's name of *santé,* or "health," has given rise to countless plays on words.

SEINE, LA (River). The Seine ranks third in length among France's rivers, being 776 kilometers long, after the Loire (1,012 kilometers) and the Rhône (812 kilometers). It drains a basin of about 78,000 square kilometers. Its source is located at an altitude of 471 meters in the Langres plateau. The city of Paris is the owner of that source, where traces were found of a Celtic cult that worshipped the river. Economically, the Seine is the busiest and most important waterway in France (*see* Ports). Paris owes its privileged position to the existence of the Île de la Cité (q.v.), which facilitates its passage. In the past, floods (q.v.) have often had catastrophic effects on the city's life, but canalization of the waterway and the construction of dams upstream now limit the risks of flooding.

During the Quaternary period, the Seine formed two arms at the location of Paris. The southern one followed the present course of the river. The northern one bordered the hills of Belleville (q.v.), Montmartre (q.v.) and Chaillot (q.v.), more or less tracing the path of Saint-Martin canal (Arsenal basin and Boulevard Richard-Lenoir), Rues du Château-d'Eau, des Petites-Écuries, Richer, de Provence, de la Pépinière, La Boétie and Marbeuf before rejoining the other arm near Pont de l'Alma. This northern arm has survived in the form of a branch, called the Ménilmontant stream, which became the Grand Égout (sewer) in the 14th century and which was embellished in a legend as an underground river called Grange-Batelière. Within the capital, the Seine has only one lesser tributary, the Bièvre (q.v.).

SENATE. *See* LUXEMBOURG (Palace).

SÉVIGNÉ, MARIE DE RABUTIN-CHANTAL, Marquise de (1626–96). Born at Place des Vosges (q.v.), then called Place Royale, Madame de Sévigné spent most of her life in Paris, in the Marais quarter (q.v.). Her daughter left her in 1671 to follow her husband to Grignan, in the Rhône valley. The inconsolable marquise spent the rest of her life writing letters that became one of the monuments of French literature and also a first-rate historical account of Parisian society at the end of the 17th century.

SÈVRES (Factory). Eleven kilometers to the west of Notre-Dame is the small town of Sèvres, which has now been swallowed up by the suburbs surrounding the capital. In order to limit the imports of English porcelain (q.v.) and to create a national industry, Louis XV encouraged the foundation of a factory at Vincennes (q.v.) in 1740. It was granted a royal charter in 1745, then transferred to Sèvres in 1756. It became a royal factory in 1759 and developed strongly after the discovery of kaolin deposits in Limousin. The Sèvres factory still exists as a state company. Its porcelain articles of exceptional quality fetch equally exceptional prices.

SORBONNE (47, Rue des Ecoles). Opened on September 1, 1257, by Robert de Sorbon, the *collège* (q.v.) that adopted the name of Sorbonne was at first just one of the many secular establishments of the University (q.v.). Its fame came from the fact that it became the seat of the all-powerful Faculty of Theology and then of the University as a whole. The first printing (q.v.) press in Paris was founded there in 1470 but its founders soon left, fleeing the harassment of the theologians. In 1481, a library was established. In 1618, the Sorbonne reinforced its repressive role when it obtained the privilege of imposing censorship on all printed texts.

In 1622, Richelieu became its protector and in 1627 he commissioned Jacques Le Mercier with reconstructing its disparate and dilapidated buildings. All that remains today is the Sainte-Ursule chapel, where Richelieu's tomb is located. The present buildings were erected by the Third Republic, which entrusted the work to Henri Paul Nénot. The sad and solemn façades are matched inside by statues and huge allegoric paintings produced by the worst practitioners of the uninspired official art of that age.

STEAMERS. The first steamboat to float on the Seine (q.v.), on August 9, 1803, was the prototype designed by the American Robert Fulton (q.v.). Navigation on the river did not actually begin until 1816, when the *Elyse* arrived from Rouen on March 29. The following April 20, the *Charles-Philippe* of Jouffroy d'Abbans ran its tests. On August 27, 1817, Jouffroy d'Abbans introduced the *Génie-du-Commerce,* which carried passengers from Paris to Saint-Cloud. By 1825, steamer navigation had been generalized, but by the 1860s the railway, which was much faster, supplanted the steamers, whose speed hardly exceeded 20 kilometers an hour.

STEINLEN, THÉOPHILE ALEXANDRE (1859–1923). Born in Lausanne, Switzerland, Steinlen arrived in Paris in 1881 and settled in Montmartre (q.v.). His friend Willette introduced him at the Chat Noir (q.v.), where he got to know Alphonse Allais, Aristide Bruant, Claude Debussy, Jean-Louis Forain (q.v.), Erik Satie and Paul Verlaine (q.v.). His work as a designer and poster artist is dominated by Paris. His most famous collection of designs, *Dans la Vie* (1901) (In Life) focuses on working-class balls, workers and the misery of the poorer quarters. In the satirical magazine *L'Assiette au Beurre,* his targets are the institutions, the Catholic Church, the army, the police (q.v.), capitalism, colonialism and the political leadership. He is less obsessed by the venality and corruption of the oppressors than the weakness and vulnerability of the oppressed. A worthy successor of Daumier, Steinlen produced works of great power that provide a pitiless chronicle of the distress in Paris during the Belle Epoque.

STRIKES. The word for strike in French is *grève*, which is derived from the Place de Grève (q.v.), nowadays called Place de l'Hôtel de Ville. In fact, up until the 1789 Revolution, workers in a large number of professions, especially masons and unskilled laborers, went to that square when they sought work and that is where the bosses went to hire them. This gathering of workers without work gave rise to the expression *faire grève*, or "go on strike," which originally meant to look for work or wait to be hired at Place de Grève. The transition to the present meaning of refusing to work took place between 1845 and 1848. Prior to this the word used for a strike was *sédition* (sedition).

SUE, MARIE JOSEPH, called EUGÈNE (1804–57). After inheriting a nice fortune when his father died in 1829, Eugène Sue turned to writing while leading the life of a debauched dandy, which sometimes aroused a scandal. He was one of the initiators of the popular serialized novel. His production, while often rather mediocre, was extremely plentiful and devoted largely to Paris. *Mathilda, ou Mémoires d'une jeune femme* (1841) (*Mathilda, or the Memoirs of a Young Lady*) created a scandal because it revealed the ugly underside of the society life of the aristocracy of the Faubourg Saint-Germain (q.v.). His most famous work, *Les Mystères de Paris* was published in serial form from 1842 to 1843 in the *Journal des Débats*. It described in an exaggerated and simplistic manner the underworld and dregs of society in the capital. It later appeared in 10 volumes.

-T-

TAXIS. Taxis initially appeared under the name of automobile fiacres (q.v.) in 1898. There were two in 1898 and 18 during the world exhibition (q.v.) of 1900. There were only two left again in 1904, and it was not until 1905 that they started to proliferate: 39 in 1905, 417 in 1906 and 465 in 1907. Starting in 1898, the horse-drawn and motorized taxis were equipped with meters to measure the time spent and the distance traveled so as to avoid any conflict over the amount to be paid for a ride. These meters were first called *taxamètres*, and then *taximètres* as of 1904, the latter being the source of the word "taxi."

The emergence of large companies, which owned half of the vehicles, caused the longest strike in the history of Parisian taxis, lasting from November 27, 1911, to April 18, 1912. Louis Aragon depicted this in his novel *Les Cloches de Bâle*. In September 1914, the Parisian taxis were requisitioned by Galliéni, the military governor of Paris, to carry 5,000 soldiers to the front, where they played a decisive role in the Battle of the Marne. In 1956, the first radio taxis appeared. At present, there are 17,500 taxi drivers, of which 1,000 are women. There are nearly 9,000 owner-drivers, while the others are paid by companies such as G7. Each vehicle covers an average of 150 kilometers a day. There are 550 parking places reserved for taxis, 122 of them equipped with telephones.

TEMPLE. The Order of the Knights of the Temple was both religious and military and was entrusted with the defense of the Holy Land. In 1139, it moved into the old temple near Saint-Gervais church. In 1147, its first chapter meeting was held in its brand-new and fortified monastery, located to the north of the Marais (q.v.) quarter. This was bounded by the present Rue du Temple, Place de la République and Rues de Turenne, de Poitou and Pastourelle—what was traditionally called the Temple quarter. After the arrest, sentencing and execution of the Knights Templar in 1314, the Temple enclosure was granted to another military order, the Knights of Saint John of Jerusalem (later, the Knights of Malta). The Temple enclosure benefited from a tax-free franchise, and the craftsmen and merchants who worked there were exempt from the obligations and burdens borne by other Parisians. The Temple Tower, or donjon, served as a prison for Louis XVI and the royal family in 1792–93. Napoléon I had it demolished in 1808, and the Temple buildings were replaced by a secondhand clothes market (q.v.), called the Carreau du Temple (Temple tiles). The annexes of the former Temple priory made way for the town hall of the 3rd arrondissement and the Square du Temple.

TERROR, THE. The Reign of Terror was a de facto system of government rooted in force and fear. The Terror was set in motion on September 5, 1793, and put under the control of the Committee of Public Safety. It was based on the Revolutionary Tribunal (q.v.) and the so-called law of suspects, adopted on the following September 27th. The Terror was political, economic and religious. It raged with particular intensity in Paris. There were two phases. During the first, which was relatively mild, it resulted on the average in only three executions a day. The Great Terror, based on the law of Prairial 22, Year II (June 10, 1794), accelerated the process and did away with all legal guarantees for those accused. It sent 1,376 persons to the guillotine (q.v.) from June 11 to July 27 — an average of 30 executions a day. The Terror ended with the execution of its mastermind, Robespierre (q.v.), on July 28, 1794.

THEATERS. The theater was born in Paris in the form of presentations of Christ's passion each year during Easter on the parvis of Notre-Dame (q.v.) Cathedral. The oldest known performance dates back to 1380. As of 1548, the amateur actors grouped in the Brotherhood of the Passion rented their hall in the Hôtel de Bourgogne to various troupes passing through the city. Until 1644, this hall remained the only permanent site for performances in the capital. At that time, another hall was opened in the Marais (q.v.) quarter. There were also halls for temporary use, in particular the Petit-Bourbon and the hall of the Palais-Royal (q.v.), built for Richelieu. Molière (q.v.) moved into the Palais-Royal in 1660, and it is there that the Comédie-Français (q.v.) plays today. Rudimentary stages were put up briefly during the fairs (q.v.). Napoléon I worried that the opposition might make use of the theater to express itself and therefore reduced the number of theater houses to nine, including the Comédie-Française. In 1852, there were about 20 theaters, almost all of them located on the grands boulevards (q.v.). Under the Second Empire (1852–70), 11 new houses were born. In 1905, there were 43 theaters and in 1990, 119. This makes Paris one of the world's theatrical capitals.

THIERS, LOUIS ADOLPHE (1797–1877). A liberal journalist at the *Constitutionnel*, Thiers acquired a reputation as a historian with his *Histoire de la Révolution française*, which appeared between 1823 and 1827. In January 1830, along with Armand Carrel and August Mignet, he founded the newspaper *Le National*, which strongly criticized the Polignac government. Thiers headed the journalists who protested against the ordinances of July 1830 that triggered the revolution and brought about the fall of Charles X. Benefiting from the revolution, Louis-Philippe rewarded Thiers by appointing him privy councillor and undersecretary of state for finance. Thiers, who hailed from Marseilles and was the deputy for Aix-en-Provence, was one of the best orators in the Chamber. He was minister of the interior in 1832 and again from 1834 to 1836 and prime minister and minister of foreign affairs in 1836 and again in 1840. It was Thiers who adopted legislation to build a fortified wall (q.v.) to protect Paris. It was erected between 1841 and 1845.

In 1848, Thiers supported the candidacy of Louis-Napoléon Bonaparte, then broke with him and went into the opposition. He was elected deputy for Paris in 1863 and opposed Napoléon III, criticizing the emperor's warlike policy that had led to the military disaster of the Franco-Prussian War of 1870. In February 1871, he was elected "head of the executive power of the French Republic" by the National Assembly. Thiers had the heavy task of negotiating a humiliating peace with Germany and the weighty burden of crushing the Commune (q.v.). On May 24, 1873, he was ousted by the monarchists, who dominated the National Assembly. Thiers finished his career as the head of the Republican party, which won shortly after his death.

TIBERI, JEAN (1936–). Repeatedly elected town councilor of the 5th arrondissement since 1965, Jean Tiberi was also the deputy for that electoral district. An eminent member of the party Rassemblement pour la République, a political formation arising out of Gaullism, in 1983 he became the first deputy of the mayor Jacques Chirac (q.v.), as well as the mayor of the 5th arrondissement. When Chirac was elected president of France, Tiberi replaced him as mayor of the capital on May 22, 1995.

TOLL. The city toll was an indirect tax collected on articles of consumption entering Paris. Its origin goes back at least to 1121, and in 1213 there existed a list of duties levied on all the goods entering the city. The toll increased the prices of standard consumer goods substantially and was therefore very unpopular with the people. In early July 1789, revolutionary disturbances began with the burning of tollgates (q.v.). This tax was abolished in 1791, but the revolutionaries had to restore it in 1798 because they were short of money. The toll was the main financial resource of the municipality and amounted to about 60 percent of its revenue throughout the 19th century. It was collected at the city gates by a small army of 2,500 employees.

With the extension of the métro (q.v.) lines to the suburbs after 1918 and the increase in automobile traffic, it became increasingly difficult and annoying to control and ensure payment of the toll. Thus, the practice gradually fell into disuse and the municipality found other sources of financing. The toll was discontinued on August 1, 1943, although it was officially abolished only on January 1, 1949, in accordance with the decree of December 9, 1948. It was replaced by a more discreet and less annoying, but much heavier, tax, namely, the *taxe sur la valeur ajoutée,* or T.V.A. (value added tax, or VAT). This enabled the state to collect about 20 percent on everything that was manufactured, sold or leased. The T.V.A. was initiated in 1954.

TOLLGATES. Parisians thought up every possible trick to avoid the heavy tolls and duties levied on all goods and merchandise that entered the capital. The Farmers General, whose duty it was to collect taxes on behalf of the king, decided to put an end to the fraud and smuggling by building a wall 3.3 meters high and 24 kilometers long around Paris. When it was constructed, between 1784 and 1787, the wall (q.v.) was equipped with doors and gates. The architect Nicolas Ledoux was asked to build tollhouses around these gates in which the tax collectors would dwell. The colossal cost of these monumental structures proposed by this megalomaniac architect caused the number of gates to be reduced to 56. There are still traces of four of them today: the gates of Trône and Denfert-Rochereau and remains of those of Monceau and La Villette.

TOULOUSE-LAUTREC, HENRI DE (1864–1901). Descended from a noble and aristocratic lineage, Henri de Toulouse-Lautrec broke first one leg and then the other in 1878 and 1879, and both stopped growing, leaving him a dwarf. Unable to engage in sports, he took up drawing and painting. In 1884, he moved into an atelier in Montmartre (q.v.), in the Rue Tourlaque, and then Rue Fontaine. He frequented Aristide Bruant and spent his nights at Moulin-Rouge (q.v.). His favorite models were Jane Avril, May Belfort, La Goulue, Yvette Guilbert and May Milton. He was also a regular client of the brothels, where he drew numerous nudes; he was always looking for natural poses that he could not find during the sittings of his models. In 1897, he moved his studio to the Rue Frochot, still in Montmartre. In relatively few years, Toulouse-Lautrec accumulated a substantial portfolio, 5,000 drawings and nearly 400 lithographs and posters. They provide a dazzling view of the gay life of Paris at the end of the 19th century.

TOUR D'ARGENT, LA (Restaurant) (17, Quai de la Tournelle).
The Tour d'Argent is the oldest restaurant (q.v.) in Paris that is still active. Its origin reaches all the way back to a tavern of the same name that was opened at 15, Quai de la Tournelle in 1582. It was there that, on March 4, 1582, Henri III learned how to use the fork that the Venetians had invented in 1574. The restaurant became famous when it became the property of Lecocq, one of the cooks of Napoléon I, early in the 19th century. Its specialty, *canard au sang* (duck with sauce made from the blood), was introduced in 1887 by Frédéric Delair. He was succeeded by André Terrail in 1912. He invented the *quenelle de brochet* (dumpling of ground pike) and transferred the 200,000 bottles of wine of the Café Anglais to the cellars of the Tour d'Argent. The restaurant has been run by Claude Terrail since 1947.

TRAIN BLEU, LE (Restaurant) (20, Boulevard Diderot). Installed in the Gare de Lyon train station (q.v.) when it was reconstructed on the occasion of the 1900 world exhibition (q.v.), Le Train Bleu restaurant was known for excellent cooking in a prestigious setting. It consisted of two large rectangular rooms and two small salons. To decorate it, the architect Marius Toudoire ordered 30 paintings from 30 different painters. They portrayed the best-known cities and tourist resorts that could be reached by train from the Gare de Lyon, including Lyon, Orange, Avignon, Arles, Marseille and Nice, but also Paris, which François Flameng painted on the roof of the main room. All these paintings were surrounded by exuberant stuccos of a remarkable quality, done by Edouard Lefèvre. Jean Giraudoux said of the Train Bleu during the 1920s: "This place is a museum, but no one knows. In the future it will be listed." He was right. The Train Bleu is now listed among the historical monuments.

TRAIN STATIONS. The oldest Parisian train station was the platform of the Paris-Saint-Germain-en-Laye line, which was inaugurated on August 26, 1837. Located at Place de l'Europe, it was the predecessor of the Saint-Lazare station. The Orléans, or Austerlitz, station, which was opened in 1843, was also preceded by a platform that began operating in September 1840. The Orsay station, intended to replace it as the terminus of the Compagnie d'Orléans, was opened in 1900 but closed down in 1939. Today it houses an art museum. The Montparnasse station was opened in 1840 as the terminus of the railway line from Paris to Versailles. Its location was changed three times, and the present station dates back to 1969. The Gare du Nord dates back to 1846, and the Gare de l'Est was built between 1847 and 1850. The Lyon station, erected between 1847 and 1852, was entirely reconstructed between 1895 and 1902.

TRAMS. The first tramline was put into service in New York in 1832. Loubat, a Frenchman who had lived in that city, obtained an authorization in 1852 to build a tramline between Place de la Concorde and the Passy tollgate (q.v.). The first test was run on November 21, 1853. Called the "American railway," the tramway was bought in 1856 by the Compagnie Générale des Omnibus (C.G.O.), which had just obtained the monopoly on public transport in Paris. It gave priority to the bus (q.v.) rather than developing the tram. In 1873, after the C.G.O. lost its monopoly, 10 tramlines were opened by the two companies, Tramways Nord and Tramways Sud. Only then did the C.G.O. decide to develop the tram network; there were 40 lines by 1878. As of 1892, the trams, which until then had been drawn by horses, became electrified. Between 1910 and 1914, draught animals were completely replaced by electricity.

In 1929, the Municipal Council condemned the trams because they apparently disturbed automobile traffic and decided to replace them with buses. The last tram made its final run on May 15, 1937. Alas, caught up in automobile traffic, the buses move very slowly nowadays, and the idea has been mooted of reintroducing trams in the capital.

TRANSNONAIN, MASSACRE OF RUE. When they learned that the city of Lyon had revolted, the Parisian Republicans rose on April 12–14, 1834. The insurrection was doomed to fail as soon as it began. There were scarcely 30 barricades (q.v.) between the Rue Saint-Martin and Rue du Temple, from west to east, and between the Rue des Gravilliers and Rue Saint-Merri, from north to south. The 50,000 men of the National Guard (q.v.) and the 40,000 soldiers of the line infantry under the command of General Bugeaud had no trouble crushing the insurgents.

The event assumed historical importance because of a massacre perpetrated by the soldiers of the 35th regiment of the line. About 5:00 A.M. on April 14, they thought that they were being fired on from a window of 12, Rue Transnonain. They broke into the building, smashed the doors to the dwellings and killed all the innocent inhabitants in their beds. A lithograph by Daumier showing one of the victims lying in a nightshirt at the foot of his bed immortalized this episode in the troubled life of Paris between 1830 and 1850.

TRANSPORT, PUBLIC. Individual paying transport got started in 1612 with the fiacres (q.v.) and in 1617 with the sedan chairs. Blaise Pascal came up with the first public transport, the "five-penny" horse-drawn carriages, named after the cost of a seat. They served five routes from 1662 until they disappeared in 1677. It was only in 1828 that

Stanislas Baudry took up Pascal's project and created a service of 100 "omnibus" cars serving 18 routes. The omnibus was drawn by horses and soon there were large numbers of them. In 1840, they formed a network of 23 lines operated by 13 companies and with 167 connection points.

In order to improve the quality of transport, Prefect Haussmann (q.v.) obliged all the companies to merge into a single Compagnie générale des omnibus, which had a monopoly on public ground transport in Paris as of 1855. The network consisted of 31 lines designated by the letters A to Z and AB to AG. The cars became larger, going from 24 to 26 seats, and then to 40 seats in 1880. The world exhibition (q.v.) of 1867 revealed the inadequacy of the omnibus network, and the trams (q.v.) were developed to remedy it. By 1906, the motorized omnibus, the autobus or bus (q.v.) was gradually replacing the horse-drawn omnibus. The last of these made its final trip on January 11, 1913. *See also* Bateau-mouche; Buses; Fiacres; Métro; Railway Line around Paris; Taxis; Trams.

TREES. The number of trees in Paris is estimated at half a million, consisting of 80 species and 300 varieties. Some 85,000 of these trees were planted along the streets, especially the plane trees (35,000), the chestnut trees (13,500), the Sophoras (7,500), the lime trees (7,300) and the maple trees (5,300). The capital's 23,000 elm trees, which became diseased, have dwindled to 1,000. The oldest tree is located in Viviani Square: it is a Robinia, or false acacia, brought from North America in 1601. The Jardin des Plantes (q.v.) (Botanical Garden) boasts many trees that have reached a ripe old age and come from afar: a Robinia, or false acacia, from 1636, a maple tree from Crete from 1702, a pistachio tree from before 1716, a cedar of Lebanon from 1734 and a Sophora and a Laricio pine from 1747. The most original tree is the *Ginkgo biloba,* known also as the "forty-crown tree" because the first five plants, which were brought back from China at the end of the 18th century, were supposedly sold for 40 crowns each, that being a lot of money at the time. Ginkgoes are the oldest living fossils on the planet. Monceau Park has the biggest tree in Paris, an Oriental plane tree with a circumference of more than seven meters.

TROIS GLORIEUSES. The Trois Glorieuses refers to the three glorious days of the insurrection of July 27, 28 and 29, 1830, which resulted in the fall of Charles X and his replacement by Louis-Philippe. The 504 victims of that uprising were buried under the Colonne de Juillet (July Column) at Place de la Bastille (q.v.). Their names were inscribed in golden letters on the shaft of the column.

TRÔNE, FOIRE DU. The origin of the Foire du Trône (Throne Fair) was apparently a bread market (q.v.) intended for the poor that was held during the Middle Ages on the parvis of Notre-Dame (q.v.) Cathedral or, according to another hypothesis, in the enclosure of Saint-Antoine Abbey. This market was held on Saturday of Holy Week and the merchants were gradually authorized to sell confections as well. At the end of the 15th century, they added rye bread and honey covered with ginger, which is why the fair also became known as the gingerbread fair. In 1841, the fair (q.v.) was moved a few hundred meters to the east and located at Place du Trône, presently Place de la Nation, which explains its other name of Foire du Trône.

The length of the fair was increased to two weeks in 1861, then three weeks, and the number of hawkers doubled between 1872 and 1880, exceeding 2,400 stalls. Over the years merry-go-rounds, lottery booths and shooting galleries were added to the stalls covered with fritters and to sellers of marshmallows and cotton candy. In 1945, the Foire du Trône stretched from Place de la Nation to Porte de Vincennes. In 1964, it was transferred to the Reuilly green in the Bois de Vincennes (q.v.). It now lasts for two months, April and May, and receives more than five million visitors.

TUILERIES (Palace). On the location of the tile works (*tuileries*) located to the west of the Louvre (q.v.), the queen mother Catherine de Médicis commissioned Philibert Delorme in 1564 to construct a palace, and the work was continued by Jean Bullant as of 1570. Henri IV linked the Tuileries to the Louvre with the Grande Galerie, which runs along the Seine (q.v.). Le Vau expanded the palace further between 1659 and 1666, while Le Nôtre redesigned the garden. The kings resided quite rarely at the Tuileries. Louis XVI and his family were installed there in October 1789, after being brought back from Versailles (q.v.) by the mob. On August 10, 1792, the taking of the Tuileries by the revolutionaries marked the end of the monarchy. Napoléon Bonaparte made it his residence as of 1800, and he was imitated by his successors, Louis XVIII, Charles X, Louis-Philippe and Napoléon III. Because it was a symbol of royal and imperial power, the Tuileries palace was burned down by the Communards in May 1871. All that remains is a huge garden (q.v.) embellished with fountains and statues. In it are also two pavilions built during the Second Empire that presently serve as art galleries, the Orangery and the Jeu de Paume.

-U-

UNIVERSITY. The Notre-Dame school, located near the cathedral, developed during the 12th century and attracted many students. However, the harassment of the canons incited the teachers and students to cross the Seine (q.v.) and settle on Mount Sainte-Geneviève (q.v.) under the more lenient tutorship of the abbot of Sainte-Geneviève. The teachers were organized into a "university" as of 1170, but it was not until 1215 that the University was officially granted its charter by Pope Innocent III. It then consisted of four faculties: theology, canon law, medicine and liberal arts. The course of studies ended with a leaving certificate, the *baccalauréat*. It was possible to teach on receiving a master's degree. Well-to-do students or those with a scholarship were lodged in some 50 *collèges* (q.v.).

The University played an important role during the theological controversies. Its turbulent students continuously upset the lives of ordinary Parisians and committed numerous crimes and misdemeanors (*see* François Villon). At the beginning of the 15th century, the University sided with the Burgundians and then the English. This explains the tenacious resentment of the kings of France. Charles VII and Louis XI put the University under tight control. During the 16th century, the University contributed to its own downfall by obstinately refusing humanism and perpetuating its cramped and constricted teaching. The intellectual and material death throes of the University continued until it was officially disbanded in 1792.

In 1806, Napoléon I recreated a university that was emancipated from the Catholic Church. During nearly two centuries it has grown and occasionally flourished, but it again faces serious problems. By 1970, the University had expanded so greatly that it had to be replaced by 13 autonomous universities in and around Paris. This, however, was not enough to solve its intellectual, financial and political woes. With 300,000 students, insufficient and unsuitable premises, diplomas of uncertain value that prepared their holders for few professions other than teaching, the University has become a potential time bomb for the government and could explode again as it did during the student uprising of May 1968.

URBAN HEATING. The urban heating network was started in 1928 with the Bercy plant. Its first kilometer served the Gare de Lyon train station. In 1935, the Hôtel de Ville (q.v.) was connected, and in 1937, the Opéra (q.v.). In 1945, there were still only 27 kilometers and 440 clients. The Urban Heating Company of Paris, of which the municipality is the main shareholder, presently runs a network of 315 kilometers with more than 4,800 users. The second biggest in Europe, after that of Finland's capital, Helsinki, it is longer but less dense than that of New York.

UTRILLO, MAURICE (1883–1955). A child of Montmartre (q.v.), Maurice Utrillo spent the better part of his life at 12, Rue Cortot and in the surrounding bistros (q.v.). A Bohemian (q.v.) and an alcoholic, he was pampered by his mother, Suzanne Valadon, and then his wife, Lucie Valore. He painted without frills, showing a surprising pictorial innocence, all of Montmartre, from the Sacré-Coeur (q.v.) to the Moulin Rouge (q.v.) and Lapin Agile, but he also did not overlook the humblest and most ordinary streets and houses. Utrillo was the painter of Montmartre par excellence.

-V-

VAL-DE-GRÂCE (Church) (277, Rue Saint-Jacques). Queen Anne of Austria vowed to build a church if she gave birth to a son. This wish was fulfilled after 23 years, perhaps thanks to Cardinal Richelieu, with the birth of the future Louis XIV (q.v.) in 1638. On April 8, 1645, the cornerstone of Val-de-Grâce was laid by the young king, since his father, Louis XIII, had passed away in 1643. The church and the convent were completed in 1667 according to plans by François Mansart. The church's dome was inspired by Saint Peter's in Rome. The interior sculpted decoration, by Michel Anguier, is exceptionally rich. The Val-de-Grâce church is the most beautiful Baroque building in Paris and the only one that was truly successful. The cloister is presently occupied by a military hospital.

VÉFOUR, LE GRAND (Restaurant) (17, Galerie de Beaujolais). Le Grand Véfour is the last nostalgic witness to the glorious era of the Palais-Royal (q.v.), between 1780 and 1840, when it was the center of Parisian life, with its many cafés (q.v.), restaurants (q.v.), gaming houses and brothels. First called Café de Chartres, it was and still remains under arcades 79 to 82 of the Palais-Royal. It has received countless political and literary figures of note. Le Grand Véfour has preserved its decor of the end of the 18th century and is still renowned for the quality of its food.

VENDÔME, PLACE (Square). In 1685, superintendent of buildings Louvois decided to create a new royal square dedicated to the glory of Louis XIV (q.v.). It was to be to the west of Paris and a counterpart to Place Royale, now Place des Vosges (q.v.), to the east. Jules Hardouin-Mansart, with the aid of Germain Boffrand, designed a rectangular site that was open only to the south on the Rue Saint-Honoré and closed to the north by the new Capuchin Convent. An equestrian statue of Louis XIV was erected in the center of the square. In 1699, the square was far from complete because buyers could not be found for the lots and the buildings to be constructed. The king then sold the lots to the city, and a new configuration was adopted. The site assumed the shape of a square with the sides cut at angles and almost closed, with a modest opening to the south on the Rue Saint-Honoré. Rather than a gallery with arcades, there was to be a ground floor with a mezzanine.

In 1806, after the Capuchin convent was demolished, Place Vendôme was opened to the north with the Rue de la Paix. The Vendôme column replaced the statue of Louis XIV, which had been destroyed in 1792. Inspired by Trajan's column in Rome, it was the work of Jacques Gondouin and Jean-Baptiste Lepère. Its sculpted bronze shaft was decorated with scenes from the 1805 campaign, which culminated in the victory at Austerlitz. A statue of Napoléon I was placed on the top. Torn down by the Commune (q.v.) in 1871, the column was put back up in 1873. Place Vendôme is the location of the most prestigious jewelry shops in the world. It also houses the Ritz Hotel (q.v.) and Ministry of Justice.

VERLAINE, PAUL MARIE (1844–96). Born in Metz, Verlaine was quite young when he arrived in Paris. From adolescence on he devoted himself to poetry and had a rough life, going from one mediocre job to another. Among his first texts was a study on Baudelaire (q.v.), another great poet of Paris. He had modest success with the *Poèmes Saturniens* (1866) and *Fêtes Galantes* (1869), through which he met the young Arthur Rimbaud, with whom he had a stormy liaison in 1872 in Montparnasse (q.v.), in the Rue Campaigne-Première. The collection *Sagesse* (1881) established his reputation. His health undermined by alcoholism, Verlaine died in misery in Paris. A large share of his work was inspired by the great city.

VERSAILLES (Château). Located about 20 kilometers to the west of the Louvre (q.v.), the Versailles plains had long been nothing more than a hunting preserve for the kings. In 1624, Louis XIII had a small hunting lodge built there. In 1661, Louis XIV (q.v.) ordered the construction of a palace. Le Vau, d'Orbay and then Hardouin-Mansart were in turn entrusted with the building, while Le Nôtre designed the huge gardens. Le Brun was in charge of the interior decoration. In 1664, the king held the splendid feast called the pleasures of the enchanted island at Versailles. On February 10, 1671, Louis XIV left Paris for Versailles, which he moved into for good on May 6, 1682, after having resided in various other places, especially Saint-Germain-en-Laye (q.v.).

The abode of the court and the site of intrigues and pleasure, Versailles helped to control and tame the nobles, but it also quickly gave the monarchy a bad image—a deplorable mixture of debauchery, corruption, irresponsibility and monumental waste of public funds. The

Estates General met in Versailles on May 5, 1789. They were convened to raise new fiscal resources for the bankrupt monarchy; in return, they demanded a constitution. On October 6, 1789, caught up in a popular demonstration coming from the capital, King Louis XVI and his family were forced to leave Versailles and were taken by the Parisian mob to Paris, where they were installed in the Tuileries (q.v.).

For some time the château was not properly maintained, but it was finally restored under Louis-Philippe, who founded a historical museum there in 1837. After the Franco-Prussian War, the National Assembly refused to sit in Paris and instead went to Versailles in March 1871, only to be joined by the government after the proclamation of the Commune (q.v.). The troops who crushed the Communards were referred to as Versaillais. The government and parliament did not leave Versailles for Paris until 1879, after the victory of the Republicans. In 1919, the Versailles Treaty concluding World War I was signed in the Galerie de Glaces. The Château de Versailles was the site of congresses of parliament and of elections of the French president until 1953, and since then of the adoption of amendments to the constitution.

VIDOCQ, FRANÇOIS EUGÈNE (1775–1857). After serving as a soldier and fighting in the battles of Valmy (1792) and Jemappes (1792), François Vidocq deserted and joined the gangs of highwaymen who plundered northern France. In 1796, he was arrested and sentenced for forgery to eight years of forced labor. He escaped from the Brest jail twice and was caught both times, but he managed to get away the third time. In 1809, Vidocq offered his services to the police (q.v.). He began as an informer, but his talents were such that, in 1811, he was made the head of a detective brigade consisting of ex-convicts. This colorful character, who knew the lowest strata of Parisian society better than anyone, inspired Honoré de Balzac (q.v.) in depicting Vautrin and treating various themes in his *Comédie humaine,* in particular the ending of *Splendeurs et misères des courtisanes.*

In 1827, Vidocq resigned and opened a paper factory, but his business did poorly and he joined the Parisian police again in 1832. He left them again shortly thereafter and set up a private police force that sometimes got into trouble with the Parisian police. On trial twice, in 1837 and 1843, Vidocq was acquitted both times thanks to intervention by high-ranking politicians. He participated actively in the election of Louis-Napoléon Bonaparte, the future Napoléon III, as president of France. In 1849, Victor Hugo (q.v.) met him and was inspired by Vidocq for the character of Jean Valjean in *Les Misérables.* Eugène Sue (q.v.) is indebted to him for a large portion of the documentation he used to write *Les Mystères de Paris.* Vidocq wrote his own *Mém-*

oires, which were interesting, but could only be trusted so far. It was through his life and his almost legendary actions that he became one of the most extraordinary figures in Paris of the first half of the 19th century.

VILLETTE, LA (Quarter). The quarter (q.v.) of La Villette, in the 19th arrondissement, is only part of the old parish and commune of La Villette, which covered the northern and western two-thirds of that arrondissement and stretched as far as Buttes-Chaumont (q.v.). La Villette Saint-Ladre or Saint-Lazare has been documented as early as 1198 as an outlying annex of the Parisian leprosarium of Saint-Ladre or Saint-Lazare. The main street of the village was the roadway of La Villette, presently the Rue de Flandre. The population consisted largely of farmers who grew wheat, barley and oats on the flatter land and vineyards (q.v.) on the heights. Bordering on Paris, on the present-day Boulevard de La Villette, outside the limits of the tollgates (q.v.), there were *ginguettes* (q.v.) where the Parisians could come to drink tax-free wine, sing, dance and have fun. In 1800, La Villette only had 1,666 inhabitants, but it grew rapidly, exceeding 12,000 souls in 1847 and 30,000 in 1860, when it was incorporated into Paris.

La Villette's expansion was related to its function as duty-free entrepôt at the gates of Paris. It developed mightily with the digging of the La Villette basin and the opening of the Ourcq Canal in 1822. The industrial boom accelerated further with the opening of an enormous cattle market (1862) and slaughterhouses (1867). Soon there were also sugar refineries, chocolate factories, distilleries, the Félix Potin preserved food plant, the works of the piano maker Erard, the vast depots of the *chiffonniers* (q.v.), the tanks of the gas company, the coach houses of the undertakers, and so on. Gradually, they left La Villette, which for a long time was the most industrialized and the most polluted place in the capital. In the place of the cattle market and slaughterhouses, there is now the City of Science and Industry and the City of Music in the midst of a large garden.

VILLON, FRANÇOIS (1431 or 1432; died after 1463). After receiving a bachelor of arts at the Paris University (q.v.) in 1449, and then a master of arts in 1452, François Villon led a dissolute life in the company of his student friends. He partook in countless brawls and killed a priest during one of them, in 1455. He obtained a pardon but continued his misdoings. About Christmas 1456, together with accomplices, he broke into the Navarre *collège* (q.v.) and stole 500 crowns. He had to flee and sought refuge in the Loire region. In 1461, he wound up in jail in Meung-sur-Loire for another crime. In 1462, he was reprieved by Louis XI and returned to Paris. On November 3,

1462, François Villon was again imprisoned for theft. He was released after he promised to return 120 golden crowns. Shortly thereafter, he got into another brawl and was condemned to be hung. The *Parlement* (q.v.) rescinded the judgment on January 5, 1463, but banned Villon from Paris for ten years. He disappeared without a trace after that date.

Nowadays François Villon is the only poet of the Middle Ages who is still well known by most French people. This is doubtlessly because of the powerful and modern cast of his writing and his themes. *Le Grand Testament, Le Petit Testament,* the *Codicille,* the *Jargon* and the *Balades* form a brief but poignant work that realistically evokes the lives of the students and outcasts of Paris and the misery and the misfortune of the disinherited.

VINCENNES (Château). King Louis VII (1137–80) established a meeting place for hunting in the Bois de Vincennes (q.v.). It was enlarged by Philippe II Auguste (q.v.), who turned it into a square manor with sides 60 meters long. Louis IX (1226–70) added a square donjon and a chapel. From 1270 to 1350, Vincennes was one of the favorite residences of the kings. Charles V (q.v.), who was born in Vincennes in 1337, turned the manor into a mighty fortress. Work began in 1361 to construct a huge keep 52 meters high and a perimeter wall 378 meters long and 175 meters wide, with nine towers and three gates. The Sainte-Chapelle de Vincennes was erected as of 1379 in flamboyant Gothic style.

By the 15th century, the Château de Vincennes was the largest fortified complex in Europe. It was neglected by the kings in the 16th century and used only as a political prison. A porcelain (q.v.) factory operated there for a few years before being transferred to Sèvres (q.v.). In 1840, the castle was turned into barracks. The Château de Vincennes was restored between 1947 and 1978 and presently houses the historical archives of the French army, navy and air force.

VINCENNES ZOO (53, Avenue de Saint-Maurice). A small zoological park was set up in the Bois de Vincennes (q.v.) during the Colonial Exhibition of 1931. It was such a success that it was decided to establish a zoo comparable in size to those in several other major European cities. The project was carried out on 14 hectares of land by Charles and Daniel Letrosne. They composed a theaterlike decor of cement and reinforced concrete—a stylized landscape, as it were. Rather than cages and fences, they preferred digging pits to keep the animals away from the public. The whole complex was crowned by a huge artificial rock 68 meters high. The Vincennes zoo was inaugurated on June 2, 1934. The variety of animal and bird species it houses makes it one of the richest zoos in Europe.

VINCENNES, BOIS DE (Woods). For a long time, Paris was surrounded by a belt of forests. The Vincennes woods were first mentioned in a text dating to 847. It became part of the royal domain in 1037. Louis VII had the monks of the Grandmont order settle there on the present location of Lake Minimes. Philippe II Auguste (q.v.) had the first portions of the Vincennes château (q.v.) built and, in 1183, surrounded the woods with stone walls. Louis XV had the woods and the alleys redesigned and opened to the public. In 1858, Napoléon III commissioned Jean Charles Alphand with completely reworking the Bois de Vincennes. Four lakes were dug, including Lake Daumesnil. In 1863, a hippodrome (race course) was installed. The Colonial Exhibition of 1931 was held in the woods. The woods are being reshaped again by an operation that began in 1983. At present, the Bois de Vincennes covers 995 hectares. It is famous for the Vincennes zoo (q.v.), flower gardens, recreational facilities and an African and Oceanian Art Museum.

VINEYARDS. Winegrowing was introduced to Gaul by the Romans 2,000 years ago. The heights dominating the center of Paris were covered with vineyards until the end of the 18th century. Winegrowing was very profitable. Even if the wine was rather mediocre, it was easy to sell in the countless *guinguettes* (q.v.) that dotted the outskirts of the city. However, urbanization and diseases such as oidium, which appeared in 1830, and mildew, which had a devastating effect as of 1880, wiped out the Parisian winegrowers.

About 1900, only some 6,000 hectares of vineyards were planted around Paris. In 1910, journalists mentioned as an oddity the last vinestocks in the capital, the trellised vineyards of the Rues Cortot, Damrémont, Lamarck and Lepic, all of them located in Montmartre (q.v.). In 1933, in Montmartre, winegrowing was given a new chance, and 2,500 vines were planted. Today, the vineyard has 3,250 plants on a plot of land measuring 800 meters by 500. It produces 400 to 500 bottles of wine at each harvest.

VOSGES, PLACE DES (Square). The Hôtel des Tournelles was torn down in 1563 at the order of Catherine de Médicis because her husband, Henri II, had died there in terrible agony. On that spot in 1605, Henri IV commanded the creation of a royal square like those being built in Italy. It is not entirely certain who drew up the plans; among those mooted were Clément and Louis Métezeau, Jacques II Androuet Du Cerceau and Claude Chastillon. On April 7, 1612, Place Royale was inaugurated, and a glorious tournament was held on that occasion.

The constructions followed a single model: 36 pavilions of brick with cornices and frames of stone, two stories high with a slate roof.

The ground floor with arcades (q.v.) was girdled with shops installed in a vaulted gallery. In the center was a garden planted with trees. This was a notorious place for duels in the 17th century. Place Royale lost its name after the fall of the monarchy on August 10, 1792. It was renamed several times before receiving its present name of Place des Vosges in 1800. This name honors the inhabitants of the Vosges département, who were the best and most punctual of all French citizens in paying their taxes.

-W-

WALLACE, SIR RICHARD (1818–90). Richard Wallace was the natural child of Viscount Beauchamp, the fourth marquess of Hertford, and Agnes Jackson, née Wallace. He was brought up in Paris, spent most of his life there and died there. An amateur art collector, he contributed substantially to the formation of the collection kept in Hertford House, London. His devotion and his generosity in providing many ambulances during the siege of Paris in 1870 were such that he was made a baronet in 1871. Owner of the Bagatelle (q.v.) and commanding a considerable fortune, in 1871 this philanthropist offered fountains to the Parisians: two fountains per arrondissement, or a total of 80. These "Wallace fountains" were a precious contribution to the supply of drinking water (*see* Water Supply) for poor Parisians, who could not afford to having running water installed in their dwellings. Some 50 of these Wallace fountains still exist.

WALLS. Paris was protected by a series of walls. Already by about 300, after the city had been looted by the Germanic invaders, the Gallo-Romans had surrounded the Île de la Cité (q.v.) with a wall. There were apparently also fortifications on the Right Bank by the 11th century, but very little remains of them. Between 1190 and 1208, Philippe II Auguste (q.v.) had a wall with a perimeter of 5,400 meters built. It was reinforced with 42 towers and the Louvre (q.v.) castle and could be entered through ten gates. Taking into account the city's expansion, Charles V had a new wall constructed solely on the Right Bank. Built between 1358 and 1383, it ran 4,900 meters from the Bastille (q.v.) to Saint-Honoré Gate. In 1566, first Charles IX, and then, from 1633 to 1636, Louis XIII, improved and enlarged the wall on the Right Bank to the west, also reinforcing its 6,200 meters with 14 bastions. Louis XIV (q.v.) had all of these walls and fortifications torn down as of 1671 and replaced them with tree-lined boulevards (q.v.) and promenades.

The next wall was built by the Farmers General, not for military but rather for fiscal reasons, so as to better collect the tolls on merchandise entering the city. Between 1784 and 1787, they had a wall constructed that was about 24 kilometers long and circumscribed Paris. It was fitted with 56 tollgates (q.v.) designed by Ledoux. It remained the administrative limit of the capital until 1860. In 1814, since the city had no defenses, it could hardly resist the allied armies that appeared at its gates. This lack was invoked to justify the construction of a modern fortified wall. Erected between 1841 and 1844 and flanked with forts in the suburbs, this wall was known as the Thiers (q.v.) fortifications, named after the prime minister who had them built in the public interest. It enclosed Paris in an ellipse of 34 kilometers, with ramparts 140 meters wide, counting 94 bastions and 16 forts on the periphery, within a radius of five kilometers. This wall became the limit of the capital in 1860 and contributed to Paris's defense during the German siege of 1870. By the law of April 19, 1919, it was decided to demolish this wall, although that was done quite slowly. *See also* Zone, La.

WATCHMEN. The watchmen emerged to ensure the safety of a city that had no public lighting (q.v.) and where anyone could be set on by thieves and thugs as of nightfall. According to tradition, this office was first established in Paris in 595, but it does not really seem to have developed until the second half of the 12th century. The town watchman seems to have evolved into a captain of the watch, under whose orders there were various types of watch: the night watch, the day watch, the trades watch, and the bourgeois watch, since this was a complex institution. Unfortunately, the watchmen do not appear to have been very effective since, in 1461, a bourgeois guard was added.

Indeed, the insecurity was such that Louis XIV (q.v.) decided to name a lieutenant general of police (q.v.) with control over the whole Parisian police force, including the watchmen. A mounted watch was established in 1666. Between the mounted watch and those on foot, there were nearly 300 men on the eve of 1789. They had been reinforced as of 1719 with a ports and ramparts guard of 255 men and, as of 1721, with an infantry company of about 200 men that assumed the name of Parisian guard in 1771. It was that Parisian guard, which had grown to about a thousand men by 1789, that had to maintain law and order when the Revolution of 1789 broke out. All of these institutions were then abolished.

WATER SUPPLY. Water supply is an essential element in the life of a city. Paris can use the water of the Seine (q.v.) and that of the phreatic and alluvial waters that meet about five meters under the ground. However, there was already considerable pollution of the Seine by the Middle Ages. Provincials and foreigners who visited Paris complained of diarrhoea and even dysentery. Haussmann (q.v.) ordered the first analyses, which confirmed that the water that the Parisians were drinking was unfit for consumption and even very dangerous, because it carried cholera and typhoid germs. With the help of Eugène Belgrand, the prefect had the pure waters of the chalky Champagne, to the east of the capital, tapped, as well as those of the Dhuis and the Vanne, and they were conveyed and stored in the Ménilmontant and Montsouris reservoirs as of 1865. Later on, the waters of the Avre, the Loing and the Lunain, to the west and south of Paris, were tapped and then, between 1922 and 1925, those of the Voulzie in Champagne.

Since 1853, the Compagnie générale des Eaux (General Water Company) has been in charge of water distribution. It is the biggest water distribution company in the world. Since 1985, it shares the Parisian market with the Lyonnaise des Eaux, which, under the name of Société Parisienne des Eaux, was allocated the Left Bank. The Service des Eaux de la Ville de Paris was entrusted with the material management of the installations until it was replaced, in 1987, by the Société Anonyme de Gestion des Eaux de Paris (SAGEP) (Water Management Company of Paris, Ltd.), of which the city owns 70 percent. The control of water quality is ensured by the Centre de Recherche, Étude, Contrôle des Eaux de Paris (CRECEP) (Center for Research, Study and Control of Water of Paris).

Some two million Parisians consume an average of 900 million liters of drinking water per day. The municipality uses 400 million liters of nonpotable water per day for cleaning the sidewalks, pavements and sewers and watering the public gardens. Water distribution is undertaken through a network of 1,700 kilometers of pipes. In each street there are two parallel pipes, one for the drinking water, the other for the nonpotable water, for use by the public authorities.

WATERMILLS. Since the Romans had all the slaves they needed, they rarely resorted to the driving power of watermills. These developed only during the Carolingian era. In the ninth century, the abbey of Saint-Germain-des-Prés owned 59 of them. The watermills were located mainly on the bridges (q.v.). In 856, Charles the Bald granted the bishop of Paris the Grand Pont and the watermills installed on its archs. After the destruction of that bridge by the flood (q.v.) of 1296, these watermills—some 13 of them—were installed on a footbridge named the Pont aux Meuniers. There were also watermills on another footbridge called Planche-Mibray. They belonged to Saint-Merri Church.

Aside from these bridges, in the Middle Ages there were about 30 watermills located on the Right Bank along the large arm of the Seine (q.v.) where the current is strongest. Floating mills were also set up on small craft in the middle of the river. One of them, the Gourdaine mill, was used to mint coins for the king. However, these watermills obstructed navigation, and they were banned at the beginning of the 19th century. They lasted longer on the Bièvre (q.v.), where, in 1860, it was still possible to see a paper mill, two flour mills and several small mills used for various industries.

WHARTON, EDITH, née JONES (1862–1937). A member of New York's high society, in 1885 Edith Jones married a Boston banker, Edward Wharton. She began to write after a nervous breakdown and published her first collection of short stories, *The Greater Inclination,* in 1899. Her first novel, *The Valley of Decision,* appeared in 1902, followed by *The House of Mirth* in 1905. As of 1907, Edith Wharton lived in France, especially Paris, where she visited Henry Adams, Bernard Berenson, Paul Bourget, Kenneth Clark, Charles du Bos, André Gide and Henry James (q.v.). Her most famous work was *Ethan Frome,* published in 1911. She won the Pulitzer Prize in 1920 for *The Age of Innocence* and wrote her autobiography, *A Backward Glance,* in 1934.

WINDMILLS. It was the Crusaders to the Holy Land who first saw windmills and brought the idea back with them. The oldest windmill in Paris was recorded in 1150 by Saint Bernard, who noted its presence on the Copeaux mound, at the location of the maze in the present Jardin des Plantes (q.v.). There is still a tower inside the Montparnasse (q.v.) cemetery, which is the remains of a windmill from the end of the 16th century. There were large numbers of them on the Right Bank, located especially on the heights of Belleville (q.v.), Chaillot (q.v.), Charonne (q.v.) and Montmartre (q.v.). The most famous and most extensively studied are the Montmartre windmills, in particular the well-known Galette mill, whose origin goes back to 1622.

Although the windmills disappeared, they were long remembered in place names. For example, a dozen streets still bear names such as Moulin-de-Beurre, Moulin-de-la-Vierge, Moulin-des-Prés, Moulin Vert or du Moulinet and des Moulins, while several dozen other roads that no longer exist had similar names. Steam power supplanted the wind power of the mills, and many of them were turned into *guinguettes* (q.v.) during the 19th century.

WORLD EXHIBITIONS. While London held the first in the series of world exhibitions in 1851, Paris takes pride in being the city that has organized the largest number, six of the 26. The second world exhibition was held in 1855 in the lower parts of the Champs-Elysées (q.v.), at the Carré Marigny and Cours-la-Reine. That of 1867 occupied the

Champ-de-Mars (q.v.). In 1878, the hill of Chaillot (q.v.) was added to the Champ-de-Mars. There were 23 million visitors to the 1889 exhibition, which was marked by the erection of the Eiffel Tower (q.v.), and 48 million to the 1900 exhibition, a record that was beaten only by Osaka in 1970. The Exhibition of Arts and Technology in Modern Life of 1937 is usually listed among the world exhibitions, but it was a disaster: sabotaged by the construction workers who really worked only on the pavilion of the Soviet Union, it turned into a confrontation between the Nazi and Communist ideologies. It also ran up a huge deficit, collecting 150 million francs in receipts against more than 1.4 billions francs in expenses. President François Mitterrand wanted Paris to organize a world exhibition in 1989, for the bicentenary of the Revolution of 1789, but the mayor, Jacques Chirac (q.v.), opposed such a financial adventure.

WORTH, CHARLES FREDERICK (1825–95). In 1845, Worth left his native England for Paris, where he worked in a shop selling fashion accessories. In 1858, he opened his own fashion house. He was the first to prepare and display a new collection each season and have it presented by live female models. The couturier for Empress Eugénie, the wife of Napoléon III, Worth could be regarded as the inventor of haute couture (q.v.).

-Z-

ZERO POINT. On the parvis of Notre-Dame (q.v.) Cathedral, there is an eight-sided bronze paving stone that weighs 80 kilograms and has a star, or compass rose, at its center bearing the arms of the city of Paris and initials indicating the cardinal points. This is the starting point, kilometer zero for the highways of France, and has been so since October 10, 1924. The origin of this zero point reaches much further back, however, as a guide to Paris that appeared in 1787 already mentioned the existence, in front of the portal of Notre-Dame, of a triangular post marking the central point for all the highways of the kingdom of France. Some historians trace this zero point back to very early times, although they cannot provide any concrete evidence.

ZOLA, ÉMILE (1840–1902). A Parisian by birth, Émile Zola was initially a journalist and art critic before moving toward naturalism and trying to write what he called "the experimental novel." In his work, he endeavored to describe the human realities of Parisian life, particularly in the *Rougon-Macquart* cycle, the "natural and social history of a family during the Second Empire," which appeared in 20 volumes from 1871 to 1893. *Nana* (1879) portrayed the life of a high-class prostitute. *Au Bonheur des Dames* (1883) (*The Ladies' Paradise*) traced the history of the birth and rise of a department store (q.v.). Zola led the movement to review the trial of Alfred Dreyfus with his article "J'accuse," which appeared in the daily *L'Aurore* on January 13, 1898.

ZONE, LA. The so-called Thiers wall (q.v.) was erected between 1841 and 1845. It was 250 meters wide and formed a ring of 35 kilometers in diameter around Paris. Very poor and marginalized people lived on the grassy slopes of the military embankment. Prostitutes exercised their trade, pimps and hoodlums met and settled their accounts there, and gangs of *Apaches* (q.v.) formed. One survey by the Seine prefecture estimated the population of the zone at 20,000 in 1913. Another survey in 1926 evaluated them at 42,300 souls. The law of April 19, 1926, condemned the fortified wall and it was decided to have it torn down. This was done slowly, being completed only around 1960. The peripheral boulevard, low-cost housing, sports fields and *lycées* replaced the shantytowns of planks, cardboard and corrugated iron.

Numerous films celebrated the low-life and slum quality of the zone, in particular *Liliom,* by Fritz Lang in 1934, and *Porte des Lilas,* by René Clair in 1957. Louis-Ferdinand Céline, Blaise Cendrars, René Fallet and Auguste Le Breton used the zone as the background for some of their novels.

Bibliography

This bibliography, which is subdivided by major subjects, presents the main works on Paris. There are more than one thousand titles from a pool consisting of more than one hundred thousand volumes. As for periodical articles, there are tens of thousands of them, but they are excluded because of the lack of space. The choice of books was designed for an English-language public, and titles in English account for 70 percent of the total. Considerable effort has been made to include recent works that are readily accessible, whether on sale in the bookshops or available in the libraries. Some 90 percent of the books have been published since 1970, and no book prior to 1945 is mentioned.

Those with a reading knowledge of French and who wish to carry out further research can consult a recent and detailed "research guide" listing more than 10,000 titles in pages 1201–1509 of the *Histoire et Dictionnaire de Paris* (1996) by Alfred Fierro. The Bibliothèque historique de la Ville de Paris (Historical Library of the City of Paris) began publishing an important collection entitled *Nouvelle Histoire de Paris* in 1970. About 20 volumes have already appeared. They cover the history of this city from its Gaulish origins, more than 2,000 years ago, until 1873. Two volumes in this collection deal with the history of town planning in Paris and the city's geography.

The *Almanach de Paris* provides a detailed chronology. Within the framework of the history of the dioceses of France, in 1987 Bernard Plongeron published a volume dealing with Paris from the beginnings of Christianity to the Revolution of 1789. Many publications have been written about the social, economic and cultural life of the Parisians, but there is no outstanding synthesis. Mention must be made of two basic dictionaries presenting the streets and monuments of Paris: *Dictionnaire historique des rues de Paris* (1963; 9th ed. 1991) by Jacques Hillaire, and *Dictionnaire des monuments de Paris* (1992). There is also an important introduction to the research and interpretation of the pictures of Paris in *Nouvelle Histoire de Paris: Histoire de l'urbanisme à Paris* by Pierre Lavedan. Finally, for those wanting a brief and accessible introduction to Paris, *A Traveller's History of Paris* (1994) by Robert Cole may be of interest.

The titles in this Bibliography are presented under the following headings:

1. GENERAL
   1.1 Bibliographies and Dictionaries
   1.2 Geography and Cartography
   1.3 Official Publications and Statistics
   1.4 Pictures
   1.5 Guidebooks

2. POLITICS AND ADMINISTRATION
   2.1 General
   2.2 Antiquity and Middle Ages (up to 1500)
   2.3 The Ancien Régime (1500–1789)
   2.4 Revolution and 19th Century (1789–1914)
   2.5 20th Century (1914–1996)

3. RELIGION

4. EDUCATION

5. SOCIETY

6. ECONOMY

7. CULTURAL AND SCIENTIFIC LIFE

8. URBANISM, ARCHITECTURE AND TOPOGRAPHY

9. AMERICANS IN PARIS

1. GENERAL

1.1 BIBLIOGRAPHIES AND DICTIONARIES

Brunel, Georges, Marie-Laure Deschamps-Bourgeon, and Yves Gagneux. *Dictionnaire des églises de Paris*. Paris: Hervas, 1995.
Dictionnaire de Paris. Paris: Larousse, 1964.
Dictionnaire des monuments de Paris. Paris: Hervas, 1992.
Fierro, Alfred. *Histoire et Dictionnaire de Paris*. Paris: R. Laffont, 1996.
Hillairet, Jacques. *Dictionnaire historique des rues de Paris*. 9th ed. 2 vols. Paris: Editions de Minuit, 1991.

1.2 GEOGRAPHY AND CARTOGRAPHY

Bastié, Jean. *Géographie du Grand Paris*. Paris: Masson, 1984.

Beaujeu-Garnier, Jacqueline. *Atlas et Géographie de Paris et de la région d'Île-de-France.* 2 vols. Paris: Flammarion; Geneva, Switzerland: Famot, 1977.

———. *Nouvelle Histoire de Paris. Paris: Hasard ou Prédestination? Une géographie de Paris.* Paris: Hachette, 1993.

Beaujeu-Garnier, Jacqueline, and Jean Bastié, eds. *Atlas de Paris et de la région parisienne.* 2 vols. Paris: Berger-Levrault, 1967.

Couperie, Pierre. *Paris through the Ages: An Illustrated Historical Atlas of Urbanism and Architecture.* London: Barrie and Jenkins, 1970.

Michel, Marie-Edmée, Alain Erlande-Brandenburg, and Catherine Quétin. *Carte archéologique de Paris.* Paris: Commission du Vieux Paris, 1991.

Pitte, Jean-Robert, ed. *Paris: Histoire d'une ville.* Paris: Hachette, 1993.

Pourquoi Paris? Une Métropole dans son environnement naturel. Paris: Association des géologues du bassin de Paris, 1986.

1.3 OFFICIAL PUBLICATIONS AND STATISTICS

Annuaire statistique de la Ville de Paris. Paris, 1880–. Annual.

Budget de la Ville de Paris. Paris, 1818–. Annual.

Bulletin municipal officiel de la Ville de Paris. Paris, 1882–. Twice a week.

Compte général des recettes et des dépenses de la Ville de Paris. Paris, 1834–. Annual.

Recueil des actes administratifs. Bulletin officiel d'information de la préfecture de Paris et de la préfecture de la Seine. Paris, 1844–. Monthly.

1.4 PICTURES

Duby, Georges, and Guy Lobrichon, eds. *L'Histoire de Paris par la peinture.* Paris: Belfond, 1988.

Fierro, Isabelle (for movies, research guide and list of nearly a thousand films) in Alfred Fierro, *Histoire et Dictionnaire de Paris.* Paris: R. Laffont, 1996, pp. 1488–1507.

Jeanne, René, and Charles Ford. *Paris vu par le cinéma.* Paris: Hachette, 1969.

Lavedan, Pierre. *Nouvelle Histoire de Paris. Histoire de l'urbanisme à Paris.* Updated ed. by Jean Bastié and Alfred Fierro. Paris: Hachette, 1993.

1.5 GUIDEBOOKS

Applefield, David. *Paris Inside Out: An Insider's Guide for Residents, Students, and Discriminating Visitors on Living in the French Capital.* 3rd ed. Paris: Parigramme, 1994.

At Home in Paris: Your Guide to Living in the French Capital. Paris: The Junior Service League of Paris, 1993.

Baillie, Kate, and Tim Salmon. *Paris: The Rough Guide.* London: The Rough Guide, 1996. Updated annually.

The Blue Guides: Paris. Paris: Hachette, 1996. Updated annually.

Dunlop, Fiona. *Fodor's Exploring Paris.* New York: Fodor, 1995.

————. *Paris Art Guide.* New York: Art Guide Publications, 1990.

Facaros, Dana, and Michael Pauls. *Paris: Cadogan City Guides.* London: Cadogan Books, 1995.

Gault, Henri, and Christian Millau. *Paris.* Paris: Gault et Millau, 1996. Updated annually.

The Green Guides: Paris. Paris: Michelin, 1996. Updated annually.

The Red Guide: Paris. Paris: Michelin, 1996. Updated annually.

Ricour de Bourgies, Maribeth. *The Chic Shoppers' Guide to Paris.* New York: St. Martin's Press, 1991.

Robertson, Ian. *Blue Guide: Paris and Environs.* 8th ed. London: A. and C. Black; New York: W. W. Norton, 1992.

Tillier, Alan, ed. *Eyewitness Travel Guides: Paris.* New York, London and Stuttgart, Germany: Dorling Kindersley, 1995. Updated annually.

Tymoczo, Julianna S., ed. *Let's Go: The Budget Guide to Paris.* Cambridge, MA: Let's Go; London: Macmillan, 1996.

Vine, Deirdre. *The Footloose Guide to Paris.* New York: Simon and Schuster, 1992.

Wells, Patricia. *Food Lover's Guide to Paris.* London: Methuen, 1989.

Wurman, Richard Saul. *Paris Access.* New York: Access Press, 1992.

2. POLITICS AND ADMINISTRATION

2.1 GENERAL

Cole, Robert. *A Traveller's History of Paris.* Moreton-in-Marsh, England: The Windrush Press, 1994.

Fierro, Alfred. *Histoire et Dictionnaire de Paris.* Paris: R. Laffont, 1996.

Fleury, Michel, et al. *Almanach de Paris.* 2 vols. Paris: Encyclopaedia Universalis, 1990.

Mollat, Michel, ed. *Histoire de l'Île-de-France et de Paris.* Toulouse, France: Privat, 1971.

Nouvelle Histoire de Paris. 20 vols. Paris: Hachette, 1970–1995.

Paris de la préhistoire à nos jours. Saint-Jean-d'Angély, France: Bordessoules, 1985.

2.2 ANTIQUITY AND MIDDLE AGES (UP TO 1500)

Allmand, Christopher. *The Hundred Years War: England and France at*

War, c. 1300–c. 1450. Cambridge, England: Cambridge University Press, 1988.

Autrand, Françoise. *Naissance d'un grand corps de l'Etat: Les gens du Parlement de Paris, 1345–1454*. Paris: Publications de la Sorbonne, 1981.

Baldwin, John W. *The Government of Philip Augustus: Foundations of the French Royal Power in the Middle Ages*. Berkeley and Los Angeles, CA: University of California Press, 1986.

Barber, Malcolm. *The Trial of the Templars*. Cambridge, England, and New York: Cambridge University Press, 1978.

Boussard, Jacques. *Nouvelle Histoire de Paris: De la fin du siège de 885–886 à la mort de Philippe Auguste, 1220*. Paris: Hachette, 1976.

Brown, Elizabeth A. R. *Customary Aids and Royal Finance in Capetian France*. Cambridge, MA: The Medieval Academy of America, 1992.

———. *Politics and Institutions in Capetian France*. Aldershot, England: Variorum, 1991.

Cazelles, Raymond. *Etienne Marcel, champion de l'unité française*. Paris: Tallandier, 1984.

———. *Nouvelle Histoire de Paris: De la fin du règne de Philippe Auguste à la mort de Charles V, 1380*. Paris: Hachette, 1972. Reprinted 1994.

Cunliffe, Barry. *Gaul*. London: Batsford, 1988.

Drinkwater, J. F. *Roman Gaul*. London: Croom Helm, 1983.

Druon, Maurice. *The History of Paris from Caesar to Saint Louis*. London: Rupert Hart-Davis, 1969.

Dunbabin, Jean. *France in the Making, 843–1180*. Oxford: Oxford University Press, 1985.

Duval, Paul-Marie. *Nouvelle Histoire de Paris: De Lutèce oppidum à Paris, capitale de la France*. Paris: Hachette, 1993.

———. *Paris antique des origines au troisième siècle*. Paris: Hermann, 1961.

Famiglietti, Richard C. *Royal Intrigue: Crisis at the Court of Charles VI, 1392–1420*. New York: AMS Press, 1986.

Favier, Jean. *Nouvelle Histoire de Paris: Paris au XVe siècle, 1380–1500*. Paris: Hachette, 1974.

Fouracre, Paul, and Richard A. Gerberding. *Late Merovingian France: History and Hagiography, 640–720*. Manchester: Manchester University Press, 1996.

La France de Philippe Auguste: Le temps des mutations. Paris: CNRS, 1982.

Freidin, Nicholas. *The Early Iron Age in the Paris Basin*. Oxford: British Archaeological Reports, 1982.

Ganshof, François Louis. *The Carolingians and the Frankish Monarchy*. London: Longman, 1971.

————. *Frankish Institutions under Charlemagne*. Providence, RI: Brown University Press, 1968.

Gibson, Margaret, and Janet L. Nelson, eds. *Charles the Bald: Court and Kingdom*. Oxford: British Archaeological Reports, 1981.

Hallam, Elizabeth M. *Capetian France, 987–1328*. London and New York: Longman, 1980.

Henneman, John Bell. *Royal Taxation in Fourteenth-Century France: The Captivity and Ransom of John II, 1356–1370*. Philadelphia, PA: American Philosophical Society, 1976.

————. *Royal Taxation in Fourteenth-Century France: The Development of War Financing, 1322–1356*. Princeton, NJ: Princeton University Press, 1971.

James, Edward. *The Franks*. Oxford: Blackwell, 1988.

————. *The Origins of France: From Clovis to the Capetians, 500–1000*. London: Macmillan, 1982.

Kaeuper, Richard W. *War, Justice and Public Order: England and France in the Later Middle Ages*. Oxford: Clarendon Press, 1988.

King, Anthony. *Roman Gaul and Germany*. London: British Museum Publications, 1990.

King, P. D. *Charlemagne*. London: Methuen, 1986.

Lasko, Peter. *The Kingdom of the Franks: North-West Europe before Charlemagne*. London: Thames and Hudson, 1971.

Latouche, Robert. *From Caesar to Charlemagne: The Beginnings of France*. New York: Barnes and Noble, 1968.

Lewis, Peter Shervey. *Later Medieval France: The Polity*. New York: St. Martin's Press, 1968.

Lombard-Jourdan, Anne. *Aux Origines de Paris: la genèse de la rive droite jusqu'en 1223*. Paris: CNRS, 1985.

————. *"Montjoie et Saint-Denis": Le centre de la Gaule aux origines de Paris et de Saint-Denis*. Paris: CNRS, 1989.

Lutèce: Paris de César à Clovis. Paris: Musée Carnavalet, 1984.

McKitterick, Rosamond. *The Frankish Kingdoms under the Carolingians, 751–987*. London and New York: Longman, 1983.

Nash, Daphne. *Settlement and Coinage in Central Gaul, c. 200–50 B.C.* Oxford: British Archaeological Reports, 1978.

Paris de la préhistoire au Moyen Age. Paris: Musée Carnavalet, 1990.

Paris mérovingien. Paris: Musée Carnavalet, 1981.

Scherman, Katherine. *The Birth of France*. New York: Paragon House, 1987.

Schmidt, Joël. *Le Baptême de la France: Clovis, Clotilde, Geneviève*. Paris: Seuil, 1996.

Thompson, Guy. *Paris and Its People under English Rule: The Anglo-Burgundian Regime, 1420–1436*. Oxford: Clarendon Press, 1991.

Velay, Philippe. *De Lutèce à Paris: l'Île et les deux rives.* Paris: CNRS, 1992.

Wallace-Hadrill, John M. *The Long-Haired Kings and Other Studies in Frankish History.* London: Methuen, 1962.

Wood, Ian. *The Merovingian Kingdoms, 450–751.* London and New York: Longman, 1994.

2.3 THE ANCIEN RÉGIME (1500–1789)

Andrews, Richard Mowery. *Law, Magistracy, and Crime in Old Regime Paris, 1735–1789.* New York and Cambridge, England: Cambridge University Press, 1994.

Babelon, Jean-Pierre. *Nouvelle Histoire de Paris: Paris au seizième siècle.* Paris: Hachette, 1986.

Baker, Keith Michael. *The Political Culture of the Old Regime.* Oxford: Pergamon Press, 1987.

Baumgartner, Frederic J. *Radical Reactionnaires: The Political Thought of the French Catholic League.* Geneva, Switzerland: Droz, 1975.

Behrens, Catherine Betty Abigail. *The Ancien Régime.* New York: Harcourt, Brace and World, 1967.

Bonney, Richard. *The King's Debts: Finance and Politics in France, 1598–1661.* Oxford: Clarendon Press, 1981.

———. *Political Change in France under Richelieu and Mazarin, 1624–1661.* Oxford: Oxford University Press, 1978.

Buisseret, David J. *Sully and the Growth of Centralized Government in France, 1598–1610.* London: Eyre and Spottiswoode, 1968.

Campbell, Peter Robert. *The Ancien Regime in France.* Oxford: Basil Blackwell, 1988.

Chagniot, Jean. *Nouvelle Histoire de Paris: Paris au dix-huitième siècle.* Paris: Hachette, 1988.

———. *Paris et l'armée au dix-huitième siècle: Étude politique et sociale.* Paris: Economica, 1985.

Dethan, Georges. *Nouvelle Histoire de Paris: Paris au temps de Louis XIV, 1660–1715.* Paris: Hachette, 1990.

Diefendorf, Barbara B. *Paris City Councilors in the Sixteenth Century: The Politics of Patrimony.* Princeton, NJ: Princeton University Press, 1983.

Egret, Jean. *The French Prerevolution, 1787–1788.* Chicago, IL: University of Chicago Press, 1977.

Hamscher, Albert N. *The Conseil Privé and the Parlements in the Age of Louis XIV: A Study in French Absolutism.* Philadelphia, PA: The American Philosophical Society, 1987.

———. *The Parlement of Paris after the Fronde, 1653–1673.* Pittsburgh, PA: University of Pittsburgh Press, 1976.

Hardy, James D. Jr. *Judicial Politics in the Old Regime: The Parlement of Paris during the Regency*. Baton Rouge: Louisiana State University Press, 1967.

Heller, Henry. *Iron and Blood: Civil Wars in Sixteenth-Century France*. Montréal, Canada: McGill-Queen's University Press, 1991.

Kettering, Sharon. *Judicial Politics and Urban Revolt in Seventeenth-Century France*. Princeton, NJ: Princeton University Press, 1978.

Kingdon, Robert M. *Myths about the St. Bartholomew's Day Massacres, 1572–1576*. Cambridge, MA: Harvard University Press, 1988.

Knecht, Robert Jean. *The French Wars of Religion, 1559–1598*. London: Longman, 1989.

Lloyd, Howell A. *The State, France and the Sixteenth Century*. London: George Allen and Unwin, 1983.

Major, James Russell. *From Renaissance Monarchy to Absolute Monarchy*. Baltimore, MD: Johns Hopkins University Press, 1994.

———. *Representative Institutions in Renaissance France, 1421–1559*. London: Greenwood Press, 1983.

Merrick, Jeffrey W. *The Desacralization of the French Monarch in the Eighteenth Century*. Baton Rouge: Louisiana State University Press, 1990.

Mettam, Roger. *Power and Faction in Louis XIV's France*. New York: Basil Blackwell, 1988.

Moote, A. Lloyd. *The Revolt of the Judges: The Parlement of Paris and the Fronde, 1643–1652*. Princeton, NJ: Princeton University Press, 1971.

Mousnier, Roland. *The Institutions of France under the Absolute Monarchy, 1598–1789*. Chicago, IL, and London: University of Chicago Press, 1979.

———. *Paris capitale au temps de Richelieu et de Mazarin*. Paris: Pedone, 1978.

Pillorget, René. *Nouvelle Histoire de Paris. Paris sous les premiers Bourbons, 1594–1661*. Paris: Hachette, 1988.

Ranum, Orest. *The Fronde: A French Revolution, 1648–1652*. London and New York: W. W. Norton, 1993.

Rogister, John. *Louis XV and the Parlement of Paris, 1735–1755*. Cambridge, England: Cambridge University Press, 1995.

Shennan, Joseph Hugh. *The Parlement of Paris*. Ithaca, NY: Cornell University Press, 1968.

Soman, Alfred, ed. *The Massacre of St. Bartholomew: Reappraisals and Documents*. The Hague: M. Nijhoff, 1974.

Stone, Bailey. *The French Parlement and the Crisis of the Old Regime*. Chapel Hill, NC: University of North Carolina Press, 1986.

———. *The Parlement of Paris, 1774–1789*. Chapel Hill, NC: University of North Carolina Press, 1981.

Sutherland, Nicola May. *Princes, Politics and Religion, 1547–1589.* London: Hambledon Press, 1984.

Treasure, Geoffrey. *Mazarin: The Crisis of Absolutism in France.* London and New York: Routledge, 1995.

Williams, Alan. *The Police of Paris, 1718–1789.* Baton Rouge: Louisiana State University Press, 1979.

Wolfe, Michael. *The Conversion of Henri IV: Politics, Power and Religious Belief in Early Modern France.* Cambridge, MA: Harvard University Press, 1993.

2.4 REVOLUTION AND 19TH CENTURY (1789–1914)

Agulhon, Maurice. *The Republican Experiment, 1848–1852.* Cambridge, England: Cambridge University Press, 1983.

Amann, Peter H. *Revolution and Mass Democracy: The Paris Club Movement in 1848.* Princeton, NJ: Princeton University Press, 1975.

Anderson, Robert David. *France, 1870–1914: Politics and Society.* London: Routledge and Kegan Paul, 1977.

Auspitz, Katherine. *The Radical Bourgeoisie, the Ligue de l'Enseignement and the Origins of the Third Republic, 1865–1885.* Cambridge, England: Cambridge University Press, 1982.

Baker, Keith Michael. *The Political Culture of the French Revolution.* Oxford: Pergamon Press, 1988.

Bergeron, Louis. *France under Napoleon.* Princeton, NJ: Princeton University Press, 1981.

Bertier de Sauvigny, Guillaume de. *Nouvelle Histoire de Paris. La Restauration, 1815–1830.* Paris: Hachette, 1977.

Bluche, Frédéric. *Septembre 1792: Logiques d'un massacre.* Paris: R. Laffont, 1986.

Bosher, John F. *The French Revolution.* New York: W. W. Norton, 1988.

Bouloiseau, Marc. *The Jacobin Republic, 1792–1794.* Cambridge, England: Cambridge University Press, 1983.

Bredin, Jean-Denis. *The Affair.* New York: George Braziller, 1986.

Christiansen, Rupert. *Paris Babylon: The Story of the Paris Commune.* New York: Penguin, 1996.

Cobb, Richard Charles. *Paris and Its Provinces, 1792–1802.* London: Oxford University Press, 1975.

———. *The Police and the People: French Popular Protest, 1789–1820.* Oxford: Clarendon Press, 1976.

Collingham, Hugh A. C., and R. S. Alexander. *The July Monarchy: A Political History of France, 1830–1848.* London and New York: Longman, 1988.

Danieri, Cheryl L. *Credit Where Credit Is Due: The Mont-de Piété of Paris, 1777–1851.* New York and London: Garland, 1991.

Doyle, William. *The Oxford History of the French Revolution*. Oxford: Clarendon Press, 1989.

Duveau, Georges. *1848: The Making of a Revolution*. Cambridge, MA: Harvard University Press, 1984.

Edwards, Stewart. *The Paris Commune, 1871*. London: Eyre and Spottis, 1971.

Edwards, Stewart, ed. *The Communards of Paris, 1871*. London: Thames and Hudson, 1973.

Elwitt, Sanford. *The Making of the Third Republic: Class and Politics in France, 1868–1884*. Baton Rouge: Louisiana State University Press, 1975.

————. *The Third Republic Defended: Bourgeois Reform in France, 1880–1914*. Baton Rouge: Louisiana State University Press, 1986.

Fehér, Ferenc. *The Frozen Revolution: An Essay on Jacobinism*. Cambridge, England: Cambridge University Press, 1988.

Fortescue, William. *Revolution and Counter-Revolution in France, 1815–1852*. Oxford: Basil Blackwell, 1988.

Furet, François. *Interpreting the French Revolution*. Cambridge, England: Cambridge University Press, 1981.

————. *Revolutionary France, 1770–1880*. Cambridge, England: Basil Blackwell, 1992.

Furet, François, and Mona Ozouf, eds. *Critical Dictionary of the French Revolution*. Cambridge, MA: Harvard University Press, 1989.

Gay, Jean. *L'Amélioration de l'existence à Paris sous le règne de Napoléon III: L'administration des services à l'usage du public*. Geneva, Switzerland: Droz, 1986.

Girard, Louis. *Nouvelle Histoire de Paris: La Deuxième République et le Second Empire, 1848–1870*. Paris: Hachette, 1981.

Godechot, Jacques. *The Taking of the Bastille, July 14th, 1789*. London: Faber, 1970.

Godfrey, James Logan. *Revolutionary Justice: A Study of Organization, Personnel and Procedure of the Paris Tribunal, 1793–1795*. Chapel Hill, NC: University of North Carolina Press, 1951.

Hampson, Norman. *Prelude to Terror: The Constituent Assembly and the Failure of Consensus, 1789–1791*. Oxford: Basil Blackwell, 1988.

Hoffman, Robert L. *More Than a Trial: The Struggle over Captain Dreyfus*. New York: Free Press, 1980.

Horne, Alistair. *The Fall of Paris: The Siege and the Commune, 1870–1871*. London: Macmillan, 1965.

————. *The Terrible Year: The Paris Commune, 1871*. London: Macmillan, 1971.

Irvine, William D. *The Boulanger Affair Reconsidered: Royalism, Boulangism, and the Origins of the Radical Right in France*. New York and Oxford: Oxford University Press, 1989.

Jardin, André, and André-Jean Tudesq. *Restoration and Reaction, 1815–1848*. Cambridge, England: Cambridge University Press, 1983.

Kates, Gary. *The Cercle Social, the Girondins and the French Revolution*. Princeton, NJ: Princeton University Press, 1985.

Kennedy, Michael L. *The Jacobin Clubs in the French Revolution*. 2 vols. Princeton, NJ: Princeton University Press, 1982–88.

Kleeblatt, Norman, ed. *The Dreyfus Affair: Art, Truth and Justice*. Berkeley and Los Angeles, CA: University of California Press, 1987.

Larkin, Maurice. *Church and State after the Dreyfus Affair: The Separation Issue in France*. London: Macmillan, 1974.

Lefebvre, Georges. *The French Revolution*. 2 vols. London: Routledge and Kegan Paul, 1962–69.

Locke, Robert R. *French Legitimists and the Politics of Moral Order in the Early Third Republic*. Princeton, NJ: Princeton University Press, 1974.

Martin, Benjamin F. *Crime and Criminal Justice under the Third Republic: The Shame of Marianne*. Baton Rouge: Louisiana State University Press, 1990.

Mayeur, Jean-Marie, and Madeleine Rebérioux. *The Third Republic from Its Origins to the Great War, 1871–1914*. Cambridge, England: Cambridge University Press, 1984.

Merriman, John M. *The Agony of the Republic: The Repression of the Left in Revolutionary France, 1848–1851*. New Haven, CT: Yale University Press, 1978.

Partin, Malcolm. *Waldeck-Rousseau, Combes and the Church: The Politics of Anti-Clericalism, 1899–1905*. Durham, NC: Duke University Press, 1969.

Pilbeam, Pamela. *The 1830 Revolution in France*. London: Macmillan, 1991.

Pinkney, David H. *Decisive Years in France, 1840–1847*. Princeton, NJ: Princeton University Press, 1986.

————. *The French Revolution of 1830*. Princeton, NJ: Princeton University Press, 1972.

Plessis, Alain. *The Rise and Fall of the Second Empire, 1852–1871*. Cambridge, England: Cambridge University Press, 1985.

Price, Roger. *Revolution and Reaction: 1848 and the Second French Republic*. London: Croom Helm; New York: Barnes and Noble Books, 1975.

Reinhard, Marcel. *Nouvelle Histoire de Paris: La Révolution, 1789–1799*. Paris: Hachette, 1971.

Rials, Stéphane. *Nouvelle Histoire de Paris: De Trochu à Thiers, 1870–1873*. Paris: Hachette, 1985.

Rigotard, Jean. *La Police parisienne de Napoléon: La préfecture de police*. Paris: Tallandier, 1990.

Roberts, John Morris. *The French Revolution*. Oxford: Oxford University Press, 1978.

Schama, Simon. *Citizens: A Chronicle of the French Revolution*. New York: Knopf, 1989.

Shapiro, Barry M. *Revolutionary Justice in Paris, 1789–1790*. Cambridge, England: Cambridge University Press, 1993.

Soboul, Albert. *The French Revolution, 1787–1799: From the Storming of the Bastille to Napoléon*. London: Routledge, 1989.

———. *The Parisian Sans-Culottes and the French Revolution, 1793–1794*. London: Greenwood Press, 1979.

Stone, Bailey. *The Genesis of the French Revolution: A Global Historical Interpretation*. Cambridge, England: Cambridge University Press, 1994.

Sutherland, Donald M. G. *France, 1789–1815: Revolution and Counterrevolution*. New York: Oxford University Press, 1986.

Tombs, Robert. *The War against Paris, 1871*. Cambridge, England: Cambridge University Press, 1981.

Tulard, Jean. *Napoléon: The Myth of the Saviour*. London: Methuen, 1984.

———. *Nouvelle Histoire de Paris: Le Consulat et l'Empire, 1800–1815*. New ed. Paris: Hachette, 1983.

———. *Nouvelle Histoire de Paris: La Révolution*. Paris: Hachette, 1989.

———. *Paris et son administration, 1800–1830*. Paris: Bibliothèque historique de la Ville de Paris, 1976.

———. *La Préfecture de Police sous la Monarchie de Juillet*. Paris: Bibliothèque historique de la Ville de Paris, 1964.

Vigier. Philippe. *Nouvelle Histoire de Paris. Paris pendant la Monarchie de Juillet, 1830–1848*. Paris: Hachette, 1991.

Vovelle, Michel. *The Fall of the French Monarchy, 1787–1792*. Cambridge, England: Cambridge University Press, 1987.

Weber, Eugen. *The National Revival in France, 1905–1914*. Berkeley, CA: University of California Press, 1968.

Woloch, Isser. *Jacobin Legacy: The Democratic Movement under the Directory*. Princeton, NJ: Princeton University Press, 1970.

———. *The New Regime: Transformation of the French Civic Order, 1789–1820*. New York: Norton, 1994.

2.5 20TH CENTURY (1914–1996)

Ambroise-Rendu, Marc. *Paris-Chirac: Prestige d'une ville, ambition d'un homme*. Paris: Plon, 1987.

Ardagh, John. *France Today*. Harmondsworth, England: Penguin, 1987.

Azéma, Jean-Pierre. *From Munich to the Liberation, 1938–1944.* Cambridge, England: Cambridge University Press, 1984.

Becker, Jean-Jacques. *The Great War and the French People.* Oxford: Berg, 1985.

Bernard, Philippe, and Henri Dubief. *The Decline of the Third Republic, 1914–1938.* Cambridge, England: Cambridge University Press, 1988.

Bernstein, Serge. *The Republic of De Gaulle, 1958–1969.* Cambridge, England: Cambridge University Press, 1993.

Caute, David. *'68: The Year of the Barricades.* London: Paladin, 1968.

Collins, Larry, and Dominique Lapierre. *Is Paris Burning?* London: Victor Gollancz, 1965.

Dank, Milton. *The French against the French: Collaboration and Resistance.* London: Cassell, 1978.

Danos, Jacques, and Marcel Gibelin. *June '36: Class Struggle and the Popular Front in France.* London: Bookmarks, 1986.

Giles, Frank. *The Locust Years: The Story of the Fourth Republic.* London: Secker, 1991.

Gordon, Bertram M. *Collaborationism in France during the Second World War.* Ithaca, NY: Cornell University Press, 1980.

Haegel, Florence. *Une Maire à Paris: Mise en scène d'un nouveau rôle politique.* Paris: Presses de la Fondation nationale des Sciences politiques, 1994.

Hall, Peter Andrew, Jack Hayward, and Howard Machin. *Developments in French Politics.* London: Macmillan, 1990.

Hanley, David L., and Anne Peterson Kerr, eds. *May '68.* London: Macmillan, 1988.

Jackson, Julian. *The Popular Front in France: Defending Democracy.* Cambridge, England: Cambridge University Press, 1988.

Keydward, Harry R. *Occupied France: Collaboration and Resistance, 1940–1944.* Oxford and New York: Basil Blackwell, 1985.

Larkin, Maurice. *France since the Popular Front: Government and People, 1936–1986.* Oxford: Clarendon Press, 1988.

Lottman, Herbert R. *The Fall of Paris: June 1940.* New York: Harper-Collins, 1992.

———. *The People's Anger: Justice and Revenge in Post-Liberation France.* London: Hutchinson, 1986.

———. *The Purge: The Purification of French Collaborators after World War II.* New York: Morrow, 1986.

McMillan, James F. *Dreyfus to De Gaulle: Politics and Society in France, 1898–1969.* London: E. Arnold, 1985.

Marrus, Michael R., and Robert O. Paxton. *Vichy France and the Jews.* New York: Basic, 1981.

Mayeur, Jean-Marie. *La Vie politique sous la Troisième République, 1870–1940.* Paris: Seuil, 1984.

Michel, Henri. *1944: La Libération de Paris*. New ed. Paris: Complexe, 1990.

————. *Paris allemand*. Paris: Albin Michel, 1981.

————. *Paris résistant*. Paris: Albin Michel, 1982.

Nivet, Philippe. *Le Conseil municipal de Paris de 1944 à 1977*. Paris: Publications de la Sorbonne, 1994.

Paxton, Robert Owen. *Vichy France: Old Guard and New Order, 1940–1944*. London: Barrie and Jenkins, 1973.

Perrault, Gilles, and Pierre Azéma. *Paris under the Occupation*. New York: Vendome, 1989.

Pryce-Jones, David. *Paris in the Third Reich: A History of the German Occupation, 1940–1944*. London: Collins, 1981.

Reader, Keith A., and Kursheed Wadia. *The May 1968 Events in France: Reproductions and Interpretations*. New York: St. Martin's Press, 1993.

Renaud, Jean-Pierre. *Paris, un Etat dans l'Etat?* Paris: L'Harmattan, 1993.

Rioux, Jean-Pierre. *The Fourth Republic, 1944–1958*. Cambridge, England: Cambridge University Press, 1987.

Soucy, Robert. *French Fascism: The First Wave, 1924–1933*. New Haven, CT: Yale University Press, 1986.

Tuppen, John. *Chirac's France, 1986–1988: Contemporary Issues in French Society*. New York: St. Martin's Press, 1991.

Wright, Vincent. *The Government and Politics of France*. 3d ed. New York: Routledge, 1989.

3. RELIGION

Adams, Geoffrey. *The Huguenots and French Opinion, 1685–1787: The Enlightenment Debate on Toleration*. Waterloo, Canada: Wilfrid Laurier University Press, 1991.

Adler, Jacques. *The Jews of Paris and the Final Solution: Communal Response and Internal Conflicts, 1940–1944*. New York: Oxford University Press, 1987.

Albert, Phyllis Cohen. *The Modernization of French Jewry: Consistory and Community in the Nineteenth Century*. Hanover, NH: Brandeis University Press, 1977.

Arnal, Oscar L. *Ambivalent Alliance: The Catholic Church and the Action Française, 1899–1939*. Pittsburgh, PA: University of Pittsburgh Press, 1985.

Benedict, Philip. *The Huguenot Population of France, 1600–1685: The Demographic Fate and Customs of a Religious Minority*. Philadelphia, PA: The American Philosophical Society, 1994.

Benveniste, Annie. *Du Bosphore à la Roquette: La communauté judéo-espagnole à Paris, 1914–1940.* Paris: L'Harmattan, 1989.

Berenson, Edward. *Populist Religion and Left-Wing Politics in France, 1830–1852.* Princeton, NJ: Princeton University Press, 1984.

Bosworth, William. *Catholicism and Crisis in Modern France: French Catholic Groups at the Threshold of the Fifth Republic.* Princeton, NJ: Princeton University Press, 1962.

Charlton, Donald J. *Secular Religion in France, 1815–1870.* New York: Oxford University Press, 1963.

Clémençot, Philippe, Florin Dumitrescue, and Françoise Since. *Guide pratique du Paris religieux.* Paris: Parigramme, 1994.

Dansette, Adrien. *Religious History of Modern France.* New York: Herder and Herder, 1961.

D'Avray, D. L. *The Preaching of the Friars: Sermons Diffused from Paris before 1300.* Oxford: Clarendon Press, 1988.

Diefendorf, Barbara B. *Beneath the Cross: Catholics and Huguenots in Sixteenth-Century Paris.* New York and Oxford: Oxford University Press, 1991.

Driancourt-Girod, Janine. *Ainsi priaient les Luthériens: La vie religieuse, la pratique et la foi des Luthériens à Paris aux dix-septième et dix-huitième siècles.* Paris: Cerf, 1992.

———. *L'Insolite Histoire des Luthériens de Paris, de Louis XIII à Napoléon.* Paris: Albin Michel, 1992.

Farge, James K. *Orthodoxy and Reform in Early Reformation France: The Faculty of Theology of Paris, 1500–1543.* Leiden, The Netherlands: Brill, 1985.

Friedmann, Adrien. *Paris, ses rues, ses paroisses, du Moyen Age à la Révolution: Origine et évolution des circonscriptions paroissiales.* Paris: Plon, 1959.

Gibson, Ralph. *A Social History of French Catholicism, 1789–1914.* London: Routledge, 1989.

Golden, Richard M. *The Godly Rebellion: Parisian Curés and the Religious Fronde, 1652–1662.* Chapel Hill, NC: University of North Carolina Press, 1981.

Gray, Janet Glenn. *The French Huguenots: Anatomy of Courage.* Grand Rapids, MI: Baker Book House, 1981.

Green, Nancy L. *Les Travailleurs immigrés juifs à la Belle Epoque: Le "Pletzl" de Paris.* Paris: Fayard, 1985.

Greengrass, Mark. *The French Reformation.* Oxford: Blackwell, 1987.

Heller, Henry. *The Conquest of Poverty: The Calvinist Revolt in Sixteenth-Century France.* Leiden, The Netherlands: Brill, 1986.

Hertzberg, Arthur. *The French Enlightenment and the Jews.* New York: Columbia University Press; Philadelphia, PA: The Jewish Publication Society of America, 1968.

Hourticq, Denise, Robert Lecomte, and Pierre Poujol. *Le Paris protestant de la Réforme à nos jours*. Paris: Les Bergers et les Mages, 1959.

Hyman, Paule. *From Dreyfus to Vichy: The Remaking of French Jewry*. New York: Columbia University Press, 1979.

Jordan, William Chester. *The French Monarchy and the Jews: From Philip Augustus to the Last Capetians*. Philadelphia, PA: University of Pennsylvania Press, 1989.

Kreiser, B. Robert. *Miracles, Convulsions and Ecclesiastical Politics in Early Eighteenth-Century Paris*. Princeton, NJ: Princeton University Press, 1978.

Larkin, Maurice. *Church and State after the Dreyfus Affair*. London: Macmillan, 1974.

Lebigre, Arlette. *La Révolution des curés: Paris, 1588–1594*. Paris: Albin Michel, 1980.

McKitterick, Rosamond. *The Frankish Church and the Carolingian Reforms, 789–895*. London: Royal Historical Society, 1977.

McManners, John. *Church and State in France, 1870–1914*. London: SPCK, 1972.

———. *The French Revolution and the Church*. London: SPCK, 1969.

Malino, Frances, and Bernard Wasserstein, eds. *The Jews in Modern France*. Hanover, NH: Brandeis University Press, 1985.

Marrus, Michael R. *The Politics of Assimilation: A Study of the French Jewish Community at the Time of the Dreyfus Affair*. Oxford: Clarendon Press, 1971.

Philippe, Béatrice. *Les Juifs à Paris à la Belle Epoque*. Paris: Albin Michel, 1992.

Piette, Christine. *Les Juifs de Paris, 1808–1840: La marche vers l'assimilation*. Laval, Canada: Presses de l'Université de Laval, 1983.

Plongeron, Bernard, ed. *Histoire des diocèses de France: Le Diocèse de Paris*. Paris: Beauchesne, 1987.

Poland, Burdette C. *French Protestantism and the French Revolution: A Study in Church and State, Thought and Religion, 1685–1815*. Princeton, NJ: Princeton University Press, 1957.

Schwarzfuchs, Simon. *Napoléon, the Jews and the Sanhedrin*. London and Boston: Routledge and Kegan Paul, 1979.

Sedgwick, Alexander. *Jansenism in Seventeenth-Century France: Voices from the Wilderness*. Charlottesville, VA: University Press of Virginia, 1977.

Stankiewicz, Wladijslaw Jozef. *Politics and Religion in Seventeenth-Century France*. Berkeley and Los Angeles, CA: University of California Press, 1960.

Sutherland, Nicola May. *The Huguenot Struggle for Recognition*. New Haven, CT: Yale University Press, 1980.

Swanson, R. N. *Universities, Academies and the Great Schism.* Cambridge, England: Cambridge University Press, 1979.

Wallace-Hadrill, John M. *The Frankish Church.* Oxford: Clarendon Press, 1983.

4. EDUCATION

Anderson, Robert David. *Education in France, 1848–1870.* Oxford: Clarendon Press, 1975.

Atkin, Nicholas. *Church and Schools in Vichy France, 1940–1944.* New York and London: Garland, 1991.

Bernstein, Allan E. *Pierre d'Ailly and the Blanchard Affair: University and Chancellor of Paris at the Beginning of the Great Schism.* Leiden, The Netherlands: Brill, 1978.

Bompaire-Evesque, Claire-Françoise. *Un Débat sur l'Université au temps de la Troisième République: La lutte contre la Nouvelle Sorbonne.* Paris: Aux Amateurs de livres, 1988.

Brockliss, L. W. B. *French Higher Education in the Seventeenth and Eighteenth Centuries: A Cultural History.* Oxford: Clarendon Press, 1987.

———. *The University of Paris in the Sixteenth and Seventeenth Centuries.* Oxford: Oxford University Press, 1976.

Chatelet, Anne-Marie, ed. *L'Ecole primaire à Paris, 1870–1914.* Paris: Délégation à l'Action artistique de la Ville de Paris, 1985.

———. *Paris à l'école, "Qui a eu cette idée folle?"* Paris: Picard, 1993.

Clark, Linda L. *Schooling the Daughters of Marianne: Textbooks and the Socialization of Girls in Modern French Primary Schools.* Albany: State University of New York Press, 1984.

Compère, Marie-Madeleine. *Du Collège au Lycée, 1500–1850: Généalogie de l'enseignement secondaire français.* Paris: Gallimard, 1985.

Ferruolo, Stephen C. *The Origins of the University: The Schools of Paris and Their Critics, 1100–1215.* Stanford, CA: Stanford University Press, 1985.

Fraser, William Rae. *Education and Society in Modern France.* London: Routledge and Kegan Paul; New York: Humanities Press, 1963.

———. *Reforms and Restraints in Modern French Education.* London: Routledge and Kegan Paul, 1971.

Gabriel, Astrik L. *The Paris Studium: Robert of Sorbonne and his Legacy.* Notre Dame, IN: University of Notre Dame; Frankfurt am Main, Germany: Josef Knecht, 1992.

Gontard, Maurice. *L'Enseignement secondaire en France de la fin de l'Ancien Régime à la loi Falloux, 1750–1850.* Aix-en-Provence, France: Edisud, 1984.

Haarhoff, Theodore Johannes. *Schools of Gaul.* 2d ed. Johannesburg, South Africa: Witwatersrand University Press, 1958.

Harrigan, Patrick J. *Mobility, Elites and Education in French Society of the Second Empire.* Waterloo, Canada: Wilfrid Laurier University Press, 1980.

Horvath-Peterson, Sandra. *Victor Duruy and French Education: Liberal Reform in the Second Empire.* Baton Rouge: Louisiana State University Press, 1984.

Huppert, George. *Public Schools in Renaissance France.* Urbana and Chicago, IL: University of Illinois Press, 1984.

Kelley, Donald. *Foundations of Modern Historical Scholarship: Language, Law and History in the French Renaissance.* New York: Columbia University Press, 1970.

Kibre, Pearl. *Scholarly Privileges in the Middle Ages: The Rights, Privileges and Immunities of Scholars and Universities at Bologne, Padua, Paris and Oxford.* Cambridge, MA: The Medieval Academy of America, 1962.

McLaughlin, Mary Martin. *Intellectual Freedom and Its Limitations in the University of Paris in the Thirteenth and Fourteenth Centuries.* New York: Arno Press, 1977.

Margadant, Jo Burr. *Madame le Professeur: Women Educators in the Third Republic.* Princeton, NJ: Princeton University Press, 1990.

Mayeur, Françoise. *L'Education des jeunes filles en France au dix-neuvième siècle.* Paris: Hachette, 1979.

———. *L'Enseignement secondaire des jeunes filles sous la Troisième République, 1867–1924.* Paris: Presses de la Fondation nationale des Sciences politiques, 1977.

Moody, Joseph N. *French Education since Napoléon.* Syracuse, NY: Syracuse University Press, 1978.

Motley, Mark. *Becoming a French Aristocrat: The Education of the Court Nobility, 1580–1715.* Princeton, NJ: Princeton University Press, 1990.

Osborne, Thomas R. *A Grand Ecole for the Grands Corps: The Recruitment and Training of the French Administrative Elite in the Nineteenth Century.* New York: Social Science Monographs, 1983.

Padberg, John W. *Colleges in Controversy: The Jesuit Schools in France from Revival to Suppression, 1815–1880.* Cambridge, MA: Harvard University Press, 1969.

Palmer, Robert Roswell. *The School of French Revolution: A Documentary History of the College of Louis-le-Grand and Its Director, Jean-François Champagne, 1762–1814.* Princeton, NJ: Princeton University Press, 1975.

Parias, Louis-Henri, ed. *Histoire générale de l'enseignement et de l'éducation en France.* 4 vols. Paris: Nouvelle Librairie de France, G.-V. Labat, 1981.

Riché, Pierre. *Education and Culture in the Barbarian West, Sixth through Eighth Centuries.* Columbia, SC: University of South Carolina Press, 1976.

Rubenstein, Diana. *What's Left? The Ecole Normale Supérieure and the Right.* Madison, WI: The University of Wisconsin Press, 1990.

Smith, Robert J. *The Ecole Normale Supérieure and the Third Republic.* Albany: State University of New York Press, 1982.

Stock-Morton, Phyliss. *Moral Education for a Secular Society: The Development of Morale Laïque in Nineteenth-Century France.* New York: State University of New York Press, 1988.

Sullivan, Thomas. *Benedictine Monks at the University of Paris, A.D. 1229–1500: A Biographical Register.* Leiden, The Netherlands; New York; Cologne, Germany: Brill, 1995.

Talbott, John E. *The Politics of Educational Reform in France, 1918–1940.* Princeton, NJ: Princeton University Press, 1969.

Tanaka, Mineo. *La Nation anglo-allemande de l'Université de Paris à la fin du Moyen Age.* Paris: Aux Amateurs de livres, 1990.

Tuilier, André. *Histoire de l'Université de Paris et de la Sorbonne.* 2 vols. Paris: Nouvelle Librairie de France, 1994.

Weisz, George. *The Emergence of Modern Universities in France, 1863–1914.* Princeton, NJ: Princeton University Press, 1983.

5. SOCIETY

The Age of Napoléon: Costume from Revolution to Empire, 1789–1815. New York: Metropolitan Museum of Art, H. N. Abrams, 1989.

Ariès, Philippe. *A Century of Childhood: A Social History of Family Life.* New York: Vintage Books, 1962.

Aron, Jean-Paul. *Essai sur la sensibilité alimentaire à Paris au dix-neuvième siècle.* Paris: Armand Colin, 1967.

Barrows, Susanna. *Distorting Mirrors: Visions of the Crowd in Late Nineteenth-Century France.* New Haven, CT: Yale University Press, 1981.

Beevor, Antony, and Artemis Cooper. *Paris after the Liberation, 1944–1949.* London: Hamish Hamilton, 1994.

Bell, David A. *Lawyers and Citizens: The Making of a Political Elite in Old Regime France.* New York: Oxford University Press, 1994.

———. *Lawyers and Politics in Eighteenth-Century Paris, 1700–1790.* Princeton, NJ: Princeton University Press, 1991.

Benedict, Philip, ed. *Cities and Social Change in Early Modern France.* London and New York: Routledge, 1992.

Berlanstein, Lenard R. *Big Business and Industrial Conflict in Nineteenth-Century France: A Social History of the Parisian Gas Com-*

pany. Berkeley, Los Angeles, Oxford: University of California Press, 1991.

————. *The Working People of Paris, 1871–1914*. Baltimore, MD: Johns Hopkins University Press, 1984.

Bernheimer, Charles. *Figures of Ill Repute: Representing Prostitution in Nineteenth-Century France*. Cambridge, MA, and London: Harvard University Press, 1989.

Bernier, Olivier. *Fireworks at Dusk: Paris in the Thirties*. Boston, Toronto, London: Little, Brown, 1993.

Bernstein, Richard. *Fragile Glory: A Portrait of France and the French*. New York: Knopf, 1990.

Berstein, Serge. *La France des années 30*. 2d ed. Paris: Armand Colin, 1993.

Bertholet, Denis. *Le Bourgeois dans tous ses états: Le roman familial de la Belle Epoque*. Paris: Olivier Orban, 1987.

Billacois, François. *The Duel: Its Rise and Fall in Early Modern France*. New Haven, CT: Yale University Press, 1990.

Bitton, Davis. *The French Nobility in Crisis, 1560–1640*. Stanford, CA: Stanford University Press, 1969.

Blanning, T. C. W. *The French Revolution: Aristocrats versus Bourgeois*. London: Macmillan, 1987.

Bonney, Richard J. *Society and Government in France under Richelieu and Mazarin, 1624–1661*. New York: St. Martin's Press, 1988.

Boussard, Jacques. *The Civilisation of Charlemagne*. London: Weidenfeld and Nicolson, 1968.

Bouthon, Cynthia A. *The Flour War: Gender, Class and Community in Late Ancien Régime French Society*. University Park, PA: Pennsylvania State University Press, 1993.

Bowman, Sara. *A Fashion for Extravagance: Art Deco Fabrics and Fashions*. London: Bell and Hyman, 1985.

Brennan, Thomas. *Public Drinking and Popular Culture in Eighteenth-Century Paris*. Princeton, NJ: Princeton University Press, 1988.

Briggs, Robin. *Communities of Belief: Cultural and Social Tensions in Early Modern France*. Oxford: Clarendon Press, 1989.

Bryant, Lawrence M. *The King and the City in the Parisian Royal Entry Ceremony: Politics, Ritual, and Art in the Renaissance*. Geneva, Switzerland: Droz, 1986.

Burgière, André, and Tamara K. Hareven. *Family and Sexuality in French History*. Philadelphia, PA: University of Pennsylvania Press, 1980.

Byrnes, Robert F. *Antisemitism in Modern France*. New York: Howard Fertig, 1969.

Capul, Maurice. *Les Enfants placés sous l'Ancien Régime*. 2 vols. Toulouse, France: Privat, 1989–90.

Caron, Jean-Claude. *Générations romantiques: Les étudiants de Paris et le Quartier latin, 1814–1851.* Paris: Armand Colin, 1991.

Chaunu, Pierre. *La Mort à Paris, seizième, dix-septième et dix-huitième siècles.* Paris: Fayard, 1978.

Chaussinand-Nogaret, Guy. *The French Nobility in the Eighteenth Century: From Feudalism to Enlightenment.* Cambridge, England: Cambridge University Press, 1985.

Chevalier, Louis. *La Formation de la population parisienne au dix-neuvième siècle.* Paris: Presses Universitaires de France, 1950.

———. *Laboring Classes and Dangerous Classes in Paris during the First Half of the Nineteenth Century.* New York: Howard Fertig, 1973.

———. *Montmartre du plaisir et du crime.* Paris: R. Laffont, 1980.

———. *Les Parisiens.* New ed. Paris: Hachette-Pluriel, 1985.

———. *Les Ruines de Subure: Montmartre de 1939 aux années 80.* Paris: R. Laffont, 1985.

Chombart de Lauwe, Paul-Henry. *Paris, essais de sociologie, 1952–1964.* Paris: Editions ouvrières, 1965.

Church, Clive H. *Revolution and Red Tape: The French Ministerial Bureaucracy, 1770–1853.* Oxford: Clarendon Press, 1981.

Clayson, Hollis. *Painted Love: Prostitution in French Art in the Impressionist Era.* New Haven, CT: Yale University Press, 1991.

Cobb, Richard. *Death in Paris: The Records of the Basse-Geôle de la Seine, October 1795–September 1801 (Vendémiaire year IV–Fructidor IX).* Oxford: Oxford University Press, 1978.

Cobban, Alfred. *The Social Interpretation of the French Revolution.* Cambridge, England: Cambridge University Press, 1964.

Coleman, Elizabeth Ann. *The Opulent Era: Fashions of Worth, Doucet and Pingat.* New York: Thames and Hudson and The Brooklyn Museum, 1989.

Coleman, William. *Death is a Social Disease: Public Health and Political Economy in Early Industrial France.* Madison, WI: University of Wisconsin Press, 1982.

Copley, Antony R. *Sexual Moralities in France, 1780–1980: New Ideas on the Family, Divorce and Homosexuality. An Essay on Moral Change.* London: Routledge, 1989.

Corbin, Alain. *The Foul and the Fragrant: Odor and the French Social Imagination.* Cambridge, MA: Harvard University Press, 1986.

Cronin, Vincent. *Paris, City of Light, 1919–1939.* London: Harper Collins, 1994.

———. *Paris on the Eve, 1900–1914.* London: Collins, 1989.

Darnton, Robert. *The Great Cat Massacre and Other Episodes in French Cultural History.* New York: Vintage, 1984.

Daumard, Adeline. *Les Bourgeois de Paris au dix-neuvième siècle.* Paris: Flammarion, 1970.

————. *La Bourgeoisie parisienne de 1815 à 1848*. Paris: SEVPEN, 1963.

————. *Maisons de Paris et propriétaires parisiens au dix-neuvième siècle, 1809–1880*. Paris: Cujas, 1965.

Daumard, Adeline, and François Furet. *Structures et relations sociales à Paris au dix-huitième siècle*. Paris: Armand Colin, 1981.

Deaucourt, Jean-Louis. *Premières Loges: Paris et ses concierges au dix-neuvième siècle*. Paris: Aubier, 1992.

Delaporte, François. *Disease and Civilization: The Cholera in Paris, 1832*. Cambridge, MA: MIT Press, 1986.

De Marly, Diana. *The History of Haute Couture, 1850–1950*. New York: Holmes and Meier, 1980.

De Pietri, Stephen, and Melissa Leventon. *New-Look to Now: French Haute Couture, 1947–1987*. New York: Rizzoli, 1989.

Dorsey, Hebe. *The Belle Epoque in the* Paris Herald. London: Thames and Hudson, 1986.

Duchen, Claire. *Feminism in France: From May '68 to Mitterrand*. London: Routledge, 1986.

Dumont, Marie-Jeanne. *Le Logement social à Paris, 1850–1930, les habitations à bon marché*. Liège, Belgium: Mardaga, 1991.

Dyer, Colin. *Population and Society in Twentieth-Century France*. London: Hodder and Stoughton, 1978.

Egbert, Virginia Wylie. *On the Bridge of Medieval Paris: A Record of Early Fourteenth-Century Life*. Princeton, NJ: Princeton University Press, 1974.

Fairchilds, Cissie. *Domestic Enemies: Servants and Their Masters in Old Regime France*. Baltimore, MD: Johns Hopkins University Press, 1984.

Farge, Arlette. *Fragile Lives: Violence, Power and Solidarity in Eighteenth-Century Paris*. Cambridge, MA: Harvard University Press, 1993.

Farr, Evelyn. *Before the Deluge: Parisian Society in the Reign of Louis XVI*. London and Chester Springs, PA: Peter Owen, 1994.

Faure, Alain. *Paris carême-prenant: Du carnaval à Paris au dix-neuvième siècle, 1800–1914*. Paris: Hachette, 1978.

Fitzsimmons, Michael. *The Parisian Order of Barristers and the French Revolution*. Cambridge, MA: Harvard University Press, 1987.

Flandrin, Jean-Louis. *Chronique de Platine: Pour une gastronomie historique*. Paris: Odile Jacob, 1992.

————. *Families in Former Times: Kinship, Household and Sexuality*. Cambridge, England: Cambridge University Press, 1979.

Ford, Franklin L. *Robe and Sword: The Regrouping of French Aristocracy after Louis XIV*. Cambridge, MA: Harvard University Press, 1953.

Forrest, Alan. *The French Revolution and the Poor*. New York: St. Martin's Press, 1981.

Fuchs, Rachel Ginnis. *Abandoned Children: Foundlings and Child Welfare in Nineteenth-Century France*. Albany: State University of New York Press, 1984.

————. *Poor and Pregnant in Paris: Strategies for Survival in the Nineteenth Century*. New Brunswick, NJ: Rutgers University Press, 1992.

Gallaher, John G. *The Students of Paris and the Revolution of 1848*. Carbondale and Edwardsville, IL: Southern Illinois University Press, 1980.

Garrioch, David. *Neighborhood and Community in Paris, 1740–1790*. Cambridge, England: Cambridge University Press, 1986.

Gasnault, François. *Guinguettes et lorettes, bals publics et danse sociale à Paris entre 1830 et 1870*. Paris: Aubier-Montaigne, 1986.

Gaxotte, Pierre. *Paris au dix-huitième siècle*. Paris: Arthaud, 1968. 2d ed., 1982.

Gelbart, Nina Rattner. *Feminine and Opposition Journalism in Old Regime France: Le Journal des Dames*. Berkeley, CA: University of California Press, 1987.

Geremek, Bronislaw. *The Margins of Society in Late Medieval Paris*. New York: Cambridge University Press, 1987.

Gibson, Wendy. *Women in Seventeenth-Century France*. Basingstoke, England: Macmillan, 1987.

Goubert, Pierre. *The Ancien Régime: French Society, 1600–1750*. New York: Harper and Row, 1973.

Greengrass, Mark. *France in the Age of Henri IV: The Struggle for Stability*. London and New York: Longman, 1984.

Haine, W. Scott. *The World of the Paris Café: Sociability among the French Working Class, 1789–1914*. Baltimore, MD: Johns Hopkins University Press, 1996.

Harsin, Jill. *Policing Prostitution in Nineteenth-Century Paris*. Princeton, NJ: Princeton University Press, 1985.

Hause, Steven C., and Anne R. Kenney. *Women's Suffrage and Social Politics in the French Third Republic*. Princeton, NJ: Princeton University Press, 1984.

Héron de Villefosse, René. *Nouvelle Histoire de Paris: Solennités, fêtes et réjouissances parisiennes*. Paris: Hachette, 1980.

Heywood, Colin. *Childhood in Nineteenth-Century France: Work, Health and Education among the "Classes Populaires."* Cambridge, England: Cambridge University Press, 1988.

Holt, Richard. *Sport and Society in Modern France*. London: Macmillan, 1981.

Hufton, Olwen H. *The Poor of Eighteenth-Century France, 1750–1789*. Oxford: Clarendon Press, 1974.

Hunt, David. *Parents and Children in History: The Psychology of Family Life in Early Modern France*. New York: Harper and Row, 1972.

Hunt, Lynn A. *Politics, Culture, and Class in the French Revolution*. Berkeley, CA: University of California Press, 1984.

Huppert, George. *Les Bourgeois Gentilshommes: An Essay on the Definition of Elites in Renaissance France*. Chicago and London: Chicago University Press, 1977.

Isherwood, Robert M. *Farce and Fantasy: Popular Entertainment in Eighteenth-Century Paris*. New York: Oxford University Press, 1986.

Isser, Natalie. *Antisemitism during the French Second Empire*. New York: Peter Lang, 1991.

Jacquemet, Gérard. *Belleville au dix-neuvième siècle*. Paris: École des Hautes Études en Sciences sociales, 1984.

Kaplow, Jeffry. *The Names of Kings: The Parisian Laboring Poor in the Eighteenth Century*. New York: Basic Books, 1972.

Kaspi, André, and Antoine Marès. *Le Paris des étrangers depuis un siècle*. Paris: Imprimerie nationale, 1989; Paris: Publications de la Sorbonne, 1994.

Kete, Kathleen. *The Beast in the Boudoir: Petkeeping in Nineteenth-Century Paris*. Berkeley, Los Angeles and London: University of California Press, 1994.

Kettering, Sharon. *Patrons, Brokers and Clients in Seventeenth-Century France*. New York and Oxford: Oxford University Press, 1986.

Kierstad, Raymond F., ed. *State and Society in Seventeenth-Century France*. New York: New Viewpoints, 1975.

Landes, Joan B. *Women and the Public Sphere in the Age of the French Revolution*. Ithaca, NY: Cornell University Press, 1988.

Langlois, Gilles-Antoine, ed. *Folies, Tivolis et attractions: Les premiers parcs de loisirs parisiens*. Paris: Délégation à l'Action artistique de la Ville de Paris, 1991.

Le Boterf, Hervé. *La Vie parisienne sous l'Occupation, 1940–1944*. 2 vols. Paris: France-Empire, 1974–75; 4 vols. Geneva, Switzerland: Famot, 1978.

Lee, Vera. *The Reign of Women in Eighteenth-Century France*. Cambridge, MA: Schenkman, 1975.

Lougee, Carolyn C. *Le Paradis des Femmes: Women, Salons, and Social Stratification in Seventeenth-Century France*. Princeton, NJ: Princeton University Press, 1976.

Lynam, Ruth. *Paris Fashion: The Great Designers and Their Creations*. London: M. Joseph, 1972.

Lynch, Katherine A. *Family, Class and Ideology in Early Industrial France: Social Policy and the Working-Class Family, 1825–1848*. Madison: University of Wisconsin Press, 1988.

Lyons, Martyn. *France under the Directory.* Cambridge, England: Cambridge University Press, 1975.

McBride, Theresa M. *The Domestic Revolution: The Modernization of Household Service in England and France, 1820–1920.* New York: Holmes and Meier, 1976.

McMillan, James F. *Housewife or Harlot? The Place of Women in French Society, 1870–1940.* New York: St. Martin's Press, 1981.

Magraw, Roger. *France, 1815–1914: The Bourgeois Century.* London: Fontana, 1983; New York: Oxford University Press, 1986.

————. *A History of the French Working Class.* Oxford: Blackwell, 1992.

Mandrou, Robert. *Introduction to Modern France, 1500–1640.* London: Edward Arnold, 1975.

Maneglier, Hervé. *Paris impérial: La vie quotidienne sous le Second Empire.* Paris: Armand Colin, 1990.

Marchand, Bernard. *Paris: Histoire d'une ville, dix-neuvième-vingtième siècle.* Paris: Seuil, 1993.

Martin, Lynn A. *The Jesuit Mind: The Mentality of an Elite in Early Modern France.* Ithaca and New York: Cornell University Press, 1988.

Martin-Fugier, Anne. *La Bourgeoise: La femme au temps de Paul Bourget.* Paris: Bernard Grasset, 1983.

————. *La Place des bonnes: La domesticité féminine à Paris en 1900.* Paris: Bernard Grasset, 1979.

————. *La Vie élégante ou la Formation du Tout-Paris, 1815–1848.* Paris: Fayard, 1990.

Maza, Sarah. *Servants and Masters in Eighteenth-Century France: The Uses of Loyalty.* Princeton, NJ: Princeton University Press, 1983.

Melzer, Sara E., and Leslie W. Rabine, eds. *Rebel Daughters: Women and the French Revolution.* New York and Oxford: Oxford University Press, 1992.

Mendras, Henri. *Social Change in Modern France: Towards a Cultural Anthropology of the Fifth Republic.* Cambridge, England: Cambridge University Press, 1991.

Merriman, John M. *The Margins of City Life: Explorations of the French Urban Frontier, 1815–1851.* New York and Oxford: Oxford University Press, 1991.

Milbank, Caroline Rennolds. *Couture: The Great Designers.* New York: Stewart, Tabori and Chang, 1985.

Milley, Jacques, Désiré Brelingard, and Louis Mazoyer. *La Vie parisienne à travers les âges.* 4 vols. Paris: Société continentale d'éditions modernes illustrées, 1965–66.

Morazé, Charles. *The Triumph of the Middle Class: A Study of European*

Values in the Nineteenth Century. London: Weidenfeld and Nicolson, 1966.

Moses, Claire Goldberg. *French Feminism in the Nineteenth Century*. Albany: State University of New York Press, 1984.

Mousnier, Roland. *Recherches sur la stratification sociale à Paris aux dix-septième et dix-huitième siècles: L'échantillon de 1634, 1635, 1636*. Paris: A. Pedone, 1976.

Munz. Peter. *Life in the Age of Charlemagne*. New York: Putnam's Sons, 1969.

Neuschel, Kristin. *Word of Honour: Interpreting Noble Culture in Sixteenth-Century France*. Ithaca, NY: Cornell University Press, 1989.

Nord, Philip G. *Paris Shopkeepers and the Politics of Resentment*. Princeton, NJ: Princeton University Press, 1986.

Oberthur, Mariel. *Cafés and Cabarets of Montmartre*. Salt Lake City: Peregrine Smith Books, 1984.

O'Brien, Patricia. *The Promise of Punishment: Prisons in Nineteenth-Century France*. Princeton, NJ: Princeton University Press, 1982.

Ory, Pascal. *Les Expositions universelles à Paris*. Paris: Ramsay, 1982.

Oster, Daniel, and Jean Goulemot, eds. *La Vie parisienne: Anthologie des moeurs parisiennes du dix-neuvième siècle*. Paris: Sand/Conti, 1989.

Ozouf, Mona. *Festivals and the French Revolution*. Cambridge, MA: Harvard University Press, 1988.

Pardailhé-Galabrun, Annik. *La Naissance de l'intime: Trois mille foyers parisiens, dix-septième–dix-huitième siècle*. Paris: Presses Universitaires de France, 1988.

Le Parisien chez lui au dix-neuvième siècle, 1814–1914. Paris: Les Presses artistiques, 1976.

Pitte, Jean-Robert. *Gastronomie française: Histoire et géographie d'une passion*. Paris: Fayard, 1991.

Price, Roger. *The French Second Republic: A Social History*. Ithaca, NY: Cornell University Press, 1972.

———. *A Social History of Nineteenth-Century France*. New York: Holmes and Meier, 1987.

Pryce-Jones, David. *Paris in the Third Reich: A History of the German Occupation, 1940–1944*. London: Collins, 1981.

Ranum, Orest. *Paris in the Age of Absolutism: An Essay*. New York: Wiley, 1968.

Rearick, Charles. *Pleasures of the Belle Epoque: Entertainment and Festivity in Turn-of-the-Century France*. New Haven, CT: Yale University Press, 1985.

Remaury, Bruno, ed. *Dictionnaire de la mode au vingtième siècle*. Paris: Editions du Regard, 1994.

Ribeiro, Aileen. *Fashion in the French Revolution*. London: B. T. Batsford, 1988.

Riché, Pierre. *Daily Life in the World of Charlemagne.* Liverpool, England: Liverpool University Press, 1978.

Rifkin, Adrian. *Street Noises: Parisian Pleasure, 1900–1940.* Manchester, England, and New York: Manchester University Press, 1995.

Roche, Daniel. *La Culture des apparences: Une histoire du vêtement, dix-septième–dix-huitième siècle.* Paris: Fayard, 1989.

———. *The People of Paris.* Berkeley, CA: University of California Press, 1987.

Rothkrug, Lionel. *Opposition to Louis XIV: The Political and Social Origins of the French Enlightenment.* Princeton, NJ: Princeton University Press, 1965.

Rudé, George. *The Crowd in the French Revolution.* London: Oxford University Press, 1967.

Saisselin, Remy. *The Bourgeois and the Bibelot.* New Brunswick, NJ: Rutgers University Press, 1984.

Sallée, André, and Philippe Chauveau. *Music-Hall et Café-Concert.* Paris: Bordas, 1985.

Salmon, John H. M. *Society in Crisis: France in the Sixteenth Century.* New York: St. Martin's Press, 1975.

La Santé des Parisiens: Bilan de santé d'une capitale. Paris: Albin Michel, 1993.

Schwartz, Robert M. *Policing the Poor in Eighteenth-Century France.* Chapel Hill, NC: University of North Carolina Press, 1988.

Sewell, William H. Jr. *Work and Revolution in France: The Language of Labor from the Old Regime to 1848.* Cambridge, England: Cambridge University Press, 1980.

Shapiro, Ann Louise. *Breaking the Codes: Female Criminality in Fin-de-Siècle Paris.* Stanford, CA: Stanford University Press, 1996.

———. *Housing the Poor of Paris, 1850–1902.* Madison, WI: University of Wisconsin Press, 1985.

Spitzer, Alan B. *The French Generation of 1820.* Princeton, NJ: Princeton University Press, 1987.

Stanton, Domna C. *The Aristocrat as Art: A Study of the Honnête Homme and the Dandy in Seventeenth and Nineteenth-Century French Literature.* New York: Columbia University Press, 1980.

Stearns, Peter N. *Paths to Authority: The Middle Class and the Industrial Labor Force in France, 1820–1848.* Urbana, IL: University of Illinois Press, 1978.

Steele, Valerie. *Paris Fashion: A Cultural History.* New York: Oxford University Press, 1988.

Stewart, Mary Lynn. *Women, Work, and the French State.* Montréal, Canada: McGill-Queens University Press, 1989.

Suleiman, Ezra N. *Elites in French Society: The Politics of Survival.* Princeton, NJ: Princeton University Press, 1978.

————. *Politics, Power and Bureaucracy in France: The Administrative Elite.* Princeton, NJ: Princeton University Press, 1974.

Sussman, George D. *Selling Mother's Milk: The Wet-Nursing Business in France, 1715–1914.* Urbana, IL: University of Illinois Press, 1982.

Tapié, Victor-Lucien. *France in the Age of Louis XIII and Richelieu.* London: Macmillan, 1974.

Taylor, Katherine Fischer. *In the Theater of Criminal Justice: The Palais de Justice in Second Empire Paris.* Princeton, NJ: Princeton University Press, 1993.

Terdiman, Richard. *Discourse/Counter-Discourse: The Theory and Practice of Symbolic Resistance in Nineteenth-Century France.* Ithaca, NY: Cornell University Press, 1985.

Tilly, Charles. *The Contentious French: Four Centuries of Popular Struggle.* Cambridge, MA: Harvard University Press, 1986.

Traer, James. *Marriage and the Family in Eighteenth-Century France.* Ithaca, NY: Cornell University Press, 1980.

Traugott, Mark. *Armies of the Poor: Determinants of Working-Class Participation in the Parisian Insurrection of June 1848.* Princeton, NJ: Princeton University Press, 1985.

Truant, Cynthia M. *The Rites of Labor: The Brotherhoods of Compagnonnage in Old and New Regime France.* Ithaca, NY: Cornell University Press, 1994.

Van de Walle, Etienne. *The Female Population of France in the Nineteenth Century.* Princeton, NJ: Princeton University Press, 1974.

Van Kley, Dale. *The Damiens Affair and the Unraveling of the Ancien Régime, 1750–1770.* Princeton, NJ: Princeton University Press, 1984.

Walton, Whitney. *France at the Crystal Palace: Bourgeois Taste and Artisan Manufacture in the Nineteenth Century.* Berkeley, Los Angeles, London: University of California Press, 1992.

Weber, Eugen. *France: Fin de Siècle.* Cambridge, MA: Harvard University Press, 1986.

Weiner, Dora B. *The Citizen-Patient in Revolutionary and Imperial Paris.* Baltimore and London: Johns Hopkins University Press, 1993.

Wheaton, Robert, and Tamara K. Hareven, eds. *Family and Sexuality in French History.* Philadelphia: University of Pennsylvania Press, 1986.

Williams, Roger. *Gaslight and Shadow: The World of Napoléon III, 1851–1870.* New York: Macmillan, 1957.

Wilson, Stephen. *Ideology and Experience: Antisemitism in France at the Time of the Dreyfus Affair.* Rutherford, NJ: Fairleigh Dickinson University Press, 1982.

Wishnia, Judith. *The Proletarianizing of the Fonctionnaires: Civil Service Workers and the Labour Movement under the Third Republic.* Baton Rouge: Louisiana State University Press, 1990.

Wright, Gordon. *Between the Guillotine and Liberty: Two Centuries of the Crime Problem in France.* New York and Oxford: Oxford University Press, 1983.

Ygaunin, Jean. *Paris à l'époque de Balzac et dans "La Comédie humaine": La ville et la société.* Paris: Nizet, 1992.

Zeldin, Theodore. *France: 1848–1945.* Oxford: Oxford University Press, 1993.

———. *The French.* San Francisco, CA: Collins, 1993.

Zuccotti, Susan. *The Holocaust, the French and the Jews.* New York: Basic Books, 1993.

6. ECONOMY

Aftalion, Florin. *The French Revolution: An Economic Interpretation.* Cambridge, England: Cambridge University Press, 1990.

Ardagh, John. *The New French Revolution: A Social and Economic Survey of France, 1945–1967.* London: Secker and Warburg, 1968.

Asselain, Jean-Charles. *Histoire économique de la France du dix-huitième siécle à nos jours.* Paris: Seuil: 1984.

Baslé, Jacqueline. *L'Economie française: Mutations, 1975–1990.* Paris: Sirey, 1989.

Baslé, Jacqueline, and Maurice Baslé. *L'État et la politique économique en France depuis 1945.* Paris: Hatier, 1982.

Bauchet, Pierre. *Le Plan dans l'économie française.* Paris: Economica, Presses de la Fondation nationale des Sciences politiques, 1986.

Baum, Warren Charles. *The French Economy and the State.* Princeton, NJ: Princeton University Press, 1958.

Bayard, Françoise. *Le Monde des finances au dix-septième siècle.* Paris: Flammarion, 1988.

Beaujeu-Garnier, Jacqueline. *Nouvelle Histoire de Paris. Paris: hasard ou prédestination? Une géographie de Paris.* Paris: Hachette, 1993.

Bellon, Bertrand. *Le Pouvoir financier et l'industrie en France.* Paris: Seuil, 1980.

Beltran, Alain, and Paul Griset. *La Croissance économique de la France, 1815–1914.* Paris: Armand Colin, 1988.

Bergeron, Louis. *Banquiers, négociants et manufacturiers parisiens du Directoire à l'Empire.* Paris: Mouton, 1978.

Bonin, Hubert. *L'Argent en France depuis 1880: Banquiers, financiers, épargnants dans la vie économique et politique.* Paris: Masson, 1989.

———. *Histoire économique de la Quatrième République.* Paris: Economica, 1987.

Bosher, John Francis. *French Finances, 1770–1795: From Business to Bureaucracy.* Cambridge, England: Cambridge University Press, 1970.

Bouvier, Pierre. *Technologie, travail, transports: Les transports parisiens de masse, 1900–1985.* Paris: Méridiens, 1985.

Braudel, Fernand, and Ernest Labrousse, eds. *Histoire économique et sociale de la France.* 8 vols. Paris: Presses Universitaires de France, 1970–82.

Cahiers du Centre de Recherches et d'Etudes sur Paris et l'Ile-de-France. Paris, 1983–. Quarterly.

Caron, François. *An Economic History of Modern France.* London: Methuen, 1979; New York: Columbia University Press, 1979.

Caron, François, Paul Erker, and Wolfgang Fischer, eds. *Innovations in the European Economy between the Wars.* Berlin: De Gruyter, 1995.

Carré, Jean-Jacques, Paul Dubois, and Edmond Malinvaud. *French Economic Growth.* Stanford, CA: Stanford University Press, 1976.

Carrez, Jean-François. *Le Développement des fonctions tertiaires supérieures internationales à Paris et dans les métropoles régionales: Rapport au Premier ministre.* Paris: La Documentation française, 1991.

Carter, Edward C., Robert Forster, and Joseph N. Moody, eds. *Enterprises and Entrepreneurs in Nineteenth- and Twentieth-Century France.* Baltimore and London: Johns Hopkins University Press, 1976.

Cassis, Youssef, ed. *Finances and Financiers in European History, 1880–1960.* Cambridge, England: Cambridge University Press, 1992.

Cassis, Youssef, François Crouzet, and Terry Gourvish. *Management and Business in Britain and France: The Age of Corporate Economy.* Oxford: Clarendon Press, 1995.

Chapman, S. D., and Serge Chassagne. *European Textile Printers in the Eighteenth Century: A Study of Peel and Oberkampf.* London: Heinemann, 1981.

Chaussinand-Nogaret, Guy. *Gens de finance au dix-huitième siècle.* Paris: Bordas, 1993.

Chemla, Guy. *Les Ventres de Paris: Les Halles, La Villette, Rungis, l'histoire du plus grand marché du monde.* Grenoble, France: Glénat, 1994.

Clough, Shepard Bancroft. *France: A History of National Economics, 1789–1939.* New York: Octagon Books, 1964.

Conjoncture en Ile-de-France. Paris, 1982–. Quarterly.

Crouzet, François, ed. *The Economic Development of France since 1870.* Aldershot, England: Elgar, 1993.

Damette, Félix, and Pierre Beckouche. *La Métropole parisienne: Système productif et organisation de l'espace.* Paris: Université de Paris I, 1990.

Damette, Félix, and Jacques Scheibling, eds. *Le Bassin parisien: Système productif et organisation urbaine.* Paris: Université de Paris I, 1992.

Darnton, Robert, and Daniel Roche, eds. *Revolution in Print: The Press in France, 1775–1800*. Berkeley, Los Angeles and London: University of California Press, 1989.

Daumard, Adeline, et al. *Les Fortunes françaises au dix-neuvième siècle*. Paris and The Hague: Mouton, 1973.

Daumas, Maurice, and Jacques Payen, eds. *Evolution de la géographie industrielle de Paris et sa proche banlieue au dix-neuvième siècle*. 3 vols. Paris: Centre de documentation d'histoire des techniques, 1976.

Delorme, Robert, and Christine André. *L'Etat et l'économie: Un essai d'explication de l'évolution des dépenses publiques en France, 1870–1980*. Paris: Seuil, 1983.

Dent, Julian. *Crisis in Finance: Crown, Financiers and Society in Seventeenth-Century France*. Newton Abbot, England: David and Charles, 1973.

Dessert, Daniel. *Argent, pouvoir et société au Grand Siècle*. Paris: Fayard, 1984.

Dunham, Arthur Louis. *The Industrial Revolution in France, 1814–1848*. New York: Exposition Press, 1955.

Eck, Jean-François. *Histoire de l'économie française depuis 1945*. 3d ed. updated. Paris: Armand Colin, 1992.

Eisenstein, Elizabeth L. *Grub Street Abroad: Aspects of the French Cosmopolitan Press from the Age of Louis XIV to the French Revolution*. Oxford: Clarendon Press, 1992.

Flood, P. J. *France 1914–18: Public Opinion and the War Effort*. London: Macmillan, 1990.

France: Business Law, Taxation, Social Law. Levallois, France: Francis Lefebvre, 1995.

France: The Economic Guide. London: Hutchinson, 1990.

Freedman, Charles E. *Joint-Stock Enterprise in France, 1807–1867*. Chapel Hill, NC: University of North Carolina Press, 1979.

———. *The Triumph of Corporate Capitalism in France, 1867–1914*. Rochester, NY: University of Rochester Press, 1993.

Geison, Gerald L., ed. *Professions and the French State, 1700–1900*. Philadelphia, PA: University of Pennsylvania Press, 1984.

Geremek, Bronislaw. *Le Salariat dans l'artisanat parisien aux treizième-quinzième siècles*. Paris, The Hague, New York: Mouton, 1982.

Godfrey, John F. *Capitalism at War: Industrial Policy and Bureaucracy in France, 1914–1918*. Leamington Spa, England: Berg, 1987.

Gordon, Colin. *The Business Culture in France*. Oxford: Butterworth-Heinemann, 1996.

Gourden, Jean-Michel. *Le Peuple des ateliers: Les artisans au dix-neuvième siècle*. Paris: Créaphis, 1992.

Heywood, Colin. *The Development of the French Economy, 1750–1914.* Basingstoke, England: Macmillan, 1992.

Hincker, François. *La Révolution française et l'économie: Décollage ou catastrophe?* Paris: Fernand Nathan, 1989.

Hodges, Richard. *Dark Age Economics: The Origins of Towns and Trade, A.D. 600–1000.* London: Duckworth, 1982.

Hoffman, Stanley. *Decline or Renewal? France since the 1930s.* New York: Viking, 1974.

L'Ile-de-France à la page. Paris, 1987–. Monthly.

Jackson, Julian. *The Politics of Depression in France, 1932–1936.* New York: Cambridge University Press, 1985.

Kaplan, Steven Laurence. *The Bakers of Paris and the Bread Question, 1700–1775.* Durham, NC: Duke University Press, 1996.

———. *Bread, Politics and Political Economy in the Reign of Louis XV.* The Hague: Martinus Nijhoff, 1976.

———. *Provisioning Paris: Merchants and Millers in the Grain and Flour Trade during the Eighteenth Century.* Ithaca, NY: Cornell University Press, 1984.

Kaplan, Steven Laurence, and Cynthia J. Koepp, eds. *Work in France: Representation, Meaning, Organization and Practice.* Ithaca, NY: Cornell University Press, 1986.

Kemp, Tom. *Economic Forces in French History.* London: Dennis Dobson, 1971.

———. *The French Economy, 1913–1939: The History of a Decline.* New York: St. Martin's Press, 1972.

Kindleberger, Charles Poor. *Economic Growth in France and Britain, 1851–1950.* Cambridge, MA: Harvard University Press, 1964.

Koch, Henri. *Histoire de la Banque de France et de la monnaie sous la Quatrième République.* Paris: Dunod, 1983.

Kuisel, Richard F. *Capitalism and the State in Modern France: Renovation and Economic Management in the Twentieth Century.* Cambridge, England: Cambridge University Press, 1981.

Lacordaire, Simon. *Les Inconnus de la Seine: Paris et les métiers de l'eau du treizième au dix-neuvième siècle.* Paris: Hachette, 1985.

Laux, James M. *In First Gear: The French Automobile Industry to 1914.* Liverpool, England: Liverpool University Press, 1976.

Lebovics, Herman. *The Alliance of Iron and Wheat in the Third French Republic, 1860–1914: Origins of the New Conservatism.* Baton Rouge: Louisiana State University Press, 1988.

Lescure, Michel. *Les Banques, l'Etat et le marché immobilier en France à l'époque contemporaine, 1820–1940.* Paris: Editions de l'Ecole des Hautes Etudes en Sciences sociales, 1982.

———. *Histoire d'une filière: Immobilier et bâtiment en France, 1820–1980.* Paris: Hatier, 1982.

Lévy-Leboyer, Maurice, and François Bourguignon. *L'Economie française au dix-neuvième siècle: Analyse macroéconomique.* Paris: Economica, 1985.

Lewis, Gwynne. *The Advent of Modern Capitalism in France, 1770–1840: The Contribution of Pierre-François Tubeuf.* Oxford: Oxford University Press, 1993.

McCauley, Elizabeth Anne. *Industrial Madness: Commercial Photography in Paris, 1848–1871.* New Haven, CT: Yale University Press, 1994.

Macready, Sarah, and F. H. Thompson, eds. *Cross-Channel Trade between Gaul and Britain in the Pre-Roman Iron Age.* London: Society of Antiquaries of London, 1984.

Marczewski, Jean, ed. *Histoire quantitative de l'économie française.* 13 vols. Paris: Cahiers de l'Institut de Sciences économiques appliquées, 1961–76.

Margairaz, Michel. *L'Etat, les finances et l'économie: Histoire d'une conversion, 1932–1952.* Paris: Comité pour l'histoire économique et financière de la France, 1991.

Merlin, Pierre. *Les Transports à Paris et en Île-de-France.* Paris: La Documentation française, 1982.

Merriman, John M., ed. *French Cities in the Nineteenth Century.* London: Hutchinson, 1982.

Meuvret, Jean. *Le Problème des subsistances à l'époque Louis XIV.* 2 vols. Paris: Editions de l'École des Hautes Études en Sciences sociales, 1977–87.

Michalet, Charles-Albert. *Les Placements des épargnants français de 1815 à nos jours.* Paris: Presses Universitaires de France, 1968.

Millard, Jean. *Paris, histoire d'un port: Du port de Paris au Port autonome de Paris.* Paris: L'Harmattan, 1994.

Miller, Michael. *The Bon Marché: Bourgeois Culture and the Department Store, 1869–1920.* Princeton, NJ: Princeton University Press, 1981.

Milward, Alan Steele. *The New Order and the French Economy.* Oxford: Clarendon Press, 1970.

Miskimin, Harry A. *Money and Power in Fifteenth-Century France.* New Haven, CT: Yale University Press, 1984.

Moncan, Patrice de. *Who Owns Paris?* Paris: SEESAM, 1990.

Moss, Bernard H. *The Origins of the French Labor Movement, 1830–1914: The Socialism of Skilled Workers.* Berkeley, Los Angeles, London: University of California Press, 1976.

Mouré, Kenneth. *Managing the Franc Poincaré: Economic Understanding and Political Constraint in French Monetary Policy, 1928–1936.* Cambridge, England: Cambridge University Press, 1991.

O'Brien, Patrick K., and C. Keyder. *Economic Growth in Britain and*

France, 1780–1914: Two Paths to the Twentieth Century. London: G. Allen and Unwin, 1978.

O'Connor, Brendan. *Cross-Channel Relations in the Late Bronze Age*. Oxford: British Archaeological Reports, 1980.

Palmade, Guy P. *French Capitalism in the Nineteenth Century*. Newton Abbot, England: David and Charles, 1972.

Papayanis, Nicholas. *The Coachmen of Nineteenth-Century Paris: Service Workers and Class Consciousness*. Baton Rouge and London: Louisiana State University Press, 1993.

Parias, Louis-Henri, ed. *Histoire générale du travail*. 4 vols. Paris: F. Sant'Andréa-J.-G. Tronche, 1959–61.

Pauchant, Etienne, and Anne Dominique Barrère. *Plan d'aménagement du tourisme parisien*. Paris: Paris Promotion, 1992.

Perrot, Michelle. *Workers on Strike: France, 1871–1890*. Leamington Spa, England: Berg, 1987.

Pinchemel, Philippe. *France: A Geographical, Social and Economic Survey*. New York: Cambridge University Press, 1987.

La Place financière de Paris: Atouts et handicaps face aux défis internationaux. Paris: Chambre de Commerce et d'Industrie de Paris, 1988.

Price, Roger. *An Economic History of Modern France, c. 1730–1914*. London: Macmillan, 1981.

—————. *The Economic Modernization of France, 1730–1880*. London: Croom Helm, 1975.

Pybus, Victoria. *Live and Work in France*. Oxford: Vacation Work, 1994.

Regards sur l'Ile-de-France. Paris, 1988–. Quarterly.

Reid, Donald. *Paris Sewers and Sewermen: Realities and Representations*. Cambridge, MA: Harvard University Press, 1991.

Roblin, Michel. *Le Terroir de Paris aux époques gallo-romaine et franque: Peuplement et défrichement dans la civitas des Parisii*. 2d ed. updated. Paris: Picard, 1971.

Rousset-Deschamps, Marcel, and Chantal Cazes. *Paris et sa région en France et dans le monde*. Paris: DREIF, 1988.

Saint-Etienne, Christian. *L'Etat français face aux crises économiques du vingtième siècle*. Paris: Economica, 1985.

Saint-Marc, Michèle. *Histoire monétaire de la France, 1800–1980*. Paris: Presses Universitaires de France, 1983.

Schuker, Stephen A. *The End of French Predominance in Europe: The Financial Crisis of 1924 and the Adaptation of the Dawes Plan*. Chapel Hill, NC: University of North Carolina Press, 1976.

Seidman, Michael. *Workers against Work: Labor in Paris and Barcelona during the Popular Fronts*. Berkeley, Los Angeles, Oxford: University of California Press, 1991.

Sheahan, John. *Promotion and Control of Industry in Postwar France*. Cambridge, MA: Harvard University Press, 1963.

Shorter, Edward, and Charles Tilly. *Strikes in France, 1830–1968.* London: Cambridge University Press, 1974.

Singer-Kerel, Jeanne. *Le Coût de la vie à Paris de 1840 à 1954.* Paris: Armand Colin, 1961.

Sivéry, Gérard. *L'Economie du royaume de France au siècle de saint Louis, vers 1180–vers 1315.* Lille, France: Presses Universitaires de Lille, 1984.

Smith, John Graham. *The Origins and Early Development of Heavy Chemical Industry in France.* Oxford: Clarendon Press, 1979.

Smith, Michael Stephen. *Tariff Reform in France, 1860–1900: The Politics of Economic Interest.* Ithaca, NY: Cornell University Press, 1980.

Sonenscher, Michael. *The Hatters of Eighteenth-Century France.* Berkeley, Los Angeles, London: University of California Press, 1987.

———. *Work and Wages: Natural Law, Politics and the Eighteenth-Century French Trades.* Cambridge, England: Cambridge University Press, 1989.

Spooner, Frank C. *The International Economy and Monetary Movements in France, 1493–1725.* Cambridge, MA: Harvard University Press, 1972.

Sulzer, Jean-Richard. *Rapport et avis sur Paris, place financière internationale.* Paris: Comité Economique et Social d'Île-de-France, 1990.

Tableaux de l'Economie de l'Ile-de-France. Paris, 1974–, Annual.

Tuppen, John. *France under Recession, 1981–1986.* London: Macmillan, 1988.

Verley, Patrick. *Nouvelle Histoire économique de la France contemporaine.* 4 vols. Paris: La Découverte, 1989.

Vinen, Richard. *The Politics of French Business, 1936–1945.* Cambridge, England: Cambridge University Press, 1991.

Weber, Henri. *Le Parti des Patrons: Le CNPF, 1946–1986.* Paris: Seuil, 1991.

Williams, James Adams. *Restructuring the French Economy: Government and the Rise of Market Competition since World War II.* Washington, DC: The Brookings Institution, 1989.

Williams, Rosalind H. *Dream Worlds: Mass Consumption in Late Nineteenth-Century France.* Berkeley, CA: University of California Press, 1982.

Zerah, Dov. *Le Système financier français: Dix ans de mutations.* Paris: La Documentation française, 1993.

7. CULTURAL AND SCIENTIFIC LIFE

Abel, Richard. *The Ciné Goes to Town: French Cinéma, 1896–1914.* Berkeley, Los Angeles, London: University of California Press, 1994.

————. *French Cinéma: The First Wave, 1915–1929*. Princeton, NJ: Princeton University Press, 1984.

Ackerknecht, Erwin H. *Medicine at the Paris Hospital, 1794–1848*. Baltimore, MD: Johns Hopkins University Press, 1967.

Adam, Antoine. *Grandeur and Illusion: French Literature and Society, 1600–1715*. Harmondsworth, England: Penguin, 1974.

Allen, James Smith. *In the Public Eye: A History of Reading in Modern France, 1800–1940*. Princeton, NJ: Princeton University Press, 1991.

Anthony, James R. *French Baroque Music from Beaujoyeulx to Rameau*. 2d ed. New York: W. W. Norton, 1978.

Antliff, Mark. *Inventing Bergson: Cultural Politics and the Parisian Avant-Garde*. Princeton, NJ: Princeton University Press, 1993.

The Art of the July Monarchy: France 1830 to 1848. Jackson, MS: University of Missouri Press, 1990.

Avril, François. *Manuscript Painting at the Court of France: The Fourteenth Century, 1310–1380*. New York: Braziller, 1978.

Avril, François, and Nicole Reynaud. *Les Manuscripts à peintures en France, 1440–1520*. Paris: Flammarion, 1993.

Bancquart, Marie-Claire. *Paris des surréalistes*. Paris: Seghers, 1972.

Benoit, Marcelle, ed. *Dictionnaire de la musique en France aux dix-septième et dix-huitème siècles*. Paris: Fayard, 1992.

Boime, Albert. *The Academy and French Painting in the Nineteenth Century*. New York: Phaidon, 1971.

————. *Art and the French Commune: Imagining Paris after the War and Revolution*. Princeton, NJ: Princeton University Press, 1995.

Boyd, Malcolm, ed. *Music and the French Revolution*. Cambridge, England: Cambridge University Press, 1992.

Bradby, David. *Modern French Drama, 1940–1980*. Cambridge, England: Cambridge University Press, 1984.

Branner, Robert. *Manuscript Painting in Paris during the Reign of Saint Louis: A Study of Styles*. Berkeley, Los Angeles, London: University of California Press, 1977.

Brody, Elaine. *Paris, the Musical Kaleidoscope, 1870–1925*. London: Robson Books, 1988.

Brown, Cynthia J. *Poets, Patrons, and Printers: Crisis of Authority in Late Medieval France*. Ithaca, NY: Cornell University Press, 1995.

Brown, Marilyn R. *Gypsies and Other Bohemians: The Myth of the Artist in Nineteenth-Century France*. Ann Arbor, MI: University of Michigan Press, 1985.

Carlson, Marvin. *The Theatre of the French Revolution*. Ithaca, NY: Cornell University Press, 1966.

Charlton, David. *Grétry and the Growth of Opéra-Comique*. Cambridge, England: Cambridge University Press, 1986.

Chatelus, Jean. *Peindre à Paris au dix-huitième siècle*. Nîmes, France: Jacqueline Chambon, 1991.

Citron, Pierre. *La Poésie de Paris dans la littérature française de Rousseau à Baudelaire*. Paris: Editions de Minuit, 1961.

Clark, Timothy J. *The Absolute Bourgeois: Artists and Politics in France, 1848–1851*. London and New York: Thames and Hudson, 1982.

————. *The Painting of Modern Life: Paris in the Art of Manet and His Followers*. Princeton, NJ: Princeton University Press, 1984.

Clébert, Jean-Paul. *Les Hauts Lieux de la littérature à Paris*. Paris: Bordas, 1992.

Cohen, Albert. *Music in the French Royal Academy of Sciences: A Study in the Evolution of Musical Thought*. Princeton, NJ: Princeton University Press, 1981.

Cohen, Margaret. *Profane Illumination: Walter Benjamin and the Paris of Surrealist Revolution*. Berkeley, Los Angeles, London: University of California Press, 1993.

Cohn, Ruby. *From "Désiré" to "Godot": Pocket Theater of Postwar Paris*. Berkeley, CA: University of California Press, 1987.

Crow, Thomas. *Emulation: Making Artists for Revolutionary France*. New Haven, CT: Yale University Press, 1995.

————. *Painters and Public Life in Eighteenth-Century Paris*. New Haven, CT: Yale University Press, 1985.

Darnton, Robert. *The Business of Enlightenment: A Publishing History of the Encyclopédie, 1775–1800*. Cambridge, MA: Harvard University Press, 1979.

————. *The Literary Underground of the Old Regime*. Cambridge, MA: Harvard University Press, 1982.

————. *Mesmerism and the End of the Enlightenment in France*. Cambridge, MA: Harvard University Press, 1968.

Demuth, Norman. *French Opera: Its Development to the Revolution*. Horsham, England: Artemis Press, 1963.

Douchet, Jean, and Gilles Nadeau. *Paris Cinéma: Une ville vue par le cinéma de 1895 à nos jours*. Paris: Du May, 1987.

Driskel, Michael Paul. *Representing Belief: Religion, Art and Society in Nineteenth-Century France*. University Park, PA: Pennsylvania State University Press, 1992.

Duby, Georges, ed. *L'Histoire de Paris par la peinture*. Paris: Belfond, 1988.

Easton, Malcolm. *Artists and Writers in Paris: The Bohemian Idea, 1803–1867*. London: E. Arnold, 1964.

Ehrlich, Evelyn. *Cinema of Paradox: French Filmmaking under the German Occupation*. New York: Columbia University Press, 1985.

Everist, Mark. *French Motets in the Thirteenth Century: Music, Poetry and Genre*. Cambridge, England: Cambridge University Press, 1994.

Fassler, Margot. *Gothic Song: Victorian Sequences and Augustinian Reform in Twelfth-Century Paris*. Cambridge, England: Cambridge University Press, 1993.

Faure, M. *Musique et Société, du Second Empire aux années 20*. Paris: Flammarion, 1985.

Ferguson, Priscilla Parkhurst. *Paris as Revolution: Writing the Nineteenth-Century City*. Berkeley and Los Angeles: University of California Press, 1994.

Fitch, Noël Riley. *Literary Cafés of Paris*. Washington, DC; Philadelphia, PA: Starrhill Press, 1989.

Flower, John E. *Writers and Politics in Modern France*. London: Hodder and Stoughton, 1977.

Forbes, Jill. *The Cinema in France: After the New Wave*. London: Macmillan, 1992.

Frank, Grace. *The Medieval French Drama*. Oxford: Clarendon Press, 1954.

Fulcher, Jane F. *The Nation's Image: French Grand Opera as Politics and Politicized Art*. Cambridge, England: Cambridge University Press, 1987.

Gelfand, Toby. *Professionalizing Modern Medicine: Paris Surgeons and Medical Science and Institutions in the Eighteenth Century*. Westport, CT: Greenwood Press, 1980.

Genêt-Delacroix, Marie-Claude. *Art et Etat sous la Troisième République: Le système des Beaux-Arts, 1870–1940*. Paris: Publications de la Sorbonne, 1992.

Gillispie, Charles Coulston. *The Montgolfier Brothers and the Invention of Aviation, 1783–1784*. Princeton, NJ: Princeton University Press, 1983.

———. *Science and Polity in France at the End of the Old Regime*. Princeton, NJ: Princeton University Press, 1980.

Goldsmith, Elizabeth. *Exclusive Conversations: The Art of Interaction in Seventeenth-Century France*. Philadelphia, PA: University of Pennsylvania Press, 1988.

Gordon, Mel. *The Grand Guignol: Theatre of Fear and Terror*. New York: Amok Press, 1988.

Gould, Cecil. *Trophy of Conquest: The Musée Napoléon and the Creation of the Louvre*. London: Faber and Faber, 1965.

Green, Christopher. *Cubisme and Its Enemies: Modern Movements and Reaction in French Art, 1916–1928*. New Haven, CT: Yale University Press, 1987.

Griffiths, Richard. *The Reactionary Revolution: The Catholic Revival in French Literature, 1870–1914*. London: Constable, 1966.

Guest, Ivor. *Le Ballet de l'Opéra de Paris: Trois siècles d'histoire et de tradition.* Paris: Théâtre national de l'Opéra, 1976.

———. *The Ballet of the Second Empire, 1858–1870.* London: A. and C. Black, 1953.

———. *The Romantic Ballet in Paris.* London: Sir Isaac Pitman and Sons, 1966.

Hahn, Roger. *The Anatomy of a Scientific Institution: The Paris Academy of Sciences, 1666–1803.* Berkeley, Los Angeles, London: University of California Press, 1971.

Hargrove, June, ed. *The French Academy: Classicism and Its Antagonists.* Newark, DE: University of Delaware Press; London and Toronto: Associated University Press, 1990.

Harvey, Sylvia. *May '68 and Film Culture.* London: British Film Institute, 1978.

Hemmings, Frederic William John. *The Theatre Industry in Nineteenth-Century France.* Cambridge, England: Cambridge University Press, 1993.

Herbert, Robert L. *Impressionism: Art, Leisure and Parisian Society.* New Haven, CT: Yale University Press, 1988.

Hesse, Carla. *Publishing and Cultural Politics in Revolutionary Paris, 1789–1810.* Berkeley, Los Angeles, Oxford: University of California Press, 1991.

Hildreth, Martha L. *Doctors, Bureaucrats and Public Health in France, 1888–1902.* New York: Garland, 1987.

Hilton, Wendy. *Dance of Court and Theater: The French Noble Style, 1690–1725.* Princeton, NJ: Princeton Book Company, 1981.

Hirschfeld, Gerhard, and Patrick Marsh, eds. *Collaboration in France: Politics and Culture during the Nazi Occupation, 1940–1944.* New York: Berg, 1989.

Isherwood, Robert M. *Music in the Service of the King: France in the Seventeenth Century.* Ithaca, NY: Cornell University Press, 1973.

Johnson, Douglas, and Madeleine Johnson. *The Age of Illusion: Art and Politics in France, 1918–1940.* New York: Rizzoli, 1987.

Johnson, James H. *Listening in Paris.* Berkeley and Los Angeles, CA: University of California Press, 1995.

Kearns, Edward John. *Ideas in Seventeenth-Century France.* Manchester, England: Manchester University Press, 1979.

Kennedy, Emmet. *A Cultural History of the French Revolution.* New Haven, CT: Yale University Press, 1988.

Kiernan, Colm. *Science and the Enlightenment in Eighteenth-Century France.* Geneva, Switzerland: Droz, 1968.

Klaits, Joseph. *Printed Propaganda under Louis XIV: Absolute Monarchy and Public Opinion.* Princeton, NJ: Princeton University Press, 1976.

Kors, Alan Charles. *D'Holbach's Coterie: An Enlightenment in Paris.* Princeton, NJ: Princeton University Press, 1976.

Kracauer, Sidney. *Orpheus in Paris: Offenbach and the Paris of His Time.* New York: Vienna House, 1972.

Kramer, Lloyd S. *Threshold of a New World: Intellectuals and the Exile Experience in Paris, 1830–1848.* Ithaca, NY: Cornell University Press, 1988.

Lacambre, Geneviève. *Les Ateliers d'artistes.* Paris: Hachette, 1991.

Lancaster, Henry Carrington. *French Tragedy in the Reign of Louis XVI and the Early Years of the French Revolution, 1774–1792.* Baltimore, MD: Johns Hopkins University Press, 1953.

———. *French Tragedy in the Time of Louis XV and Voltaire, 1715–1774.* 2 vols. Baltimore, MD: Johns Hopkins University Press, 1950.

———. *Sunset: A History of Parisian Drama in the Last Years of Louis XIV, 1701–1715.* Baltimore, MD: Johns Hopkins University Press, 1945.

Lehoux, Françoise. *Le Cadre de vie des médecins parisiens aux seizième et dix-septième siècles.* Paris: A. et J. Picard, 1976.

Leroy, Dominique. *Histoire des arts du spectacle en France: Aspects économiques, politiques et esthétiques, de la Renaissance à la Première Guerre mondiale.* Paris: L'Harmattan, 1990.

Lesch, John. *Science and Medicine in France: The Emergence of Experimental Physiology, 1790–1855.* Cambridge, MA: Harvard University Press, 1984.

Lethève, Jacques. *The Daily Life of French Artists.* New York: Praeger, 1972.

Levin, Miriam R. *Republican Art and Ideology in Late Nineteenth-Century France.* Ann Arbor, MI: UMI Research Press, 1986.

Littlewood, Ian. *Paris, a Literary Companion.* London: J. Murray, 1987.

Lottman, Herbert R. *The Left Bank: Writers, Artists and Politics from the Popular Front to the Cold War.* Boston: Houghton Mifflin, 1982.

Lough, John. *Paris Theatre Audiences in the Seventeenth and Eighteenth Centuries.* Oxford: Oxford University Press, 1957.

McClellan, Andrew. *Inventing the Louvre: Art, Politics and the Origins of the Modern Museum in Eighteenth-Century Paris.* New York and London: Cambridge University Press, 1994.

Mainardi, Patricia. *Art and Politics of the Second Empire: The Universal Expositions of 1855 and 1867.* New Haven, CT: Yale University Press, 1987.

———. *The End of the Salon: Art and the State in the Early Third Republic.* Cambridge, England: Cambridge University Press, 1993.

Marlais, Michel. *Conservative Echoes in Fin-de-Siècle Parisian Art Criticism.* University Park, PA: Pennsylvania State University, 1992.

Marriman, Michael. *Painting Politics for Louis-Philippe: Art and Ideology in Orleanist France.* New Haven, CT: Yale University Press, 1988.

Mather, Betty Bang, and Dean M. Karns. *Dance Rhythms of the French Baroque: A Handbook for Performance.* Bloomington and Indianapolis: Indiana University Press, 1987.

Milner, John. *The Studios of Paris: The Capital of Art in the Late Nineteenth Century.* New Haven, CT: Yale University Press, 1988.

Morris, Frances. *Paris Post War: Art and Existentialism, 1945–1955.* London: Tate Gallery, 1993.

The Nabis and the Parisian Avant-Garde. New Brunswick, NJ: Rutgers University Press, 1988.

Nori, Claude. *French Photography from Its Origins to the Present.* New York: Pantheon Books, 1979.

Page, Christopher. *The Owl and the Nightingale: Music Life and Ideas in France, 1100–1300.* London: Dent, 1989.

Paris au dix-neuvième siècle: Aspects d'un mythe littéraire. Lyon, France: Presses Universitaires de Lyon, 1984.

Paris in Literature. New Haven, CT: Yale University Press, 1964.

Paul, Charles B. *Science and Immortality: The "Eloges" of the Paris Academy of Sciences, 1699–1791.* Berkeley, CA: University of California Press, 1980.

Pecker, André. *La Médecine à Paris du troisième au vingtième siècle.* Paris: Hervas, 1984.

Perl, Jed. *Paris without End: On French Art since World War I.* San Francisco, CA: North Point Press, 1988.

Pitou, Spire. *The Paris Opera: An Encyclopedia of Operas, Ballets, Composers, and Performers.* 2 vols. London: Greenwood Press, 1983–85.

Pozharskaya, M. N. *The Russian Seasons in Paris: Sketches of the Scenery and Costumes, 1909–1929.* Moscow: Iskusstvo Art Publishers, 1988.

Prendergast, Christopher. *Paris and the Nineteenth Century.* Oxford and Cambridge, MA: Blackwell, 1992.

Ramsey, Matthew. *Professional and Popular Medicine in France, 1770–1830: The Social World of Medical Practice.* Cambridge, England: Cambridge University Press, 1988.

Raser, George Bernard. *Guide to Balzac's Paris: A Analytical Subject Index.* Choisy-le-Roi, France: Imprimerie de France, 1964.

Reader, Keith A. *Intellectuals and the Left in France since 1968.* London: Macmillan, 1987.

Reff, Theodore. *Manet and Modern Paris.* Chicago, IL: University of Chicago Press, 1982.

Robertson, Anne Walters. *The Service Books of the Royal Abbey of St.*

226 • Bibliography

Denis: Images of Ritual and Music in the Middle Ages. Oxford: Clarendon Press, 1991.

Root-Bernstein, Michèle. *Boulevard Theater and Revolution in Eighteenth-Century Paris*. Ann Arbor, MI: UMI Research Press, 1984.

Rubin, David Lee, ed. *Sun King: The Ascendance of French Culture during the Reign of Louis XIV*. Washington, DC: Folger Shakespeare Library; London and Toronto: Associated Universities Press, 1992.

Rudolf, Conrad. *Artistic Change at St. Denis: Abbot Suger's Program and the Early Twelfth-Century Controversy over Art*. Princeton, NJ: Princeton University Press, 1990.

Saisselin, Remi G. *The Literary Enterprise in Eighteenth-Century France*. Detroit, MI: Wayne State University, 1979.

The Second Empire, 1852–1870: Art in France under Napoléon III. Philadelphia, PA: Philadelphia Museum of Art, 1978.

Sègre, Monique. *L'Art comme institution: l'Ecole des Beaux-Arts, dix-neuvième-vingtième siècle*. Cachan, France: Editions de l'Ecole Normale Supérieure-Cachan, 1993.

Sherman, Daniel. *Worthy Monuments: Art Museums and the Politics of Culture in Nineteenth-Century France*. Cambridge, MA: Harvard University Press, 1989.

Siegel, Jerrold. *Bohemian Paris. Culture, Politics and the Boundaries of Bourgeois Life, 1830–1930*. New York: Viking, 1986.

Siegfried, Susan L. *The Art of Louis-Léopold Boilly: Modern Life in Napoleonic France*. New Haven, CT: Yale University Press, 1995.

Silver, Kenneth E. *Esprit de Corps: The Art of the Parisian Avant-Garde and the First World War, 1914–1925*. Princeton, NJ: Princeton University Press, 1989.

Silverman, Debora L. *Art Nouveau in Fin-de-Siècle France: Politics, Psychology and Style*. Berkeley, CA: University of California Press, 1989.

Solomon, Howard M. *Public Welfare, Science and Propaganda in Seventeenth-Century France: The Innovations of Théophraste Renaudot*. Princeton, NJ: Princeton University Press, 1972.

Sonn, Richard David. *Anarchism and Cultural Politics in "Fin de Siècle" France*. Lincoln, NE: University of Nebraska Press, 1989.

Souchal, François. *French Sculpture of the Seventeenth and Eighteenth Centuries: The Reign of Louis XIV*. 4 vols. Oxford: B. Cassirer, 1977–87.

Sterling, Charles. *La Peinture médiévale à Paris, 1300–1500*. 2 vols. Paris: Bibliothèque des Arts, 1987–91.

Stroup, Alice. *A Company of Scientists: Botany, Patronage and Community at the Seventeenth-Century Parisian Royal Academy of Sciences*. Berkeley and Los Angeles, CA: University of California Press, 1990.

————. *Royal Funding of the Parisian Académie Royale des Sciences during the 1690s.* Philadelphia, PA: American Philosophical Society, 1987.

Thomas, Marcel. *The Golden Age: Manuscript Painting at the Time of Jean, Duke of Berry.* New York: G. Braziller, 1979.

Todd, Christopher F. *Political Bias, Censorship and the Dissolution of the "Official" Press in Eighteenth-Century France.* Lewiston, NY: E. Mellen Press, 1991.

————. *Le Triomphe des mairies: Grands décors républicains à Paris, 1870–1914.* Paris: Ville de Paris, 1986.

Verba, Cynthia. *Music and the French Enlightenment: Reconstruction of a Dialogue, 1750–1764.* Oxford: Clarendon Press, 1993.

Vidal, Mary. *Watteau's Painted Conversations: Art, Literature and Talk in Seventeenth- and Eighteenth-Century France.* New Haven, CT: Yale University Press, 1992.

Wechsler, Judith. *A Human Comedy: Physiognomy and Caricatures in Nineteenth-Century Paris.* Chicago, IL: University of Chicago Press, 1982.

Weisz, George, and Robert Fox, eds. *The Organization of Science and Technology in France, 1808–1914.* Cambridge, England: Cambridge University Press, 1980.

Williams, Alan. *Republic of Images: A History of French Filmmaking.* Cambridge, MA: Harvard University Press, 1992.

Wright, Craig. *Music and Ceremony at Notre-Dame of Paris, 500–1550.* Cambridge, England: Cambridge University Press, 1989.

Wrigley, Richard. *The Origins of French Art Criticism from the Ancien Régime to the Restoration.* Oxford: Clarendon Press, 1993.

8. URBANISM, ARCHITECTURE AND TOPOGRAPHY

Adams, William Howard. *The French Garden, 1500–1800.* New York: George Braziller, 1979.

Ausseur, Christine. *Le Guide littéraire des monuments de Paris.* Paris: Hermé, 1992.

Babelon, Jean-Pierre. *Demeures parisiennes sous Henri IV et Louis XIII.* 3d ed. Paris: F. Hazan, 1991.

————. *Le Palais de Justice, la Conciergerie, la Sainte-Chapelle.* Nancy, France: Imprimerie A. Humblot, 1973.

Ballon, Hilary. *The Paris of Henri IV: Architecture and Urbanism.* Cambridge, MA: Architectural History Foundation and MIT Press, 1991.

Barozzi, Jacques. *Guide des 400 jardins publics de Paris.* Paris: Hervas, 1992.

Barthélemy, Guy. *Les Jardiniers du Roy: Petite histoire du Jardin des Plantes de Paris*. Paris: Le Pélican, 1979.

Beaumont-Maillet, Laure. *L'Eau à Paris*. Paris: F. Hazan, 1991.

Béhar, Michèle, and Manuelle Salama. *Paris Nouvelle/New Architecture: Guide*. Paris: Regirex-France, 1985.

Berger, Robert W. *In the Garden of the Sun King: Studies on the Park of Versailles under Louis XIV*. Washington, DC: CAA Monographs, 1985.

―――. *The Palace of the Sun: The Louvre of Louis XIV*. University Park, PA: Pennsylvania State University Press, 1993.

―――. *Versailles: The Château of Louis XIV*. University Park, PA: Pennsylvania State University Press, 1985.

Bergeron, Louis, ed. *Paris: Genèse d'un paysage*. Paris: Picard, 1989.

Bernard, Léon. *The Emerging City: Paris in the Age of Louis XIV*. Durham, NC: Duke University Press, 1970.

Biver, Paul. *Abbayes, monastères et couvents de femmes à Paris, des origines à la fin du dix-huitième siècle*. Paris: Presses Universitaires de France, 1975.

Biver, Paul, and Marie-Louise Biver. *Abbayes, monastères et couvents de Paris, des origines à la fin du dix-huitième siècle*. Paris: Editions d'Histoire et d'Art, 1970.

Blunt, Anthony. *Art and Architecture in France, 1500–1700*. Harmondsworth, England: Penguin, 1982.

Borsi, Franco, and Ezio Godoli. *Paris Art Nouveau: Architecture et décoration*. Paris: Marc Vokar, 1989.

Boudon, Françoise, André Chastel, Hélène Couzy, and François Hamon. *Système de l'architecture urbaine: Le quartier des Halles à Paris*. Paris: Editions du CNRS, 1977.

Bowie, Karen, ed. *Les Grandes Gares parisiennes au dix-neuvième siècle*. Paris: Délégation à l'Action artistique de la Ville de Paris, 1987.

Braham, Allen. *The Architecture of French Enlightenment*. Berkeley and Los Angeles, CA: University of California Press, 1980.

Bresc-Bautier, Geneviève. *Le Louvre: Histoire, architecture et décors*. Paris: Assouline, 1995.

Brunel, Georges, Marie-Laure Deschamps-Bourgeon, and Yves Gagneux. *Dictionnaire des églises de Paris, catholique-orthodoxe-protestant*. Paris: Hervas, 1995.

Cahiers de l'Institut d'Aménagement et d'Urbanisme de la Région d'Ile-de-France. Paris. 1964–. Quarterly.

Champion, Virginie, Bertrand Lemoine, and Claude Terreaux. *Les Cinémas de Paris, 1945–1995*. Paris: Délégation à l'Action artistique de la Ville de Paris, 1995.

Chaslin, François. *Les Paris de François Mitterrand: Histoire des grands projects architecturaux*. Paris: Gallimard, 1985.

Chemetov, Paul, and Bernard Marrey. *Architectures: Paris, 1848–1914*. Paris: Dunod, 1980.

Chenebault, Christophe, and Marie Gaussel. *Guide des cinémas à Paris/Guide to Cinemas in Paris*. Paris: Syros-Alternatives, 1992.

Chevalier, Louis. *The Assassination of Paris*. Chicago, IL: University of Chicago Press, 1993.

Christ, Yvan, Jean-François Barrielle, Thérèse Castieau, and Antoinette Lenormand-Romain. *Champs-Elysées, faubourg Saint-Honoré, plaine Monceau*. Paris: H. Veyrier, 1982.

Christ, Yvan, Jacques Silvestre de Sacy, and Philippe Siguret. *Le Faubourg Saint-Germain*. Paris: H. Veyrier, 1985.

———. *L'Ile Saint-Louis, l'île de la Cité, le quartier de l'ancienne Université*. Paris: H. Veyrier, 1984.

———. *Le Marais*. Paris: H. Veyrier, 1985.

Clausen, Meredith. *Frantz Jourdain and the Samaritaine: Art Nouveau Theory and Criticism*. Leiden, The Netherlands: E. J. Brill, 1987.

Cohen, Jean-Louis, Monique Eleb, and Antonio Martinelli. *The Twentieth Century Architecture and Urbanism, Paris*. Tokyo: A+U, 1990.

Cohen, Jean-Louis, and Bruno Fortier. *Paris, la ville et ses projets/A City in the Making*. Paris: Editions Babylone, Pavillon de l'Arsenal, 1992.

Cohen, Jean-Louis, and André Lortie. *Des Fortifs au Périf: Paris, les seuils de la ville*. Paris: Picard, 1992.

Coural, Jean. *Le Palais de l'Elysée: Histoire et décor*. Paris: Délégation à l'Action artistique de la Ville de Paris, 1994.

Culbertson, Judi, and Tom Randall. *Permanent Parisians: An Illustrated Guide to the Cemeteries of Paris*. Chelsea, England: Chelsea Green Publishing, 1986.

Delorme, Jean-Claude. *L'Ecole de Paris: Dix architectes et leurs immeubles, 1905–1937*. Paris: Editions du Moniteur, 1981.

Des Cars, Jean, and Pierre Pinon. *Paris-Haussmann, le "pari d'Haussmann."* Paris: Picard, 1991.

Dictionnaire des monuments de Paris. Paris: Hervas, 1992.

Drexler, Arthur, ed. *The Architecture of the Ecole des Beaux-Arts*. New York: MIT Press, 1977.

Egbert, Donald Drew. *The Beaux-Arts Tradition in French Architecture*. Princeton, NJ: Princeton University Press, 1980.

Eleb, Monique, and Anne Debarre. *L'Invention de l'habitation moderne: Paris, 1880–1914*. Paris: Hazan, 1994.

Erlande-Brandenburg, Alain. *Notre-Dame de Paris*. Paris: Fernand Nathan, 1991.

Etlin, Richard Allan. *The Architecture of Death: The Transformation of the Cemetery in Eighteenth-Century Paris*. Cambridge, MA: MIT Press, 1984.

Eveno, Claude. *Paris perdu: Quarante ans de bouleversements d'une ville.* Paris: Carré, 1991.
———. *Paris perdu réactualisé.* 3d ed. Paris: Carré, 1995.
Evenson, Norma. *Paris: A Century of Change, 1878–1978.* New Haven, CT: Yale University Press, 1979.
Fermigier, André. *La Bataille de Paris: Des Halles à la Pyramide, chroniques d'urbanisme.* Paris: Gallimard, 1991.
Fierro, Alfred, ed. *Patrimoine parisien, 1789–1799: Destructions, Créations, mutations.* Paris: Délégation à l'Action artistique de la Ville de Paris, 1989.
Fortier, Bruno, ed. *La Politique de l'espace parisien à la fin de l'Ancien Régime.* Paris: CORDA, 1975.
Frémy, Dominique. *Guide de la Tour Eiffel.* Paris: R. Laggont, 1989.
Gabriel, André. *Guide de l'architecture des monuments de Paris/Guide to the Architecture of Monuments of Paris.* Paris: Syros-Alternatives, 1991.
Gady, Alexandre. *Le Marais: Guide historique et architectural.* Paris: Carré, 1994.
Gaillard, Jeanne. *Paris, la ville, 1852–1870: L'urbanisme parisien à l'heure d'Haussmann.* Paris: H. Champion, 1977.
Gaillard, Marc. *Quais et Ponts de Paris: Guide historique.* Amiens, France: Martelle, 1993.
Gallet, Michel. *Paris Domestic Architecture of the Eighteenth Century.* London: Barrier and Jenkins, 1972.
———. *Stately Mansions: Eighteenth-Century Paris Architecture.* New York: Praeger, 1972.
Goubert, Jean-Pierre. *La Conquête de l'eau: L'avènement de la santé à l'âge industriel.* Paris: Hachette-Pluriel, 1987.
———. *Du Luxe au confort.* Paris: E. Belin, 1988.
Gournay, Isabelle. *Le Nouveau Trocadéro.* Liège, Belgium: P. Mardaga, 1985.
Guide du promeneur. 20 vols., one for each arrondissement. Paris: Parigramme, 1993–97.
Hamon, Philippe. *Expositions, Literature and Architecture in Nineteenth-Century France.* Berkeley, CA: University of California Press, 1992.
Hargrove, June. *The Statues of Paris.* New York: Vendome, 1989.
Hazlehurst, F. Hamilton. *Gardens of Illusion: The Genius of André Le Nostre.* Nashville: Vanderbilt University Press, 1980.
Hillairet, Jacques. *La Colline de Chaillot.* Paris: Editions de Minuit, 1978.
———. *Dictionnaire historique des rues de Paris.* 2 vols. 9th ed. Paris: Editions de Minuit, 1991.
———. *Le Douzième Arrondissement.* Paris: Editions de Minuit, 1972.
———. *Gibets, piloris et cachots du vieux Paris.* Paris: Editions de Minuit, 1989, reprint of the 1956 ed.

———. *L'Île de la Cité*. Paris: Editions de Minuit, 1969.

———. *L'Île Saint-Louis, rue par rue, maison par maison*. Paris: Editions de Minuit, 1967.

———. *Le Palais du Louvre, sa vie, ses grands souvenirs historiques*. Paris: Editions de Minuit, 1961.

———. *Le Palais royal et impérial des Tuileries et son jardin*. Paris: Editions de Minuit, 1965.

———. *La Rue de Richelieu*. Paris: Editions de Minuit, 1966.

———. *La Rue Saint-Antoine*. Paris: Parigramme, 1988, reprint of the 1970 ed.

———. *Le Village d'Auteuil*. Paris: Editions de Minuit, 1978.

Hoyet, Jean-Michel, ed. *Guide: L'Architecture contemporaine à Paris/Contemporary Architecture in Paris*. Paris: Techniques et Architecture, Altedia Communication, 1994.

Imbert, Dorothée. *The Modernist Garden in France*. New Haven, CT: Yale University Press, 1993.

Jestaz, Bertrand. *L'Hôtel et l'Eglise des Invalides*. Paris: Picard, 1990.

Jordan, David P. *Transforming Paris: The Life and Labors of Baron Haussmann*. New York: The Free Press, 1995.

Kalnein, Wend von. *Architecture in France in the Eighteenth Century*. New Haven, CT: Yale University Press, 1995.

Lacaze, Jean-Paul. *Paris, urbanisme d'Etat et destin d'une ville*. Paris: Flammarion, 1994.

Large, Pierre-François. *Des Halles au Forum: Métamorphose au coeur de Paris*. Paris: L'Harmattan, 1992.

Lavedan, Pierre. *Nouvelle Histoire de Paris: Histoire de l'urbanisme à Paris*. New ed. updated by Jean Bastié and Alfred Fierro. Paris: Hachette, 1995.

Le Dantec, Denise, and Jean-Pierre Le Dantec. *Reading the French Garden: Story and History*. Cambridge, MA: MIT Press, 1990.

Le Hallé, Guy. *Les Fortifications de Paris*. Paris: Horvath, 1986.

Leith, James A. *Space and Revolution: Projects for Monuments, Squares and Public Buildings in Paris, 1789–1799*. Montreal-Kingston, Canada: McGill-Queen's University Press, 1991.

Le Moël, Michel. *L'Architecture privée à Paris au Grand Siècle*. Paris: Service des Travaux historiques de la Ville de Paris, 1990.

———. *Paris, la place Royale, place des Vosges*. Paris: Tourelle, 1986.

Lemoine, Bertrand. *La Cité internationale universitaire de Paris*. Paris: Hervas, 1990.

———. *Les Halles de Paris*. Paris: L'Equerre, 1980.

———. *Les Passages couverts en France*. Paris: Délégation à l'Action artistique de la Ville de Paris, 1989.

Lemoine, Bertrand, and Philippe Rivoirard. *Paris: L'architecture des années 30*. Lyon, France: La Manufacture, 1987.

Leniaud, Jean-Michel, and Françoise Perrot. *La Sainte-Chapelle*. Paris: Nathan and CNMHS, 1991.

Léri, Jean-Marc. *Montmartre*. Paris: H. Veyrier, 1983.

Liberty: The French-American Statue in Art and History. New York: Harper and Row, 1986.

Livre du centenaire de la reconstruction de l'Hôtel de Ville, 1882–1982. Paris: Bibliothèque administrative de la Ville de Paris, 1982.

Loyer, François. *Paris Nineteenth Century*. New York: Abbeville Press, 1988.

Lucan, Jacques, ed. *Eau et gaz à tous les étages: Paris, cent ans de logement*. Paris: Picard Editions du Pavillon de l'Arsenal, 1992.

McClure, Bert, and Bruno Régnier. *Architectural Walks in Paris*. Paris: La Découverte/Le Monde, 1989.

Marrey, Bernard. *Le Fer à Paris, architectures*. Paris: Picard, 1989.

Marrey, Bernard, and Marie-Jeanne Dumont. *La Brique à Paris*. Paris: Picard and Editions du Pavillon de l'Arsenal, 1991.

Martin, Hervé. *Guide de l'architecture moderne à Paris/Guide to Modern Architecture in Paris, 1900–1990*. Paris: Syros-Alternatives, 1991.

Mead, Christopher Curtis. *Charles Garnier's Paris Opera: Architectural Empathy and the Renaissance of French Classicism*. Cambridge, MA: MIT Press, 1991.

Michel, Christian. *Les Halles: La renaissance d'un quartier, 1966–1988*. Paris: Masson, 1988.

Middleton, Robin, ed. *The Beaux-Arts and the Nineteenth-Century French Architecture*. Cambridge, MA: MIT Press, 1982.

Mignot, Claude. *Le Val-de-Grâce, l'ermitage d'une reine*. Paris: CNRS, 1994.

Moncan, Patrice de, and Christian Mahout. *Le Guide des passages de Paris*. Paris: SESSAM, 1991.

———. *Les Passages de Paris*. Paris: SEESAM, 1991.

Neumann, Robert. *Robert de Cotte and the Perfection of Architecture in Eighteenth-Century France*. Chicago, IL: University of Chicago Press, 1994.

Olsen, Donald J. *The City as a Work of Art*. New Haven, CT: Yale University Press, 1986.

Paris: Balade au fil du temps. Paris: Sélection du Reader's Digest, 1995.

Paris et ses réseaux: Naissance d'un mode de vie urbain, dix-neuvième-vingtième siècles. Paris: Hôtel d'Angoulême-Lamoignon, 1990.

Paris, la rue: Le mobilier urbain parisien du Second Empire à nos jours. Paris: Société des Amis de la Bibliothèque historique, 1976.

Pérouse de Montclos, Jean-Marie, ed. *Le Guide du patrimoine: Paris*. Paris: Hachette, 1994.

Picon, Antoine. *French Architects and Engineers in the Age of Enlightenment*. Cambridge, England: Cambridge University Press, 1992.

Pinkney, David H. *Napoléon III and the Rebuilding of Paris*. Princeton, NJ: Princeton University Press, 1958.

Pret, Nadia. *Guide des marchés à Paris/Guide to Markets in Paris*. Paris: Syros-Alternatives, 1991.

Quoniam, Pierre, and Laurent Guinamard. *Le Palais du Louvre*. Paris: F. Nathan, 1988.

Reuterswärd, Patrik. *The Two Churches of the Hôtel des Invalides: A History of Their Design*. Stockholm: Nationalmuseum, 1965.

Roblin, Michel. *Quand Paris était à la campagne: Origines rurales et urbaines des vingt arrondissements*. Paris: Picard, 1985.

Rouleau, Bernard. *Le Tracé des rues de Paris: Formation, typologie, fonctions* . . . New ed. Paris: CNRS, 1988.

———. *Villages et faubourgs de l'ancien Paris: Histoire d'un espace urbain*. Paris: Seuil, 1985.

Salvadori, Renzo. *Architect's Guide to Paris*. Sevenoaks, England: Butterworth Architecture, 1990.

Siguret, Philippe, and Vincent Bouvet. *Chaillot, Passy, Auteuil, le bois de Boulogne: Le seizième arrondissement*. Paris: H. Veyrier, 1982.

Silver, Nathan. *The Making of Beaubourg: A Building Biography of the Centre Pompidou Paris*. Cambridge, MA: MIT Press, 1994.

Sutcliffe, Anthony. *The Autumn of Central Paris: The Defeat of Town Planning, 1850–1970*. Montréal, Canada: McGill-Queen's University Press, 1971.

———. *Paris: An Architectural History*. New Haven, CT: Yale University Press, 1993.

Thomason, David. *Renaissance Paris: Architecture and Growth, 1475–1600*. Berkeley and Los Angeles, CA: University of California Press, 1984.

Troy, Nancy. *Modernism and the Decorative Arts in France: Art Nouveau to Le Corbusier*. New Haven, CT: Yale University Press, 1991.

Vallois, Thirza. *Around and About Paris*. 3 vols. London: Iliad Books, 1996.

Van Deputte, Jocelyne. *Ponts de Paris*. Paris: Sauret and Paris-Musées, 1994.

Van Zanten, David. *Building Paris: Architectural Institutions and the Transformation of the French Capital, 1830–1870*. Cambridge, England: Cambridge University Press, 1994.

———. *Designing Paris: The Architecture of Duban, Labrouste, Ducand, Vaudoyer*. Cambridge, MA: MIT Press, 1987.

Vie et histoire . . . 20 vols., one for each arrondissement. Paris: Hervas, 1985–1988.

Walton, Guy. *Louis XIV's Versailles*. Chicago, IL: University of Chicago Press, 1986.

Willemin, Véronique. *Guide du promeneur à Paris/Guide to Walks in Paris*. Paris: Syros-Alternatives, 1991.

9. AMERICANS IN PARIS

Alsop, Susan Mary. *Yankees at the Court: The First Americans in Paris*. New York: Doubleday, 1982.

Beach, Sylvia. *Shakespeare and Company*. New ed. London: Plantin Paperbacks, 1987.

Benstock, Shari. *Women of the Left Bank: Paris, 1900–1940*. Austin: University of Texas Press, 1986.

Bertier de Sauvigny, Guillaume de. *La France et les Français vus par les voyageurs américains, 1814–1848*. 2 vols. Paris: Flammarion, 1982–85.

Bizardel, Yvon. *Les Américains à Paris pendant la Révolution*. Paris: Calmann-Lévy, 1972.

———. *American Painters in Paris*. New York: Macmillan, 1960.

Campbell, James. *Paris Interzone: Richard Wright, Lolita, Boris Vian and Others on the Left Bank, 1946–1960*. London: Secker and Warburg, 1994.

Carpenter, Humphrey. *Geniuses Together: American Writers in Paris in the 1920s*. London: Unwin Hyman, 1987.

Delanoe, Nelcya. *Le Raspail vert: L'American Center à Paris, 1934–1994. Une histoire des avant-gardes franco-américaines*. Paris: Seghers, 1994.

Fabre, Michel. *From Harlem to Paris: Black American Writers in France, 1840–1980*. Urbana, IL: University of Illinois Press, 1991.

Fink, Lois Marie. *American Art at the Nineteenth-Century Paris Salons*. Washington, DC: National Museum of American Art, Smithsonian Institution; Cambridge, England: Cambridge University Press, 1990.

Fitch, Noël Riley. *Sylvia Beach and the Lost Generation: A History of Literary Paris in the Twenties and Thirties*. New York: Norton, 1983; London: Souvenir Press, 1984.

Ford, Hugh. *Four Lives in Paris*. San Francisco, CA: North Point Press, 1987.

———. *Published in Paris: American and British Writers, Printers and Publishers in Paris, 1920–1939*. New York: Macmillan; London: Garnstone Press, 1975.

Greenfeld, Howard. *They Came to Paris*. New York: Crown Publishers, 1975.

Gysin, Brion. *The Last Museum*. London: Faber and Faber; New York: Grove Press, 1986.

Haight, Mary Ellen Jordan. *Walks in Gertrude Stein's Paris: A Peregrine Smith Book.* Salt Lake City: Gibbs M. Smith, 1988.

Hansen, Arlen J. *Expatriate Paris: A Cultural and Literary Guide to Paris of the 1920s.* New York: Arcade, 1990.

Jouve, Daniel. *Paris: Birthplace of the U.S.A.* Paris: Gründ, 1995.

Kennedy, J. Gerald. *Imagining Paris: Exile Writing and American Identity.* New Haven, CT: Yale University Press, 1993.

Méral, Jean. *Paris in American Literature.* Chapel Hill, NC: University of North Carolina Press, 1989.

Morton, Brian N. *Americans in Paris: An Anecdotal Street Guide.* Ann Arbor, MI: The Olivia and Hill Press, 1984.

Paris-New York: Echanges littéraires au vingtième siècle. Paris: Centre national d'Art et de Culture Georges Pompidou, 1977.

Petit, Solange. *Les Américains de Paris.* Paris and The Hague: Mouton, 1975.

Pizer, Donald. *American Expatriate Writing and the Paris Moment: Modernism and Place.* Baton Rouge: Louisiana State University, 1996.

Rood, Karen Lane, ed. *American Writers in Paris, 1920–1939.* Detroit, MI: Gale Research Company, 1980.

Sawyer-Lauçanno, Christopher. *The Continual Pilgrimage: American Writers in Paris.* London: Bloomsbury, 1992.

Weinberg, H. Barbara. *The Lure of Paris: Nineteenth-Century American Painters and Their French Teachers.* New York and London: Abbeville Press, 1991.

Wickes, George. *Americans in Paris, 1903–1939.* New York: Doubleday, 1969.

Wiser, William. *The Great Good Place: American Expatriate Women in Paris.* New York: W. W. Norton, 1991.

Statistical Appendixes

APPENDIX 1. AREA OF PARIS

	Hectares*
52 B.C.	8
250	52
1180	200
1220	273
1380	439
1553	483
1635	567
1638	1,000
1672	1,103
1715	1,337
1788	3,370
1818	3,402
1860	7,802
1926	8,622
1946	10,516
Since 1954	10,540

*One hectare equals 100 acres or 10,000 square meters (2.471 acres).

APPENDIX 2. POPULATION OF PARIS

	Inhabitants*
Circa 250	6,000
1328	200,000
Circa 1422	100,000
Circa 1500	150,000
1565	294,000
1590	200,000
Circa 1600	300,000
1637	415,000
Circa 1680	500,000
Circa 1709	510,000
Circa 1752	576,000
Circa 1780	600,000
1789	650,000
1801	546,856
1811	622,636
1817	713,966
1831	785,866
1836	899,313
1841	936,261
1846	1,053,897
1851	1,053,261
1856	1,174,346
1861	1,696,141
1866	1,825,274
1872	1,851,792
1876	1,988,806
1881	2,269,023
1886	2,344,550
1891	2,447,957
1896	2,536,834
1901	2,714,068
1906	2,763,393
1911	2,888,107
1921	2,906,472
1926	2,871,429
1931	2,891,020
1936	2,829,746
1954	2,850,189
1962	2,790,091
1968	2,590,771
1975	2,290,852
1982	2,176,243
1990	2,154,678

*Estimates until the first census in 1801.

APPENDIX 3. NUMBER OF STREETS IN PARIS

1300	310
1407	310
1555	468
1636	515
1723	960
1763	967
1791	1,169
1819	1,190
1848	1,474
1859	1,694
1860 (new limits)	3,186
1865	3,750
1892	4,090
1898 (official statistics)	4,304
1912 (official statistics)	4,414
1928 (official statistics)	4,608
1946 (official statistics)	5,073
1956 (official statistics)	5,207
1974 (official statistics)	5,281
1992 (official statistics)	5,414

APPENDIX 4. HOUSING IN PARIS

	Houses	Families or flats
1328		61,098
1553	12,000	
1571	14,625	
1637	20,300	
1684	23,223	81,280
1714	22,000	
1755	23,565	
1817 (census)	26,801	224,922
1841 (census)	28,699	332,669
1851 (census)	30,770	385,191
1859 (census)	32,734	451,374
New limits		
1861 (census)	55,160	567,917
1872 (census)	64,203	759,352
1886 (census)	68,126	
1896 (census		810,400
1911 (census)	80,639	1,123,634
1921 (census)	82,127	1,149,366
1962 (census)		1,241,903
1968 (census)		1,221,954
1975 (census)		1,238,732
1982 (census)		1,279,730
1990 (census)		1,304,398

APPENDIX 5. FOREIGNERS DWELLING IN PARIS (1991)

From

Germany	6,879
Italy	13,220
Portugal	53,317
Spain	27,709
United Kingdom	9,370
Total European Community	122,216
Algeria	48,640
Morocco	34,796
Tunisia	32,595
Total North Africa	116,098
Mali	9,024
Senegal	8,677
Total Africa	48,973
China	7,951
Japan	5,587
Total East and South Asia	17,114
Iran	5,803
Lebanon	9,111
Turkey	9,658
Total Middle East	30,948
U.S.A.	9,537
Total North America	11,172
Total Latin America	11,545
Other Countries (Eastern Europe, ex-USSR, Pacific)	6,242
TOTAL	364,308

15.9% of the population of Paris

APPENDIX 6. PRINCIPAL SOURCES
OF IMPORTS AND EXPORTS (1991)

	(Millions of French Francs)			
	Imports (to Paris)		Exports (from Paris)	
Germany	5,576	8.2%	5,168	9.3%
Italy	10,250	15.0%	3,145	5.7%
Netherlands	3,567	5.3%	4,087	7.4%
United Kingdom	6,140	9.0%	3,379	6.1%
Total European Community	31,283	46.0%	22,059	39.9%
Switzerland	2,697	3.9%	4,963	9.0%
U.S.A.	5,348	7.9%	4,092	7.4%
Japan	5,203	7.7%	3,749	6.8%
Total other OECD Countries	16,629	24.5%	15,781	28.5%
TOTAL PARIS	67,927		55,311	
ÎLE-DE-FRANCE	402,225 31.0% of Imports		235,280 19.6% of Exports	

APPENDIX 7. TOURISM IN PARISIAN HOTELS (1991)

	Guests	Nights
Belgium and Luxembourg	215,700	420,900
Germany	881,600	2,070,400
Italy	860,500	2,344,600
Netherlands	297,000	710,500
Spain	439,300	1,133,100
United Kingdom and Ireland	969,100	2,247,600
Total Europe	4,582,300	11,486,600
Algeria, Morocco and Tunisia	149,100	462,200
Total Africa	263,400	747,600
Canada	135,300	357,300
U.S.A.	861,200	2,228,000
Total America	1,200,100	3,141,000
Middle East	154,600	412,500
Japan	755,500	1,684,700
Other countries of Asia	151,300	334,200
Australia	57,900	154,200
New Zealand	14,900	34,100
TOTAL STRANGERS	7,584,900	18,785,900
FRENCH TOURISTS	5,017,200	9,483,400
GRAND TOTAL	12,602,100	28,269,300

About the Author

ALFRED FIERRO (École des Chartes, archivist-paleographer diploma; École pratique des Hautes Études, Ph.D.) was a librarian at the National Library of Paris, beginning in the Bibliographical Service of the Catalog Room (1965–71), then chief of the service of French history (1971–80), and finally librarian of the French Geographical Society at the Department of Maps (1980–88). Since 1988, he has been a chief librarian of the Historical Library of the City of Paris. To date, he has published nine books on the history of Paris, including studies on the Louvre and the 4th, 12th, 14th, 18th and 19th arrondissements. He has also written the *Histoire et Dictionnaire de la Révolution Française.* His latest work is the *Histoire et Dictionnaire de Paris,* a survey of more than 1,500 pages containing the first research guide on the history of Paris since 1908.

JON WORONOFF (Interpreters' School, University of Geneva, translator-interpreter diploma; Graduate Institute of International Studies, Geneva, License des sciences politiques) started off as a translator and interpreter for international organizations, including the United Nations, FAO, UNESCO and others. He later ran language service companies in Hong Kong, Tokyo and New York. Since then he has become a journalist, writer and editor of various series of historical dictionaries for Scarecrow Press, including this one. Presently living in a remote corner of France, his favorite city is Paris.